CONTEMPORARY MUSICIANS

ISSN 1044-2197

CONTEMPORARY MUSICIANS

PROFILES OF THE PEOPLE IN MUSIC

MICHAEL L. LaBLANC,
Editor

VOLUME 1

Includes Indexes

 Gale Research Inc. • Book Tower • Detroit, Michigan 48226

STAFF

Michael L. LaBlanc, *Editor*

Peter M. Gareffa, *Supervising Editor*

David Collins, *Assistant Editor*

Nancy H. Evans, Anne Janette Johnson, Tim LaBorie, Calen D. Stone, Nancy Stone,
Barbara Stratyner, and Elizabeth Thomas, *Contributing Editors*

Linda Metzger, *Senior Editor*

Jeanne Gough, *Permissions Manager*
Patricia A. Seefelt, *Picture Permissions Supervisor*
Margaret A. Chamberlain, *Permissions Coordinator*
Pamela A. Hayes, *Permissions Assistant*
Lillian Quickley, *Permissions Clerk*

Mary Beth Trimper, *Production Manager*
Marilyn Jackman, *External Production Assistant*
Arthur Chartow, *Art Director*
Cynthia Baldwin, *Graphic Designer*

Laura Bryant, *Production Supervisor*
Louise Gagné, *Internal Production Associate*
Shelly Andrews and Sharana Wier, *Internal Production Assistants*

Cover Illustration: John Kleber

Copyright © 1989 by Gale Research Inc.
ISBN 0-8103-2211-0
ISSN 1044-2197

Computerized photocomposition by
Roberts/Churcher
Derby Line, Vermont

Printed in the United States of America

Published simultaneously in the United Kingdom
by Gale Reseach International Limited
(An affiliated company of Gale Reseach Inc.)

Contents

Introduction   ix

Photo Credits   xi

Subject Index   251

Musicians Index   253

Introduction

Fills the Information Gap on Today's Musicians

Contemporary Musicians profiles the colorful performers and composers who create or influence the music we hear today. Until now, no quality reference series has provided comprehensive information on such a wide range of artists despite keen and ongoing public interest. To find biographical and critical coverage, an information seeker had little choice but to wade through the offerings of the popular press, scan television "infotainment" programs, and search for the occasional published biography or expose. *Contemporary Musicians* is designed to serve that information seeker, providing in one ongoing source in-depth coverage of the important figures on the modern music scene in a format that is both informative and entertaining. Students, researchers, and casual browsers alike can use *Contemporary Musicians* to fill their needs for personal information about the artists, find a selected discography of the musician's recordings, and read an insightful essay offering biographical and critical information.

Provides Broad Coverage

Existing single-volume biographical sources on musicians are limited in scope, focusing on a handful of performers from a specific musical genre or era. In contrast, *Contemporary Musicians* offers researchers and music devotees a comprehensive, informative, and entertaining alternative. *Contemporary Musicians* is published twice yearly, with each volume providing information on 80 to 100 musical artists from all the genres that form the broad spectrum of contemporary music—pop, rock, jazz, blues, country, new wave, New Age, folk, rhythm and blues, gospel, bluegrass, and reggae, to name a few, as well as selected classical artists who have achieved "crossover" success with the general public.

Includes Popular Features

In *Contemporary Musicians* you'll find popular features that users value:

- **Easy-to-locate data sections**—Vital personal statistics, chronological career summaries, listings of major awards, and mailing addresses, when available, are prominently displayed in a clearly marked box on the second page of each entry.

- **Biographical/critical essays**—Colorful and informative essays trace each personality's personal and professional life, offer representative examples of critical response to each artist's work, and provide entertaining personal sidelights.

- **Selected discographies**—Each entry provides a comprehensive listing of the artist's major recorded works.

- **Photographs**—Most entries include portraits of the artists.

- **Sources for additional information**—This invaluable feature directs the user to selected books, magazines, and newspapers where more information on listees can be obtained.

Helpful Indexes Make It Easy to Find the Information You Need

Contemporary Musicians features a Musicians Index, listing names of individual performers and musical groups, and a Subject Index that provides the user with a breakdown by primary musical instruments played and by musical genre.

We Welcome Your Suggestions

The editors welcome your comments and suggestions for enhancing and improving *Contemporary Musicians*. If you would like to suggest musicians or composers to be covered in the future, please submit these names to the editors. Mail comments or suggestions to:

The Editor
Contemporary Musicians
Gale Research Inc.
Book Tower
Detroit, MI 48226
Phone : (800) 521-0707
Fax: (313) 961-6241

Photo Credits

Permission to reproduce photographs appearing in *Contemporary Musicians,* Volume 1, was received from the following sources:

AP/Wide World Photos: pp. 1, 4, 8, 11, 18, 26, 29, 35, 39, 42, 47, 50, 55, 58, 61, 64, 70, 73, 76, 80, 83, 86, 88, 91, 97, 101, 104, 106, 112, 117, 121, 124, 126, 128, 133, 138, 142, 145, 148, 151, 154, 158, 161, 169, 172, 175, 185, 188, 196, 200, 203, 206, 209, 211, 218, 222, 225, 231, 238, 241, 243, 246; **Reuters/Bettmann Newsphotos:** pp. 14, 180, 248; **UPI/Bettmann Newsphotos:** pp. 22, 31, 52, 94, 109, 114, 163, 192, 214, 228, 234; **Melodie Gimple/ Warner Bros., courtesy of Night After Night Ltd.:** p. 136.

CONTEMPORARY MUSICIANS

Alabama

Country group

Alabama is the most successful country group of the 1980s in terms of albums sold and awards bestowed. Consisting of three cousins born in Alabama—Randy Owen, Teddy Gentry, and Jeff Cook— and a Massachusetts-born drummer, Mark Herndon, the band won Entertainer of the Year honors from the Country Music Association three consecutive years, making history as the first multi-member group to earn the coveted award. Recognition and million-selling albums have come after years of struggle for Alabama; according to Suzan Crane in *Country Music* magazine, the band's music "has the unpretentious sincerity of the truest country tune."

Saturday Evening Post contributor Bob Allen likewise commented that because of the band's many fallow years before success came, the music "is redolent of a sense of belonging, of a sense of home and of gratitude for the emotional ties that bind." Bill C. Malone elaborated on Alabama's sound in his book *Country Music U.S.A.:* "Alabama discovered a winning commercial formula by judiciously mixing romantic ballads such as

For the Record. . .

Originally formed in Fort Payne, Ala., in 1969 as Wild Country; name changed to Alabama, 1977; original group members include **Randy Owen** (born 1949 in Fort Payne, Ala.), guitar and vocals; **Teddy Gentry** (born 1952 in Fort Payne, Ala.), bass and vocals; **Jeff Cook** (born 1949 in Fort Payne, Ala.), guitar and keyboards. **Mark Herndon** (born 1955 in Massachusetts) joined Alabama as its sixth drummer in 1979 (also sings).

Awards: Named instrumental group of the year and vocal group of the year by Country Music Association, 1982; entertainer of the year awards from County Music Association, 1982, 1983, and 1984; entertainer of the year awards from Academy of Country Music, 1982, 1983, 1984, and 1985; named "country artist of the 1980s" by Academy of Country Music, 1989.

Addresses: *Management*—c/o Dale Morris Management, 818 19th Ave. S., Nashville, TN 37203. *Record company*—RCA Records 1133 Avenue of the Americas, New York, NY 10036-6758.

'Feels So Right' and 'An Old Flame Burning in Your Heart' with rousing uptempoed tunes like 'Mountain Music' and 'Tennessee River.' The results have been a balanced and fruitful melange which has brought Alabama an enthusiastic and broad audience of both mainstream country listeners and youthful devotees."

Three of Alabama's four principal members were born and raised near Fort Payne, a small town in the Appalachian region of Alabama. Gentry and Owen lived on neighboring farms, where they helped to eke a bare subsistence living from the thin soil. Gentry told the *Saturday Evening Post* that neither family could afford such basics as indoor plumbing, television, or radio. As boyhood chums, Gentry and Owen sang together at the Lookout Mountain Pentecostal Holiness Church; both came from musical families in the rural gospel tradition. In high school the boys met a distantly related cousin, Jeff Cook, whose Fort Payne family was slightly more affluent.

Cook owned a veritable "arsenal of musical equipment," to quote Crane, and he teamed with his country relatives to form a band. Their first performance in a local talent show resulted in a first prize—tickets to Nashville's Grand Ole Opry. Soon they were playing at theme parks and in small lounges in the vicinity of Fort Payne. Although they wanted to be full-time musicians, they took salaried jobs as carpet layers and as an electrician in order to make ends meet. They shared a

rented house, where they spent their off-hours practicing and composing music. Cook told *Country Music* that late at night, "even with the lights off we'd lay there in the dark and sing until one by one we'd drift off to sleep."

Finally, in 1972, the young men decided to quit their secure jobs to devote themselves entirely to the band. Calling themselves Wild Country, they hit the road in a battered Dodge van, playing gigs at Holiday Inns and honky tonk bars all across the South. One regular venue was The Bowery, in the seaside resort of Myrtle Beach, South Carolina; the band members would perform and then sell albums they had produced at their own expense. No one in Alabama remembers those lean years with any fondness. "After six months another group would've given up," Owen told *People* magazine. "We started playing music as a business rather than just treating it like a big party." Cook told the *Saturday Evening Post:* "We had just about every reason to quit. But we went on anyhow."

Wild Country changed its name to Alabama in 1977. Cook gave several reasons for the switch to the *Satur-*

> "Alabama will never put on a show you couldn't take your children to see."

day Evening Post: "Alabama is a good short name, and you can't copyright a state name. It's also a good alphabetical place to be in a music store. That's the first album that's gonna be in there." In 1979 drummer Rick Scott left the band and was replaced by Mark Herndon. Within six months Alabama had its first recording contract. Dallas-based MDJ Records released the single "I Wanna Come Over," and the song made the top thirty on the country charts. The group's debut professionally produced album, *My Home's in Alabama* (1980), also hit the country charts quickly and remained there for thirteen weeks. In the wake of that success, Alabama signed with RCA and became, in four short years, the best selling group in the history of country music.

Crane wrote that Alabama's lyrics "take the listener on a journey through their past; bringing us to their home, introducing us to their lovers, and inviting us to share some of their experiences. It's a scenic ride on American roads and through human emotions. The music won't allow you to stay in one place too long, though, as tempos and sentiments change with every song. You get to like these boys on vinyl, their honesty and integrity, and especially their loyalty to their roots."

By all accounts the members of Alabama have remained as down-home genuine as their music. They all still live in Fort Payne, now with their wives and children; they do an annual benefit concert that helps finance numerous local charities, and they forbid public drinking among their retinue during concerts. According to Allen, "You can call it country or you can call it rock, but one thing is certain: Alabama will never put on a show you couldn't take your children to see."

Owen explained the band's philosophy in the *Saturday Evening Post*: "To me, all these awards we've won are something to live up to," he said. "We're not a bunch of angels, by any means. But we do believe in promoting the positive things . . . the kinds of things you've got to be aware of as far as the way you live your life." Having earned country music's most prestigious awards for songs they have written and performed themselves, Alabama's members have achieved their greatest goals. Owens told *People*, however, that he and his partners still nurture ambitions for the future. He called the country music business "a never ending process of wanting to be bigger and go further."

Selected discography

My Home's in Alabama, RCA, 1980.
Feels So Right, RCA, 1981.
Mountain Music, RCA, 1982.
The Closer You Get, RCA, 1983.
Roll On, RCA, 1984.
Greatest Hits, RCA, 1986.
The Touch, RCA, 1986.
Just Us, RCA, 1987.
Southern Star, RCA, 1989.

Also recorded *Alabama Christmas* and *40 Hour Week*, both with RCA.

Sources

Books

Malone, Bill C., *Country Music U.S.A.*, revised and enlarged edition, University of Texas Press, 1985.

Periodicals

Country Music, October, 1980.
People, May 3, 1982.
Saturday Evening Post, May, 1985.

—*Anne Janette Johnson*

Laurie Anderson

Performance artist; violinist

A performance artist "treads the high-wire between art and popular culture, between 'refined consciousness' and 'dumbness'. But by appropriating aspects of both—a well-worn tradition in avant-garde art—Anderson simply succeeds in creating an extraordinarily virtuosic in-joke." So wrote Sally Banes in the *Village Voice* in 1980, at the mid-point of Laurie Anderson's career in performance art. Thanks to a long-term recording contract with Warner Bros., Anderson has become the most popularly recognized figure in that ever-changing field of music—art and solo performance. She is a multitalented musician, once described as "a recording artist who can do her own MTV videos and record cover graphics," who is one of the most controversial artists of our times.

Raised outside of Chicago in a musical family, Anderson studied violin before moving to New York to take a degree in Art History from Barnard College in 1969. She earned an M.F.A. in Sculpture from Columbia University in 1972 and studied with noted minimalist artist Sol Le Witt. Anderson began to perform as an element of her own "installation pieces," combined exhibitions and events in small art galleries, museums and post-modern dance spaces. They included text, films or videos, as in the narrative of her own photographs, *Story Show,* that she exhibited in 1972. *Automotive,* which she described as her first performance piece, was a setting of car horns in an open space in Rochester, Vermont, that year.

From 1973 to the present, Anderson has created installations at galleries or museums that require her performance as a musician. She is associated with the electric and/or altered violin—an instrument that can be plucked or bowed as if it were a conventional accoustic fiddle. But she frequently experiments with its extraordinary sound capabilities. She has rigged her violins with prerecorded music, as in her *Duets on Ice,* so that she played a duet on accoustic violin with the tape of herself hidden inside her tape-bow violin. On each occasion in New York and in Genoa, the "duet" was performed on blocks of ice and lasted, at each performance, until the ice melted. More recently, she composed *Like a Stream* for her tape-bow altered violin accompanied by the St. Paul Chamber Orchestra in 1978.

Anderson also alters her voice for performance. In her six-hour-long *United States I-IV,* she used a Vocoder to split and sample her own voice into a variety of effects including a "vocal transformation from female to male . . . [that] reminded one of Lily Tomlin's use of transvestism to make anti-sexist statements," as Stephen Holden described a "works-in-progress" appearance in 1982. She can also alter the "age" of her voice electronically, re-creating herself as a chorus of children, adolescents, mature adults, or the elderly.

Her installations, requiring a limited present audience, have become less important to her career than recordings, which can be taped for a much wider audience. She had originally been attracted by the impermanence of art, telling Robert Palmer in the *New York Times* that "That was very important to me, because it made the work so much about memory. The only way to document it, really, is to use your memory, I refused to even let people take pictures of it for a long time." As Tom Johnson described one installation in his *Village Voice* column in 1977, Anderson soon adapted the technology of permanence of music to her art. "Anyone who wandered into the Holly Solomon Gallery last month was confronted by, of all things, a jukebox. It was a big stereo model, all lit up in the usual way. If you pushed a few buttons, it would play any one of 124 singles by Laurie Anderson. . . . The singles in Anderson's jukebox were in an artsy sort of semi-popular vein. . . . Number 121 admitted a number of extraneous sounds, such as a boat horn and a parrot. Number 100 featured a talking jew's harp that conveyed a text almost comprehensibly. Number 103, 'Like a CB,' lamented the intrusion of CB signals on home stereo equipment and itself had a brief CB-type intrusion."

Selections of her works were included in two significant anthology albums in the 1970s—*Airwaves* (1977) and *New Music for Electronic and Recorded Material* (1977). Her song, "O Superman" (1981), became a surprise number one hit in Great Britain and brought her to the attention of Warner Bros. Records. The beat that came naturally to her, having grown up in the rock and roll era, brought her odd sounds and unusual lyrics to an enormous audience and Anderson became performance art's first rock star and Warner Bros. first conceptualist. Anderson described the process of her recording to Robert Palmer's "The Pop Life" column in the *New York Times:* "On [*Big Science*], I tried to integrate the music, the singing and the talking. . . . But I try to lock those elements a little tighter [for] listening. I'm so used to depending on music, language and a third thing, the picture, that making this album was like—gulp."

Much of the work of performance artists like Anderson or Philip Glass, who combine minimalist music with overwhelming visual spectacle, has been compared to opera. Anderson's massive multi-media work, *United States I-IV,* has often been so desribed. She told Michael VerMeulen in *In Performance* that it grew out of her social experiences abroad, "sitting at dinner tables in Europe and having people ask me: 'How can you Americans be behaving that way? How could you have elected that guy? What's wrong with you people? What's wrong with your cities? Why are they rotting? Why don't you care about sick people? How can you live in a society run by computers? Why do you spend so much time in your cars? Why don't you care about your mothers and fathers?'"

United States I-IV was a work in progress for much of Anderson's career. Part I, "Americans on the Move," about transportation as a metaphor for change, was premiered at The Kitchen, a New York performance space, in 1979. The second part, on politics, was first presented at a proscenium theater in New York. Part Three, about money, was seen in partial previews in Anderson's concerts during 1983, while Part Four, concerning love, was given its premiere at the Brooklyn Academy of Music's prestigeous Next Wave Festival in 1984.

Critics from mainstream theatre/music and the avant garde world were disappointed with the work. In a retrospective article on performance art, the *New York Times* reported that it "was meant to be a portrayal of this country, composed of a mixture of visual images, music, Zen koans [chants] and theatrical gesture . . . suggesting an American society that is all technological surface and commerce, empty slogans and formulaic language. . . . The result—far from being an avant-garde challenge to American culture—was as formulaic as the questions [she] was inspired by. [It], in fact, displayed many of the characteristics Miss Anderson seemed to think belong to the United States—preoccupation with technological novelty, celebrations of cliches and surface."

The *Village Voice* assigned two critics to the premiere—theatre editor Erika Munk and performance art specialist Sally Banes. As Munk described the event, "Anderson's work leans heavily on charm, suggestion and light irony, but these don't explain its fleeting quality either. There's something disturbing under the charm, and it's not, I think, a disturbance she intends. Anderson gives us songs and anecdotes, imagery, a persona, an enviroment, but basically she is performing an attitude—towards the means of art, its subjects, its interplay with the audience—which embraces all these things, and taken over the hours, diminishes them."

Banes was also disappointed. "Must a performance about a trivial culture—or trivial aspects of a very

---

Basically she is performing an attitude—towards the means of art, its subjects, its interplay with the audience— which embraces all these things and diminishes them.

---

complex culture—be as shallow and pretentious as the life it describes? . . . The references to popular culture are eerie and empty, rather than vibrant. They dessicate, rather than vitalize, the world they describe. Yet some of the most powerful songs in *United States* quote from 30's culture rather than the 80's. . . . Graphic imagery from the 30's crops up throughout the four sections. Some of Anderson's appeal has to do with her technology-futurism hype, but some of it also has to do with depression nostalgia."

Now best known for her recordings, Anderson continues to create live art works that depend on combinations of environmental and technological determinates. Every performance requires the recreation of the human voice and all instruments through electric and computerized programming. She has recently attempted to recreate the performance mode on recordings. She includes photographs, diagrams, and instructions in her albums to develop a multi-layering effect of hearing on audio equipment what musicians are performing on audio equipment in order to sound like different instruments.

Many of Anderson's installation pieces have been published by galleries as a permanent art form, among them *Transportation/Transportation* (1973; Pace University Print Shop) and *Performance by Artists* (1979; Art Metropole, Toronto). She has also published the illustrated text of *United States* (Harper & Row, 1984). Her "high-tech, one-woman show," *What Do You Mean We?*, was shown on the Public Broadcasting Service series dedicated to experimental and performance art, "Alive from Off Center," in 1986. Her film, "Home of the Brave" (Warner Bros., 1986) has also been seen on the Public Broadcasting Service.

Recently, Anderson has returned to less stagey events. Her concert at the "Serious Fun Festival" at Lincoln Center in 1988 was admired by John Rockwell in the *New York Times* as "heartwarming." "Her singing seemed new because there was so much of it and it sounded strong compared with her mostly spoken story-songs of the past or her mousy vocalizations of a couple of years ago. The accompaniment consisted of herself alone, bereft of a quasi-rock band . . . it was fascinating and somehow ingratiating to see her alone on stage the way she used to be back at the Kitchen and other haunts, mustering up an extraordinary range of vocal and instrumental textures all be herself."

Anderson's future in music and performance art will undoubtedly lead to more controversy. She is experimenting more with videos and has discussed the possibilities of making works directly on to video discs, without any live performances. She has been able to enlarge the audience for mixed-media work by her mainstream recording contracts and appearances on MTV. Many audiences now anticipate her next moves.

Selected discography

Big Science, (includes "O Superman"), Warner Brothers, 1982.
Mister Heartbreak, Warner Brothers, 1984.
United States Live (five-LP set), Warner Brothers, 1984.
Home of the Brave (motion picture soundtrack), Warner Brothers, 1986.

Work has also appeared on music anthologies, including *Airwaves*, One Ten Records, 1977, and *New Music for Electronic and Recorded Material*, 1750 Arch Street Records, 1977.

Writings

United States (illustrated text of performance piece and record album of the same name), Harper, 1984.

Sources

Artforum, February, 1982.
In Performance, Volume 2, Number 5.
Los Angeles Reader, September 11, 1981.
New York Times, October 27, 1980; April 21, 1982; February 6, 1983; March 10, 1983; August 12, 1984; September 6, 1986; July 23, 1988.
Newsweek, June 29, 1981.
Village Voice, February 28, 1977; October 11, 1980; June 8, 1982; February 22, 1983; March 13, 1984; July 24, 1984.

—Barbara Stratyner

Claudio Arrau

Claudio Arrau is among the most durable and versatile pianists of the twentieth century. His career extends more than eighty years, and in that time he has distinguished himself in a phenomenal range of music—from Baroque master J. S. Bach to Romantics such as Robert Schumann and Franz Liszt, and from the towering genius Ludwig van Beethoven to key Impressionist Claude Debussy. Throughout much of his career Arrau has also performed at a pace that might prove exhausting to less disciplined musicians: in his most hectic period, stretching from the 1920s into the 1960s, he annually gave more than one hundred performances and still managed to produce a vast catalog of recorded works. Even into the 1970s and '80s his schedule has remained relatively formidable. Arrau, however, seems undaunted by the demands of his career, and he dismisses the belief that a performer's abilities must inevitably decline. "I think an artist in his development doesn't necessarily have an up and down," he told Joseph Horowitz in the *New York Times*. "In most cases an artist's development only goes *up*."

Arrau was born in Chile in 1903. A prodigy, Arrau prospered under the tutelage of his mother, a piano instructor. At age five he held his first public performance, playing works by Mozart and Schumann. Within two years he was known among Chilean music afficianados as a remarkable talent, and in 1910 he was given a ten-year scholarship for studying in Germany's music center, Berlin. Arrau's greatest teacher there was Martin Krause, a former pupil of Liszt's. Krause devoted himself extensively to educating young Arrau in nearly all matters, from music—Beethoven's compositions were especially emphasized—to nutrition, aesthetics, and even etiquette.

In the mid-1910s Arrau performed his first Berlin recital and earned several awards. Soon afterwards he began performing outside Germany and with such conductors as Wilhelm Furtwangler, who became one of Arrau's favorite musical collaborators. Arrau's career seemed to be developing impressively, but he faltered when Krause died in 1918. Without his mentor, Arrau suffered a devastating loss of self-confidence, and after a mismanaged tour of the United States he found himself in despair back in Berlin.

Through therapy with psychoanalyst Hubert Abrahamsohn, who had studied under Carl Jung, Arrau gradually recovered from his depression and found greater awareness of himself as an interpretive artist. By the late 1920s Arrau was once again realizing success, winning a prestigious piano competition in Switzerland and commencing another concert tour. Europe, however, was teeming with musicians, and in order to sustain public interest and draw further attention, Arrau undertook a publicity stunt in 1935 by playing J. S. Bach's

For the Record. . .

Born February 6, 1903, in Chillan, Chile; naturalized U.S. citizen, 1979; son of Carlos (an oculist) and Lucrecia (a piano teacher; maiden name, Leon) Arrau; married Ruth Schneider, July 8, 1937; children: Carmen, Mario, Christopher.

Concert pianist, 1908—. Performed extensively throughout Europe during 1920s and 1930s, came to United States during World War II, toured U.S. during 1940s, toured Mexico and South America during 1950s, still performs over fifty concert dates per year. Established Claudio Arrau Fund for Young Musicians, 1967.

Awards: Winner of numerous awards and prizes, c. 1910—, including Gustav Hollander Award, c. 1910s; Liszt Prize (two-timer winner) c. 1910s; Gran Prix International des Pianists, Geneva, Switzerland, 1927; gold medal from Chilean government, c. 1950s; Chilean National Arts Prize; Mexico's Order of the Aztec Eagle; Commander of the French Legion of Honor; and the UNESCO Music Prize, 1983.

Addresses: *Home*—Douglaston, N.Y. *Manager*—ICM Artists Ltd., 40 W. 57th St., New York N.Y. 10019.

was known throughout the Western world for his musical prowess, and though he sustained that awareness through near-continual touring, he also found time to record, with particular emphasis on Beethoven's sonatas and concertos. Towards the end of the decade, after complete sets of the Beethoven compositions, he undertook similarly extensive recordings of works by Romantic masters Schumann, Chopin, and Liszt. These records earned Arrau still further accolades as an artist of astounding interpretive powers and range.

Acclaim continued to be accorded Arrau as he began realizing pivotal birthdays and anniversaries. In 1978, he celebrated his seventy-fifth year by giving nearly one hundred performances in a total of fourteen countries. Among this tour's highlights was a New York City recital featuring Beethoven's *"Les Adieux" Sonata,* Liszt's *B Minor Sonata,* and Brahms's *F Minor Sonata. Newsweek* reported that Arrau "attacked the pieces in typical Arrau fashion: with fierce aplomb and with scrupulous respect for the notes as written." Another career highlight occurred in 1984 when he returned again to his native Chile and performed a nationally broadcast recital.

> *"In 1978, [Arrau] celebrated his seventy-fifth year by giving nearly one hundred performances in a total of fourteen countries."*

Despite his age, Arrau has maintained a demanding work pace into the 1980s. He still performs at least fifty concerts and recitals each year and continues devoting himself to recording and re-recording the vast piano literature. Among his recording projects in the 1980s are new interpretations of the Beethoven concertos and selected Beethoven sonatas—his Beethoven recordings alone number more than eighty—as well as Mozart sonatas and some Schubert compositions. In 1978, by which time Arrau had already been performing for seventy years, he explained his work pace to *Newsweek:* "I'm afraid if I stop I won't have the courage to start again."

complete keyboard compositions in a series of twelve recitals. When this series earned Arrau considerable praise, he followed in 1936 with a series devoted to Mozart's entire keyboard works, and two years later he gave the first of his many series presenting Beethoven's thirty-two sonatas.

The success of these artistically demanding—and physically exhausting—feats established Arrau in Europe as an artist of phenomenal range and stamina. In America, though, he was unknown, and when he fled there after World War II erupted he found himself once again forced to develop an audience. American critics, however, quickly rallied behind Arrau, who powerfully impressed them with his versatility and unusual stamina. At the end of World War II, by which time Arrau had given more than two hundred concerts and recitals, he was widely acclaimed as an artist of distinguished interpretive powers as well. More than one critic remarked that Arrau produced probing, dramatic interpretations whether playing Bach or Mozart or Schumann.

During the 1950s Arrau broadened his appeal by performing extensively in Mexico and South America. Returning to his native Chile proved particularly triumphant, with audiences providing wildly enthusiastic ovations and the Chilean government granting him a gold medal for his achievements. By the 1960s Arrau

Selected discography

Beethoven, Ludwig van, *Piano Concerto No. 4 in G, Opus 58,* Phillips.
Beethoven, *Piano Concerto No. 5 in E Flat, Opus 73,* Phillips.

Beethoven, *Piano Sonata No. 21 in C, Opus 53 ("Waldstein")*, Phillips.

Brahms, Johannes, *Piano Concerto No. 1 in D, Opus 15*, Angel.

Brahms, Johannes, *Piano Sonata No. 3 in F, Op. 5*, Phillips.

Chopin, Frederic, *24 Preludes, Opus 28*, Odyssey.

Chopin, *Andante Spianato and Grand Polonaise, Opus 22* [and] *Kradowiak, Opus 14*, Phillips.

Chopin, *Piano Concerto No. 1 in E, Opus 11*, Phillips.

Debussy, Claude, *Preludes, Book One*, Phillips.

Liszt, Franz, *Twelve Transcendental Etudes for Piano*, Phillips.

Liszt, *Piano Sonata in B*, Phillips.

Liszt, *Piano Concerto No. 1 in E Flat*, Columbia.

Mozart, Wolfgang Amadeus, *Piano Sonata No. 12 in F, K. 332*, Phillips.

Schubert, Franz, *Piano Sonata in A, Opus Posthumous, D. 959*, Phillips.

Shumann, Robert, *Kreisleriana, Opus 16*, Columbia.

Schumann, *Kinderszenen, Opus 15*, Phillips.

Sources

Books

Dubal, David, *Reflections From the Keyboard: The World of the Concert Pianist*, Summit Books, 1984.

Horowitz, Joseph, *Conversations With Arrau*, Knopf, 1982.

Periodicals

Christian Science Monitor, July 28, 1983.

Life, August 25, 1972.

Newsweek, February 20, 1978.

New York Times, February 5, 1978.

Burt Bacharach

Composer, songwriter, pianist, and singer

A unique love song may be the hardest project for any contemporary composer, but Burt Bacharach has been able to create over two hundred ballads, tunes, and themes that make contact with the emotions of his stage, screen, and recording audiences. From "Walk On By" to "That's What Friends Are For," the Bacharach sound has been on the airwaves for over thirty astoundingly succesful years.

Born in Kansas City, Missouri, in 1929, Bacharach grew up in Queens, New York, where his father served as a fashion industry journalist. He learned to play the piano and spent his adolescence listening to a wide range of musical styles. Bacharach's formal studies in composition and form were under three experimenters in flexible rhythms and free-flowing melodies who were willing to support his developing personal style—Darius Milhaud, at the New School for Social research in New York; Boleslav Martineau at the Mannes School of Music there; and Henry Cowell at the Music Academy of the West in Santa Barbara, California. He later told *ASCAP Today* that his early influences had also included Maurice Ravel, Dizzy Gillespie, and Charlie Parker. Bacharach's music, with its shifting rhythms, wide melodic jumps and unusual structures, owe much to all six of these teachers.

Military service in Korea and Germany brought Bacharach experience with performing as a concert pianist and as an accompanist for popular vocalists. After returning to New York, he played for Vic Damone, Polly Bergen, the Ames Brothers, and many others, most memorably Marlene Dietrich, with whom he toured as conductor and arranger from 1958 to 1961. He has since consigned to oblivion his first published song, "The Night Plane to Heaven," and many others from the early 1950s. But his meeting with lyricist Hal David at the Paramount Music Corporation in 1957 brought their two first succesful songs, "Magic Moments" and "The Story of My Life." After his three years with Dietrich, he returned to a partnership with David that lasted until 1976.

That long-lasting partnership included over 200 individual songs (most written for Dionne Warwick), title songs for major Hollywood films, and a musical comedy, *Promises, Promises,* that was a hit on Broadway and in London. Their collaborative works represent a combination of both the American popular love song tradition and the experiments of Bacharach's mentors. They have been compared to the best of Irving Berlin, Jerome Kern, and Rodgers and Hart's conversational ballads because the lyrics are set as if they were spoken. Lines are seldom broken in mid-sentence, but instead flow throughout a vast melodic range. Bacharach has always denied that his music is other than normal songwriting, as he did to *Newsweek* at the height of the collaboration: "I look back at songs and wish I could have simplified them. Its not done to be clever. You've got less than two minutes in a song and you want every second to count. Forget rules. Just listen and feel. My trouble is that these so-called abnormalities seem conventional and normal to me."

Bacharach was able to hear his songs at all because singer Dionne Warwick had become a third member of the partnership with Hal David. He had met Warwick when one of his early songs, "Mexican Divorce," was recorded by the drifters for Scepter Records in 1960. Warwick was a member of the Gospelaires, the backup group for that recording session. In 1962, she recorded

their "Don't Make Me Over" for Scepter—soon reaching the top ten on the pop charts. Over the next five years, Warwick made hits out of Bacharach and David's "Anyone Who Had a Heart," "Walk On By," "Reach Out for Me," "The Look of Love," "This Guy's in Love With You," "Do You Know the Way to San Jose?," and "What the World Needs Now."

At first, writers questioned Bacharach's experiments with the popular love song and analyzed their hits as oddities, such as the fourteen time signatures in "Anyone Who Had a Heart." But Warwick proved the "singability" of the tunes by selling over 12.5 million copies of Bacharach/David songs by 1970. They soon became popular with a wide variety of performers. "What's New Pussycat," for example, was recorded by Warwick, Tom Jones, and The Chipmunks. Other artists who included Bacharach/David songs on their albums were rockers Joe Cocker, Stevie Wonder, and Issac Hayes; jazz stylists Bill Evans and Billy Vaughn; vocalists Barbra Streisand and Vic Damone; and Bacharach himself. The uncredited author of a 1965 *Newsweek* article praised Bacharach's inventiveness and stated that he was "not afraid of melodies . . . has the soft touch and sets up his songs for surprising explosions or dramatic fadeouts . . . a witty composer who kids his own melodies with tinny pianos and punctuates tender tunes with sudden bumps and grinds."

With Hal David, Bacharach was also becoming known for scores and title songs for Hollywood films, many of them contemporary comedies, including *Send Me No Flowers* and *Promise Her Anything,* that required an up-to-date theme song as an advertising lure. "The Look of Love" was created for the James Bond thriller "Casino Royale" (1967) and their Oscar-winning "Raindrops Keep Fallin' on My Head" was written for the Paul Newman/Robert Redford cowboy film, "Butch Cassidy and the Sundance Kid" (1970). The former song way outshone its film, but both "Raindrops . . ." (as performed by B.J. Thomas) and "Butch Cassidy" were enormously popular for years. "Raindrops . . ." was also recorded by Perry Como, guitarist Buddy Merrill, Andy Williams, and Dionne Warwick. Among their many other film themes that became popular as individual songs were the title songs for *What's New Pussycat* and *Alfie,* for which Bacharach won a Grammy for best instrumental arrangement. Bacharach has also provided complete scores for many films, most notably "The Man Who Shot Liberty Valance" and "Butch Cassidy and the Sundance Kid." For the latter film, he won a Grammy for best original soundtrack recording and an Oscar for best original score.

Bacharach and David next took on the challenge of creating a full score of characterizational solos, duets, and ensembles for a plotted Broadway musical, "Promises, Promises." An adaptation by Neil Simon of the Billy Wilder film "The Apartment," the musical amassed a very succesful 1281 performances on Broadway before moving to London (for 560 performances) and a fourteen-month national tour. The title song and "I'll Never Fall in Love Again" both acheived top ten status as singles for Warwick. Critical response was favorable, with Brendan Gill of the *New Yorker* "telling two hundred millions of my fellow citizens . . . to go and see it as quickly as possible." "Promises, Promises" was one of the first musicals on Broadway to adapt the technology of the recording studio to the live theatre, as well as adapting the totally contemporary sound of Bacharach and David's songs to the requirements of a plot. The show was scored for electric organ, guitar, and organ and Broadway's first pit chorus of four women was installed in the Shubert Theater. The original cast recording of the show was honored by NARAS as the best of 1969.

With hit films, a hit show, and songs all over the play list, Bacharach returned to the concert tour in 1970—this time as the composer, conductor, and featured performer. Since, as fellow songwriter Sammy Cahn put it succinctly, "he is the only composer who doesn't look like a dentist," Bacharach enjoyed the status of a celebrity sex symbol. He appeared with his father in a well-received series of print advertisements endorsing Jim Beam Bourbon. He performed his own songs on successful albums for A&M under a long-term contract and starred in television specials devoted to his work. In 1971, in fact, his first television special, "The Burt Bacharach Special" (CBS, 1970) beat his second, "Another Evening with Burt Bacharach" (NBC, 1970), for an Emmy.

Bacharach's professional and personal lives changed in the late 1970s when he and David split their partnership. This led to a rift with Warwick, who had been guaranteed by contract songs for one album per year for another three years. Her suit against Bacharach and David was eventually settled out of court. Bacharach's solo projects included *Women,* a recording with the Houston Symphony, and songs for Carly Simon and Libby Titus. The score for the re-make of "Lost Horizon" was praised, but the film was not succesful. His second marriage, to actress Angie Dickenson, ended.

In 1979, however, he began a new collaboration (and, eventually, marriage) with lyricist Carole Bayer Sager. Their romantic ballads, such as "Easy to Love Again" on the *Sometimes Late at Night* album, are markedly less complex than his works with David and more fitted to Sager's less-vernacular lyrics and personal singing style. Sager described it as a "concept album, a song cycle in which each track ties into the next," in *People* magazine. Their most succesful colaborative song, "That's What Friends are For," was created in 1985 as a benefit recording for a medical charity that promoted AIDS research. As performed by Dionne Warwick, it has earned millions for its cause.

Compositions

Composer (with lyricist Hal David, 1957-76; and with Lyricist Carole Bayer Sager, 1979—) of numerous songs, including "Alfie," "Always Something There to Remind Me," "Any Day Now," "Anyone Who Had a Heart," "Baby, It's You," "Blue on Blue," "(They Long to Be) Close to You," "Do You Know the Way to San Jose?," "Don't Make Me Over," "I Just Don't Know What To Do with Myself," "I'll Never Fall in Love Again," "I Say a Little Prayer," "The Look of Love," "Make It Easy on Yourself," "The Man Who Shot Liberty Valance," "Message to Michael," "One Less Bell to Answer," "Only Love Can Break a Heart," "Promises, Promises," "Raindrops Keep Fallin' on My Head," "This Guy's in Love with You," "Tower of Strength," "Trains and Boats and Planes," "Twenty-four Hours from Tulsa," "Walk on By," "What the World Needs Now is Love," "What's New, Pussycat?," "Who's Been Sleeping in My Bed?," "Wishin' and Hopin'," and "Wives and Lovers."

Selected discography

Promises, Promises, Liberty/Capitol, 1968.
Butch Cassidy and the Sundance Kid, A&M, 1969.
Burt Bacharach's Greatest Hits, A&M, 1987.
Burt Bacharach, A&M, 1988.

Sources

ASCAP Today, August 1970.
New York Times, December 2, 1968; May 11, 1971; June 10, 1985.
New Yorker, December 7, 1968.
Newsweek, August 2, 1965; June 22, 1970.
People, June 1, 1981.
San Francisco Chronicle, July 30, 1975.

—*Barbara Stratyner*

Joan Baez

Singer, songwriter, guitarist

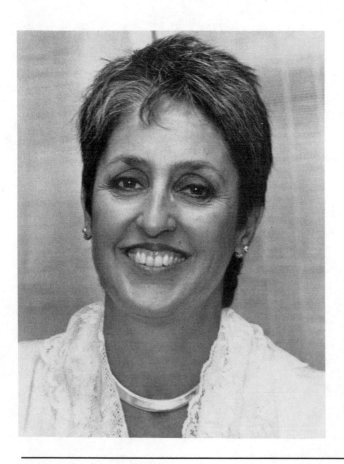

The voice can be a powerful instrument in music and social activism. For Joan Baez, through many years of performance, writing, and speaking out, the voice is a symbol of an individual's power to effect change. She was born in Staten Island, New York, January 9, 1941, the daughter of Dr. Albert Baez, a physicist. Baez's autobiography, *And a Voice to Sing With,* details her childhood as a faculty child in Ithaca, New York, and in Bagdad, Redlands, and Palo Alto, California, where she attended high school and began to play the guitar. Relocated to the Boston area, where her father had joined the faculty at the Massachusetts Institute of Technology, she attended Boston University and began to perform professionally at small clubs, such as Tulla's Coffee Grinder. Her two years of apprenticeship in the Boston area brought her to the attention of Bob Gibson, who invited her to participate in the 1959 Newport Folk Festival.

Baez began a long association with Vanguard Records, then America's foremost folk label, in 1960 with her album *Joan Baez.* It brought acclaim and invitations to perform in folk clubs and concert halls throughout the college circuit and major cities. She soon became a symbol of the folk revival and was featured on the cover of *Time.* Her voice, described by Robert Shelton in a 1960 review of an early concert in the *New York Times,* was a "a soprano voice, surprisingly never trained, that has a purity, penetrating clarity and control that not a few art singers would envy. With seeming effortlessness, Miss Baez produced a purling, spun-gold tone particularly suited to the lyric Anglo-American songs and ballads that made up most of her program." The phrase, "achingly pure soprano," cited often by critics over the last 25 years, also dates from this first concert tour. She has denied the importance of the "purity" of her voice in interviews throughout her long career. In a 1963 article by Nat Hentoff, for example, she praised interpretation over mere quality: "I think of a rural folk singer—Doc Watson's mother—whose voice might not seem beautiful to some people. But her voice has a straightness, an honesty, a purity. On the other hand, a voice may have all the tone quality and all the vibrato you could ask for, and yet it'll sound so bland that it has no beauty at all." Baez's voice, her songs, guitar style, and even her long flowing hair set a pattern for a generation of young folk singers and balladeers. The hair was cut in 1968, and the soprano has darkened and mellowed but the influence remains strong.

Her tour of campuses was also noteworthy for Baez's refusal to perform in segregated arenas and concert halls—a decision that led her to limit the Southern part of her tours to black colleges. Raised as a Quaker, she also refused to pay that part of her Federal Income Tax which, the Society of Friends believed, was used for military spending. Part of her income from performing and recording went to found the Institute for the Study of Nonviolence (now called the Resource Center for Nonviolence) in Carmel Valley, California. Her social activism also led to her support for the civil rights movement and its concurrent voting rights protests, as well as anti-war events around the world. She was arrested and jailed for non-violent protests of the Vietnam-era draft, as was her husband, David Harris, who spent much of their marriage in jail. Her focus throughout her life has been on nonviolent protest as a means of ending wars, war-related industries and national budgets, and discrimination. She has worked through Amnesty International since 1972 and Humanitas since its founding in 1979.

Although most of her audience supported the same beliefs that she did, Baez's activities were often criticized publically by others. Her parodied but recogniz-

able image was included in Al Capp's "Li'l Abner" comic strip as "Joanie Phonie" in 1967. Also that year, in a move that reminded many of the banning of famed black soprano Marian Anderson thirty years earlier, she was denied permission by the Daughters of the American Revolution to perform in Constitution Hall (capacity: 3800), and so she appeared instead before a crowd of over 30,000 at the Washington Monument. Baez's most controversial activity was her participation in a tour of (then North) Vietnam in 1972, which produced the album *Where are You, My Son?*

The almost continuous concert tours and recordings for a decade brought Baez and her message to an ever wider audience. In a 1979 joint interview with Judy Collins, she told the *New York Times* that performance and the message are interrelated: "The concert becomes a context of its own, and that's what's beautiful about being able to stand up there—that I can say what I want, put the songs where I want them and, hopefully, give people an evening of beautiful music as well." She has appeared on most college campuses, in Carnegie Hall and major concert halls, and in outdoor festivals. Baez was one of only four musical acts that participated in both Woodstock, the defining event of the late 1960s music scene, and in LiveAid, the 1985 international rock concert to raise money for African relief, an irony that she described in her autobiography. Both events reached a wide audience—Woodstock became a film from Warner Brothers; LiveAid was broadcast on worldwide television. Many of Baez's solo tours were also filmed as documentaries, among them, the Rolling Tunder Revue (with Bob Dylan, 1975) and Live Europe '83, which produced a French television film and an award-winning album of the same name. A 1970 documentary, "Carry It On" covers her life at the time of Harris's arrest, but also includes 13 songs in concerts.

The folk revival of the 1960's brought widespread attention to traditional folk forms and to the young folksingers who were writing new music, most notably, Baez and Bob Dylan. They performed together often at the start of their careers, as in her 1963 Forest Hills Music Festival concert in New York at which she devoted half of the program to Dylan songs, sung by him, by her, and as duets. The *New York Times* review of that summer concert praised her programming decision: "To have her so closely align herself with Mr. Dylan's charismatic poetry resulted in an unforgettable evening." They also toured together in the mid-1970's. Her performance of his "Blowin' in the Wind," was included on the Grammy Award presentations of 1983 as an example of "Music has a message." Other Dylan songs, such as "That's Allright" and "A Hard Rain's a-Gonna Fall," remain in her repertoire.

Baez was criticized at the onset of her career for mixing her musical messages and not limiting herself to music on a specific theme or from a specific genre, as was traditional with folk singers in the 1950's. she defended herself to Nat Hentoff in the November 1963 *HiFi-Stereo Review:* "[The historical] aspect of folk music has always been so secondary with me. It's as if there were a mysterious string in me. If something I hear plucks that string, then I'll sing that song. It can be funny or serious, or it can be in another language. I can't analyze what qualities a song must have to do that to me." This generalism has become a major selling point in her later career. Baez's albums, like her concert appearances, always mix genres, including new songs (often about her son, Gabriel), American spirituals, Scottish hymns, and protest statements from different cultures. She has made recordings of folk songs paired with country-and-western numbers, as on her *David's Album,* which featured "Carry It On," as well as her popular cut of "Green Grass of Home." She stresses ballads and anthems by her and other contemporary writers, such as Leonard Cohen's "Suzanne," and Lennon/McCartney's "Imagine" and "Long and Winding Road"; but also includes ballad standards from the

---

Like Pete Seeger and the folk singers of the earlier generation, her voice is her conscience.

1940s and 1950s, including Julie London's "Cry Me a River" on her *Blowin' Away* album. Her music follows its sources into their music heritages, and she was one of the first American singers to perform reggae songs, like her 1983 "Warriors of the Sun," Latin American non-salsa styles, and the now-popular new African genres.

A 1977 *Village Voice* feature suggested that Baez's diversity had rescued her career and praised her use of rock-and-roll rhythms. In her 1987 *Recently* and on its tour, her repertory included, as it was described in the *New York Times:* "a spare, moving rendition of Dire straits' pacifist hymn, 'Brothers in Arms', a version of the Marian Anderson staple, 'Let Us Break Bread Together,' that finds the singer buoyed by a gospel chorus, and two equally strong renditions of songs evoking the agony of South Africa: Peter Gabriel's elegaic incantation 'Biko' and John Clegg's passionate 'Asimbonanga.'"

Baez's "achingly pure soprano" has deepened into a "richer, more dramatic" and fluid alto in recent years. A *New York Times* review of a 1983 concert praised her rendition of the spiritual "Swing Low Sweet Chariot": "Her rendition swept through two octaves with an authority and passion that few other singers could hope to muster."

The dual role of Joan Baez as a performer and as, in the words of *Rolling Stone's* John Grissim, Jr., "as a purveyor of an enjoined social consciousness and responsibility," has given her a place in American music that supports her activism. Like Pete Seeger and the folk singers of the earlier generation, her voice is her conscience. But for Baez, like Marian Anderson, the quality of her vocal production brings authority to her message.

Selected discography

Joan Baez, Vanguard, 1960.
Joan Baez 2, Vanguard, 1961.
In Concert, Vanguard, 1962.
In Concert 2, Vanguard, 1963.
Joan Baez 5, Vanguard, 1964.
Farewell, Angelina, Vanguard, 1965.
Noel, Vanguard, 1966.
Portrait, Vanguard, 1966.
Joan, Vanguard, 1967.
Baptism, Vanguard, 1968.
Any Day Now, Vanguard, 1968.
David's Album, Vanguard, 1969.
One Day at a Time, Vanguard, 1970.
First Ten Years, Vanguard, 1970.
Blessed Are, Vanguard, 1971.
Carry It On, Vanguard, 1972.
Come from the Shadows, A&M, 1972.
Where Are You Now, My Son?, A&M, 1973.
Gracias a la Vida (Here's to Life), A&M, 1974.
Diamonds & Rust, A&M, 1975.
Live in Japan, Vanguard, 1975.
Love Song Album, Vanguard, 1976.
From Every Stage, A&M, 1976.
Gulf Winds, A&M, 1976.
Blowin' Away, Portrait, 1977.
Golden Hour, Pye, 1972.
Hits: The Greatest and Others, Vanguard, 1973.
Best of Joan Baez, A&M, 1977.
Golden Hour 2, Pye.
House of the Rising Sun, Musidisc, 1978.
Honest Lulaby, Portrait, 1979.
Country Music, Vanguard, 1979.
Spotlight on Joan Baez, Portrait, 1980.
Live in Concert, Portrait, 1980.
The Magic of Joan Baez, K Tel, 1981.
Early Joan Baez I and II, Metronome.
Recently, Goldcastle, 1987.

Joan Baez in Concert, Vanguard, 1988.

Sources

Books

Baez, Joan, *And a Voice to Sing With,* Summit Books, 1987.

Periodicals

Hi Fi/Stereo Review, November, 1963.
New York Times, November 7, 1960; August 19, 1963; March 14, 1966; July 6, 1979; November 18, 1983; July 8, 1987; October 12, 1987; November 21, 1987.
Rolling Stone, December 7, 1968.
Time, June 1, 1962; November 23, 1962.
Village Voice, May 30, 1977.

—*Barbara Stratyner*

The Beach Boys

American rock group

O ne of the world's top-drawing rock music groups, the Beach Boys have riveted audiences for more than twenty-five years with songs celebrating the California dream. Promising a sundrenched paradise of fast cars and fast girls, where the surf's always up and the summer never ends, the all-American-looking musicians dominated the contemporary music scene for a good part of the 1960s. Unlike so many of their long-forgotten peers, however, the Beach Boys have remained popular year after year. In hits like "Surfer Girl," "Surfin' U.S.A.," "Help Me, Rhonda," and "Good Vibrations," the musicians combined catchy melodies with fantasy-filled lyrics to create a sound and a myth that continues to earn them scores of devoted fans. Indeed, pieces first regarded as faddish teen tunes have since won acclaim as original contributions to popular music, and many of the group's songs—like the Beach Boys themselves—are now considered classics.

The core of the Beach Boys was formed around the Wilson brothers, Brian, Carl, and Dennis (drowned in

1983); completing the group are cousin Mike Love and friend Al Jardine. The three brothers grew up in Hawthorne, California, a working-class suburb of Los Angeles several miles from the Pacific Ocean. Although the brothers received almost no formal musical training, they all demonstrated an interest in music fairly early in life. Brian, generally regarded as the genius behind the Beach Boys, is reported to have begun humming complete tunes at age eleven months and singing at age three; at sixteen, he was creating four-part harmonies with a simple tape recorder. Carl, a self-taught guitarist, also demonstrated a curiosity about music as a toddler. And by the time he was in his teens, Dennis, too, had become involved in the family pastime.

The boys' talents were fostered both by their father, Murry, a machine-shop owner and unsuccessful songwriter, and by their mother, Audree, who enjoyed singing. Family get-togethers, which included the Love relatives, frequently featured sing-alongs and gave cousin Mike plenty of opportunity to prove he had perfect pitch. The music-making was pretty much restricted to family gatherings, however, until Brian,

Dennis, Carl, and Mike competed in their local high school's talent show one year. Billed as Carl and the Passions, a name created to persuade the hesitant Carl to participate with them, the boys viewed the venture as something of a lark.

Not long afterwards, however, Brian, who had entered El Camino Junior College, began singing with fellow student and folk musician Al Jardine. The two thought it might be fun to start their own group and soon asked Mike, Carl, and Dennis to join them. Calling themselves the Pendletones, the five youths hoped to secure an audition with a recording company. When informed that they needed an angle and some original music to distinguish themselves from all the other aspiring musicians, the amateurs rose to the challenge. Dennis, a surfer, suggested capitalizing on the surfing craze that was just beginning to sweep California. As a result, Brian and Mike collaborated on a song they called "Surfin'."

The number interested the owners of Guild Music, the small recording and publishing operation that had published some of Murry's songs, and they arranged for the boys to record it. Although apparently put down live on a single track in just about an hour, "Surfin'" had a sound that appealed to the people at Candix, a local label, and they agreed to release the single for the group, renamed the Beach Boys, in 1961.

In short order the Beach Boys realized they had scored a success. The song appeared on the local charts and then, in mid-January, as number 118 on the *Billboard* charts. By the end of March "Surfin'" had reached number seventy-five, with sales hovering around fifty thousand copies. But more importantly, the single had attracted attention at Capitol Records, a pop label mainstay, and it wasn't long before the group signed a contract with Capitol that would carry them through the sixties. Their careers were launched.

The Capitol Record years are widely regarded as the Beach Boys' most productive. Although much of their earliest material was significantly influenced by the pop sound of a 1950s vocal group called the Four Freshmen (Brian's favorite) and by rock and roller Chuck Berry (Carl's preference), the boys had managed to create a new sound for themselves and are often credited as the originators of surfing music. One of their initial singles for Capitol, the June 1962 release "Surfin' Safari," was a hit, and their *Surfin' Safari* album, released in 1963, became their first gold record.

A landmark year, 1963 saw the Beach Boys leap to national celebrity, their success far outstripping all expectations. As their popularity escalated, so did demand for live concerts, and the rising stars found themselves constantly on the road. After several years, Brian, the group's main composer, decided to stop touring; while he stayed home to create new material for the group, Bruce Johnston replaced him live. By the end of 1964, the Beach Boys had recorded six albums for Capitol. Their future looked promising, and in the middle sixties the group assured their star status with hits that included such favorites as "Fun, Fun, Fun," "I Get Around," "Help Me, Rhonda," "California Girls," and "Barbara Ann."

Impressively, the Beach Boys were one of only a handful of American acts to survive the British Invasion of 1964 that was spearheaded by the Beatles and the Rolling Stones. Their music not only tapped into the surfing mania and the subsequent car craze, but it had also unfolded as a creative new sound distinguished by pure, joyous harmonies. In 1966 the group released their most sophisticated and successful song until that time, "Good Vibrations." By the end of the year polls were showing them to be the most popular group around, surpassing even the Beatles.

> "The Wilsons' happy myth of an untrammeled life of endless summers struck a chord in American suburbia in a way no other popular musicians had done."

Nineteen sixty-six had also seen the release of their extraordinary *Pet Sounds* album, an unusual, innovative recording that critics acclaimed as one of the most brilliant in the annals of popular music. A departure from the Beach Boys' traditional fun in the sun themes, *Pet Sounds* employed extraordinary production techniques to help present an emotional exploration of the various states of mind experienced on the way to maturity. Perhaps too sophisticated for the typical Beach Boy fan of the day, Brian's brainchild album fared better with the critics than with the average audience.

Before 1967 was half over, many people believed the Beach Boys were washed up. They had issued no new recordings for months and there was evidence of turmoil in the stars' personal lives as well as rumors of divisiveness within the group. In addition, their long-awaited *Smile* album, expected to be Brian's masterpiece, was scrapped (a few recovered cuts appeared on *Smiley Smile,* issued in lieu of the original). In retrospect, however, it appears that the Beach Boys'

careers were only in remission. After their obscurity during the late 1960s, they made a successful European showing in 1970, reclaimed status in the United States the following year, and hit another peak when their 1974 album *Endless Summer* went double platinum. In 1975 *Rolling Stone* magazine named the Beach Boys band of the year.

Although the Beach Boys in fact never quite regained the adulation they commanded during their heyday, the musicians have succeeded in remaining among the most popular, and most versatile, live entertainers in the business. They have survived not only extraordinary changes in popular music, but strife amongst themselves and their changing membership as well, including the 1983 death of Dennis Wilson. Woes notwithstanding, the group has continued to find itself in demand throughout the 1980s—albeit as "oldies" entertainment—and in recognition of their achievement, the members of the original Beach Boys were inducted into the Rock and Roll Hall of Fame in 1988.

Beloved by fans around the world, the Beach Boys, according to Timothy White in the *New York Times,* are regarded by many music lovers as "the most successful musical group in American history." Trying to sum up the reasons for the group's appeal, White suggested that "The Wilsons' happy myth of an untrammeled life of endless summers struck a chord in American suburbia in a way no other popular musicians had done. The essence of the American Dream is the belief that anyone can escape the limits and sorrows of his background by reinventing himself. . . . The Beach Boys themselves embodied and celebrated that dream."

Selected discography

Singles; For Candix

"Surfin'," 1961.
"Luau," 1961.
"Surfer Girl," 1962.
"Surfin' Safari," 1962.
"Judy," 1962.
"Karate," 1962.

Albums; For Capitol, except as noted

Surfin' Safari, 1962.
Surfin' U.S.A., 1963.
Surfer Girl, 1963.
Little Deuce Coupe, 1963.
Shut Down (two songs), 1963.
Shut Down, Volume 2, 1964.
All Summer Long, 1964.
Christmas Album, 1964.

Beach Boys Concert, 1964.
Beach Boys Today, 1965.
Summer Days (and Summer Nights), 1965.
Beach Boys Party, 1965.
Pet Sounds, 1966.
Smiley Smile, Brother, 1967.
Wild Honey, 1967.
Friends, 1968.
20/20, 1969.
Sunflower, Reprise, 1970.
Surf's Up, Reprise, 1971.
Carl and the Passions: So Tough, Reprise, 1972.
Holland, Reprise, 1973.
Beach Boys in Concert, Reprise, 1973.
Live in London, 1976.
Fifteen Big Ones, Reprise, 1976.
Beach Boys Love You, Reprise, 1977.
MIU, Reprise, 1978.
L.A. (Light Album), Caribou, 1979.
Keepin' the Summer Alive, Caribou, 1980.
The Beach Boys, CBS, 1985.
Be True to Your School.
California Girls.

Also released numerous anthologies, including *Best of the Beach Boys,* 1966, Volume 2, 1967, *Endless Summer,* 1974, *Spirit of America,* 1975, *Stack of Tracks,* 1976, *Ten Years of Harmony,* 1985, and *Golden Harmonies,* 1986.

Sources

Books

Gaines, Steven, *Heroes and Villains,* New American Library, 1986.
Leaf, David, *The Beach Boys and the California Myth,* Grosset & Dunlap, 1978.
Milward, John, *The Beach Boys Silver Anniversary,* Doubleday, 1985.
Preiss, Byron, *The Beach Boys,* revised edition, St. Martin's, 1983.
Tobler, John, *The Beach Boys,* Chartwell Books, 1978.

Periodicals

Newsweek, January 27, 1986; August 1, 1988.
New York Times, June 26, 1988.
People, January 16, 1984.
Rolling Stone, June 7, 1984; November 5-December 10, 1987.

—*Nancy H. Evans*

Chuck Berry

Singer, songwriter, guitarist

"If there were a single fountainhead for rock guitar, Chuck Berry would be it," wrote Gene Santoro in *The Guitar*. Indeed, the list of artists influenced by the "father of rock and roll" is nearly endless. From the Beach Boys and the Beatles to Jimi Hendrix and on to Van Halen and Stevie Ray Vaughan, every popular musician knows the impact that Chuck Berry has had on popular music. As Eric Clapton stated, there's really no other way to play rock 'n' roll.

Born in 1926, Berry didn't take up the guitar until he was in junior high school thirteen years later. With the accompaniment of a friend on guitar, the two youths played a steamy version of "Confessin' The Blues" which surprised, and pleased, the student audience. The reaction from the crowd prompted Berry to learn some guitar chords from his partner and he was hooked from then on. He spent his teen years developing his chops while working with his father doing carpentry. But, before he could graduate from high school, Berry was arrested and convicted of armed robbery and served three years in Algoa (Missouri). A year after his release on October 18, 1947, he was married and working on a family, swearing that he was forever cured of heading down the wrong path again.

In addition to carpentry, he began working as a hairstylist around this time, saving as much money as he could make (a trait that would cause him considerable grief later in his life). Near the end of 1952 he received a call from a piano player named Johnnie Johnson asking him to play a New Year's Eve gig at the Cosmopolitan Club. Berry accepted, and for the next three years the band literally ruled the Cosmo Club (located at the corner of 17th and Bond St. in East St. Louis, Illinois). At the beginning the band (which included Ebby Hardy on drums), was called Sir John's Trio and played mostly hillbilly, country, and honky tonk tunes. Berry's influence changed not only their name (to the Chuck Berry Combo) but also their style. He originally wanted to be a big band guitarist but that style had died down in popularity by then. Berry cited sources like T-Bone Walker, Carl Hogan of Louis Jordan's Tympani Five, Charlie Christian, and saxophonist Illinois Jacquet as his inspirations, borrowing from their sounds to make one of his own.

While the swing guitarists had a major impact on his playing, it was the blues, especially that of Muddy Waters, that caught Berry's attention. He and a friend went to see the master perform at a Chicago club, and with some coaxing, Berry mustered the nerve to speak with his idol. "It was the feeling I suppose one would get from having a word with the president or the pope," Berry wrote in his autobiography. "I quickly told him of my admiration for his compositions and asked him who

I could see about making a record. . . . Those very famous words were, 'Yeah, see Leonard Chess. Yeah, Chess Records over on Forty-seventh and Cottage.'" Berry flatly rejects the story of him hopping on stage and showing up Waters. "I was a stranger to Muddy and in no way was I about to ask my godfather if I could sit in and play." But he did take the advice and went to see the Chess brothers, Leonard and Phil. They were interested in the young artist but wanted to hear a demo tape before actually cutting any songs. So Berry hurried back home, recorded some tunes and headed back to Chicago.

"He was carrying a wire recorder," Leonard Chess told Peter Guralnick in *Feel Like Going Home,* " and he played us a country music take-off called 'Ida Red.' We called it 'Maybellene.' . . . The big beat, cars, and young love. . . . It was a trend and we jumped on it." Phil chess elaborated, "You could tell right away. . . . He had that something special, that—I don't know what you'd call it. But he had it." After the May 21, 1955,

recording session they headed back to the Cosmo Club, earning $21.00 per week and competing with local rivals like Albert King and Ike Turner. Unbeknownst to him, Berry shared writing credits for "Maybellene" with Russ Fralto and New York disc jockey Alan Freed as part of a deal Chess had made (also known as payola). The scam worked for the most part because by mid-September the song, which had taken 36 cuts to complete, was number 1 on the r&b charts. Berry was bilked out of two-thirds of his royalties from the song, but in later years he would reflect upon the lesson he learned: "let me say that any many who can't take care of his own money deserves what he gets," he told *Rolling Stone.* "In fact, a man should be able to take care of most of his business himself." Ever since the incident that's just what Berry has done. He insists on running his career and managing his finances the way he sees fit.

The next few years, up till 1961, would see at least ten more top ten hits, including "Thirty Days," "Roll Over Beethoven," "Too Much Monkey Business," "Brown Eyed Handsome Man," "School Days," "Rock and Roll Music," "Sweet Little Sixteen," "Johnny B. Goode," "Carol," and "Almost Grown." Berry was a tremendous hit on the touring circuit, utilizing what is now known as his trademark. He explained its development in his autobiography:

"A brighter seat of my memories is based on pursuing my rubber ball. Once it happened to bounce under the kitchen table, and I was trying to retrieve it while it was still bouncing. Usually I was reprimanded for disturbing activities when there was company in the house, as there was then. But this time my manner of retrieving the ball created a big laugh from Mother's choir members. Stooping with full-bended knees, but with my back and head vertical, I fit under the tabletop while scooting forward reaching for the ball. This squatting manner was requested by members of the family many times thereafter for the entertainment of visitors and soon, from their appreciation and encouragement, I looked forward to the ritual.

"An act was in the making. After it had been abandoned for years I happened to remember the maneuver while performing in New York for the first time and some journalist branded it the 'duck walk.'"

The money from touring and record royalties were filling his pockets enough for Berry to start spending on some of the dreams he had long held. Around 1957 he opened Berry Park just outside of Wentzville, Missouri. With a guitar-shaped swimming pool, golf course, hotel suites, and nightclub, it was, next to his fleet of Cadillacs, his pride and joy. "Now that's what I call groovy," he told *Rolling Stone*. "To own a piece of land is like getting the closest to God, I'd say."

Things seemed to be going smoothly until 1961, when Berry was found guilty of violating the Mann Act. [Berry was charged with transporting a teenage girl across a state line for immoral purposes.] He spent from February 19, 1962 until October 18, 1963 behind bars at the Federal Medical Center in Springfield, Missouri. For years Berry denied this, claiming he was acquitted and never served time. He finally admitted the truth in his autobiography. He used his prison term constructively though, taking courses to complete his high school education and also by penning some of his most notable songs: "Tulane," "No Particular Place To Go," and "Nadine."

By the time he was released from jail the British Invasion was about to take over. Groups like the Beatles were churning out cover versions of Berry classics and turning whole new audiences on to him. While some artists might have cried rip-off (the Stones have done over ten of his tunes), Berry sees only the positive aspects. "Did I like it? That doesn't come under my scrutiny," he told *Guitar Player*. "It struck me that my material was becoming marketable, a recognizable product, and if these guys could do such a good job as to get a hit, well, fantastic. I'm just glad it was my song." Even so, remakes of Berry hits are more often than not considerably weaker than his originals. While it is a style that's remarkably simple, it's also next to impossible to duplicate with the same feel, humor and touch.

"Chuck Berry dominated much of the early rock scene by his complete mastery of all its aspects: playing, performing, songwriting, singing and a shrewd sense of how to package himself as well," wrote Santoro. As shrewd as Berry was, by the mid-1960s his type of rock was losing ground to improvisors like Eric Clapton, Mike Bloomfield, and Jimi Hendrix (all three of whom acknowledged Berry's influence, but were trying to break new ground). A switch from Chess to Mercury Records from 1966 to 1969 did little to help. He would continue touring throughout the 1960s without the aid of a regular backup band.

Berry's method since the late 1950s has been to use pickup bands comprised of musicians from the city he's playing in. This has led to many complaints from fans and critics alike that his performances are sometimes shoddy and careless. In his book, Berry gives his own reasons, stating that "drinks and drugs were never my bag, nor were they an excuse for affecting the quality of playing so far as I was concerned. A few ridiculous performances, several amendments to our band regulations, and the band broke up, never to be reconstructed. Whenever I've assembled other groups

and played road dates, similar conditions have prevailed." (Berry reportedly accepts no less than $10,000 per gig and plays for no more than 45 minutes; no encores.)

By 1972 he was back with Chess and produced his biggest seller to date, "My Ding-a-Ling," from *The London Chuck Berry Sessions*. Selling over two million copies, it was his first gold record and a number 1 hit on both sides of the Atlantic according to *The Illustrated Encyclopedia of Rock*. He had hit paydirt, but his obsession to have a bank account with a $1 million figure led to another run-in with the law. In 1979 Berry was convicted of tax evasion and spent just over three months at Lompoc Prison Camp in California. Perhaps the one thing that has caused him more pleasure/pain than money is his fancy for women, stated simply in his book: "The only real bother about prison, to me, is the loss of love." He hopes to write a book one day devoted solely to his sex life.

While Berry's career has had the highest peaks and some pretty low valleys, he has survived while most of

---

"Chuck Berry dominated much of the early rock scene by his complete mastery of all its aspects: playing, performing, songwriting, singing, and a shrewd sense of how to package himself."

---

his contemporaries have vanished. In 1986 Rolling Stones guitarist Keith Richard, perhaps the ultimate student of the Chuck Berry School of Guitar, decided to put it all together with a 60th birthday-party concert to be filmed and released as a movie, "Hail! Hail! Rock 'n' Roll." It took place at St. Louis's Fox Theater, a venue which had at one time refused a youthful Berry entrance because of his skin color. The show featured Berry's classic songs with Richard, Johnnie Johnson, Robert Cray, Etta James, Eric Clapton, Linda Ronstadt, and Julian Lennon also performing. Berry has also been honored with a star in the Hollywood Walk of Fame, and induction into the Rock and Roll Hall of Fame. If that's not enough, "Johnny B. Goode" is riding around in outer space on the *Voyager I* just waiting to be heard by aliens.

Despite the accolades, in his own book Berry shrugs off his contributions, stating that "my view remains that I do not deserve all the reward directed on my account for the accomplishments credited to the rock 'n' roll bank of music." Nevertheless, *Rolling Stone's* Dave Marsh's words seem to be more appropriate: "Chuck Berry is to rock what Louis Armstrong was to jazz."

Compositions

Composer of numerous songs, including "Almost Grown," "Carol," "Johnny B. Goode," "Maybelline," "Memphis," "My Ding-a-Ling," "Nadine," "No Particular Place to Go," "Reelin' and Rockin'," "Roll Over Beethoven," "School Day (Ring! Ring! Goes the Bell)," (with Brian Wilson) "Surfin' U.S.A.," "Sweet Little Sixteen," and "Too Much Monkey Business."

Selected discography

Hit singles; all released on Chess

"Maybelline," July 1955.
"Roll Over Beethoven," June 1956.
"Too Much Monkey Business"/"Brown Eyed Handsome Man," October 1956.
"School Day (Ring! Ring! Goes the Bell)," March 1957.
"Rock and Roll Music," October 1957.
"Sweet Little Sixteen"/"Reelin' and Rockin'," January 1958.
"Johnny B. Goode"/"Around and Around," April 1958.
"Carol," August 1958.
"Sweet Little Rock and Roller," November 1958.
"Little Queenie"/"Almost Grown," March 1959.
"Memphis"/"Back in the U.S.A.," June 1959.
"Nadine," March 1964.
"No Particular Place to Go," May 1964.
"My Ding-a-Ling," August 1972.

LPs

(With others) *Rock, Rock, Rock* (motion picture soundtrack), Chess, 1956; reissued, 1987.
After School Session, Chess, 1957.
One Dozen Berrys, Chess, 1958.
Chuck Berry Is On Top, Chess, 1959; remastered and reissued, 1987.
Rockin' At The Hops, Chess, 1960; reissued, 1987.
New Juke Box Hits, Chess, 1961.
Chuck Berry Twist, Chess, 1962.
Chuck Berry On Stage, Chess, 1963.
Chuck Berry's Greatest Hits, Chess, 1964.
The Latest And Greatest, Chess, 1964.
(With Bo Diddley) Two Great Guitars, Chess, 1964.
You Never Can Tell, Chess, 1964.
St. Louis To Liverpool, Chess, 1964.
Chuck Berry In London, Chess, 1965.

Fresh Berrys, Chess, 1965.
Golden Hits, Mercury, 1967.
Chuck Berry's Golden Decade (six-record set), Chess, 1967.
In Memphis, Mercury, 1967.
Live At The Fillmore, Mercury, 1967.
From St. Louis To Frisco, Mercury, 1968.
Concerto In B. Goode, Mercury, 1969.
Back Home, Chess, 1970.
San Francisco Dues, Chess, 1971.
St. Louis To Frisco To Memphis, Mercury, 1972.
The London Chuck Berry Sessions, Chess, 1972.
Johnny B. Goode, Pickwick, 1972.
Golden Decade, Vol. 2, Chess, 1973.
Bio, Chess, 1973.
Golden Decade, Vol. 3, Chess, 1974.
Chuck Berry, Chess, 1975.
Live In Concert, Magnum, 1978.
American Hot Wax (motion picture soundtrack), A & M, 1978.
Rock It, Atco, 1979.
Rock! Rock! Rock 'n' Roll!, Mercury, 1980.
The Great Twenty-Eight (two-record set), Chess, 1982.
Toronto Rock 'n' Roll Revival, 1969, Vols. 1 & 2, Accord, 1982.
Chess Masters, Chess, 1983.
Rock 'n' Roll Rarities, Chess, 1986.
More Rock 'n' Roll Rarities, Chess, 1986.
(With others) *Hail! Hail! Rock 'n' roll* (motion picture soundtrack), 1987.

Sources

Books

Berry, Chuck, *The Autobiography*, Fireside, 1988.
Guralnick, Peter, *Feel Like Going Home*, Vintage, 1981.
Kozinn, Alan, and Pete Welding, Dan Forte, and Gene Santoro, *The Guitar*, Quill, 1984.
Logan, Nick, and Bob Woffinden, *The Illustrated Encyclopedia of Rock*, Harmony Books, 1977.
Rock Revolution, by the editors of *Creem* magazine, Popular Library, 1976.
The Rolling Stone Interviews, by the editors of *Rolling Stone*, St. Martin's Press/Rolling Stone Press, 1981.
The Rolling Stone Record Guide, edited by Dave Marsh and John Swenson, Random House/Rolling Stone Press, 1979.

Periodicals

Guitar Player, February, 1981; May, 1984; June, 1984; January, 1985; January, 1987; November, 1987; December, 1987; March, 1988.
Guitar World, March, 1987; November, 1987; December, 1987; March, 1988; April, 1988.

—Calen D. Stone

David Bowie

Singer, songwriter

After playing in obscure groups in England during the 1960s—like George and the Dragons and David Jones and the Lower Third—David Jones took the name David Bowie to avoid being confused with Davey Jones, the rising star of the television-based pop group, The Monkees. His first album to be released in the United States, *David Bowie: Man of Words/Man of Music,* included the 1969 single "Space Oddity," which brought him a great deal of favorable attention on both sides of the Atlantic. Thus began the career that Bowie would pursue in many different personas, such as those of Ziggy Stardust and Aladdin Sane, through many different types of music, from rock to danceable funk. As Jay Cocks put it in *Time* magazine, "Musically, . . . Bowie always seems to know what time it is." In addition to being a rock trendsetter for two decades, Bowie has made successful appearances as an actor on Broadway and in films.

Born in 1947 in Brixton, a deprived section of London, England, Bowie had a difficult childhood. His parents did not marry until after his birth, his brother was eventually confined to a psychiatric hospital, and Bowie's teenage fighting in his bad neighborhood led to the paralysis of his left eye, the pupil of which is permanently dilated. He has revealed in various interviews, however, that he noticed music from an early age, and that his parents provided him with the recordings of early American rock pioneers such as Fats Domino and Little Richard. Bowie also learned to play the guitar and the saxophone as a child.

But having varied talents and interests, Bowie was undecided as a young man as to which of the arts he wished to specialize in. He studied commercial art at Bromley Technical High School in London, and left before earning a degree in order to work at an advertising agency, but soon quit because he disliked the work he was doing. He also studied with the Lindsay Kemp Mime Troupe for two and a half years, painted, and acted in small stage roles. At one time Bowie even considered entering a Buddhist monastery.

Meanwhile, he continued playing in rock groups until meeting his future wife, Angela Barnet, who convinced a friend at Mercury Records to listen to Bowie's music. He followed his successful *David Bowie: Man of Words-Man of Music* with *The Man Who Sold the World,* which featured him wearing a dress and makeup on the cover. While this garnered the artist controversial attention and foreshadowed the glitter rock personas soon to come from him, Bowie went back to what most reviewers referred to as his 1960s pop style, reminiscent of singers Bob Dylan and Anthony Newley, for his 1971 recording for RCA, *Hunky Dory.* The well-received album includes the hit single "Changes," and

For the Record. . .

Born David Robert Hayward Jones, January 8, 1947, in London, England; son of Hayward (a publicist) and Margaret Mary (a movie theater usher; maiden name, Burns) Jones; married Angela Barnet, 1970 (divorced, 1980); children: Joey (name originally Zowie).

Worked in advertising and with the Lindsay Kemp Mime Troupe prior to musical career; performed with various bands during the 1960s, including David Jones and the Buzz, David Jones and the Lower Third, The Kon-rads, and George and the Dragons; solo performer since late 1960s. Actor in motion pictures, 1976—, including "The Man Who Fell to Earth," "Just a Gigolo," "The Hunger," "Merry Christmas, Mr. Lawrence," "Labyrinth," and "Absolute Beginners"; also appeared in theatrical production of "The Elephant Man."

Addresses: *Home*—Switzerland. *Office*—c/o 641 Fifth Ave., #22-Q, New York, NY 10022.

was described by John Mendelsohn in *Rolling Stone* as Bowie's "most easily accessible, and thus his most enjoyable work."

But Bowie did not really become a rock superstar until he released *The Rise and Fall of Ziggy Stardust and the Spiders From Mars* in 1972. On the album, and in related concert appearances, Bowie took on the persona of Ziggy Stardust, an androgynous, space-alien rock star dressed in an outrageous costume, whose music was filled with great power. *Ziggy* was a story album, and chronicled the Stardust persona's adventures on earth, ending with his spiritual demise as portrayed in the final song, "Rock'n'Roll Suicide." As Cocks explained, "When he first hit the stage as Ziggy, decked out in makeup, dye job and psychedelic costume, the rock world was ready. Too much karma, too much good vibes, too much hippy dippy: audiences wanted decadence with a difference. Bowie was there."

The singer found himself heralded as the king of glitter rock, a movement in the early 1970s that saw rock performers dressing in gaudy and often sexually ambiguous outfits. At about the same time, despite being married to Angela Barnet and having a son, Bowie told an interviewer that he was bisexual. As the first rock star to come out into the open on this subject, he was the object of a great deal of controversy. Later Bowie told Kurt Loder in *Rolling Stone:* "The biggest mistake I ever made . . . was telling that . . . writer that I was bisexual. Christ, I was so *young* then. I was *experimenting.*"

Bowie went from Ziggy Stardust to Aladdin Sane, made up with a lightning bolt drawn across his face and a painted-on tear drop; to the Thin White Duke, who slicked his hair back and wore white suits. In this last persona he recorded the 1975 *Young Americans* album, which included his hit duet with the late ex-Beatle John Lennon, "Fame." As disco music was peaking in popularity, in "Fame" Bowie turned to a funk beat. But he told a *Playboy* interviewer: "'Fame' was an incredible bluff that worked," because "my rhythm and blues are thoroughly plastic."

During the mid-1970s Bowie staggered under the weight of drug abuse problems. He confided to Loder that he sustained "incredible losses of memory. Whole *chunks* of my life. I can't remember, for instance, any—*any*—of 1975." He eventually went to Berlin to recover. While he fought to overcome the excesses of his former lifestyle, he still put out albums, including *Heroes, Lodger,* and *Scary Monsters (and Super Creeps).* Bowie's music from this period is noted for its emphasis on electronic sounds.

In 1980 he divorced Angela, retaining custody of his son, named Zowie in Bowie's glitter days but now

---

"Audiences wanted decadence with a difference. Bowie was there."

---

called Joey. After signing a deal for five albums with EMI America, Bowie produced 1983's *Let's Dance.* The single of the same name, a danceable tune with a heavy, booming beat, became his biggest seller ever. As he told Loder, Bowie had changed his outlook on life and was now interested in producing positive music. He also broke into the field of music videos, and saw them as a chance to expose people to social issues— hence the video for "Let's Dance" protests the treatment of Australia's aboriginal people. Bowie explained to Loder: "I know this is very *cliche,* but I feel that now that I'm thirty-six years old, and I've got a certain position, I want to start utilizing that position to the benefit of my . . . brotherhood and sisterhood. . . . I think you can't keep on being an artist without actually saying anything more than . . . 'this is an interesting way of looking at things.'"

In 1976, Bowie made his film debut in "The Man Who Fell to Earth," the story of a man who comes to Earth in a spaceship looking for water to take back to his own planet, which suffers from drought. He received high praise for his acting ability; Richard Eder in the *New York Times* lauded Bowie's performance as "extraordinary." In l983 Bowie had a highly praised supporting role as a British prisoner in a Japanese war camp in the film, *Merry Christmas, Mr. Lawrence*. The film's director, Nagisa Oshima, according to Loder, picked Bowie after seeing him perform on Broadway in "The Elephant Man" because he projected "an inner spirit that is indestructible." Bowie's other films include "Just a Gigolo," "The Hunger," "Labyrinth," and the musical "Absolute Beginners."

As of 1987, Bowie still professed a desire to make positive music, but told Loder in another *Rolling Stone* interview that his album, *Never Let Me Down,* "sounds so much more . . . as though the continuity hasn't been broken from *Scary Monsters*. It's almost as though *Let's Dance* [was] in the way there." He also expressed interest in making his own films, and claimed that he and fellow rock superstar friend Mick Jagger were attempting to write a screenplay.

Compositions

Composer of numerous songs, including "All the Young Dudes," "Changes," "Fame," "Golden Years," "Move On," "Space Oddity," "Starman," "Stay," "Suffragette City," "TVC 15," and "Young Americans."

Selected discography

David Bowie: Man of Words/Man of Music (includes "Space Oddity"), Mercury, 1969, later reissued as *Space Oddity*, RCA, 1984.
The Man Who Sold the World (includes "She Shook Me Cold" and "Savior Machine"), Mercury, 1971.

Hunky Dory RCA, 1971.
The Rise and Fall of Ziggy Stardust and the Spiders From Mars (includes "Ziggy Stardust," "Starman," "Moonage Daydream," "Five Years," and "Rock'n'Roll Suicide"), RCA, 1972.
Aladdin Sane, RCA, 1973.
Pin Ups, RCA, 1973.
Diamond Dogs, RCA, 1974.
Young Americans RCA, 1975.
Low, RCA, 1977.
Heroes, RCA, 1977.
Lodger, RCA, 1979.
Scary Monsters (and Super Creeps), RCA, 1980.
Let's Dance (includes "Let's Dance" and "China Girl"), EMI America, 1983.
Tonight, EMI America, 1984.
Never Let Me Down, EMI America, 1977.

Sources

Books

Cann, Kevin, *David Bowie: A Chronology,* Simon & Schuster, 1984.
Edwards, Henry, and Tony Zanetta, *Stardust: The David Bowie Story,* McGraw-Hill, 1986.
Tremelett, George, *The David Bowie Story,* Warner Books, 1975.

Periodicals

Newsweek, July 18, 1983.
New York Times, May 20, 1976.
Playboy, September, 1976.
Rolling Stone, January 6, 1972; October 4, 1979; May 12, 1983; October 25, 1984; April 23, 1987.
Time, July 18, 1983.

—*Elizabeth Thomas*

Betty Buckley

Singer, songwriter, actress

For her popular roles, from "Abby Bradford" to "Grizabella," Betty Buckley has won a wide and devoted audience. She has received high critical praise on television, in film, on and off-Broadway, and in the recording studio. In twenty years in music and theater, she has become known as a performer who is not afraid to take chances with her appearence, her roles, her voice, and her career.

A self-described "Air Force brat" raised in Fort Worth, Texas, Buckley fell in love with the theater after seeing her first show, "Pajama Game," as she later told the *New York Post,* "with Bob Fosse's original choreography. And when they got to the 'Steam Heat' number, I said, 'Oh, wow. I want to do that, whatever that is, for the rest of my life.'" Buckley's memories of her childhood also include a self-imposed apprenticeship to the great song stylists of recordings. "I remember a specific image of myself," she told the *Los Angeles Times* in 1985, "I'm 13 years old and I'm in a bathtub . . . listening to *Judy Garland at Carnegie Hall.* . . . I'm a very good listener and I knew every note of that album. Judy Garland taught me singing and Ella Fitzgerald taught me phrasing." Buckley earned a degree in journalism and toured with a Miss America USO troupe (as Miss Fort Worth) before moving to New York to be in the theater. She was cast as "Martha Jefferson" in the Broadway hit "1776" after her very first audition in 1969 and spent the next five years playing leading roles in musical comedies on and off-Broadway and in London.

Buckley became famous nation-wide when, in 1977, she was cast as "Abby Bradford," the stepmother to the "Eight is Enough" family on the ABC hit series. The dramatic role brought her fans and critical acclaim for her sympathetic portrayal of a young second wife. Film roles followed, including her portrayal of the ex-wife of a country-and-western singer (Robert Duvall) in the 1983 "Tender Mercies." Buckley appeared in the feminist musical comedy, "I'm Getting My Act Together and Taking It on the Road," by Gretchen Cryer, in Los Angeles and New York during breaks from other projects in the late 1970s and early 1980s.

However, her greatest challenge came with her return to Broadway as "Grizabella" in "Cats." The British musical by Andrew Lloyd Webber and T.S. Elliot was still selling out every performance in London when auditions began for its New York run. The success of the show was due in part to the widespread popularity of "Grizabella's" ballad, "Memories." Not only was the London cast recording, with the "Grizabella" of Elaine Page, widely known in America, but new singles of the ballad by such stars as Judy Collins and Barbra Streisand were becoming top sellers. The song comes at the end of the long musical and precedes a dangerous ascent to the theatre ceiling (called "the heavyside layer") on a

For the Record...

Full name, Betty Lynn Buckley; born 1948, in Big Spring, Tex.; father was in the U.S. Air Force and later worked in construction; mother worked for Ft. Worth (Tex.) Music Fair; married Peter Flood (an acting coach), 1972 (divorced, 1979). *Education:* Texas Christian University, B.A. in journalism, c. 1968. *Religion:* Jain Buddhist.

Actress in films, Broadway musicals, and on television; stage appearances include "1776," 1969, "I'm Getting My Act Together and Taking It on the Road," "Cats," 1982, "The Mystery of Edwin Drood," 1985, "Song and Dance," 1986, "Into the Woods," 1987, and "Carrie," 1988; feature films include "Carrie," 1976, and "Tender Mercies," 1983; regular member of cast of television series "Eight Is Enough," 1977-81. Also has performed a cabaret act in clubs; songwriter, 1973—.

Awards: Tony Award for best featured actress in a musical, 1983, for "Cats."

Addresses: *Agent*—International Creative Management, 49 West 57th St., New York, NY 10019.

cherry-picker/tire. To make things even worse, the show's sophisticated body microphone system failed just before Buckley's entrance. As she later told Tom Tomasulo of the *New York Daily News:* "It was a different kind of pressure where you had to deliver better than your best. . . . When you come from behind with a show, people don't know what to expect—it's easier to delight people. Whereas when you have such expectations placed upon you, its very hard to impress people. . . . I just went out and sang as loud as I could."

Buckley impressed so many people as "Grizabella" that she was awarded the Tony Award as best featured actress in a musical in 1983. When the Broadway cast recording was released later that year, her performance of "Memories" received high praise. Buckley has never been afraid to appear in odd roles or, following her triumph with "Memories," in roles premiered by other actresses. After "Cats" and dramatic film roles, she portrayed "Alice Nutting," the male impersonator who appeared as Edwin Drood in "The Mystery of Edwin Drood," a 1985 musical comedy by Rupert Holmes based on Charles Dickens's final, unfinished novel. Since Dickens had never solved his mystery, the musical version invited the audience to vote on its own solution at each performance. The cast had to learn alternative final scenes depending on the audience's interpretation of the clues. In recent seasons, Buckley

has replaced Bernadette Peters in Lloyd Webber's "Song and Dance" (1986) for the last six weeks of its Broadway run and has performed in the workshop version of Stephen Sondheim's "Into the Woods" (1987).

Her most recent role on stage was a return to a film property with which she had long been associated. Having played the sympathetic role of the gym teacher in Brian De Palma's thriller, "Carrie" (1976), she accepted the highly negative role of the mother, "Margaret," in the 1988 musical version. Buckley had to replace Barbara Cook, the Broadway legend who created the role in England but, as she told Diana Maychick in the *New York Post,* she was thrilled by the challenge of creating the emotionally charged character of "a Bible-spouting hellfire." "I gave Margaret a history. Although it's not clear in the book [by Stephen King] or the movie or even in our version here, I chose to believe that Margaret wasn't married when she had Carrie. Consequently, she feels tremendous guilt over her own sexuality. . . . She's fearful for her daughter making the same mistakes at the same time she feels punished by Carrie's existence. . . . The show is a metaphor for life . . . a ballad of high school as life."

Buckley has been writing songs ("mostly heartbreak ballads") since 1973 and often includes them in her cabaret acts. She described her 1987 Atlantic City act as "very musical, very soothing [with] a lot of really good songs in it, but songs people are not familiar with. I do 'Memories,' of course, but about 70% of the music people haven't heard before." She has recorded her own feminist ballads on the album that bears her name which was recorded live at St. Bartholomew's Church in New York.

Selected discography

1776 (original cast recording), Columbia, 1969.
Cats (original cast recording), Geffen, 1982.
The Mystery of Edwin Drood (original cast recording), Polydor, 1985.
Betty Buckley, Rizzoli, 1987.

Sources

Drama-logue, July 2-8, 1981.
Louisville Courier-Journal & Times, December 2, 1973.
Los Angeles Times, June 30, 1983.
New York Daily News, March 1, 1983; November 24, 1985; December 10, 1986; February 27, 1987.
New York Post, May 12, 1988.

—*Barbara Stratyner*

Johnny Cash

Singer, songwriter, guitarist

For more than thirty years the craggy-faced Johnny Cash has been one of America's most popular country singers. Cash's appeal has even extended beyond the bounds of country and western music to embrace pop, blues, and folk audiences who often reject the pure country sound. A member of the Country Music Hall of Fame since 1980, Cash is renowned for his combination of rural music traditions—especially gospel and ballads—with innovation and experimentation from a number of contemporary sources.

Additionally, critics of modern music have noted that Cash's performances are greatly enhanced by his carefully-crafted stage persona, based on a pastiche of rough-hewn backwoodsmen from a bygone era. In Johnny Cash, writes Henry Pleasants in *The Great American Popular Singers,* "the artist is the man rather than the art. . . . The man—the life story, the successes, the humiliations, the disasters, the fascinating juxtaposition of the sinister and the charming, the suggestion of unpredictability—is an attractive figure."

Pleasants also comments that possibly more important "is the figure he seems to represent: the frontier American. . . . Johnny Cash entered upon the musical scene at a moment in history when America . . . had grown unsure of itself and its direction. It looked back nostalgically to a time when life was simpler, closer to nature, less tortured by tempo and doubt. Johnny had sprung from a backwater of that earlier environment, and he revived it in song as had no previous singer." In *The Best of the Music Makers,* George T. Simon characterizes Cash as "a man of experience and magnetism who, for years, has conveyed to millions the truth and emotion of country music."

Cash was born in Kingsland, Arkansas, February 26, 1932, the fourth of seven children of Ray and Carrie Cash. Although the Great Depression hit hard in Arkansas, it is unfair to describe the Cash family as poverty-stricken. In 1935 they moved to Dyess, Arkansas, where they worked together to grow cotton. Eventually, through hard labor and frugality, they prospered to the extent that they were able to buy the forty-acre farm on which they lived.

Johnny Cash grew up in a charismatic religious environment—he is descended on both sides from Baptist missionaries and preachers—and gospel music was a staple in the home. When he was four his parents bought a battery-powered radio (Dyess had no electricity), and the youngster was exposed to such country music pioneers as the Carter Family, Jimmie Rodgers, and Ernest Tubb. In *Stars of Country Music,* Frederick E. Danker writes: "For the Cashes, their old hymns and the newer Carter Family versions seemed central to their lives."

For the Record. . .

Born February 26, 1932, in Kingsland, Ark.; son of Ray (a farmer) and Carrie (Rivers) Cash; married Vivian Liberto, 1954 (divorced, 1966); married June Carter (a singer), March 1, 1968; children: (first marriage) Rosanne, Kathy, Cindy, Tara; (second marriage) John Carter. *Education:* Graduated from Dyess High School, Dyess, Ark., 1959. *Religion:* Baptist.

Worked in a General Motors auto assembly plant in Pontiac, Mich., and in an oleomargarine factory in Evadale, Ark., 1949-50; sold electrical appliances door-to-door in Memphis, Tenn., 1954.

Singer, songwriter, musician, 1955—. Founder of Johnny Cash and the Tennessee Two (also included Marshall Grant on bass and Luther Perkins on guitar), 1955, band's name changed to Johnny Cash and the Tennessee Three (with addition of W.S. Holland on drums), 1960, Bob Wootton replaced Perkins, 1969. Also sings with wife, June Carter.

Actor in theatrical release and made-for-TV movies, including ''A Gunfight,'' 1970, ''Pride of Jessee Hallam,'' 1981, and ''Stagecoach,'' 1986, and television miniseries, including ''North and South,'' 1985. Star of television variety show ''The Johnny Cash Show,'' 1969-71. Producer, co-writer, and narrator of film ''The Gospel Road,'' 1973. Composer of music for screenplays, including ''The True West,'' ''Little Fauss and Big Halsy,'' and ''Pride of Jesse Hallam.'' *Military service:* U.S. Air Force, 1950-54; worked with radio code.

Awards: Winner or co-winner of seven Grammy Awards; has recorded nine Gold Albums; winner of six Country Music Association awards, including best male vocalist, entertainer of the year, best single, best album, best vocal group, and outstanding service award; named to the Country Music Hall of Fame, 1980. L.H.D. from National University of San Diego, 1976.

Addresses: *Home*—711 Summerfield Dr., Hendersonville, TN 37075. *Agent*—Agency for the Performing Arts, 9000 Sunset Blvd., Suite 1200, Los Angeles, CA 90069.

Late in the 1930s Cash's brother Roy formed a band, and Johnny vowed he would someday do the same—he had no affection for the long hours and rough work of cotton farming. Cash graduated from Dyess High School in 1950 and worked briefly in a Pontiac, Michigan, auto plant and an Arkansas oleomargarine factory before joining the Air Force for a four-year stint. He was stationed in Germany, and it was there that he learned to play the guitar. He had long written poetry, but in Germany, with the help of some friends, he began turning his verses into songs.

After he was discharged in 1954 he married Vivian Liberto and settled in Memphis, where he sold electrical appliances door-to-door. Pleasants suggests that had Cash been a more successful salesman he might never have become a professional entertainer. In 1954 he teamed with two new friends, Marshall Grant and Luther Perkins, to form a small gospel band. They played informally for several months, then Cash's financial situation impelled him to try to find a recording contract—or at least some profitable gigs.

Luckily, an innovative producer named Sam Phillips was living in Memphis at the time; his Sun record label had introduced Elvis Presley, Jerry Lee Lewis, Carl Perkins, and Roy Orbison, to name a few. Cash approached Phillips early in 1955 for an audition. He was denied a contract but given some valuable advice, namely to retire his gospel repertoire and work in a commercial vein. Several months later Johnny Cash and the Tennessee Two returned to the Sun studios with new material, and Phillips put them under contract.

Success came quickly after that. The band's first single, ''Cry, Cry, Cry,'' was a regional hit. The next year, 1956, Cash and the Tennessee Two had a dual country and pop hit with ''I Walk the Line,'' also recorded on the Sun label. According to Gene Busnar in *Superstars of Country Music,* Cash's career ''took off. In the years to come he would sell tens of millions of records, host his own prime-time television show, star in movies, and secure a position as one of the true superstars of country music.'' Busnar makes another point, however: ''Too often fame and fortune can create more problems than they solve. For a long time, Johnny Cash's success was little more than a heavy cross to bear.''

That statement may be an exaggeration, but it is certain that drug abuse almost claimed Cash's life in the mid-1960s. In 1958 he resigned from his regular appearance on Nashville's Grand Ole Opry—considered the pinnacle of the country music profession—in favor of national touring and mainstream television appearances. The decision was a sound one artistically, but the physical and emotional toll of constant travel was severe. Cash began to take amphetamines and barbiturates; he and his band members pulled pranks and sometimes wound up in scrapes with the law as they moved from show to show across the country.

For seven years Cash was addicted to dangerous drugs; his first marriage ended in 1966, his voice began to fail, and at one point his weight dropped from 200 to 153 pounds. He was cared for on more than one occasion by June Carter, whose group, the Carter Family, toured with him. Finally, an almost-fatal overdose scared him into a series of rehabilitation programs. He married Carter in 1968 and credited her—and his renewed Christian faith—with his salvation.

Ironically, Cash's struggles with substance abuse had little effect on the quality of his music. Not only was the singer able to keep his band and his backup troupe constant throughout the period, he also managed to make "key achievements in repertory expansion, recording activity, and road-show innovations," observed Danker. Cash reached beyond the country tradition into folk and blues, performed "message music" about the plight of Native Americans and prison inmates, and recorded songs written by such maverick artists as Kris Kristofferson and Bob Dylan.

Busnar concluded that Cash "achieved a national recognition by the end of the sixties that was unmatched in country music history." A 1968 live album, *At Folsom Prison,* afforded Cash his biggest crossover success. As its title suggests, the album was recorded before an audience of prisoners; Danker maintains that the work reveals "the finest troupe and most polished road

---

Cash sings with his soul as well as his voice.

---

show" ever mounted in country music. *At Folsom Prison* propelled Cash to the top of the Country Music Association Awards in 1969. He won "best male vocalist," "entertainer of the year," "best single," "best album," an "outstanding service" award, and, with Carter, "best vocal group." From 1969 until 1971 he hosted his own television variety show, and when that was cancelled he returned to touring with Carter and his friend Carl Perkins, who had joined his retinue in 1966.

Cash has also written books and starred in films. His 1975 autobiography, *Man in Black,* sold 250,000 hardcover copies, and his 1986 novel *Man in White,* about Saint Paul, has been optioned for a movie. Cash's own movie roles, including "A Gunfight" and "Stagecoach," capitalize on the same image that he projects in concert, an image *People* magazine contributor Andrea Chambers described as "scarred . . . like a strip-mined Appalachian mountainside, . . . dark and somber, . . . [with a] deep, rumbling voice that would rather converse with God or the dogwoods than almost anybody else."

Assessments of Cash's talent highlight two characteristics of the charismatic "Man in Black." First, he writes much of his own material, drawing on his own past, his nation's mythic Western history, social problems, family and romantic love, and religious faith. Danker contends that this highly personal style of writing-performing "continues as one of country music's distinctive features" through the efforts of artists like Cash.

Second, Cash's unusually deep voice and his mix of singing and speaking in his tunes has produced an original—and subsequently much-imitated—style. "With Johnny Cash, as with other country and blues singers, the context is oratorical rather than melodic or harmotic," writes Pleasants. "The lyric is more important than the tune. Since the singer is working closer to the less precise intonation and inflections of speech, imprecision in the identification and articulation of pitches becomes, if not necessarily a virtue, at least a compatible idiosyncrasy."

To put it succinctly, Cash sings with his soul as well as his voice, and the resulting gravelly baritone can sustain the moods of a surprising variety of songs. Now into his third decade as a performer, Cash gives more than seventy-five concerts a year. He still struggles with the seductive dangers of substance abuse but is helped by the concern of his wife, his four daughters, his son, and numerous grandchildren. "I had some bad old days," Cash told *People.* "I always remember that God forgives, though, and one of the worst things you can do is not to forgive yourself."

Selected discography

Johnny Cash with His Hot and Blue Guitar, Sun, 1957.
The Fabulous Johnny Cash, Columbia, 1958.
Ride This Train, Columbia, 1960.
Blood, Sweat, and Tears, Columbia, 1963.
Ring of Fire, Columbia, 1963.
I Walk the Line, Columbia, 1964.
Bitter Tears: Ballads of the American Indian, Columbia, 1964.
Orange Blossom Special, Columbia, 1965.
Ballads of the True West, Columbia, 1965.
Mean As Hell, Columbia, 1966.
Everybody Loves a Nut, Columbia, 1966.
Greatest Hits: Volume I, Columbia, 1967.
Carrying on with June Carter, Columbia, 1967.
From Sea to Shining Sea, Columbia, 1968.
At Folsom Prison, Columbia, 1968.
Old Golden Throat, Columbia, 1968.
Holy Land, Columbia, 1969.
At San Quentin, Columbia, 1969.
Johnny Cash, Harmony, 1969.
Original Golden Hits: Volume I and II, Sun, 1969.

Show Time with the Tennessee Two, Sun, 1970.
Story Songs of Trains and Rivers with the Tennessee Two, Sun, 1970.
Hello, I'm Johnny Cash, Columbia, 1970.
The World of Johnny Cash, Columbia, 1970.
Singing Storyteller with the Tennessee Two, Sun, 1970.
(With June Carter) *Jackson*, Columbia, 1970.
Living Legend, Sun, 1970.
Little Fauss and Big Halsy, Columbia, 1970.
Get Rhythm, Sun, 1970.
The Johnny Cash Show, Epic, 1970.
Rough Cut King of Country Music, Sun, 1970.
Sunday Down South with Jerry Lee Lewis, Sun, 1970.
Show, Columbia, 1971.
Johnny Cash: The Man, the World, His Music, Sun, 1971.
Man in Black, Columbia, 1971.
(With Jerry Lee Lewis) *Johnny Cash Sings Hank Williams*, Sun, 1971.
Collections: Great Hits Volume II, Columbia, 1971
Original Golden Hits Volume III, Sun, 1972.
A Thing Called Love, Columbia, 1972.
Folsom Prison Blues, Columbia, 1972.
(With Carter) *Give My Love to Rose*, Harmony, 1972.
America, Columbia, 1972.
Johnny Cash Songbook, Harmony, 1972.
Any Old Wind That Blows, Columbia, 1973.
I Walk the Line, Nash, 1973.
(With Carter) *Johnny Cash and His Woman*, Columbia, 1973.
Ragged Old Flag, Columbia, 1974.
Junkie and Juicehead, Columbia, 1974.
Johnny Cash Sings Precious Memories, Columbia, 1975.
John R. Cash, Columbia, 1975.
Look at Them Beans, Columbia, 1975.
Destination Victoria Station, Columbia, 1976.
Strawberry Cake, Columbia, 1976.
One Piece at a Time, Columbia, 1976.
Last Gunfighter Ballad, Columbia, 1977.
The Rambler, Columbia, 1977.
I Would Like to See You Again, Columbia, 1978.
Gone Girl, Columbia, 1978.
Johnny Cash's Greatest Hits: Volume III, Columbia, 1979.
Silver, Columbia, 1979.
A Believer Sings the Truth, Columbia, 1980.
Rockabilly Blues, Columbia, 1980.

The Baron, Columbia, 1981.
(With Lewis and Carl Perkins) *The Survivors*, Columbia, 1982.
(With Willie Nelson, Waylon Jennings, and Kris Kristofferson) *Highwayman*, Columbia, 1985.
Classic Cash, Columbia, 1986.
Believe in Him, Columbia, 1986.
(With Jennings) *Heroes*, Columbia, 1986.
Johnny Cash Is Coming to Town, Mercury, 1987.
(With Bob Dylan, George Harrison, Jeff Lynn, Roy Orbison, and Tom Petty) *The Traveling Wilburys*, 1988.

Writings

Man in Black (autobiography), Zondervan, 1975.
Man in White (novel), Harper & Row, 1986.

Sources

Books

Busnar, Gene, *Superstars of Country Music*, J. Messner, 1984.
Cash, Johnny, *Man in Black*, Zondervan, 1975.
Grissim, John, *Country Music: White Man's Blues*, Coronet Communications, 1970.
Malone, Bill C., *Country Music U.S.A.*, revised and enlarged edition, University of Texas Press, 1985.
Malone, Bill C. and Judith McCulloh, editors, *Stars of Country Music*, University of Illinois Press, 1975.
Pleasants, Henry, *The Great American Popular Singers*, Simon & Schuster, 1974.
Simon, George T., *The Best of the Music Makers*, Doubleday, 1979.
Wren, Christopher, *Winners Got Scars, Too: The Life and Legends of Johnny Cash*, Dial Press, 1971.

Periodicals

New York Times Magazine, March 25, 1979.
People, November 3, 1986.

—Anne Janette Johnson

Ray Charles

Singer, songwriter, pianist

A living legend, Ray Charles is generally regarded as one of the most influential figures in contemporary music. The multitalented musician has seen both artistic and commercial success, surmounting personal tragedy to become an exceptional singer, songwriter, instrumentalist, and bandleader. He has also proven himself the master of almost every conceivable musical style, ranging from jazz and rhythm-and-blues to pop, rock, and even country-and-western. But in a career that has thus far spanned four decades, Charles remains best known as the Genius of Soul, the man who fused gospel with rhythm-and-blues to create an entirely new style of black popular music.

The Southern-born Charles took an early interest in music, reportedly teaching himself to play the piano at age three. Although struck with an illness that caused him to start going blind at age five and rendered him totally blind by age seven, he continued to develop his musical talents. At the St. Augustine School for the Blind in Florida, the youth learned to play trumpet, saxophone, clarinet, and organ. He also learned to compose musical scores in Braille, and in 1945, after being orphaned, he left school to begin his career.

During the next ten years Charles experimented with a variety of musical styles before finding his own sound. He traveled through the South with rhythm-and-blues bands, headed up a notable black jazz trio in Seattle, toured with bluesman Lowell Fulson as well as solo, and distinguished himself as an arranger. He tried modeling himself after the great American singer/pianist Nat "King" Cole and absorbed the lessons of such talents as Charles Brown, Guitar Slim, and Lloyd Glenn. But according to *Esquire* contributing editor Guy Martin, probably "the most radical change in the man's life occurred" when he stopped imitating others and began "singing like himself."

As a result, Charles emerged as one of the most innovative entertainers of the 1950s. He recorded a couple of rhythm-and-blues hits in the early fifties, then saw the 1954 "It Should Have Been Me" reach number one. He made recording history, however, with "I've Got a Woman" in 1955. His own composition, the song combined the emotional fervor of gospel with the sexuality of the blues to establish an altogether new kind of music. Later called soul, the new music was considered revolutionary not simply because it united two traditions, but because of the emotional intensity with which it was presented. According to Charles, the musician had to feel the music before the audience could feel it.

"I've Got a Woman" became a national hit, and its debut helped alter the course of popular music. Indeed, although Charles continued his work in jazz and

For the Record. . .

Full name, Ray Charles Robinson; born September 23, 1930 (some sources say 1932), in Albany, Ga.; son of Bailey (a mechanic and handyman) and Areatha ([one source lists given name as Reather] a saw mill employee) Robinson; married Della Antwine (a singer); children: three. *Education:* Attended St. Augustine School for the Blind.

Musician, singer, and composer. Began professional career touring with a combo in the South, 1945; performed with Seattle-based jazz trio, c. 1947-49; toured with bluesman Lowell Fulson, 1950-52; toured as soloist; formed own band, 1954, subsequently adding a female vocal group, the Raelettes (originally spelled Raylettes), and speciality acts; founded Ray Charles Enterprises (recording, publishing, and management company), Los Angeles, Calif.; recording artist with Swing Time, 1951-52, with Atlantic Records, 1952-59, with ABC-Paramount, 1959-65, with Tangerine Records, 1965-73, with Crossover Records, 1973-77, re-signed with Atlantic, 1977. Makes regular concert tours; plays nightclubs and appears on television.

Awards: Winner of *down beat* magazine's International Jazz Critics Poll, 1958 and 1961-64; named top male singer in sixteenth International Jazz Critics Poll, 1968; named best soul and rhythm-and-blues artist in *down beat*'s critics poll, 1984; named to Playboy Jazz and Pop Hall of Fame and to Songwriters Hall of Fame; named honorary life chairman of Rhythm-and-Blues Hall of Fame; inducted into Rock and Roll Hall of Fame, 1986; honored by John F. Kennedy Center for the Performing Arts, 1986; recipient of at least ten Grammy Awards from Academy of Recording Arts and Sciences.

Addresses: *Home*—Los Angeles, CA. *Other*—2107 W. Washington Blvd. #2, Los Angeles, CA; c/o Triad Artists Inc., 90200 Sunset Blvd. Suite 823, Los Angeles, CA 90069.

performer into the public eye. As greater attention than ever was focused on his work, Charles found his music appealing to a broader and broader audience. In fact Charles, perhaps more than any other artist of the time, is credited with popularizing traditional black music—what Geoffrey C. Ward, in a review for *American Heritage,* attested was once called "race music"—among white audiences. As Ward remembered, it "seemed raw, ardent, unabashed, above all, compelling—unlike anything most of us had ever heard before."

Charles's eclecticism greatly contributed to his success. Ever inventive, and indifferent to labels, the artist has always been willing to experiment. As he told Martin, "If I like it, I don't give a damn what it is. I'll sing it." As a result, the growing star continued to expand his range. In 1961 he recorded a country and western hit album titled *Modern Sounds in Country and Western Music,* and one of its spin-off singles, "I Can't Stop Loving You," became a 1962 country, rhythm-and-blues, and pop hit. From 1961 through 1965 Charles was named the United States's top male vocalist in *down beat* magazine's poll of international jazz critics.

> *Ray Charles has secured a place for himself among the most important figures in post-World War II American music.*

Credited with influencing countless musicians, including such greats as Aretha Franklin, Stevie Wonder, and James Brown, the entertainer elected, during the mid-1960s, to begin working the nightclub circuit. Although some critics saw the decision as an admission of declining appeal, Charles's continuing success has all but vanquished those claims. Indeed, the musician is so versatile that he has been impossible to stereotype—and has thereby been free to pursue his own agenda. And given a choice, Charles prefers to sing and play the piano. In fact, despite his remarkable songwriting talents, Charles does not view himself as a composer at heart. He told Martin, "If you say to me, what is it that is *you*? Then I say singing a song, sitting at the piano and singing."

And that's just what the artist has been doing in the seventies and eighties. He spends nearly half the year in concert, giving polished, professional performances. His audiences, as always, remain diverse, reflecting his widespread appeal. As Martin described, Charles "has consistently been too popular for pure jazz, too jazzy for

rhythm-and-blues, it was his new sound, the granddaddy of pop, rock, and soul, that consistently drew rave reviews. Scoring top-ten hits became almost routine for the star as he recorded such now-vintage tunes as "This Little Girl of Mine," "Hallelujah I Love Her So," "Right Time," and "What'd I Say."

Toward the end of the 1950s, the pioneering musician decided to switch from Atlantic Records to ABC/Paramount. The move proved fortuitous. His first hit for the label, the 1960 release "Georgia on My Mind," became a commercial turning point, with outstanding sales shattering previous records and propelling the young

pure blues, too bluesy for pure pop. Musical fashion was naturally something he made, but most of the time it was cut to fit his defiantly catholic ear." And if the musician himself has anything to say about it, he'll continue making music that way forever. As he revealed in his conversation with the *Esquire* editor: "Music is just as much a part of me as your breathin' or your bloodstream is to you. So they ain't no retiring from it; I'm gonna do it . . . till I die. This is all I know, and all I wanna know."

If it were up to reviewer Ward, Charles would be named a "National Living Treasure." From his beginnings as a jazz and rhythm-and-blues man in the 1940s to his peak as an innovator in the fifties and sixties to his continuing excellence as a performer in the seventies and eighties, the entertainer has consistently defied expectations. Indeed, as one of those rare musicians whose talents span a variety of musical styles as well as decades of musical history, Ray Charles has secured a place for himself among the most important figures in post-World War II American music.

Selected discography

Major single releases

"Baby Let Me Hold Your Hand," Swing Time, 1951.
"Kiss Me Baby," Swing Time, 1952.
"It Should Have Been Me," Atlantic, 1954.
"I've Got a Woman," Atlantic, 1955.
"Hallelujah I Love Her So," Atlantic, 1956.
"What'd I Say?," Atlantic, 1959.
"Let the Good Times Roll," Atlantic, 1960.
"Come Rain or Come Shine," Atlantic, 1960.
"One Mint Julep," Impulse, 1960.
"Georgia On My Mind," ABC, 1960.
"Ruby," ABC, 1960.
"Hit the Road Jack," ABC, 1961.
"Unchain My Heart," ABC, 1961.
"I Can't Stop Loving You," ABC, 1962.
"Born to Lose," ABC, 1962.
"You Don't Know Me," ABC, 1962.
"Busted," ABC, 1963.
"I Got a Woman," ABC, 1965.
"Crying Time," ABC, 1965.
"Living For the City," Crossover, 1975.

Albums

Ray Charles, Atlantic, 1957.
The Great Ray Charles, Atlantic, c. 1958.
Ray Charles at Newport, Atlantic, 1958.
Yes Indeed, Atlantic, 1958.
(With Milt Jackson) *Soul Brothers*, Atlantic, c. 1958.
What'd I Say, Atlantic, 1959.

The Genius of Ray Charles, Atlantic, 1959.
Ray Charles Sextet, Atlantic, 1960.
Ray Charles In Person, Atlantic, 1960.
The Genius Hits the Road, ABC, 1960.
The Genius Sings the Blues, Atlantic, c. 1960.
The Genius After Hours, Atlantic, 1961.
Dedicated to You, ABC, 1961.
Genius + Soul = Jazz, Impulse, 1961.
Ray Charles and Betty Carter, ABC, c. 1960.
Modern Sounds in Country and Western, ABC, 1961.
Modern Sounds in Country and Western, Volume 2, ABC, 1962.
(With Milt Jackson) *Brothers in Soul: Soul Meeting*, Atlantic, 1962.
Ingredients in a Recipe for Soul, ABC, 1963.
Sweet and Sour Tears, ABC, 1963.
Have a Smile With Me, ABC, 1964.
Live in Concert, ABC, 1965.
Together Again, ABC, 1965.
Cincinnati Kid (film soundtrack) MGM, 1965.
Crying Time, ABC, 1966.
Ray's Moods, ABC, 1966.
Ray Charles Invites You to Listen, ABC, 1967.
In the Heat of the Night (film soundtrack) UA, 1967.
A Portrait of Ray, ABC, c. 1968.
Love Country Style, ABC, c. 1969.
I'm All Yours Baby, ABC, c. 1969.
Doing His Thing, ABC, 1969.
My Kind of Jazz, Tangerine, 1970.
Volcanic Action of My Soul, ABC, 1971.
Ray Charles Presents the Raelettes, Tangerine, 1972.
Jazz Number Two, Tangerine, 1973.
A Message From the People, ABC, 1972.
Through the Eyes of Love, ABC, c. 1972.
Come Live With Me, Crossover, 1974.
Live in Japan, Crossover, 1975.
My Kind of Jazz, Volume 3, Crossover, 1975.
Renaissance, Crossover, 1975.
(With Cleo Laine) *Porgy and Bess*, RCA, 1976.
True to Life, Atlantic, 1977.
Love and Peace, Atlantic, 1978.
Ain't It So, Atlantic, 1979.
Brother Ray Is at It Again, Atlantic, 1980.
From the Pages of My Mind, Columbia, 1986.

Also released numerous anthologies, including *The Ray Charles Story*, four volumes, Atlantic, 1962-64, *A Man and His Soul*, ABC, 1967, *Twenty-fifth Anniversary Salute*, ABC, 1971, and *Rockin' With Ray*, Archive of Folk and Jazz Music, 1980. More than thirty additional albums feature the Ray Charles Singers.

Sources

Books

Charles, Ray and D. Ritz, *Brother Ray: Ray Charles' Own Story*, Dial Press, 1978.

Periodicals

American Heritage, August-September, 1986.
Esquire, May, 1986.
Jet, December 9, 1985.
Rolling Stone, February 13, 1986; February 17, 1986.
Stereo Review, February, 1986.

—Nancy H. Evans

Cher

Singer, actress

Performing artist Cher has been a mainstay of the Hollywood *glitterati* for more than two decades, and her personal star seems to be waxing still. Few would quarrel with *Mademoiselle* contributor Diana Maychick, who calls Cher "a breed unto herself" who "has lived enough lives to fill a novel." Professionally, the statuesque performer has had equal success as a singer, a comedienne, and an actress, with Gold Records and Academy Award nominations to her credit. Personally, a series of tempestuous relationships with several rock stars, producers, and actors has helped keep her name in the news even when her career stagnated.

As a reporter for *Time* magazine noted, the arc of Cher's rise to stardom "proves that at least one American dream lives: she gives evidence that show biz can still reach out among the adolescent millions and—with a little luck and a lot of hype—transform a mildly talented young woman into a multimillion dollar property." Ironically, though known for her cool onstage demeanor and effectively understated acting, Cher admits to a chronic case of stage fright. "I've been *running* on fear," she told *Mademoiselle.* But, she added, she has learned that "you take your terror and you do it."

A younger generation might recognize Cher as simply a film actress, but it was as a popular singer that she first gained national notoriety. Her initial success in the music industry can be attributed to her former husband/partner Sonny Bono; they married in 1964 when Cher was only seventeen. Bono had had some prior experience as a songwriter and record producer, and he recognized Cher's star potential. However, noted the *Time* reporter, "they both must have known that she needed him. Her ambition may have been fierce, but like her talent it was vague and undefined." First Bono talked Cher into concentrating on singing rather than acting, her art of choice. Then, after she had done some studio backup work for other artists, he began to write songs specifically for her.

Bono told *Time* that Cher "was too frightened to perform by herself," so he provided vocal harmony "just to be with her." After a short stint as "Caesar and Cleo" they began singing as Sonny and Cher, and their third record release—the 1965 soft-rock tune "I Got You, Babe"—sold more than four million copies and made them instant headliners. By the fall of that year they had five singles on the Top-40 charts simultaneously and were playing at major rock concerts in the United States and Europe.

The Sonny and Cher sound drew on folk and rock roots, especially the work of Bob Dylan. A critic for the *Rolling Stone Record Guide* contends that the couple "always cultivated an exuberant vulgarity in order to disarm

For the Record. . .

Full name, Cherilyn LaPiere; born Cherilyn Sarkesian, May 20, 1946, in El Centro, Calif.; daughter of John and Georgia (a model; maiden name, Holt) Sarkesian; stepdaughter of Gilbert LaPiere (a bank manager); married Sonny (Salvatore Philip) Bono (a record producer, songwriter, and entertainer), October 27, 1964 (divorced, May, 1975); married Gregg Allman (a musician), June, 1975 (divorced); children: (first marriage) Chastity; (second marriage) Elijah Blue.

Singer, with husband, Sonny Bono, in duo Sonny and Cher, 1964-75, and 1977; has also recorded and performed as a soloist, 1965—. Star of musical variety television shows "The Sonny and Cher Comedy Hour," 1971-74, "Cher," 1975-76, and "The Sonny and Cher Show," 1977. Member of rock group Black Rose, 1979-80. Actress in feature films, including "Good Times," 1966, "Chastity," 1969, "Come Back to the Five and Dime, Jimmy Dean, Jimmy Dean," 1982 (also performed role on Broadway), "Silkwood," 1983, "Mask," 1985, "The Witches of Eastwick," 1987, and "Moonstruck," 1988.

Awards: Academy Award nomination for best supporting actress, 1983, for "Silkwood"; Academy Award for best actress, 1988, for "Moonstruck."

Addresses: *Home*—2727 Benedict Canyon Dr., Beverly Hills, CA 90210.

dy Hour" was seen weekly by more than thirty million viewers. Simultaneously, Cher began a solo singing career in the pop format; her best known hits were "Half Breed" and "Gypsies, Tramps, and Thieves," both of which reached number one on the charts. By virtue of her glamorous Bob Mackie gowns and ever-changing hairstyles—a look *Rolling Stone* correspondent Lynn Hirschberg called "ridiculously sexy for television"— Cher cultivated an image of materialistic excess that was tempered by the themes of hurt and vulnerability in her music. "Television always made Cher accessible," Hirschberg wrote. "She seemed like a lot of fun. . . . She appealed to the junky impulses in everyone."

In 1975, Sonny and Cher divorced; both starred in their own variety shows, but only Cher's was a success. Still, the dissolution of Sonny and Cher marked the beginning of a difficult period for her. Gradually her show declined in popularity, and her personal life was made chaotic by her marriage and divorce of band leader Gregg Allman and extended liasons with producer David Geffen and Gene Simmons, actor and member of the colorful rock group Kiss. By 1977, she told *Rolling Stone,* her career "cooled down to an ice cube." Musically she experimented with a fully-orchestrated studio

> "Cher not only triumphs as an actress, but finally vanquishes her glitzy Vegas image."

sound on the 1977 album *I'd Rather Believe In You* and then turned to disco on the 1978 *Take Me Home.* Neither record achieved the popularity of her previous offerings.

Cher's last attempt at musical innovation came in 1980 when she formed the hard rock band Black Rose. The effort was a critical disaster; Jim Farber reported in *Rolling Stone* that "newspaper reviews were pointedly negative," singling out Cher for their barbs even though she deliberately understated her role in the band. "The critics panned us," Cher told *Rolling Stone.* "And they didn't attack the record. They attacked me. It was like, 'How dare Cher sing rock & roll?'"

Stung by this defeat, Cher returned to her more conventional Las Vegas stage show and tried to inch her way onto a stage or into a film as a serious actress. In the latter capacity—as an actress—she has met with unexpected but welcome critical favor. In movies such as "Silkwood," "Mask," and "Moonstruck," to quote *Newsweek* contributor Cathleen McGuigan, "Cher not

Sixties songwriting . . . to push it into a more comfortably sentimental direction." This "exuberant vulgarity" extended to their wardrobes as well; both favored hip-hugging bell-bottom pants and a gaudy array of hippy-style shirts and vests. Then, observes the *Time* reporter, "fashion changed. Hard rock, acid rock, were suddenly in, and Sonny and Cher were out."

Their sudden plunge in popularity was accelerated by their vocal criticism of drug use. Cher told *Time* that after she and Sonny made a public service film denouncing drugs, their fans "thought we were stupid." Deeply in debt after a movie project called "Chastity" bombed, the couple were forced to reassess their act and make drastic changes. Against Cher's wishes they opted for a more mainstream approach in sound and style, and they turned to nightclubs for performing venues. It was in this environment that Sonny and Cher developed the comic repartee and musical variety formula that they would take to television so successfully.

Between 1971 and 1974, "The Sonny and Cher Come-

only triumphs as an actress, but finally vanquishes her glitzy Vegas image."

Although she has won respect for her acting, the ambitious performer has not relinquished her musical career. She still sings in New York, Las Vegas, and Atlantic City, and she is constantly entertaining the idea of starring in a movie musical. *Time* suggested that by whatever medium she chooses, Cher will continue "to woo the world through performance." Cher herself told *Time:* "From the time I could talk I began to sing. Singing just came from the inside—something I'd do without thinking whenever I felt good or was really blue. . . . It released my tensions."

Selected discography

With Sonny and Cher

Look At Us, Atco, 1965.
Wonderous World, Atco, 1966.
In Case Your In Love, Atlantic, 1967.
Good Times, Atlantic, 1967.
The Best of Sonny & Cher, Atlantic, c. 1968.
Sonny & Cher Live, Kapp, c. 1969, re-released, MCA, 1972.
All I Ever Need Is You, Kapp, 1971, re-released, MCA, 1974.
Baby Don't Go, Reprise.
Live In Las Vegas, MCA, 1974.
Greatest Hits, MCA, 1975.
The Beat Goes On, Atco, 1975.

Solo albums

All I Really Want to Do, Imperial, 1965.
Sonny Side of Cher, Imperial, 1966.
Cher, Imperial, 1967.
With Love, Imperial, 1968.
Backstage, Imperial, 1968.
Golden Greats, 1968.
3614 Jackson Highway, Atco, c. 1969.
Cher, Kapp, 1972.

Foxy Lady, MCA, 1972.
Hits of Cher, United Artists, 1972.
Bittersweet White Light, MCA, 1973.
Dark Lady, MCA, 1974.
Half Breed, MCA, 1974.
Stars, Warner Bros., 1975.
This Is Cher, Sunset.
Greatest Hits, MCA, 1975.
I'd Rather Believe In You, Warner Bros., 1977.
Cherished, Warner Bros., 1977.
Take Me Home, Casablanca, 1978.
Prisoner, Casablanca, 1979.
The Best of Cher, EMI America, 1987.
Cher, Geffen, 1988.
Sings the Hits, Springboard.
Greatest Hits, Springboard.
Live.
The Two of Us.
This Is Cher.
Allman and Woman.

With Black Rose

Black Rose, Casablanca, 1980.

Sources

Books

The Rolling Stone Record Guide, Random House, 1979.

Periodicals

Mademoiselle, June, 1985.
Newsweek, March 18, 1985.
People, April, 10, 1978; October 22, 1979.
Rolling Stone, October 16, 1980; March 29, 1984.
Time, March 17, 1975.

—*Anne Janette Johnson*

Eric Clapton

Guitarist, singer, songwriter

"I think I'm probably the 50th [best guitarist] if anything," Eric Clapton told *Rolling Stone*. If he's not the best, he certainly is the most modest. It would be hard to come up with five, much less forty-nine, better guitar players than Clapton, especially when dealing with the blues. "Yes, that's what I do best. That is really my personal style," he said in *The Guitar Player Book*. From the Yardbirds to Cream, Blind Faith, Derek and the Dominos, and various backup bands, Clapton has played styles as diverse as heavy metal, pop, sweet love songs, and even reggae. But, throughout a career that has spanned nearly 25 years, he has always remained true to his blues roots. "If I'm put into any other kind of situation, I'd have to fly blind," he told Dan Forte in *The Guitar*. "In the blues format I can just almost lose consciousness; it's like seeing in the dark."

Clapton was born illegitimately in Ripley, England, on March 30, 1945. His mother left him to be raised by his grandparents, Rose and John Clapp, when he was a small child. He was brought up thinking they were his parents until his real mother returned home when he was nine years old. The family pretended that his mother was his sister, but he soon found out the truth from outside sources. "I went into a kind of . . . shock, which lasted through my teens, really," he said in *Musician,* "and started to turn me into the kind of person I am now . . . fairly secretive, and insecure, and madly driven by the ability to impress people or be the best in certain areas."

Around this time Clapton began hearing American blues musicians like Sonny Terry, Brownie McGhee, Muddy Waters, and Big Bill Broonzy. He was knocked out by the sound and took up the guitar trying to emulate them. Soon he discovered a few friends that were also into this mysterious music from the States and they formed their own clique. "For me, it was very serious, what I heard. And I began to realize that I could only listen to this music with people who were equally serious about it," he told *Rolling Stone*'s Robert Palmer. "And, of course, then we had to be purists and seriously dislike other things."

The seventeen-year-old was soon playing folk blues in coffee houses, and in 1963 he joined his first band, the Roosters. They stayed together for only a few months before Clapton moved on to Casey Jones and the Engineers, which lasted an even shorter period. By then Clapton had begun to hear some of the electric blues that were coming into England, and he switched over from acoustic. "Hearing that Freddie King single ('I Love The Woman') was what started me on my path," he said in *Rolling Stone*.

Word began to spread around town about the hot new guitarist, and in late 1963 the Yardbirds asked Clapton

For the Record. . .

Name originally Eric Patrick Clapp; born March 30, 1945, in Ripley, Surrey, England; illegitimate son of Patricia Clapp; raised by grandparents, John and Rose Clapp; married Patti Boyd Harrison March 27, 1979 (divorced, 1988); children: (by Lory Del Santo) one. *education:* Expelled from Kingston College of Art, 1962.

Professional musician, 1963—. Guitarist with The Roosters, 1963, Casey Jones and the Engineers, 1963, The Yardbirds, 1963-65, John Mayall's Bluesbreakers, 1965-66, Cream 1966-68, Blind Faith, 1969-70, Delaney and Bonnie & Friends, 1970, and Derek and the Dominos, 1970-71; solo artist, 1974—. Has also appeared in motion pictures, including "Tommy" and "Water."

Awards: Recipient of *Melody Maker* magazine's World's Top Musician award, 1969; winner of *Guitar Player* magazine's Readers' Poll in rock category, 1971-74, in overall category, 1973, and in electric blues category, 1975, and 1980-82; co-winner of Grammy Award for album of the year, 1972, for *The Concert for Bangla Desh;* co-recipient (with Michael Kamen) of British Academy of Film and Television Arts Award for original television music, 1985, for "Edge of Darkness."

Addresses: *Office*—67 Brook St., London W1, England. *Record company*—Warner Bros., 75 Rockefeller Plaza, New York, NY 10019.

to join their band, replacing Tony "Top" Topham. With the Rolling Stones' popularity verging on worldwide, the Yardbirds took over as houseband at the Crawdaddy Club in Richmond. The group specialized in rave-ups: driving music that starts low and steady, building to a frentic climax before dying down and then repeating again. Clapton was developing his chops on the bluesier numbers and was also gaining a loyal following.

Band manager Giorgio Gomelsky nicknamed him "Slowhand" at this time in reference to his fluid and speedy playing and also as a pun to the slow hand clapping Clapton received whenever he broke a string on stage. The band was becoming anxious to cash in on the success of other British bands like the Beatles and decided to record more commercial material, which Clapton was totally against."Single sessions are terrible. I can't take them at all," he told *Rolling Stone*'s Jann Wenner. "No matter what the music is like, it's got to be commercial, it's got to have a hook line, you've got to have this and that and you just fall into a very dark hole."

Clapton's disgust during the "For Your Love" recording coupled with an embarrassing session with Sonny Boy Williamson (the bluesman said that Englishmen didn't know how to play authentic blues) prompted him to leave the Yardbirds in 1965. "For Your Love" became a hit for the band, as Clapton figured it would, and he was replaced by Jeff Beck, and later by Jimmy Page, whose style was more compatible with the band's.

Clapton worked with his grandfather for a time, doing construction work. A popular myth has Clapton locking himself in his room with nothing but his guitar for a year, but actually he went and stayed with his friend from the Roosters, Ben Palmer, for a month. "I was all screwed up about my playing," he said in *Rock 100*. "I realized that I wanted to be doing it for the rest of my life, so I'd better start doing it right." Clapton devoted his playing to pure blues, and by the end of 1965 John Mayall recognized the talent and asked him to join the Bluesbreakers. By then Clapton had formed his own style, which borrowed from the traditional masters, yet was easily recognized as something special.

Gene Santoro commented in *The Guitar:* "The boy had it all. The characteristic hesitations and syncopations, the punching buildups toward chord changes, the lilting phrases punctuated by bent blues notes tumbling into abrupt finishes that accent the power and beauty of the line, the sure-fingered variety of attack, the breathtaking reaches up to the twelfth fret and beyond, the heavy sustain, the flawless timing—it must have been difficult to be a guitarist listening in the audience without being overwhelmed completely."

Clapton was becoming much more than an underground hero. The blues revival of the 1960s was in full swing and the group's album debuting the 21-year-old sensation, *Bluesbreakers,* went all the way to number 6 on the English *pop* charts. The now-famous slogan, "Clapton is God," began appearing on subway walls in England and guitarists everywhere were searching for the key to his magical sound. By 1966 Clapton was growing weary of the strict diet of Chicago-style blues the band was playing and decided to form a new band with former Bluesbreaker bass player Jack Bruce (Clapton was replaced by Peter Green and Mick Taylor, who went on to join Fleetwood Mac and the Stones respectively).

Cream, the new band, also included virtuoso drummer Ginger Baker, whom Clapton originally thought "was just too good for me to play with, too jazzy," he said in *Rock 100*. Although the three improvised *a la* jazz, the sound was pure rock and blues, played in a manner which has become synonymous with today's heavy metal. As Charley Walters wrote, "The formula was easy and deceptively limiting: start off simply, explode into a lengthy free-for-all, and end as begun. The brilliant moment occasionally surfaced, but self-indulgence was the general rule." The group released four albums, which contained some live cuts in addition to the studio tracks. Clapton's guitar set-up established the sound for future rock and rollers: "Two 100-watt Marshalls. I set them full on everything, full treble, full bass and full presence, same with the controls on the guitar," he said in *Rolling Stone*.

With psychedelia and the Vietnam War happening, Cream epitomized the times and rode a crest of success. While the fans just couldn't get enough guitar licks, critics like Jon Landau had had more than enough. Landau cited Clapton as the master of the blues cliche in one of his *Rolling Stone* reviews, and it struck home. "The ring of truth just knocked me backward; I was in a restaurant and I fainted," Clapton told Palmer. "And after I woke up, I immediately decided that that was the end of the band." Cream played their final performance at London's Albert Hall in November 1968.

A few months later, Clapton and Baker joined forces with Steve Winwood and Rick Grech to form the first super-group, Blind Faith. Amidst media hype and little rehearsal time, the group played their first gig; a free concert in front of 36,000 fans at Hyde Park in London. Their planned 24-hour tour of the United States proved to be too much too soon and they broke up in January of 1970 with only one album under their belt.

During the tour Clapton converted to Christianity, which was an unusual move at a time when most of his contemporaries were exploring Eastern religions. He was unhappy with the adulation Blind Faith received, feeling that it was unwarranted. He felt the opening act, Delaney and Bonnie & Friends, were playing the type of music he could relate to, so he joined them. Delaney pushed Clapton to develop his singing and writing skills during his stint as a sideman with them. In 1970 he released his first solo album, *Eric Clapton,* with the help of Delaney and Bonnie and their band. Afterwards, Carl Radle and Bobby Whitlock asked Delaney for a raise and he fired them.

Clapton seized the opportunity and picked them up for his own band, Derek and the Dominos, adding Jim Gordon on drums. Clapton befriended Duane Allman while recording in Florida and the guitarist was asked to play with them. The collaboration had an enormous impact on Clapton's style, and the twin guitars produced some of the finest music in rock and roll. "I think what really got me interested in it (slide guitar) as an electric approach was seeing Duane take it to another place," he told Forte. "No one was opening it up until Duane showed up and played it a completely different way. That sort of made me think about taking it up."

Clapton formed the Dominos and wrote the songs as a way of reaching a certain woman he yearned for: ex-Beatle George Harrison's wife Patti. The song he wrote for her, "Layla," is "perhaps the most powerful and beautiful song of the Seventies," according to *Rolling Stone*'s Dave Marsh. Patti stuck by her husband though, causing Clapton to lose his faith and to start on a path of self-destruction. The Dominos were already heavily into drugs, which eventually caused their breakup, but Clapton was now using heroin as a means of easing his emotional pains. "Not Patti herself, as a person, but as an image, she was my excuse. That was the catalyst, a very big part of it," he told Ray Coleman in *Clapton!* "It was a symbol, my perfect reason for embarking on this road which would lead me to the bottom."

The addiction forced Clapton to take a three-year hiatus after the Dominos, performing only at the 1971 Bangladesh concert and at the 1973 Rainbow Concert (arranged by Pete Townshend of the Who as a means to get Clapton back into circulation). He eventually underwent electroacupuncture treatment successfully and spent some time on a farm in Wales relaxing and working.

> *Clapton formed the Dominos and wrote the songs as a way of reaching a certain woman he yearned for: ex-Beatle George Harrison's wife Patti.*

After his recovery, Clapton stated in *Rolling Stone* that "the thing about being a musician is that it's a hard life and I know that the minute I get on the road I'm going to be doing all kinds of crazy stuff. It's just that kind of life." Manager Robert Stigwood booked Clapton into a Miami studio for the recording of his comeback LP, *461 Ocean Blvd.* One of his finest to date, it includes "I Shot the Sheriff" and "Mainline Florida," two tunes that Clapton still performs in concert.

Clapton eventually won Patti and the two were married in 1979. He wrote one of his most requested and popular songs, "Wonderful Tonight," for her and it appeared on his *Slowhand* album. Clapton has continued releasing solo albums (14 to date) and playing on other artists' records. His fans still cry out "Clapton is God" at his concerts and they're still waiting for him to cut loose on his guitar like he did with Cream, but he refuses to revert back to that style. Another reason Clapton plays less guitar is fear. "I lost confidence because I thought I'd done it all. . . . That's why I didn't play as much lead guitar on those albums in the Seventies. I was very, very nervous that I'd said it all," he told *Rolling Stone*. Even though he had kicked heroin, Clapton's obsessive behavior led him to another vice, alcohol. Oddly enough, he kicked that too, at the same time his Michelob beer ads began to appear on television.

He has also done work in films, appearing in Ken Russell's "Tommy" and the movie "Water." He also scored "Lethal Weapon" and the British television series "Edge of Darkness." In 1983 the three former guitarists from the Yardbirds, Clapton, Beck, and Page, were reunited at the ARMS benefit concert for musician Ronnie Lane. And while Clapton's 1980s albums seem to be heading back to his older style of playing of committment and passion, there is talk of a Cream reunion (Clapton and Bruce jammed at a New York club in 1988). His 1986 tour to promote *August* featured Phil Collins on drums and a four-piece band, his smallest since the 1960s.

His personal life is still unsteady, as he and Patti were divorced in 1988 after Clapton fathered a child by Italian actress Lory Del Santo. But to fans, critics, and fellow musicians his music remains the primary focus. An excellent summary of his career thus far can be found on the 6-LP package *Crossroads*, which was released in 1987 and reached number 1 on *Billboard*'s compact disc chart.

Compositions

Composer of numerous songs, including "Badge," "Bell Bottom Blues," "Hello Old Friend," "Lay Down Sally," "Layla," "Strange Brew," "Sunshine of Your Love," "Watch Out for Lucy," "Wonderful Tonight." Co-wrote (with Michael Kamen) musical score for British television series "Edge of Darkness"; wrote musical score for motion picture "Lethal Weapon."

Selected discography

With the Yardbirds

Sonny Boy Williamson and The Yardbirds, Fontana, 1964.
For Your Love, Epic, 1965.

With John Mayall's Bluesbreakers

Bluesbreakers, Decca, 1966.

With Cream

Fresh Cream, Atco, 1966.
Disraeli Gears, Atco, 1967.
Wheels of Fire, Atco, 1968.

Goodbye, Atco, 1969.
Cream Live, Atco, 1970.
Cream Live 2, Atco, 1971.

With Blind Faith

Blind Faith, Atco, 1969.

With Derek and the Dominos

Layla, And Other Assorted Love Songs, Atco, 1971.
Derek and the Dominos—Live In Concert, RSO, 1973.

Solo albums

Eric Clapton's Rainbow Concert, RSO, 1973.
461 Ocean Boulevard, RSO, 1974.
There's One In Every Crowd, RSO, 1975.
E.C. Was Here, RSO, 1975.
No Reason to Cry, RSO, 1976.
Slowhand, RSO, 1977.
Backless, RSO, 1978.
Just One Night, RSO, 1980.
Another Ticket, RSO, 1981.
Money and Cigarettes, Warner Bros., 1983.
Behind the Sun, Warner Bros., 1985.
August, Warner Bros., 1986.
Crossroads, Polygram, 1987.

Has also appeared as a sideman on numerous albums, including *The Beatles* [The White Album] (on "While My Guitar Gently Weeps"), *The Concert For Bangla Desh, The Last Waltz,* and *Stephen Stills.*

Sources

Books

Coleman, Ray, *Clapton!,* Warner Books, 1985.
Dalton, David, and Lenny Kaye, *Rock 100,* Grossett & Dunlap, 1977.
Evans, Tom, and Mary Anne Evans, *Guitars: Music, History, Construction, and Players From the Renaissance to Rock,* Facts on File, 1977.
The Guitar Player Book, by the editors of *Guitar Player* magazine, Grove Press, 1979.
Kozinn, Allan, and Pete Welding, Dan Forte, and Gene Santoro, *The Guitar,* Quill, 1984.
Logan, Nick, and Bob Woffinden, *The Illustrated Encyclopedia of Rock,* Harmony Books, 1977.
The Rolling Stone Interviews, by the editors of *Rolling Stone* magazine, St. Martin's Press/Rolling Stone Press, 1981.
The Rolling Stone Record Guide, edited by Dave Marsh and Jon Swenson, Random House/Rolling Stone Press, 1979.
Shapiro, Harry, *Slowhand,* Proteus, 1984.
What's That Sound?, edited by Ben Fong-Torres, Anchor Press, 1976.

Periodicals

Detroit Free Press, April 19, 1987.

down beat, March, 1987.

Guitar Player, July, 1980; December, 1981, January, 1984; July, 1985; January, 1987; December, 1987; July, 1988; August, 1988.

Guitar World, September, 1983; March, 1985; January, 1986; March, 1987; April, 1987; June, 1988; January, 1989.

Musician, November, 1986.

Rolling Stone, June 20, 1985; August 25, 1988.

—Calen D. Stone

Roy Clark

The affable Roy Clark, longtime co-host of "Hee Haw" on syndicated television, is recognized as a virtuoso of country-style banjo and guitar. Clark has been performing since his teens, and his serious musicianship is sometimes overshadowed by his hayseed comedy routines, especially on television. Neil Hickey noted in *TV Guide,* however, that the corny "Hee Haw" was the vehicle that propelled Clark "from the penumbral half-light of minor celebrity to the blinding glare of full public favor" and therefore gave the star a national following for his music.

Named Country Music Association Entertainer of the Year in 1973, Clark has extended his popularity beyond America's borders to include Europe and the Soviet Union, where he has toured to enthusiastic ovations. The extent of his appeal, obviously, is wider than the southern states where country music dominates. This is because Clark has been a ground-breaker in adapting country picking styles to classical and popular melodies—his repertory includes the Spanish dance "Malaguena," "Lara's Theme," and "Yesterday When I Was Young." Hickey quotes "Hee Haw" producer Frank Peppiatt, who has said of Clark: "It took a long time for him to be discovered, but he deserves his success because he is one of the best musicians alive."

Clark was born into a musical family. His father and uncles were amateur performers who played guitar, banjo, and fiddle at small socials in the Washington, D.C., area. While a child, Clark toyed with a cigar-box ukelele his father made for him; by his teens he had graduated to the banjo and guitar, both of which he mastered without learning how to read music. Soon he was playing with his family and contemplating a show business career. Clark was also an excellent athlete as a youngster. He was invited to spring training by the St. Louis Browns but had no money for the train fare to Florida. He also boxed professionally as a light heavyweight, winning fifteen bouts before losing one and deciding to retire.

At the age of fourteen Clark won the prestigious banjo competition at the National Country Music Championships in Warrenton, Virginia. He won again in 1948 and earned television contracts in Washington, D.C., and occasional appearances at Nashville's Grand Ole Opry. By 1950 he had his own band and had added fiddle, piano, trumpet, trombone, and drums to his list of instruments played. He also worked up a comedy act that he performed during the band's breaks, and he discovered that he enjoyed making people laugh.

Slowly Clark began to make his way in the competitive country music industry. In the mid-1950s he played lead guitar first for Jimmy Dean's Texas Wildcats, then for the Marvin Rainwater Ensemble. A 1956 guest

For the Record. . .

Full name, Roy Linwood Clark; born April 5, 1933, in Meherrin, Va.; son of Hester (a federal government employee) Clark; divorced first wife; married second wife, Barbara Joyce, 1957; children: (first marriage) two. *Education:* Vocational high school graduate.

Professional country musician, 1948—, comedian, 1950—. Professional boxer, 1951. Lead guitarist with Jimmy Dean's Texas Wildcats, the Marvin Rainwater Ensemble, and Wanda Jackson's band, 1953-61; toured with Hank Thompson, 1961; guest host of "The Tonight Show," 1962; regular performer on "Swingin' Country" (NBC-TV), 1966; host, with Buck Owens, of "Hee Haw," syndicated television comedy/variety show, 1969—.

Has also made guest appearances on television shows, including "The Beverly Hillbillies," "Grand Ole Opry," "The Flip Wilson Show," "The Jonathan Winters Show," "Country Music Hit Parade," and numerous talk shows.

Awards: National Country Music Banjo Championship winner, 1947 and 1948; recipient of entertainer of the year awards from Country Music Association, 1973, and Academy of Country Music, 1973-74; Country Music Star of the Year citation from American Guild of Variety Artists, 1974; Instrumentalist of the Year awards from Country Music Association, 1977, 1978, and 1980; named Guitarist of the Year by *Guitar Player* and *Playboy* magazines, 1977 and 1978.

Addresses: *Home*—Tulsa, OK. *Office*—c/o 1800 Forrest Blvd., Tulsa, OK 74114. *Agent*—Jim Halsey Company, Inc., 3225 S. Norwood Ave., Tulsa, OK 74135.

appearance on the "Arthur Godfrey Show" led to even wider exposure; by 1960 he was touring the nation and playing Las Vegas as backup to Wanda Jackson and Hank Thompson. In 1962 Clark got the chance to be a guest host of "The Tonight Show," and he played the rural wisecracker so successfully that other television offers poured in. He appeared several times as Cousin Roy and Big Mama Halsey on "The Beverly Hillbillies" and was a guest star on numerous variety shows.

His early albums, *Lightning Fingers of Roy Clark, Superpicker,* and *Yesterday When I Was Young* did well on the country charts; the latter also made the pop charts. In 1969 Clark was working with "The Jonathan Winters Show" when he was asked to co-host a country comedy/variety series on CBS. He agreed, and "Hee Haw," starring Clark and Buck Owens, premiered in May of 1969.

Fast-paced but uncompromisingly hokey, "Hee Haw" was an instant hit, not only among rural viewers, but with mainstream audiences as well. *Country Music U.S.A.* author Bill C. Malone observed that the show's appeal "suggested that the humor of country music was more traditional than its music" but added that the performers in the ensemble cast "won a national exposure through the show that most earlier country comedians had only dreamed of."

"Hee Haw" was more than just a silly comedy program, however. Each episode featured an old-fashioned gospel quartet number, with Clark providing vocals and guitar accompaniment, and both hosts were given a solo song in almost every show. Clark used his solo time primarily to perform his guitar and banjo instrumentals, some of which bore little resemblance to the stereotypical hillbilly tenor of "Hee Haw.". While one week he might pick the ever-popular "Orange Blossom Special" or "Jesse James," the next week he would offer a jazz tune like "St. Louis Blues" or "Georgia on My Mind."

Clark's performance styles likewise were quite varied, from traditional stringband methods to complex classical fingering to innovative uses of a guitar pick. CBS cancelled "Hee Haw" in 1971 because the network wanted to urbanize its image, but the show continued in syndication. It is still on the air throughout rural America, the longest continuously-running television program in history.

Surprisingly, "Hee Haw" consumes only three to five weeks of Clark's time each year. The rest of the time he travels, giving live performances and appearing on television talk shows, variety specials, and charity telethons. In *The Encyclopedia of Country & Western Music,* Rick Marschall suggested that because of his engaging personality, Clark "is more popular in performance than on record. . . . His voice can be described as a permanently hoarse tenor, and the emotion he brings to heart-songs sounds like every drop of feeling has been wrung out for the task." It is as a comedian and an instrumentalist that Clark has made his mark, however. Long-time friend Jimmy Dean is quoted in *The Encyclopedia of Folk, Country, and Western Music* as saying of Clark: "Everybody loves him. When he walks out on stage with his bungling attitude as though he didn't know what was going to happen next, the audience is immediately on his side. It's like cheering for the underdog or the hometown boy."

Selected discography

Lightning Fingers of Roy Clark, Capitol, 1962.
Best of Roy Clark, Dot.
Country, Dot.
Do You Believe This?, Dot.
The Entertainer, Dot.
Entertainer of the Year, Capitol.
Everlovin' Soul, Dot.
The Greatest!, Capitol.
Guitar Spectacular, Capitol.
He'll Have to Go, Pickwick.
Incredible, Dot.
I Never Picked Cotton, Dot.
Honky Tonk, Pickwick.
Live!, Dot.
Live Fast, Love Hard, Pickwick.
The Magnificent Sanctuary Band, Dot.
The Other Side of Roy Clark, Dot.
Roy Clark, Pickwick.
Silver Threads and Golden Needles, Hilltop.
Superpicker, Dot.
Take Me As I Am, Hilltop.
Urban, Suburban, Dot.
Yesterday When I Was Young, Dot.
Roy Clark Sings Gospel, Word.
Classic Clark, Dot.
Family and Friends, Dot.
Roy Clark's Greatest Hits, Volume I, Dot.
Heart to Heart, Dot.

Hookin' It, ABC.
Live with Me, Dot.
(With Buck Trent) *A Pair of Fives*, Dot.
Sincerely Yours, Paramount.
So Much to Remember, Capitol.
Introducing Roy Clark, Ember.
The Very Best of Roy Clark, Capitol.
Country Standard Time, MCA, 1986.

Also recorded *Happy to Be Unhappy*, *Family Album*, *Back to the Country*, and with Trent, *Banjo Bandits*.

Sources

Books

Malone, Bill C., *Country Music U.S.A.*, revised and enlarged edition, University of Texas Press, 1985.
Marschall, Rick, *The Encyclopedia of Country and Western Music*, Exeter Books, 1985.
Stambler, Irwin and Grelun Landon, *The Encyclopedia of Folk, Country, and Western Music*, St. Martin's, 1969.

Periodicals

People, September 26, 1977.
TV Guide, August 24, 1973.

—*Anne Janette Johnson*

Richard Clayderman

Pianist

Richard Clayderman's billing as the world's most popular pianist was put to the test during an interview on the "Late Night with David Letterman" show. The *Christian Science Monitor* reported that Letterman, in order to judge Clayderman's reputation as a household name, placed a random telephone call to a home in Norway. The family not only knew him but owned several of his albums.

Born in France with the name Phillipe Pages, he took the stage name Clayderman (from his great-grandmother) because his real name was pronounced differently in every country. His father was a piano teacher and began teaching him classical piano at a young age. Clayderman entered the Paris Conservatory at age 12 and won first prize for piano at 16. When he found it difficult to make a living as a classical pianist, he turned to popular music and toured with French rock musician Johnny Hallyday. The turning point for Clayderman came when two record producers asked him to record "Ballad pour Adeline." That record, which helped launch his career into popular music, has sold over 20 million copies in 38 countries.

Clayderman's shift from classical to popular music not only allowed for his remarkably successful career but moved him into an area of music which he feels more closely reflects his personality. Although he still plays classical music on stage, for his United States concerts he focuses on romantic interpretations of popular American melodies. "I think there is a need for this kind of romantic music," he told the *Christian Science Monitor,* "because we live in a world [where] terrible things are happening, and people need music to feel a bit cool and relaxed. I think a proportion of my audience also listens to other styles. For example, I'm sure the young people like rock 'n roll music. But through my playing they discover a new kind of music—classical, because sometimes I play that on stage."

In a review of his 1985 New York debut at Carnegie Hall, *Variety* suggested that, besides his repertoire and lush playing style, "Clayderman's main appeal lies in his youth and boyish good looks. . . . Coupled with his gentlemanly charm and his thick French accent, they promise to rope in the romantically inclined middle-aged Yank ladies who cotton to this ilk of soothing entertainment." The *Los Angeles Times,* also reporting on a performance from his first American tour, objected to the canned quality and cuteness of his audience interaction, but praised the show as "otherwise well constructed, with a good balance of original and established songs, and of romantic ballads and high-stepping rhythm pieces."

For his American concerts he performed with a 16-piece orchestra and offered romantic crowd pleasers like "Feelings," "The Way We Were," and "Chariots of Fire." The *Christian Science Monitor* remarked that, heard along with the orchestra, his performance had the "solidity and strength that spring from his training as a classical pianist." His concerts are marked by standing ovations and multiple encores.

For *People* to accuse Clayderman of displaying "all the emotions of a turnip" and for *Rolling Stone* to describe him as a "schlock pianist" is perhaps unfair. He may not be Horowitz but his music does fill a need as evidenced by over two hundred gold and platinum records and international sales reported at over 40 million albums. "If the sales figures Columbia claims are true," *Stereo Review* noted in 1987, "he is probably the most successful pianist in the world today."

Selected discography

American releases—on Columbia

From Paris with Love, 1985.
Amour, 1985.
A Romantic Christmas, 1985.
Plays Love Songs of the World, 1986.
Romantic America, 1988.

Released on Teldec in 1986

Rhapsodie (with the Royal Philharmonic Orchestra).
Ti Amo.
Traumereien.
Traumereien 2.
Traumereien 3.
Zeit Zum Traumen.

Sources

Christian Science Monitor, January 6, 1986.
Los Angeles Times, January 26, 1985.
People, October 28, 1985.
Rolling Stone, April 25, 1985.
Stereo Review, April 1985; May 1987.
Variety, February 20, 1985.

—Tim LaBorie

James Cleveland

Singer, songwriter, pianist

Variously hailed as the King of Gospel Music and the Crown Prince of Gospel, the Reverend James Cleveland has combined his talents as preacher, composer, singer, producer, and philanthropist to become one of the most outstanding exponents of the modern gospel sound. Indeed, with a voice that has earned acclaim as one of gospel's greatest, and a religious fervor that has refused the lure of secular music, Cleveland, more than any artist of his generation, has served as a champion of gospel in its purest form. As he explained to Ed Ochs in an interview for *Billboard,* gospel is not only "a music, but . . . a representation of a religious thinking. Gospel singing is the counterpart of gospel teaching. . .. It's an art form, true enough, but it represents an idea, a thought, a trend."

Born in Depression-era Chicago, the son of hard-working, God-fearing parents, Cleveland grew up in an environment where gospel flourished. His grandmother introduced him to Chicago's Pilgrim Baptist Church, where the budding musician was influenced by choir director Thomas A. Dorsey—also known as the father of gospel music. Under Dorsey's tutelage, the youth made his solo debut with the choir at the age of eight. The vocalist subsequently taught himself to play piano, often recounting how he practiced on imaginary keys until his parents could afford to purchase an upright for him. As Tony Heilbut quoted the star in *The Gospel Sound:* "My folks being just plain, everyday people, we couldn't afford a piano. So I used to practice each night right there on the windowsill. I took those wedges and crevices and made me black and white keys. And, baby, I played just like Roberta [Martin]. By the time I was in high school, I was some jazz pianist."

Roberta Martin, a Dorsey disciple and one of the Chicago gospel pioneers to gain international recognition, was among Cleveland's idols. It was her group, the Roberta Martin Singers, who first helped shape the youth's singing and piano style, with Roberta Martin herself inspiring the youngster to begin composing. By the time he was a teenager, Cleveland was singing with a neighborhood group, the Thorn Gospel Crusaders. And once the group began featuring Cleveland's compositions, the artist found himself piquing the interest of prominent gospel talents. In 1948 Cleveland's "Grace Is Sufficient," performed at a Baptist convention, prompted Martin to begin publishing the new composer's work.

The next decade proved a productive one for Cleveland. He made his recording debut on the Apollo label in 1950, singing "Oh What a Time" with the Gospelaires. He composed songs for Roberta Martin, including "Stand By Me," "Saved," and "He's Using Me." He worked frequently with the Caravans, first establishing

For the Record. . .

Born December 23, 1932 (some sources say 1931), in Chicago, Ill.; son of Ben Cleveland (a WPA worker); children: LaShone (daughter).

Minister and gospel singer, songwriter, and pianist. Singer with The Thorn Gospel Crusaders, 1940s; The Gospelaires, 1940s; Mahalia Jackson, early 1950s; The Caravans, beginning in 1954; The Gospel All Stars, late 1950s; The Gospel Chimes, 1959; co-director of music for New Bethel Baptist Church, Detroit, Mich., beginning in 1960; minister of music for Prayer Tabernacle, Detroit, beginning c. 1960; recording artist with Savoy Records, 1960—; founded James Cleveland Singers, 1963; founded Southern California Community Choir, 1969. Makes concert tours. Ordained minister, early 1960s; Cornerstone Institutional Baptist Church, Los Angeles, Calif., founder and pastor, 1970—.

Awards: Award from National Association of Negro Musicians, 1975; Image Award from NAACP, 1976; *Billboard* magazine's Trendsetter Award; *Ebony* magazine's Artist Award; NATRA's award as best gospel artist; *Billboard*'s award for best album and best male singer in soul/gospel for *Live at Carnegie Hall*; Grammy Award from Academy of Recording Arts and Sciences; six gold albums.

Addresses: *Home*—Los Angeles, CA. *Office*—c/o Ed Smith, Gospel Artists Association, P. O. Box 4632, Detroit, MI 48243.

During the 1960s Cleveland also formed the James Cleveland Singers, gradually built an international reputation, and became one of the best paid of the gospel music entertainers. And although two of Cleveland's former pupils—Aretha Franklin and Billy Preston—went on to achieve celebrity status, the master himself declined to expand his audience by moving into secular music, choosing instead to devote himself strictly to gospel.

Indeed, in the early sixties Cleveland became a minister and served Los Angeles's New Greater Harvest Baptist Church as pastor until he was able to build his own Cornerstone Institutional Baptist Church in 1970. For him, gospel music and gospel teaching are inseparable—different mediums conveying the same message. As the minister-musician explained to Ochs: "If we can't preach to people in a dry, talking sermon and get their attention, we'll sing it to them, as long as we get the message across. We have been instrumental in drawing more people to the church in recent years through singing and getting them to find favor with

> *Cleveland, more than any artist of his generation, has served as a champion of gospel in its purest form.*

something in the church they like to identify with. Then when we get them into church, putting the same message into words without music is not as hard, for we have set some type of precedent with the music to get them into the church and get them focused on where we're coming from."

For Cleveland, gospel music is so vital that in 1968 he organized the first Gospel Music Workshop of America. Designed both to help preserve the gospel tradition and to feature new talent, the workshop has grown to include more than five hundred thousand members representing almost every state. "My biggest ambition is to build a school somewhere in America, where we can teach and house our convention," Cleveland told *Village Voice* interviewer David Jackson. This is the best way, in the artist's opinion, to assure that gospel's legacy continues.

As a musical artist for more than forty years and a minister for nearly thirty, Cleveland remains not only one of the most successful and popular gospel artists of all time, but also one of the staunchest supporters of

himself as a superlative gospel arranger, then emerging as a singer—the Caravans scored their earliest hits, in fact, with Cleveland as lead vocalist on such tunes as "Old Time Religion" and "Solid Rock." And he founded the first of his own groups, the Gospel Chimes, which helped showcase his talents as composer, arranger, and singer.

By 1960 Cleveland, who had incorporated blues riffs and what Heilbut described as "sheer funkiness" in his work, had become associated with a new tenor in gospel music. That year "The Love of God," a song he recorded with Detroit's Voices of Tabernacle choir, was a sensation, and its success helped Cleveland secure a recording contract with Savoy Records, for whom he has since recorded more than sixty albums. The artist passed another milestone with Savoy's 1963 release *Peace Be Still.* A recording pairing Cleveland with the Angelic Choir of Nutley, New Jersey, the album, which held a spot on the gospel charts for more than fifteen years, has sold more than one million copies, an almost unheard of achievement for a gospel recording.

gospel in its purist form. Remaining true to the gospel heritage, Cleveland perpetuates an understanding of gospel music and gospel teaching as part of the same religious experience, believing that the music devoid of the mission is not genuine gospel. As Jackson articulated: "What Cleveland has been saying since he first started composing and performing gospel music is that God seeks to bring us peace—to reconcile us with ourselves. Through classics like 'Peace Be Still,' 'Lord Remember Me,' 'Father, I Stretch My Hands to Thee,' and 'The Love of God,' Reverend Cleveland retells a biblical love story for the plain purpose of reconciling people to God and to one another." And as his scores of devoted followers attest, concluded Jackson, "his message is widely appreciated and applauded."

Compositions

Composer of numerous gospel songs, including "Grace is Sufficient," "Jesus," "The Man," "He's Using Me," and "God Specializes."

Selected discography

Albums; released by Savoy Records

All You Need
At the Cross
Bread of Heaven
Christ Is the Answer
Down Memory Lane
Everything Will Be All Right
Free At Last
Give Me My Flowers
God's Promises
Grace of God
Greatest Love Story
Hark the Voice
He's Working It Out
Heaven Is Good Enough
His Name Is Wonderful
How Great Thou Art
I Stood on the Banks
I Walk With God
If I Perish
I'll Do His Will
I'm One of Them
It's Real
Jesus Is the Best Thing
Live at Carnegie Hall
Lord, Do It
Lord, Help Me

Lord Let Me Be an Instrument
Merry Christmas
Miracle Worker
New Day
99 1/2 Won't Do
No Failure in God
No Ways Tired
One and Only James Cleveland
Out on a Hill
Parade of Gospel
Peace Be Still
Pilgrim of Sorrow
Reunion
Somebody Knows
Songs Mother Taught Me
Songs of Dedication
Soul of James Cleveland
Stood on Banks
Sun Will Shine
Trust In God
Try Jesus
When I Get Home
Where Can I Go
Without a Song
You'll Never Walk Alone

Also released numerous recordings for Savoy in collaboration with other artists, including albums with The Charles Fold Singers, The Angelic Choir of Nutley, N.J., The L.A. Gospel Messengers, The New Jerusalem Baptist Church Choir, and many others. Several early recordings released by such labels as Hob (Detroit) and States (Chicago).

Sources

Books

Broughton, Viv, Black Gospel: An Illustrated History of the Gospel Sound, Blandford Press, 1985.
Heilbut, Tony, The Gospel Sound: Good News and Bad Times, Simon & Schuster, 1971.

Periodicals

Billboard, September 27, 1980.
Ebony, December, 1984.
Village Voice, April 16, 1979.

Other

Baker, Barbara, "Black Gospel Music Styles: 1942-1979," Ph.D. dissertation, University of Maryland, 1978.
Casey, M. E., "The Contributions of James Cleveland," thesis, Howard University, 1980.

—Nancy H. Evans

Natalie Cole

Singer

Rhythm and blues singer Natalie Cole rose to stardom almost overnight and then fell into obscurity just as precipitously. The spirited daughter of the late Nat "King" Cole was one of the top black performers in the mid- to late-1970s; awarded a Grammy in 1975 as best new artist of the year, she seemed destined to duplicate her famous father's career—without echoing his sound. According to *Ebony* contributor Herschel Johnson, Cole's albums have shown her voice "to have considerable style and facility, [easily] handling everything from the sizzling rhythmic strains . . . to the tender ballad lines. . . . And her phrasing, like that of her late father, is expertly sympathetic."

Cole became a superstar at twenty-five and was showered with acclaim and awards over the next three years. By 1982, however, ill health, drug abuse, and a failed marriage had sidetracked her career. She has yet to recover her earlier level of success, although she continues to perform and to handle her own affairs. Reflecting on her life's low points, Cole told *Newsweek:* "I managed to survive the worst things any entertainer could possible go through."

Natalie Maria Cole was born in 1950, the second of Nat and Maria Cole's five children. Throughout the 1950s her father was one of the highest paid performers in the world, with his own prime-time television show and a string of bestselling albums. "On stage, he was a star," Cole told *Ebony,* "but at home he was an ordinary father—a companion." Raised in wealth and luxury, Cole learned to love music under the influence of both of her parents; her mother had been a principal singer with the Duke Ellington orchestra before her marriage. Still, young Natalie was not encouraged to pursue music as a career. Instead she attended college at the University of Massachusetts, eventually earning a Bachelor's degree in child psychology.

Cole began singing professionally quite by chance, when she went looking for summer work as a waitress and wound up fronting a local band. Good club bookings followed—but they were invariably based on the strength of her father's name. Cole found this "humiliating" at times but accepted it as an opportunity to bypass the years of struggle some artists must endure. "It was only natural that I should resent it," she told *High Fidelity* magazine in 1977, "because I wanted to be recognized for my own talent, but at the same time it made me realize just how famous my father was. And I guess if I had been Ann Smith, I'd probably still be struggling and maybe just now being able to get ahead."

Cole may have gotten a start on her father's coattails, but once she took the stage she developed her own style and repertoire, based on influences as various as Ella Fitzgerald, Aretha Franklin, Carole King, and the

Beatles. In *Ebony,* Louie Robinson writes that the young singer "exploded on the national scene . . . rising to the top like cream with a dazzling flourish of versatility: ballads, torch-rock, rhythm-and-blues." According to John Storm Roberts in *High Fidelity,* the core of Cole's sound, "both in quantity and quality, is a joyous pop-soul singing: The sound of early Motown soul, Marvin Gaye, the Supremes, and above all, the early Aretha Franklin."

Cole's success on her own terms was greatly aided by producer/songwriters Chuck Jackson and Marvin Yancy, who provided her with material and helped to engineer her albums for Capitol Records. With their support, her 1975 debut album, *Inseparable,* with its chart-topping single "This Will Be," went platinum and won her two Grammy awards. Roberts called the Cole-Jackson-Yancy relationship "a partnership that obviously can't be faulted commercially; but it also works well musically, never dominating [Cole] or giving the impression that she is being jammed art-first into some unsuitable sack marked 'What's happening.'"

Once established—and married to Yancy—Cole seemed reluctant to experiment stylistically. Roberts suggests that she seemed satisfied to be a "club singer with an almost perfect command of the current hip-pop middle ground. . . . Black middle of the road, you might call it, not simply all-American middle of the road sung by black singers, but . . . with specifically black references: hip but slightly deodorized rhythm and blues, gospel-soul, the jazz-ballad tradition and a nostalgia for the great period of soul when its audience was kids."

By the early 1980s, Cole was quarreling with her manager, her band, and the executives at Capitol, all of whom she claimed were ignoring her wishes. Her marriage to Yancy ended in divorce in 1979. To quote *Essence* correspondent Jack Slater, "her fabled zest for life was turning sour, and the sourness compounded the loneliness and her growing inability to cope. Things began to fall apart." Depressed and alone, Cole turned to cocaine. "I must say that I did succumb to the weakness," she told *Essence* of her drug abuse. "At one time I would stay in my bedroom for hours on end. I didn't do anything but that." To make matters worse, she developed throat polyps that had to be removed surgically—a potentially career-ending condition.

In 1982 Cole's mother sued for control of her daughter's finances, and eventually the troubled singer was able to find the privacy and therapy to regain her health. She returned to work—and to the responsibility for her assets—in 1983. Cole told *High Fidelity:* "I remember

> "I managed to survive the worst things any entertainer could possibly go through."

my father saying that 'hits are not important—it's longevity that matters.'" It is just this "longevity" that Cole is striving for now. She maintains a professional association with Yancy and has returned to live club performance on a regular basis.

Cole told *Ebony* that she feels a singer "should be a human instrument. So whatever I [do] with my voice, I [want] to make it work *with* the music and not sing *against* the music or stand *above* it, but enhance it, like flavoring and seasoning." According to Roberts, Cole has achieved the goal of being that "human instrument." Roberts concludes: "In a period of decadence, fatigue, and gimmicks, she returns to the central issues of voice, tune, and spirit. To reinterpret the ethos of the young Aretha, to keep it all clean and tight and youthful, to back herself with classically joyous, shouting gospel-soul chorus and jumping musicians, is to return to what classic r & b was all about."

Selected discography

Inseparable, Capitol, 1975.
Dangerous, Capitol, 1975.
Thankful, Capitol, 1978.
I'm Ready, Epic, 1983.
Everlasting, Capitol, 1987.
Modern, Capitol.
Natalie Cole Collection, Capitol.

Sources

Ebony, September, 1973; December, 1975; May, 1978.
Essence, October, 1973.
High Fidelity, February, 1977.
Newsweek, August 25, 1975; May 30, 1983.
People, May 8, 1978.

—Anne Janette Johnson

Sam Cooke

Singer, songwriter

Soul singer Sam Cooke was acclaimed as "a bravura vocal stylist who blazed the path for a generation of singers from Otis Redding and Wilson Pickett to Aretha Franklin and Al Green," by Jim Miller in *Newsweek*. A prominent feature on the music scene from the early 1950s, when he sang with the black gospel group the Soul Stirrers, through a solo pop career that ended when he was shot to death in late 1964, Cooke "became famous for letting his voice glide over every syllable of a song in a sustained lyrical caress," according to Miller. Popular with black and white audiences alike, Cooke—who wrote most of his own material—is remembered for such hit songs as "You Send Me," "Only Sixteen," "Wonderful World," "Cupid," and "Chain Gang."

Cooke, one of eight children in his family, was born in Chicago, Illinois. His father, the Reverend Charles Cooke, was a Baptist minister, and Sam began singing gospel songs in his father's church as a child. While still attending Chicago's Wendell Phillips High School, he and one of his brothers sang in a gospel group called the Highway Q.C.'s. But Cooke did not begin to achieve fame for his vocal abilities until he joined the already well-established Soul Stirrers.

Cooke quickly became the Soul Stirrers' featured tenor, and sang the lead on their hits "Pilgrim of Sorrow" and "Touch the Hem of His Garment." Gene Busnar asserted in his book, *It's Rock'n'Roll,* that "many knowledgeable listeners consider these two gospel performances the best of [Cooke's] career." In addition, Cooke, "with his good looks and dreamy voice . . . lowered the age of the average female attendee of a gospel program by about thirty years," according to Ed Ward in *Rock of Ages: The Rolling Stone History of Rock and Roll.*

But even while a Soul Stirrer, Cooke was showing interest in more secular forms of musical expression. He released a pop single called "Loveable" in 1956 on the Specialty label that recorded the Stirrers' music, but was credited with the name "Dale Cooke" instead of his own. Art Rupe, the owner of Specialty, feared that the Stirrers' fans would be offended at their lead singer cutting a pop tune. He also felt that Cooke's voice was too mellow and smooth to make much of a dent in the pop music scene, and tried to discourage the singer from following that direction. Cooke did record a few more pop tunes for Specialty, however, including "I'll Come Running Back to You."

Despite Rupe's negative attitude, Cooke was undaunted in his mainstream musical ambitions. He left the Stirrers, and with Bumps Blackwell—who had produced his pop efforts for Specialty—broke with Rupe and signed with the fledgling label, Keen. Cooke's first hit for Keen was the 1957 release that he wrote with his brother, L. C. Cooke, "You Send Me," which sold 1.7 million copies in 1957 alone.

Cooke was an instant solo success; the "B" side of "You Send Me," "Summertime," also made the charts, and he followed this up with another double-sided hit released later in the year, "Desire Me," and "For Sentimental Reasons." As Busnar explained, these songs "introduced the public to a voice that was unlike any that they had ever heard. Cooke had a delicate but intense voice. His clear diction and timbre reminded some people of Nat King Cole. But Cooke had a depth of emotion below his polish which Cole could not touch."

Cooke had several other hits for Keen, including "Win Your Love For Me," "Everybody Likes to Cha-Cha-Cha," "Only Sixteen," and "Wonderful World" before moving to RCA in 1960. His first big hit for his new label was "Chain Gang," a song describing the sufferings of convict labor that rose to second place on the record charts. In 1961 he released "Cupid," his hit song of supplication to the Roman god of love, and in 1962 he capitalized on the new dance craze, the Twist, with "Twistin' the Night Away."

Cooke also introduced black phrases into the popular music lover's vocabulary with songs like his 1962 hit "Bring It on Home to Me," on which he was backed up by soul singer Lou Rawls in a call and response style, and his posthumous release "A Change Is Gonna Come," which gave new social overtones to a familiar black expression. In the early 1960s Cooke was also working as a record producer on his own independent label, Sar, which released cuts like "Soothe Me," by the Sims Twins, and "Rome Wasn't Built in a Day," by Johnny Taylor.

The circumstances surrounding Cooke's death are somewhat cloudy. In December 1964 he was vacationing in Los Angeles, California. In *Rock of Ages* Geoffrey

Stokes claimed that Cooke, though he had married his high school sweetheart, Barbara Campbell, in 1959, checked into a motel room with Elisa Boyer as Mr. and Mrs. Cooke. He allegedly tried to rape her, and she fled. In the confusion that ensued, Cooke pounded at the motel manager's door, "eventually breaking in on the 55-year old manager, Bertha Franklin. She shot him three times with a .22 revolver. . . . He was dead when

> *"Cooke blazed the path for a generation of singers from Otis Redding and Wilson Pickett to Aretha Franklin and Al Green."*

the police arrived." Despite the sordid aspects of his death, Cooke was perceived as a martyr by many of his fans, according to Miller. "Thousands of distraught fans mobbed A. R. Leak's Funeral Home in Chicago to catch a last glimpse of their idol," Miller noted. Cooke left some recorded but unreleased material when he died, thus 1965 added "A Change Is Gonna Come" and "Shake" to his list of hit records.

Compositions

Composer of numerous songs, including (with brother, L.C. Cooke) "Another Saturday Night," "Bring It On Home to Me," "A Change Is Gonna Come," "Cupid," "Frankie and Johnnie," "Good News," "Having a Party," "It's Got the Whole World Shakin'," "Shake," "Sweet Soul Music," and "Twistin' the Night Away."

Selected discography

Major single releases

(Under name Dale Cooke) "Loveable," Specialty, 1956.
"You Send Me," Keen, 1957.
"For Sentimental Reasons," Keen, 1957.
"There, I've Said It Again," Keen, 1959.
"Wonderful World," Keen, 1960.
"Chain Gang," RCA, 1960.
"Cupid," RCA, 1961.
"Twistin' the Night Away," RCA, 1962.
"Bring It on Home to Me," RCA, 1962.
"Another Saturday Night," RCA, 1963.
"Little Red Rooster," RCA, 1963.

"Ain't That Good News?" RCA, 1964.
"Shake," RCA, 1965.
"A Change Is Gonna Come," RCA, 1965.

LP collections

Best of Sam Cooke Volume 1, RCA, 1962.
Gospel Soul of Sam Cooke, Specialty, 1964.
Gospel Soul Volume 2, Specialty, 1965.
Best of Sam Cooke Volume 2, RCA, 1965.
Unforgettable Sam Cooke, RCA, 1966.
Man Who Invented Soul, RCA, 1968.
Sam Cooke Live at the Harlem Square Club, RCA, 1985.

Also featured vocalist on gospel recordings by the Soul Stirrers, including "Pilgrim of Sorrow," and "Touch the Hem of His Garment."

Sources

Books

Busnar, Gene, *It's Rock'n'Roll,* Messner, 1979.
Ward, Ed, Geoffrey Stokes, and Ken Tucker, *Rock of Ages: The Rolling Stone History of Rock and Roll,* Summit Books, 1986.

Periodicals

Newsweek, June 3, 1985.

—*Elizabeth Thomas*

Ileana Cotrubas

Singer

Ileana Cotrubas is among the opera world's most beloved singers. Her lyric soprano does justice to the most fanciful melodies of Mozart and Donizetti, and her extraordinary stage presence and command of acting technique lend further credibility to her performances in both lighthearted operas such as Mozart's *The Abduction From the Seraglio* and more dramatically demanding fare such as Verdi's *Don Carlo* and Puccini's *La Boheme.* She is, in short, an extremely compelling performer. As George Movshon noted in the *New York Times,* "Even her laughter—and she laughs readily—comes in neat, musical clusters of chromatic eighth-notes."

Cotrubas was born in 1939 in Galati, Romania. Although she grew up in a fairly musical family—her father and mother both sang—she aspired, when a child, to an acting career in Hollywood. Before adolescence, however, she had joined a children's chorus that occasionally performed on Romanian radio and in local opera presentations. Within a few years she had reached solo status in the chorus, and when her family moved from Galati to Bucharest, Romania, in the early 1950s, she entered a music school. She devoted her first two years there to a variety of studies, including conducting, playing piano and violin, and acting. In her mid-teens, she finally began concentrating on singing. Her voice, however, was considered too modest, and she was initially rejected for further study by a Bucharest conservatory. After an additional year of music theory and practice Cotrubas reapplied to the conservatory in 1958 and gained acceptance.

Under the guidance of her teachers, notably Constantin Stroescu, Cotrubas shaped her singing voice into one featuring a more adult range. This work occupied much of her time at the conservatory, though she was also able to continue her piano studies and indulge in athletics. She also studied several languages, including those in which most operas are written—Italian, German, and French. It was as a singer of the latter language that she first appeared as a soloist in 1964 with Debussy's *Pelleas et Melisande* at the Bucharest Opera. During the next year Cotrubas also appeared in company productions of Gounod's *Faust* and Verdi's *Don Carlo* and *Un Ballo in Maschera.* Her most impressive feat during this period, though, was as triple winner at an important Dutch vocal competition. Scoring victories in the key categories of opera, oratorio, and lieder, Cotrubas consequently appeared on the Dutch stage in Mozart's *Magic Flute* and *The Abduction From the Seraglio.* The following year Cotrubas scored another triumph at a West German competition, and her career was assured.

Throughout the remainder of the 1960s Cotrubas continued to sing in Europe. Among her greatest successes at this time was as Melisande at a Glyndebourne Festival production in 1969 under conductor John Pritchard. The next year she again thrilled British audiences when she appeared at London's Covent Garden—home of the Royal Opera House—in a production of Tchaikovshy's *Eugene Onegin.* Cotrubas's sensitive portrayal in the latter work proved especially endearing, and in the ensuing years the British public came to hold her in what Movshon described in the *New York Times* as "unusual affection."

After her first British appearances, however, Cotrubas returned to the continent and sang for three years with the Vienna State Opera. Among her greatest performances with the Vienna company was as the tubercular courtesan Violetta in Verdi's drama *La Traviata.* This role has been an especially befitting one for Cotrubas, as it allows her to express the vulnerability that is her specialty. Years later, she recorded the role opposite celebrated tenor Placido Domingo in what *Newsweek*'s Annalyn Swan described as a "supurb" rendition, one that "ranks with the best available." Swan, who also assessed Cotrubas's 1981 performances of *La Traviata* at New York City's Metropolitan Opera, noted that "from the moment

she sweeps onstage . . . hers is a memorable Violetta—sweet, vulnerable and infinitely touching." Cotrubas, Swan added, "transforms a domestic drama into something approaching tragedy."

Cotrubas's first triumph in America, however, had come eight years earlier when she appeared as Mimi in the Chicago Lyric Opera's presentation of Puccini's *La Boheme.* Like Violetta in *La Traviata,* Mimi is tubercular, and like Violetta, the role of Mimi affords Cotrubas ample opportunity to display her gifs for endearingly expressive vocalization and expression. Puccini's opera has also proved a key work for Cotrubas, as it was the opera with which she made her debuts at two of the world's greatest opera houses—La Scala and the Metropolitan. At La Scala, she was a last-minute replacement in 1975 opposite the great Luciano Pavarotti who, upon learning that scheduled soprano Mirella Freni was ill, reportedly cried, "Get Cotrubas!" Recalling the event, Cotrubas told the *New York Times,* "In the end they shouted and shouted, and Pavarotti . . . left me alone for the applause. And I thanked God."

She was similarly successful in *La Boheme* at the Metropolitan, where her performance prompted *New York Times* reviewer Raymond Ericson to describe her as "an unusually fine artist." Following her successes in the mid-1970s with *La Traviata* and *La Boheme,* Cotrubas has consolidated her reputation with a variety of performance on stage and record. At the Metropolitan, she has appeared in works such as Verdi's *Rigoletto* and Mozart's *Idomeneo* (both performances were televised); at Glyndebourne she drew praise for her work in Verdi's *Don Carlo* and Benjamin Britten's *A Midsummer Night's Dream* (both productions have been recorded on video tape); and in Chicago she triumphed in a mid-1980s production of Puccini's *La Rondine.* Aside from *La Traviata,* Cotrubas's greatest operatic recordings include Donnizetti's *L'Eliser d'Amore* (opposite Domingo) and Mozart's *The Magic Flute.* In addition, she has appeared on recordings of Hugo Wolf's lieder and Haydn's *The Seasons.*

Though diminuitive and endearing, Cotrubas has also developed a reputation as an exacting, demanding performer, one who is adamant in her refusal to compromise her work. As such, she is sometimes characterized as egomaniacal and uncooperative. She disputed these charges to *Opera News* interviewer Thomas Lanier, to whom she explained: "I'm demanding a lot from other people because I'm giving. I have to give, because I have some special qualities; like any artist, I have to transmit these feelings, and I can't do this without a good conductor, understanding colleagues, and a serious director." Cotrubas is not without confidence, though. Pondering the British public's particular enthusiasm for her, she mused to the *New York Times*, "Maybe it is because I am good."

Selected discography

Arias by Mozart, Donizetti, Verdi, and Puccini, Columbia, 1977.
Gaetano Donizetti, *L'Elisir d'Amore,* Columbia, 1977.
Giuseppe Verdi, *La Traviata,* Deutsche Grammophon, 1977.
Franz Joseph Haydn, *The Seasons,* London, 1978.
Verdi, *Rigoletto,* Deutsche Grammophon, 1981.
Giacomo Puccini, *Gianni Schicchi,* Columbia.

George Bizet, *Carmen,* Deutsche Grammophon.
Wolfgang Amadeus Mozart, *The Marriage of Figaro.*
Mozart, *The Magic Flute,* RCA.
Englebert Humperdinck, *Hansel and Gretel.*

Sources

High Fidelity, June, 1978.
Newsweek, April 6, 1981.
New York Times, March 25, 1977; April 10, 1977.
Opera News, September, 1975; December, 1977; March 28, 1981.

Miles Davis

Trumpeter, composer

"The way you change and help music is by tryin' to invent new ways to play, if you're gonna ad lib and be what they call a jazz musician," Miles Davis told *down beat*. Using that criterion, Davis is perhaps the consummate jazz artist of all time. During a career that began in the late forties and is still going strong, he has been the spearhead of at least five different stages in music: hard bop, cool jazz, orchestral jazz, modal improvising, and fusion.

Miles Dewey Davis III was born in Alton, Illinois, on May 25, 1926; his family moved to East St Louis a year later. Davis's father, Miles II, was a dental surgeon who raised his family in a middle class atmosphere that stressed the importance of money. After receiving a trumpet for his thirteenth birthday, Davis began taking lessons from a local teacher named Buchanan. It was at this early stage that Davis acquired his trademark sound characterized by the lack of vibrato. In just two years he had joined the musicians union and was working in a St Louis band led by Eddie Randall called the Blue Devils.

Like his mentor at the time, Clark Terry, Davis began using a Heim mouthpiece, which produces a higher quality tone but is much more difficult to play. His sound was gaining recognition in jazz circles, and before he was out of high school Davis was earning $85.00 a week gigging with pianist 'Duke' St. Clare Brooks's group. The Billy Eckstine Band, featuring Charlie 'Bird' Parker and Dizzy Gillespie, was in town for a two-week stint and asked Davis to sit in with them. The experience wetted his appetite for a shot at the Big Apple and the chance to play with the jazz heavy-weights.

His mother, recognizing her son's musical talent, yet fully aware of the difficult life of a jazzman, agreed to let him go to New York, but only if he would attend the Juilliard School of Music to study the classics. Davis was already a husband and a father by now (having been married at age 17), and after graduation, he and his wife and child left for the East Coast. Davis began juggling his time between strict lessons at Juilliard and free-style jam sessions in the nightclubs of 52nd Street. At Minton's Playhouse in Harlem he met Freddy Webster, a trumpeter who would have an enormous impact on the youngster. "I used to love what he did to a note," Davis said in *Esquire*. "He didn't play a lot of notes; he didn't waste any. I used to try to get his sound. . . . Freddie was my best friend. I wanted to play like him."

Davis felt that he already knew what was being taught at Juilliard and decided to drop out and concentrate solely on jazz. On May 4, 1945, he played on his first recording session with sax man Herbie Fields, and years later he would tell *down beat* that "I was too nervous to play, and I only performed in the ensembles—no solos." His inexperience must not have shown through too often, because by the end of the year he had joined Charlie Parker's group playing at the Three Deuces club. And, at the tender age of 19, Davis appeared alongside Bird, Diz, and Max Roach on one of the first bebop recordings (November 26, 1945). Although the material was well-received by the critics, Davis's performance did not go over as well and he was slammed by a reviewer in *down beat.*

New York's jazz clubs were drying up at the time, so Parker and Gillespie headed to California to try out their new sound while Davis went back to East St. Louis. He hooked up with Benny Carter whose band was also going to the West Coast to work. Once there, Davis was asked by Parker to replace Dizzy who was fed up with the lack of response their music was getting. On March 28, 1946, the group recorded in Hollywood, and the results won Davis the *down beat* award for New Star on Trumpet that year. Shortly after, he began to work with Charles Mingus and then replaced Fats Navarro in Billy Eckstine's band, working his way back east.

In 1947, Parker and Davis formed a quintet in New York that lasted 18 months. It was a period that saw Parker playing at his best with Davis acting as musical director of the group. On May 8, Davis made his debut as a composer when the quintet recorded for the Savoy label. He was also starting to develop his own sound instead of playing the usual licks that Dizzy had made famous. In August they recorded four more tunes of which Ian Carr said, "The solos too—and for the first time, Miles shares the honours on equal terms with Parker—echo the smooth fluency of the themes. Miles is poised and assured, tending to understate and imply melodic ideas."

Also in 1947, Davis befriended Gil Evans, a composer who was 14 years his senior. Evans would look over Davis's work and help him to write less cluttered tunes. The two formed a partnership that would last for nearly four decades. By late 1948, Davis quit Parker and started to lead his own nine-piece group at the Royal Roost club. He began trimming down his sound, making it lighter and saying more with fewer notes. Saxophonist Gerry Mulligan, who was undergoing a similar process, stated, "Miles dominated the band completely; the whole nature of the interpretation was his." Although the group was not a big hit, they did leave behind some broadcast recordings that mark the beginnings of Miles's ability to influence those who play with him.

He signed his first recording contract with Capitol (for twelve sides at 78 rpm; about three minutes each) and brought the band into the studio to tape. The selections were all later released in 1957 as *The Birth of Cool* and became the foundation for the West Coast Jazz School. Davis headed to Europe to play the Paris Jazz Festival where he was a huge success. But it was a different story back in the States; when he returned he found no jobs available. Like many musicians of the time, Davis turned to heroin and became an addict for the next four years.

He joined Eckstine's band again, and while on tour he was arrested on suspicion of being a heroin addict. The charges were later dropped, but the bad publicity caused him to move to Chicago to do session work to pay for his habit. While other trumpet players who were indebted to Davis were gaining noteriety, he was going nowhere and decided to quit heroin cold turkey. By 1954 he was leading his own group again and recording some of the best performances in jazz history. He would also begin to use the amplified sound of the metallic harmon mute with its stem removed, which according to Ian Carr, "sounded so right and was so immediately attractive, that it spawned imitators everywhere." The song "Oleo" is a prime example of this tone.

After trying various groups through 1955, Davis finally settled on what has come to be known as "the rhythm section": Philly Joe Jones—drums, Paul Chambers—bass, and Red Garland—piano. The group also included John Coltrane on tenor sax. Their first album, *The New Miles Davis Quintet,* was just the beginning of a prolific period in which they would record enough material for over five albums in one year alone. Columbia Records offered Davis $4,000 to join their label, but he still owed Prestige four more albums. They worked out a compromise that allowed Davis to record for both labels: (*Cookin', Relaxin', Workin',* and *Steamin'* for Prestige and *Round About Midnight* for Columbia were all released in 1956.)

After the recordings, Davis went to Europe to work. When he came back to New York, he and Gil Evans collaborated on the seminal LP *Miles Ahead.* With orchestral arrangements by Evans and Davis on flugelhorn, the album met with rave reviews by the critics. Davis and Evans joined forces again in 1958, working on their version of Gershwin's opera, *Porgy and Bess,* called "a major contribution to twentieth-century music" by Ian Carr. "It is outstanding in the way that a sustained dialogue is created between a great improvising soloist and a great orchestrator." Two years later their third orchestral-jazz masterpiece, *Sketches of Spain,* would be released.

During this same period, Davis's combo was recording also. For awhile Coltrane was joined on sax by Sonny Rollins. Coltrane quit soon after to kick his heroin habit, working with Thelonious Monk in the meantime, developing a style of his own with the pianist. Back working with Davis, he was able to put his new theories to use. "Miles' music gave me plenty of freedom," Coltrane told *down beat.* "It's a beautiful approach." The addition of Cannonball Adderely on second sax helped to create two superb albums for the sextet, *Milestones* and *Kind of Blue.*

The early sixties saw still more changes for Davis. He was remarried, this time to dancer Frances Taylor. Columbia assigned musician and producer Teo Macero to be his A&R (artist and repertoire) man, a relationship that would have some extreme highs and lows. Davis was once again in trouble with the law, this time for fighting with the police. In addition, his group was going through many personnel changes, missing gigs and having to cancel ones they couldn't make. The 1963 lineup included Tony Williams on drums, Ron Carter on bass, Herbie Hancock on keyboards, and George Coleman on sax. They released a fine studio effort, *Seven Steps to Heaven,* in addition to a few live LPs. At the same time, Columbia released *Quiet Nights,* which consisted of previous material by Davis and Evans. Unhappy with the selections, Davis was so mad at Macero that the two did not talk for over two years.

In 1965 Davis recorded *ESP,* an abstract jazz album where the solos have no set chorus length. This same format was also used on three other albums: *Miles Smiles, The Sorcerer,* and *Nefertiti.* Davis wrote none of the tunes for the last two, utilizing instead concepts developed by his sidemen. He began leaving the tape machines rolling whenever they were in the studio, later splicing ideas together to form the songs. Davis would later tell *down beat,* "Listening to what they do and feeding it back to them is how any good bandleader should lead his musicians."

By late 1968 Davis had a new wife and more musicians to work with. Dave Holland was brought in on bass, and Chick Corea was added on keyboards. Davis is credited with writing all the tunes, but *Filles de Kilimanjaro* has the stamp of Gil Evans on it. It would be the last album the two would work on together. It would also mark the period known as jazz-rock. "Yes, Miles is the daddy of the whole thing," Chick Corea told *Rolling Stone.* "He structured the music mostly by predicting the way interrelationships between musicians develop. He would write out little or nothing, but he would put the musicians together and nudge them with comments in such a way that he would in effect be structuring the

> *The impact of electronics and musicians who were mastering them forced Davis to reevaluate his music and to come up with something fresh and exciting, thus fusion.*

music. Whatever the individuals came up with from his directions was OK."

Musicians like John McLaughlin, Joe Zawinul, and Jack DeJohnette were brought in to fuel the fire on these landmark LPs: *In A Silent Way,* "which left the listener feeling suspended in space," wrote Mikal Gilmore; *Jack Johnson,* "mood music for a vacation on the moon," according to Robert Christgau; and *Bitches Brew,* the one that made rock and rollers take a listen to jazz. The impact of electronics and musicians who were mastering them (like Jimi Hendrix) forced Davis to reevaluate his music and to come up with something fresh and exciting, thus fusion.

The early 1970s started off badly for Davis. He was in trouble with the law again, both his sons were hooked on dope, he broke both his legs in a car accident, and he fought against a number of health problems (pneumonia, arthritis, bad hip joint, leg infection, and bursitis). He has since remarried, this time to actress Cicely Tyson. More importantly, he continues to tour and record (with occasional pauses for health reasons) with over 40 albums to his credit. While his latest records may not offer anything as dramatically different as the jazz world has come to expect from him, as recently as 1985-86 he has won the *down beat* readers' and critics' polls for best electric jazz group. "Miles is a leader in jazz because he has definite confidence in what he likes and he is not *afraid* of what he likes," said Gil Evans. "He goes his own way."

Selected discography

The Complete Birth of the Cool, Capitol, 1957.
Workin', Steamin', Relaxin', and *Cookin',* Prestige, 1956.
Round About Midnight, Columbia, 1956.
Miles Ahead, Columbia, 1957.
Milestones, Columbia, 1958.
Someday My Prince Will Come, Columbia, 1961.
In Person at The Blackhawk, Columbia.
Kind Of Blue, Columbia, 1959.
Seven Steps to Heaven, Columbia, 1963.
My Funny Valentine, Columbia.
"Four" And More, Columbia.
Porgy and Bess, Columbia, 1958.
Quiet Nights, Columbia.
Sketches of Spain, Columbia, 1960.
Miles Smiles, Columbia, 1966.
E.S.P., Columbia, 1967.
Sorcerer, Columbia, 1967.
Nefertiti, Columbia, 1967.
Miles in the Sky, Columbia.
Filles de Kilimanjaro, Columbia, 1968.
In a Silent Way, Columbia, 1969.
Water Babies, Columbia, 1978.
Bitches Brew, Columbia, 1970.
At Fillmore, Columbia, 1970.

Black Beauty, CBS.
Jack Johnson, Columbia, 1970.
Live-Evil, Columbia, 1971.
On the Corner, Columbia, 1972.
Big Fun, Columbia, 1974.
Get Up With It, Columbia, 1974.
Agharta, Columbia, 1976.
The Man With the Horn, Columbia, 1981.
We Want Miles, Columbia, 1982.
Star People, Columbia, 1983.
Decoy, Columbia, 1983.
You're Under Arrest, Columbia.
Tutu, Warner Bros.
Siesta, Warner Bros.
The Columbia Years, 1955-1985, Columbia, 1988.

Sources

Books

Carr, Ian, *Miles Davis,* Quill, 1984.
Christgau, Robert, *Christgau's Record Guide,* Ticknor & Fields, 1981.
Fong-Torres, Ben, editor, *What's That Sound?,* Anchor Books, 1976.
Hentoff, Nat, *The Jazz Life,* Panther Books, 1964.
Marsh, David, editor, *The Rolling Stone Record Guide,* Random House, 1979.

Periodicals

down beat, September 29, 1960; April 6, 1967; August, 1987; October, 1988; November, 1988; December, 1988.
Esquire, March, 1959.
Guitar Player, November, 1982; September, 1984.
Guitar World, September, 1983.
Rolling Stone, March 11, 1976.

—*Calen D. Stone*

Paco de Lucia

Guitarist

"The portrait of studied concentration and pristine perfection: stiff backed and stern faced, with a distinguished air about him that some might misread as haughtiness," wrote Bill Milkowski describing the great flamenco guitarist, Paco de Lucia, in *down beat*. "He's proud and majestic, like a regal Arabian steed prancing with grace and elegance, yet able to reveal great power."

Born Francisco Sanchez Gomez in December of 1947 in the Gypsy area of southern Spain known as Algeciras, he would later use his mother's name, Lucia, after becoming a professional. He first took up the guitar at age seven and began receiving lessons from his father, Antonio de Algeciras (stage name) and his brother, Ramon. "I was playing for more than ten years when Paco first began to play the guitar," the elder brother stated in *Guitar Player*. "I taught him, although I wasn't his only influence by any means. Paco had a great deal of talent from the very beginning." De Lucia studied the toques of his idol, Nino Ricardo, almost exclusively until he was twelve years old.

After winning a local competition a year later, he was asked by Jose Greco to join the dancer's company and travel to America to play. It was here that one of the flamenco masters, Sabicas, was so impressed by the youth's talent that he urged him to devote his time to developing a style of his own. At age fourteen he was deemed too young to play for the main prize in the La Catedra de Flamencologia in Jerez, but his performance was so stunning that he was awarded a special prize: El Premio Internacional de Acompanamiento. He would enter the recording studio just a year later.

De Lucia also began to tour with Ramon under the Algeciras name, backing up singers and dancers as he had during most of his life. It was his teaming with Gypsy singer Camaron de la Isla and their mixture of contemporary and traditional styles that would mark the beginning of his controversial and successful career. Having already mastered the technical aspects of flamenco music, de Lucia began incorporating chords and scales that were usually associated with jazz. "The feeling is very much the same in both flamenco and jazz," he explained in *down beat*. The difference is that flamenco "is really much more anarchic."

In 1976 de Lucia recorded a rumba, "Entre Dos Aguas", which had never been done before in flamenco history. High sales figures for the single, which made the Spanish Top 20, immediately established him as an international superstar. Flamenco purists were outraged and considered the single a bastardization of their music. De Lucia defended his concept though, stating that he would remain true to the traditional form but that there must also be room for change. "I was brought up in a flamenco atmosphere, and I only really feel flamenco, and after that I play what I want to play without worry," he said in *Guitar*.

He continued to explore new territories in 1977 by recording on American fusion guitarist Al DiMeola's album, *Elegant Gypsy*. Traditionalists were even more upset upon hearing the mostly electric album, but DiMeola defended the Spaniard in *down beat,* stating, "He's not leaving flamenco, he's expanding it." For such an emotional player as de Lucia (he does not even read music), who has admitted influences as experimental as Jimi Hendrix, it must have been very hard to try and grow and yet remain faithful to his past. "I cannot do with flamenco all that I should like because then it loses its identity," he told *down beat*. Regardless of what his mentors were saying, de Lucia was forging a new style that was more than welcome by his audiences. From 1977 to 1981 he won the *Guitar Player* Readers' Poll Award for best flamenco guitarist and became a member of the magazine's Gallery of Greats.

Although he continued recording, his rise to the top and continuous creativity would take a toll. "I have had so many periods of anxiety and nervousness since becoming more popular, and fame can eat you," he told

Guitar Player. "You always have so much pressure to repeat your successes." But de Lucia was able to create magic once again in 1980 with the help of DiMeola and John McLaughlin. The three formed an acoustic-guitar super trio that stunned audiences with their brilliant musicianship. Evidence of their virtuosity and comraderie can be heard on the live 1981 album, *Friday Night in San Francisco.* McLaughlin explained the group's conception to *Guitar Player*'s Tom Wheeler: "Al and I had the same idea—to play with Paco. I heard Paco on the radio, and it was love at first hearing. I said, 'I have to play with this man, and that's all I know.' And so I looked for him until I found him." Two years later the trio would enter the studio to record an appropriately titled follow-up LP, *Passion, Grace and Fire.*

De Lucia is still playing the flamenco music that is so much a part of the rich Gypsy heritage, but in a way that is both rooted in the past and easily accessible to today's audiences. Those who may doubt his commitment to either should take note. ". . . I play guitar not for me, but for flamenco," de Lucia told *Guitar Player.* "I don't want to be a star, or a rich man. I am working for my village, for my country, for my music, for the tradition of the art form, and I want to make the music better."

Selected discography

Solo albums

La Guitarra Fabulosa de Paco de Lucia, Philips.
Fuente y Caudal, Philips.
Almoraima, Philips.
Paco, Island.
Entre Dos Aguas, Philips.
Meister der Spanischen Gitarre, Philips.
Motive, Philips.
Plays Manuel de Falla, Philips.
Solo Quero Caminar, Philips.

With brother, Ramon de Algeciras

Dos Guitarras Flamencas en America Latina, Philips.
Paco de Lucia y Ramon de Algeciras en Latino America, Philips.

With Ricardo Modrego

12 Canciones de Garcia Lorca para Dos Guitarras en Stereo, Philips.
12 Exitos para Dos Guitarras Flamencas, Philips.
Dos Guitarras Flamencas, Philips.

With Al DiMeola

Elegant Gypsy, Columbia, 1977.

With John McLaughlin and Larry Coryell

Castro Marin, Philips.

With Paco Pena

Paco Doble, Philips.

With Al DiMeola and John McLaughlin

Friday Night in San Francisco, Columbia, 1981.
Passion, Grace and Fire, Columbia, 1983.

Sources

Books

Evans, Tom, and Mary Anne Evans, *Guitars From the Renaissance to Rock,* Facts on File, 1977.

Periodicals

down beat, April, 1981; November, 1985.
Guitar, April, 1976.
Guitar Player, June, 1977; May, 1979; March, 1981.

—Calen D. Stone

John Denver

Singer, songwriter, guitarist

John Denver is a pop star whose name is synonymous with music that celebrates life's simple pleasures. Wearing granny glasses and relatively long hair, the singer/songwriter first charmed audiences in the 1970s with his country-boy appeal and lyrics that extolled goodness, love, and natural beauty. Indeed, hit songs like "Take Me Home, Country Roads" and "Rocky Mountain High" brought him national recognition and eventual acclaim as the "nature-loving singer who shaped a whole musical ethos during the seventies," reported Alice Steinbach in the *Saturday Review*.

Even as he reached stardom, however, the entertainer had begun to slight his musical career, choosing instead to concentrate on efforts to preserve the environment and find solutions to the problem of world hunger. Only in the mid-1980s, after a long hiatus from the spotlight, has Denver begun to express an interest in renewing his musical career. In fact, the musician-turned-political activist told Steinbach in a 1985 interview that in the future he hopes to return to music and "become a role model for young people."

Denver received his first guitar as a gift from his grandmother when he was in the seventh grade. He failed to take much of an interest in the instrument, though, until Elvis Presley revolutionized the music world. Excited by the King's example, the teenager started playing the guitar in earnest, becoming good enough to perform with local groups and to entertain at parties. After entering Texas Tech University as an architecture student, he continued to indulge his interest in music, earning an income by doing solo gigs, singing with a trio, and playing guitar in a band. Finally, midway through his junior year, the college student left school to pursue his musical calling.

The aspiring musician initially headed for Los Angeles, California, where his skills sparked some interest at Capitol Records. He cut a demonstration record for the label and even, after some prompting by Capitol, changed his surname to Denver (from the original Deutschendorf), but the recording company failed to release the singles. From Los Angeles the young artist traveled to New York City, where he successfully auditioned for a place with the [Chad] Mitchell Trio. He spent three years with the group, singing, playing guitar and banjo, and witnessing the release of the first album featuring his talents, *The Mitchell Trio: That's the Way It's Gonna Be*.

When the group folded in 1968, Denver struck out on his own. While with the trio he had composed his first hit, "Leaving on a Jet Plane" (recorded by folk singers Peter, Paul, and Mary), and the publicity from that success helped him line up engagements playing for coffee house and college audiences. Before long, he

Real name, Henry John Deutschendorf, Jr.; born December 31, 1943, in Roswell, N.M.; son of Henry John (a U.S. Air Force career man) and Erma Deutschendorf; married Ann Martell, June, 1967 (divorced, c. 1983); children: (adopted) Zachary, Anna Kate. *Education:* Attended Texas Tech University, two-and-a-half years.

Singer and songwriter, 1960s—; began career while a college student, early 1960s; vocalist and instrumentalist (guitar and banjo) with the New York City-based Mitchell Trio, 1965-68; played in coffee houses and on college campuses, 1968-69; signed recording contract with RCA Victor, 1969; formed John Denver Enterprises; provided soundtrack for the CBS television film "Sunshine"; actor in the film "Oh God"; associated with CBS movie "A Christmas Present," 1986. Political activist, 1970s—.

Awards: Named poet laureate of Colorado; named male vocalist of the year by the Academy of Country Music, 1975; named country music entertainer of the year by the Country Music Association, 1975; "Back Home Again" named song of the year by the Country Music Association, 1975.

Addresses: *Home*—Aspen CO; *Office*—John Denver Concerts Inc., P.O. Box 1587, Aspen CO 81612.

had signed a recording contract with RCA and his career was launched.

During the early 1970s Denver enjoyed celebrity as one of pop music's superstars. He released the million-selling single "Take Me Home, Country Roads" in 1971 and followed it in 1972 with the platinum album *Rocky Mountain High* and in 1974 with the successful *Back Home Again.* Although the musician and his compositions impressed some critics as corny, the star more often captivated listeners with his honesty and unabashed enthusiasm and was frequently invited to appear on television variety specials as well as to guest star in dramatic series.

Concurrent with his music career, Denver was pursuing his interest in a number of causes important to him, and by the mid- to late 1970s issues like the environment and hunger had superceded the place of music in his life. In 1977 he helped found the World Hunger Project and was appointed by President Jimmy Carter to the Commission on World Hunger; he also began playing benefit concerts, including one for NASA, and he has made unofficial goodwill musical tours of the

Soviet Union and China. Although involved in a host of projects, Denver has remained most dedicated to eradicating what he calls "the obscenity of world hunger" and has spent recent years, according to Steinbach, "donating money, raising money and working on hunger and agrarian reform commissions."

Once regarded as the "Tom Sawyer of Rock," Denver is now, in Steinbach's estimation, "a thoughtful, serious and socially-committed man." But he is also a man who

> *Although involved in a host of projects, Denver has remained most dedicated to eradicating what he calls "the obscenity of world hunger."*

believes that youngsters need additional role models to choose from in today's world. The artist's album *Dreamland Express* marks one step toward returning to a musical career that he hopes will enable him to inspire young people. He told Steinbach, "I want people to look outside of the narrow focus we all get caught up in and see that whether you live in Aspen or in Africa, underneath we are all the same." The multitalented Denver, concluded Linda Feldman for *McCalls,* "is every bit the Renaissance man."

Compositions

Composer of more than fifty songs, including "Leaving on a Jet Plane," "Rocky Mountain High," and "Take Me Home, Country Roads."

Selected discography

(With the Mitchell Trio) *The Mitchell Trio: That's the Way It's Gonna Be,* Mercury, 1965.
Rhymes and Reasons, RCA, 1969.
Take Me to Tomorrow, RCA, 1970.
Whose Garden Was This, RCA, 1970.
Poems, Prayers, and Promises, RCA, 1971.
Aerie, RCA, 1972.
Rocky Mountain High, RCA, 1972.
Farewell Andromeda, RCA, 1973.
Back Home Again, RCA, 1974.
The Best of John Denver, RCA, 1974.

Rocky Mountain Christmas, RCA, 1975.
An Evening With John Denver, RCA, 1975.
Windsong, RCA, 1975.
Live in London, RCA, 1976.
Spirit, RCA, 1976.
I Want to Live, RCA, 1977.
The Best of John Denver, Volume 2, RCA, 1977.
John Denver, RCA, 1979.
A Christmas Together With the Muppets, RCA, 1979.
Autograph, RCA, 1980.
Some Days Are Diamonds, RCA, 1981.
Perhaps Love, CBS, 1981.
Seasons of the Heart, RCA, 1982.
Its About Time, RCA, 1983.
Collection, Telstar, 1984.
Spirit, RCA, 1984.
Dreamland Express, RCA, 1985.

Sources

Books

Fleischer, Leonore, *John Denver,* Flash, 1976.
Morse, Charles, *John Denver,* Creative Ed., 1974.

Periodicals

McCalls, December, 1987.
Newsweek, December 20, 1976.
People, February 26, 1979.
Saturday Evening Post, January, 1974.
Seventeen, March, 1974.
Saturday Review, September/October, 1985.

—Nancy H. Evans

Neil Diamond

Singer, songwriter, guitarist

Neil Diamond is pop music's perennial chart-topper, a singer-songwriter with a devoted international following. In *The Best of the Music Makers,* George T. Simon calls Diamond "a balance between sexy superstar and nice boy from Brooklyn" who ". . . has a broad appeal to an audience that cuts across age levels, sophistication levels, and the traditional musical-preference categories." Diamond has been performing his own compositions since 1966, and his long list of hits—from "Cherry, Cherry" to "You Don't Bring Me Flowers" and "Heart Light"—has spanned some 15 years. While Simon describes the singer's work as "rock domesticated for everyone," *Time* magazine contributor Jay Cocks sees Diamond otherwise. "Neil Diamond is . . . fronting a big sound," Cocks writes. "He has written and sung some of the smoothest and best contemporary pop, yet he remains a performer in search of a tradition, a megabucks pilgrim looking for roots he never had and a place in which to settle." Rock, even soft-rock, has never been Diamond's milieu; it is equally wrong to categorize him as a club singer in the Frank Sinatra/Wayne Newton vein. In fact, Cocks concludes, Diamond "is revealed as a rouser, a showman, a kind of bandmaster of the American mainstream." According to Robert Christgau in the New York *Daily News,* Diamond's singing "combines rawness and control in a way that can please both rock fans . . . and stylish young adults."

Some of Diamond's best lyrics reflect a certain confusion about identity and disillusionment overcome only by immersing oneself in song. The adult personality who writes such unconventional pop verses can be traced to Neil Leslie Diamond, an insecure Jewish boy who grew up in Brooklyn, New York. Diamond changed schools nine times as a child, and as he was intensely shy, he had great difficulty making friends. Instead, he immersed himself in a fantasy world populated by imaginary characters and idolized the singing cowboys he saw in movies.

When Diamond was 16 he bought a second-hand guitar, learned some chord progressions, and began to compose songs. He also began to sing with the Erasmus Hall High School chorus group, a 100-member glee club that included Barbra Streisand. Diamond was a good student, so after high school he enrolled in premedical studies at New York University. He was in his senior year at NYU when the Sunbeam Music Company, a Tin Pan Alley songwriting mill, offered him a 16-week contract. He dropped out of college and never returned. "It just absorbed me and became more and more important as the years passed."

Between 1962 and 1965 Diamond worked at a number of Tin Pan Alley companies, trying to crank out main-

For the Record. . .

Full name, Neil Leslie Diamond; born January 24, 1941, in Brooklyn, N.Y.; son of Kieve (a dry goods store proprietor) and Rose Diamond; married; second wife's name, Marcia Murphy; children: (first marriage) Marjorie, Elyn; (second marriage) Jesse, Micah. *Education:* Attended New York University.

Songwriter for Sunbeam Music Company and other songwriting shops, 1962-65; songwriter, singer, musician and recording artist, 1965—; composer of soundtracks for films "Jonathan Livingston Seagull," 1973, "Every Which Way But Loose," 1978, and "The Jazz Singer," 1980; actor in film "The Jazz Singer," 1980; host of television variety specials "The Neil Diamond Special," 1977, and "I'm Glad You're Here with Me Tonight," 1977, both NBC.

Awards: More than twenty gold and platinum records; received Grammy Award, Golden Globe Award, and Academy Award nomination, all 1974, all for "Jonathan Livingston Seagull" soundtrack; received Grammy Award nomination, with Barbara Streisand, for song "You Don't Bring Me Flowers," 1979.

Addresses: *Office*—c/o Columbia Records, 1801 Century Park W., Los Angeles, Calif., 90067.

stream tunes to order. Finally, in 1965, he decided to begin writing songs that he wanted to sing himself. He performed his work at the Bitter End, a Greenwich Village nightclub, where he attracted the attention of Bert Berns, a producer who was beginning a new label, Bang Records. In 1966 Diamond cut three hit singles for Bang: "Solitary Man," "Cherry, Cherry," and "I Got a Feelin'." He also contributed a song, "I'm a Believer," to the Monkees, who propelled it to a 10 million-selling, number one hit. Diamond went on in 1967 to release several more bestselling songs, including "Kentucky Woman" and "You Get to Me."

The young artist was not satisfied with Berns and Bang Records, however, so in 1968 he moved to the Uni label (a division of MCA's Universal Studios) in Los Angeles. With greater control over his own material and more artistic latitude, Diamond blossomed into an unusual mainstream singer whose work reflected irony, inner turmoil, and psychological depth. He made the Billboard top ten with songs as diverse as the jaunty "Cracklin' Rosie," the satirical "Brother Love's Travelling Salvation Show," and cryptic "I Am, I Said." By 1972 he was a major force in pop music. He became the first pop-rock artist to headline a musical perform-

ance on Broadway at the prestigious Winter Garden Theatre, and he also travelled widely, giving concerts in every major American city.

The strain caught up with Diamond after his Winter Garden engagement, and he went into temporary retirement. The hiatus lasted forty months; he spent the time undergoing intense psychotherapy, regaining his family ties, and studying music theory. Ironically, his few recordings during this period were among his most successful. His 1973 soundtrack for the film *Jonathan Livingston Seagull* won a Grammy Award, a Golden Globe Award, and an Oscar nomination. Still, Simon notes, "some predicted that he would be forgotten if he stayed out of the tour circuit for long."

Diamond surprised the doubters when he returned to a full schedule in 1976. He played to sellout crowds in New Zealand and Australia, then returned for a three-performance, $500,000 stint at the Aladdin Hotel in Las Vegas. Simultaneously, his concept album *Beautiful Noise* —and its single "If You Know What I Mean"—

> *"He has written and sung some of the smoothest and best contemporary pop, yet he remains a performer in search of a tradition, a megabucks pilgrim looking for roots he never had . . . ."*

went gold. The following year Diamond starred in two television specials on NBC, "The Neil Diamond Special," and "I'm Glad You're Here with Me Tonight." He was also working under a million-dollar-advance-per-album contract with Columbia records.

Such continued success had its drawbacks, however. Diamond's work has always received mixed-to-negative reviews; critics were particularly savage about his starring role in "The Jazz Singer," a 1980 film. An album reviewer for the *Rolling Stone Record Guide* perhaps summarizes the disdain some rock critics have felt for Diamond. "Diamond was writing potboilers, and his thirst was for Pulitzer-level poesy," the critic contends. "Unfortunately, his imagination and the very blandness of his voice condemned him to setting a model for the radical-[middle-of-the-road] singer/songwriter style of the Seventies. . . . Like so many of his pop predecessors, his talent is greatest when he reaches for less, not more."

Diamond himself had admitted in *People* magazine that he used to struggle with doubts about his songs. "After years of working with a psychiatrist," he said, "I have finally forgiven myself for not being Beethoven." Diamond may not be Beethoven, but the emotions he stirs among his millions of fans cannot be discounted—he has endured too long. *People* quotes screenwriter Stephen Foreman on Diamond's talent: "When you see a crowd of paunchy, middle-aged auto executives in Detroit get up and start dancing in the aisles, you realize something pretty unusual is going on." That "something unusual" is a bond created between Diamond and his audience by his meaningful lyrics, his soulful performances, and his comfortable, catchy tunes. "My music says what I am," Diamond told the *New York Post*. "It speaks about what I feel as a person, what I dream about, what I hope to be."

Selected discography

The Feel of Neil Diamond, Bang, 1966.
Shilo, Bang, 1968.
Velvet Gloves & Spit, Uni, 1969.
Brother Love's Travelling Salvation Show, Uni, 1969.
Touching Me, Touching You, Uni, 1969.
Gold, Uni, 1970.
Tap Root Manuscript, Uni, 1970.
Stones, Uni, 1971.
Moods, Uni, 1972.
Hot August Night, MCA, 1972.
Rainbow, MCA, 1973.
Jonathan Livingston Seagull, Columbia, 1973.
Serenade, Columbia, 1974.
Beautiful Noise, Columbia, 1976.
Love at the Greek, Columbia, 1977.

I'm Glad You're Here with Me Tonight, Columbia, 1977.
You Don't Bring Me Flowers, Columbia, 1978.
September Morn, Columbia, 1980.
The Jazz Singer, Capitol, 1980.
Best of Neil Diamond, World, 1981.
On the Way to the Sky, Columbia, 1981.
Love Songs, MCA, 1981.
Song Sung Blue, Columbia, 1982.
Heart Light, Columbia, 1982.
Neil Diamond's Twelve Greatest Hits, Columbia, 1982.
Primitive, Columbia, 1984.
Classics of the Early Years, Columbia, 1984.
Headed for the Future, Columbia, 1986.
Neil Diamond, Columbia, 1986.

Sources

Books

The Rolling Stone Record Guide, Random House, 1979.
Simon, George T., *The Best of the Music Makers,* Doubleday, 1979.

Periodicals

Chicago Tribune, December 14, 1980.
Daily News (New York), October 6, 1972.
New York Post, October 30, 1972.
New York Times, October 1, 1972.
People, January 22, 1979; April 5, 1982.
Rolling Stone, September 23, 1976.
Time, January 26, 1981.

—Anne Janette Johnson

Placido Domingo

"**S**ingers who become successful conductors must be as rare as conductors who become successful singers. The two callings, while presupposing certain similarities in temperament, require such different levels of musical training that the appearence of a tenor in the pit conducting the New York City Opera's *La Traviata* on Sunday afternoon raised eyebrows to the scalp level." Donal Henahan opened his *New York Times* review of Placido Domingo's 1973 American conducting debut with these words. Henahan concluded that "he came through with considerable success." For Domingo, in the prime years of his career as a tenor, conducting was merely a new facet in his lifelong career of musicality.

Placido Domingo was born in Madrid on January 21, 1941, the son of Don Placido Domingo and Pepita Embil, internationally famous singers in the popular field of *zarzuela*. This comic opera genre was as popular in the Spanish-speaking countries of Latin America as it was in Madrid, and in the early 1950s, the Domingo-Embil troupe relocated in Mexico City. Young Domingo studied piano and voice at the National Conservatory of Music in Mexico City, where Carlo Morelli coached him upwards from the baritone to tenor range. He made his profesional debut as a tenor as "Alfredo," the hero of *La Traviata,* in Monterrey, Mexico, in 1961. Soon, he was appearing in Texas, where he had the opportunity to perform with two of the great divas of the opera world. In 1961, he sang "Arturo" with Joan Sutherland in *Lucia di Lammermoor* for the Dallas Civic Opera, and in 1962, he sang the larger role of "Edgardo" in *Lucia* for the farewell performance of Lily Pons in Fort Worth.

Domingo and his wife, soprano Marta Ornelas, joined the Israel National Opera where he learned to enlarge and project his voice by re-learning to breathe. In a process that he described to the *New York Times Magazine* in 1972 as "being reborn," he developed the muscular control necessary to thrust the diaphragm down and abdomen out to provide a pressurized column of air for the vocal chords.

He began a long association with the New York City Opera in 1965 and became prominent during the company's debut season at Lincoln Center in 1966. Among his most succesful roles with that company were as the hero of *Don Roderigo,* a 12-tone work by contemporary Argentine composer Alberto Ginastera, and as the Earl of Essex in Donizetti's *Roberto Devereux,* featuring Beverly Sills. William Bender described their performances as "a true meeting of romantic equals" and praised her "unsurpassed coloratura" and his "tender gestures that can thrill girls on both sides of the footlights" in *Time* in 1970. As "Alfredo," Domingo's stage presence and ability to add depth to his characteriza-

For the Record. . .

Born January 21, 1941, in Madrid, Spain; son of Placido and Pepita Embil Domingo (both *zarzuela* singers); married briefly as a young man; married Marta Ornelas (an opera singer), c. 1962; children: (first marriage) one son; (second marriage) two sons. *Education:* Studied piano and voice at National Conservatory of Music, Mexico City.

Made professional debut as a tenor in *La Traviata* in Monterrey, Mexico, 1961; has appeared in numerous operas throughout the world, including *Lucia di Lammermoor, La Traviata, Les Comtes d'Hoffmann, Carmen, Otello, Rigoletto, La Boheme, Don Carlo, Il Trovatore, Lohengrin,* and *I Pagliacci;* former member of Israel National Opera Company and New York City Opera. Has toured and recorded extensively, singing popular songs, operettas, and *zarzuela* music, as well as opera; has made many appearances on television programs, including "The Muppet Show," in addition to his own specials; has also appeared in a number of filmed operas; conductor.

Addresses: *Home*—Spain; Mexico City; and New Jersey. *Agent*—Eric Semon Associates, 111 West 57th St., New York, NY 10019.

tions was especially noted in the latter role in a performance in which, as Gerald Walker wrote in the *New York Times Magazine,* in 1972, "[opera director Frank] Corsaro had instructed Domingo to carry the dying 'Violetta' to the couch, where they were to begin singing. At one point, Domingo was late in picking up [Patricia] Brooks and starting for the couch, so he began singing while holding her in his arms. Most singers shrink from singing while lifting a weight or bending because it interferes with their breath control. Domingo finished the duet and said, 'It would be a wonderful idea to hold her during the performance and make it move like a lullaby.' They kept it in."

He performed extensively in Europe receiving praise for his "Rich vocal endowment" in Verona and his "effortless elan" in Hamburg. On October 2, 1968, he was scheduled to appear for the first time at the Metropolitan Opera in New York in *Adriana Lecouvreur,* but he made his actual debut in that opera four days earlier, replacing an ailing Franco Corelli. Both performance received high praise.

"God must have been in excellent spirits the day He created Placido," legendry soprano Birgit Nilsson was quoted as saying in a *New York Times Magazine* article in 1972. "He has everything needed for one of the

greatest careers ever seen; an incredibly beautiful voice, great intelligence, an unbelievable musicality and acting ability, wonderful looks, a great heart, and he's a dear, dear colleague. He is almost the perfect linguist—but, alas, he has not yet learned how to say no in any language." Domingo sings more operas than most tenors—over 80 roles in all genres. For much of his career, critics have written advisory articles warning him that the number of performances, variety of roles, and intensity of travel required for a twentieth century opera star could damage his voice. Domingo has stated, and has proven through the longetivity of his career, that he could protect his voice despite the strain of singing. He has passed many of the milestones of the repertory encompassing roles that, because of their range, intensity, or length, are considered threats to a continued career. His first "Otello," in the Verdi opera, was a triumph at the Hamburg State Opera in 1978 and was followed by appearances in that role around the world and on film. He told Peter G. Davis in *New York* in 1982 that singing "Otello" had actually improved his overall vocal quality: "The secret is to keep a smooth texture and retain flexibility while you develop the power. My voice has grown warmer since singing 'Otello,' but not darker, I feel that the role has helped solidify my sound—it has given me a foundation on which I can build and manipulate the tone more freely."

As early as 1979, when he opened the Metropolitan Opera with *Otello,* some critics began to list his awesome statistics. Hubert Saal, in *Newsweek,* estimated that he had sung 80 operas, had recorded 50, and had totaled up 1400 performances. But Saal praised that performance, which was telecast nationwide on PBS's "Live from the Met" as being "as electric as a third rail, a figure of quivering nerve ends, of emotions running into each other. He not only has the Devil on his back in 'Iago,' but has devils running amok within him. If anything distinguishes him onstage, it's his ferocious concentration and the intensity of a runaway train." Only once did Domingo himself have publicly stated doubts about accepting a role. He questioned his decision to accept the role of "Aeneas" in Berlioz's *Les Troyens* for the Metopolitan Opera in 1983 but did, in fact, do the performances.

Non-operatic music appeals to Domingo who has made recordings of Requiems by Verdi and Andrew Lloyd Webber, the latter a world-wide top seller. He has followed the tradition of tenors in the era of recorded sound begun by Enrico Caruso of recording traditional, folk, and popular songs. His album with John Denver, *Perhaps Love* (1981), sold millions of copies and introduced him to new listeners unfamiliar with opera. A 1983 *New York Times Magazine* article quoted a spokesman for CBS Masterworks, which released the album, as targeting "mainly people over 25 and mainly women. . . . Domingo is eating into this audience from his end of the spectrum just as Willie Nelson is from the other." Domingo defended his pop recordings to *New York* in 1982 as a trade-off for recording obscure works, such as Weber's *Oberon* and claimed that singing popular English language ballads helped him "to become even more conscious of words in an opera, to project character and verbal nuances more meaningfully." Among his many other pop recordings are collections of tangos, of songs from Viennese operettas, *Dein ist Mein Ganzes Herz* and *Vienna, City of My Dreams,* and of his family's native *zarauela, Zarzuela Arias* and *Zarzuela Arias and Duets.*

Non-operatic music has also been the focus of Domingo's television and live performances. He co-starred with Carol Burnett in a highly acclaimed variety special (CBS, January 27, 1984) on which he sang "Be a Clown" and "Vesti la giubba" (from *I Pagliacci)* and partnered Burnett in Cole Porter's "Night and Day." His own special, "Steppin' Out with the Ladies" (NBC, May 14, 1985), featured Domingo singing pop standards and duets from Broadway musicals with Maureen McGovern, Marilyn McCoo, Leslie Uggams, and Patti LaBelle, as well as "Tevye's" monologue, "If I Were a Rich Man" from "Fiddler on the Roof." He sang with Miss Piggy on "The Muppet Show" and revived their partnership at Radio City Music Hall in a benefit for the Actors' Fund of America in 1982. Domingo is also the focus of a European television special that has been aired on PBS and cable systems, "Placido: A Year in the Life of Placido Domingo."

Domingo has also starred in *zarzuela* performances all over the Spanish speaking world. He appeared in the newly composed *Il Poeta* by Federico Moreno Torroba in Madrid in 1980 and has sung recitals and concerts from the repertory, most notably on the successful tour "Antologia de la Zarzuela" in 1985. Robert C. Marsh, writing in the *Chicago Sun-Times,* described it as a triumph for Domingo: "He seemed to be having the greatest satisfaction singing this music, which, needless to say, he sings with complete authority and artistry, since it is more than a symbolic return to his musical roots. . . . The opera of Spain is *zarzuela* and seeing him and hearing him in this music reveals to us basic truths about him as a man and an artist that we are richer for knowing." Domingo had discussed the importance of presenting *zaruela* as early as 1981, when he told *Dial* of his preliminary plans to present the Spanish-language operas in American cities, because "these communities are too much deprived of their own cultural forms."

As televised and filmed opera became more popular in

the 1980s, Domingo's dignified presence and intense acting made him a natural star. His appearances in fully staged operas and recitals on the Public Broadcasting Service's "Live from Lincoln Center" and "Live from the Met" received high praise. In the PBS program guide, *Dial,* he talked to John Kobler about his television preparation. He reads avidly the source material for each opera, since most nineteenth century operas were based on popular novels or historical plays. He also studies the political and cultural climate surrounding the opera's creation and the events that the libretto portrays. Finally, he adapts his acting style to the camera, as in the party scene of the first act of *La Traviata:* "Normally, Alfredo would raise his glass high, but if he does this on television, the glass will go right off the screen. He must keep it at the level of the chest. Again, many singers close their eyes when they are singing an aria. On television, this looks foolish. You should keep them open." Domingo's opera films have also been tremendously popular in theaters and now on video. His intensely romantic *La Traviata,* directed by Franco Zefferelli with Theresa Stratas as "Violetta," and Zefferelli's *Otello, Cavalleria Rusticana,* and *I Pagliacci* were lush and theatrical. The controversial *Carmen,*

> "God must have been in excellent spirits the day he created Placido."
> —Soprano Brigit Nilsson

---

with Julia Migines-Johnson in the title role, was praised for its sensual realism.

Domingo's career continued at its rapid pace until September 1985 when Mexico City was devastated by earthquakes. He lost several members of his family and took time out from opera performances to sing benefits for the city. He lives in Spain but also maintains homes in Mexico City and the New York metropolitan area.

Conducting has become a major focus of Domingo's career, although he expects to sing until the mid-1990s. His ability to make that eyebrow-raising switch from singer to conductor is based, many colleagues believe, on his inate musicianship. Zubin Mehta told *Newsweek* in 1982 that "the signals that come out of a conductor are understood by all musicians but not always by all singers. Placido understands them." *Time* then quoted Domingo himself saying that "I have a tremendous advantage being a real musician because I never have to think about the music. It flows." It seems likely that Domingo will be providing music—as a singer and conductor—in live performances, television, and film for decades to come.

Selected discography

Carmen, London, 1975.
Carmen (soundtrack), RCA, 1984.
Otello, RCA, 1978.
Perhaps Love, CBS, 1981.
Tangos, Pansera/DG, 1981.
Andrew Lloyd Weber, *Requiem,* Angel, 1985.

Sources

Books

Domingo, Placido, *My First Forty Years,* Knopf, 1983.

Snowman, Daniel, *The World of Placido Domingo,* McGraw, 1985.

Periodicals

Chicago Sun-Times, August 19, 1985.
Dial, September, 1981.
New York, March 1, 1982.
New York Times, October 9, 1973; March 13, 1977; September 26, 1983.
New York Times Magazine, February 27, 1972; January 30, 1983.
Newsweek, October 8, 1979.
Opera News, January 19, 1963; April 16, 1966; September 20, 1969.
Time, October 26, 1970.

—*Barbara Stratyner*

Billy Eckstine

Singer, bandleader

Handsome and elegant, Billy Eckstine was one of the nation's most popular singers in the years between the end of World War II and the advent of rock and roll. Eckstine achieved renown primarily as a solo crooner whose "vocal lower register was often a sound of rare beauty," according to George T. Simon in *The Big Bands;* however, Eckstine's contribution to modern jazz as a band leader is also significant. In *The Pleasures of Jazz,* Leonard Feather writes that the Billy Eckstine Band, founded in 1944 and disbanded in 1946, was "the first big bebop band, musically apocalyptic but too far ahead of the public taste." Arnold Shaw also comments in *Black Popular Music in America* that Eckstine's orchestra—staffed by such giants as Charlie Parker, Miles Davis, Dizzy Gillespie and Sarah Vaughan—"left a permanent mark on Jazz history." Eckstine's own mark on music history rivals that of his contemporaries Frank Sinatra, Perry Como, and Nat "King" Cole. As Simon notes in *The Best of the Music Makers,* Eckstine's fame at its zenith in the early-to mid-1950s "equaled that of any popular singer of his time. First dubbed 'The Sepia Sinatra,' then 'The Great Mr. B.,' Billy Eckstine had a host of imitators, set trends in male fashions, and was pursued by bobby soxers. Responsible for a new and influential style of romantic singing, he was also the first black singer to become a national sex symbol and to make the front cover of *Life* magazine."

William Clarence Eckstine was born in Pittsburgh, Pennsylvania, on July 8, 1914. He grew up in Pittsburgh and in Washington, D.C., where he attended Armstrong High School. His parents emphasized education, so after high school he enrolled in college, first at St. Paul Normal and Industrial School in Lawrenceville, Virginia, then at Howard University in the nation's capitol. After only a year of college he won an amateur music contest at the Howard Theater and decided to sing full time. From 1934 until 1939, Eckstine—who changed the spelling of his name because a club owner thought it looked "too Jewish"—performed as a vocalist with small dance bands in the mid-Atlantic region. He joined the Earl Hines Orchestra as a soloist in 1939, learned to play the trumpet, and met many of the pioneers of modern jazz. Eckstine's first hit was "Jelly, Jelly," released in 1940. He followed that success with other blues tunes and romantic ballads such as "Somehow," "You Don't Know What Love Is," and "Skylark." In 1943 Eckstine left the Hines group to try to form his own band. The next year he assembled an impressive ensemble of talented musicians for the Billy Eckstine Band. In addition to Parker, Davis, Vaughan, and Gillespie, Eckstine hired Fats Navarro, Gene Ammons, Dexter Gordon, and drummer Art Blakey. Touring the South in 1944, the band grossed $100,000 in its first ten weeks.

For the Record. . .

Full name, William Clarence Eckstine; surname originally Eckstein; born July 8, 1914, in Pittsburgh, Pa.; son of William and Charlotte Eckstein; married a singer, 1942; children: five sons; two daughters. *Education:* Attended St. Paul Normal and Industrial School and Howard University.

Began working as a singer, 1934; soloist with Earl Hines Orchestra, 1939-43; solo performer, 1943-44; founder and leader of Billy Eckstine Band, 1944-46; solo performer, 1946—; has toured and recorded as a vocalist, trumpeter, and trombonist.

Awards: Named top male vocalist by *Metronome* magazine, 1949 and 1950; voted most popular singer in *down beat* readers poll, 1949 and 1950; winner of *Billboard* college poll, 1951.

Addresses: *Home*—Encino, CA. *Office*—c/o Polygram Records, 810 Seventh Ave., New York, NY 10019.

Eckstine's band was full of artists who were seeking new forms of musical expression. They introduced rhythmic and melodic innovations that transformed the standard jazz of the 1920s—primarily dancing music with a steady beat—to bebop, a music of offbeat accents and orchestral improvisations. Although Hines's and other big bands had experimented with the new sounds, Eckstine's was the first group to highlight them; hence, he is credited with forming the first big bop band. Unfortunately, bebop did not provide the best formula to set off a singer, and according to Simon in *The Big Bands,* Eckstine's recordings "sounded so bad that they made few . . . converts." Nor was it easy to meet the large payroll and unify so many unconventional temperaments.

After only two years Eckstine disbanded his orchestra and returned to solo performing. Simon notes in *The Best of the Music Makers* that bebop's loss "was Eckstine's gain. Unfettered by the band, he soon produced a string of hits, mostly stylized, smooth romantic ballads." The sensuous music found a mainstream audience, and the stylish Eckstine, who headlined with the George Shearing Quintet and the Count Basie orchestra, became a fashion trend-setter. By 1950 he was MGM's top-selling popular singer and was drawing record-breaking crowds at the Oasis Club in Los Angeles and New York's Paramount Theater. On November 11, 1950, he gave a solo concert at Carnegie Hall, leading a *New York Herald Tribune* critic to write: "Mr. Eckstine begins with considerably more voice

than the average crooner, and therefore he is not driven to the usual faking procedures popularized by others. He sings, for the most part, on pitch, cleanly, clearly, and with the standard breast-beating and catch-in-the-voice technique that seem the stock-in-trade of novelty crooners. But there is real vocal color to his work, and it is a color which he varies according to the expressive dictates of the song."

As a black man, Eckstine was not immune to the prejudice that characterized the 1950s. Quincy Jones is quoted in *The Pleasures of Jazz* as saying of Eckstine: "They never let him become the sex symbol he might have become. If he'd been white, the sky would have

> *"He was the first black singer to become a national sex symbol and to make the front cover of* Life *magazine."*

been the limit. As it was, he didn't have his own radio or TV show, much less a movie career. He had to fight the system, so things never quite fell into place." Jones's assessment is accurate; denied the television and movie exposure his fame seemed to warrant, Eckstine gradually returned to semi-obscurity. He has never lacked for work in Las Vegas, Miami, and California—he still performs regularly—but the international acclaim that still greets his contemporaries has passed him by. Eckstine still finds an audience, though, and he also has time to indulge his passions for golf and classical music. In *The Best of the Music Makers,* Simon concludes that the years have been kind to Eckstine, keeping his voice clear and his looks youthful. "Fads don't last," writes Simon, "but talent does."

Selected discography

I Stay in the Mood for You, Deluxe.
I'll Wait and Pray, Deluxe.
She's Got the Blues for Sale, National.
In the Still of the Night, National.
Cool Breeze, National.
Prisoner of Love, National.
Fools Rush In, MGM.
Everything I Have Is Yours, MGM, 1947.
You Go to My Head, MGM.

Caravan, MGM, 1949.
My Foolish Heart, MGM, 1950.
I Apologise, MGM, 1951.
Gentle on My Mind, Motown.
Stormy, Enterprise.
Senior Soul, Enterprise.
Billy Eckstine's Greatest Hits, Polydor.

Also recorded *Feel the Warm, If She Walked into My Life, The Legendary Big Band of Billy Eckstine, The Soul Sessions, Prime of My Life,* 1963, *For the Love of Ivy,* 1967, and *My Way,* 1967.

Sources

Books

Feather, Leonard, *The Pleasures of Jazz,* Horizon, 1976.

Shaw, Arnold, *Black Popular Music in America,* Schirmer Books, 1986.
Simon, George T., *The Best of the Music Makers,* Doubleday, 1979.
Simon, *The Big Bands,* 4th edition, Schirmer Books, 1981.

Periodicals

Life, April 24, 1950.
Negro Digest, November, 1950.
Newsweek, May 16, 1949.
New York Herald Tribune, November 12, 1950.
Time, June 20, 1949.

—*Anne Janette Johnson*

The Fabulous Thunderbirds

Blues band

"If you searched all the roadhouses and border juke joint dives in Texas, chances are you couldn't find a tighter goodtime band. Anyone who argues that good white blues and r & b are getting hard to find has never dipped a needle into the grooves of a Fabulous T-Bird LP." Since that record review (of *What's the Word*) appeared in *Guitar Player* in 1980, the Fabulous Thunderbirds have released five more albums, each one proving the above statement to be indisputable. Their fifth effort, 1986's *Tuff Enuff,* stayed on the *Billboard* charts for 25 weeks, topping off at No. 13, while the title track reached No. 10. After nearly twelve years of playing 250 to 300 dates annually and receiving little, if any, radio air play, the band finally was given the national exposure and success that was long overdue.

The T-Birds were formed in 1974 by guitarist Jimmie Vaughan, the only original member remaining in the group. Vaughan played in various bands around the Dallas area, beginning in 1963 with the Swinging Pendulums. Covering tunes by Hendrix and Clapton in bands like Sammy Loria and the Penetrations, the

Chessmen, Texas, and Texas Storm, Vaughan was gradually paring his style down from the flash of rock to the rawness of blues. Having already built up an impressive reputation, he left for Austin in 1970 to form Storm along with guitarist Denny Freeman. "I think Jimmie Vaughan influenced more bass players, drummers, guitarists, and just the public in general, and had more influence in the whole state of Texas than probably any other unsigned musician," said Freeman in *Guitar Player*'s July 1986 cover story on Vaughan.

After a brief period in California he moved back to Austin and started Jimmie Vaughan and the Fabulous Thunderbirds (after the Nightcaps' song "Thunderbird") with singer Lou Ann Barton and drummer Otis Lewis. Bassist Keith Ferguson, who played with Vaughan in Storm and with brother Stevie Ray Vaughan in the Nightcrawlers, joined shortly after Barton and Lewis quit in 1974. Ferguson had played up and down the West Coast in the late 1960's with Sunnyland Special and was even offered a spot with ZZ Top by guitarist Billy Gibbons.

The T-Birds hooked up with vocalist-harmonica player Kim Wilson while jamming at Alexander's, an Austin rib-joint. Wilson was visiting from Minnesota when he blew the T-Birds' harp player off the stage, impressing Vaughan enough to ask him to join the band. With influences like Big Walter Horton, James Cotton, and Lazy Lester, Wilson became the group's chief songwriter and musical director. Dan Forte wrote, "If Jimmie Vaughan has few peers among blues guitarists, Kim Wilson has fewer among harmonica players—among singer/songwriters of his genre and generation, he has next to none."

With the addition of Mike Buck on drums, the T-Birds became one of the most solid and authentic blues bands in the state, if not the entire country. The group was fortunate enough in 1975 to hook up with Clifford Antone who had just opened up a club dedicated strictly to blues music, Antone's. The T-Birds became the house band, headlining their own shows and gaining invaluable experience by backing up nearly every major blues act that played there. "About the first year or two we stayed in Austin," Wilson told *down beat,* "and then Muddy Waters got us on the road—it was his suggestion. And he spread our name around all over the place."

By then the band had become nearly legendary in Texas, and it was time to branch out. Their music was lowdown blues mixed with a bit of Cajun and Tex-Mex, played with a style that stopped other bands in their tracks. After the T-Birds played the San Francisco Blues Festival in 1978, festival promoter Tom Mazzolini told *Guitar Player* that "The Thunderbirds were very self-assured, and the effect was awesome—almost overnight. The local bands had to clean up their act. Before, they were all sort of drifting, but the T-Birds gave them a focus."

A year later they signed with Takoma records and released their self-titled first LP. The corny 1950's-style cover did little to prepare listeners for what was inside. Vaughan's tremolo-laden rhythms and clean economical solos lived up to his original idea for the band: "Bo Diddley on acid." An impressive debut, with six originals and five cover tunes, it received minimal promotion, as did their follow up a year later, *What's the Word.*

With nine more originals and songs like "The Crawl" and "Sugar-Coated Love," this was no-frills party music. "We just set up in a big circle with boom mikes and go," Vaughan said in *Guitar Player.* "That's why it's kind of caveman sounding—ancient." Drummer Fran Christina replaced Buck (who went on to form the Le Roi Brothers) midway through the recording. The original drummer for Roomful of Blues, Christina left them in 1972, played a few gigs with the T-Birds years later on the East Coast, and then joined Texas's Asleep At The Wheel for eighteen months. The T-Birds called him in to finish the record and kept him afterwards.

As raunchy as they were on record, live remained the best way to fully appreciate their sound. European audiences got a taste in 1980 as the T-Birds played their first tour overseas by opening for Dave Edmunds and Nick Lowe's Rockpile. They came back to the States to record their third album, *Butt Rockin',* bringing along members of Roomful's horn section and Anson Funderburgh on second guitar. Wilson collaborated with Lowe on "One's Too Many," and the group once again dug up obscure gems from the past like "Mathilda" and "Cherry Pink and Apple Blossom White."

Their first three albums were produced by their manager, Denny Bruce, and seemed to authentically reproduce the sound of old blues recordings. In 1982, the T-Birds switched producers. With Nick Lowe at the controls, their fourth LP, *T-Bird Rhythm,* sounded more modern and contained only a few up-tempo numbers. Although a fine album, Chrysalis nevertheless dropped the band after its release.

The next four years saw the band struggling for a record contract, playing endlessly on the road and going through more changes. Bassist Ferguson ended his nine years with the group over internal conflicts. "On the one hand we had people saying we weren't commercial and never would be; at the same time, they were saying, 'If you don't change, you'll never sell any records.' Pretty soon, you start letting people tell you how to play," he told *Guitar Player.* "To me, I was perfectly content to play better blues and rhythm and blues than anyone in the world." Ferguson's replacement was also a former member of Roomful of Blues, Preston "Pinky" Hubbard. After four years with Roomful, he left in 1976 to play with Atlanta's Alley Cats and then with the Memphis Rockabilly Band. He rejoined Roomful briefly before coming to the T-Birds.

The Fabulous Thunderbirds have come a long way since Alexander's rib-joint.

The group went to London where Dave Edmunds produced ten of their songs. They then had to shop around for a contract. Finally, in 1986, CBS signed them, and their careers took a sharp upward turn. They released their fifth LP, *Tuff Enuff,* recorded two videos, hired a new manager, and started opening for bands like the Rolling Stones, Santana, ZZ Top, and Tom Petty. With the record's pop production, die-hard fans were crying "sell-out," but as Vaughan told Dan Forte: "You change with each record. Each one of our records sounds different, even though it still sounds like us. I figured if we're going to make records, we might as well sell records." While scoring the movie "Gung Ho," Stevie Ray played the title cut for director Ron Howard, who liked it enough to put it in the film.

With their newfound success, the T-Birds wasted little time by following up a year later with the LP *Hot Number.* Again, Edmunds produced, but the emphasis was on soul music this time around. With the Memphis Horns backing them up, the T-Birds faithfully reproduced the feel of early Stax recordings. With an appearance in Paul Schrader's film "Light Of Day" and various soundtrack performances, the Fabulous Thunderbirds have come a long way since Alexander's rib-joint.

Selected discography

The Fabulous Thunderbirds (includes "Wait On Time," "Scratch My Back," "Rich Woman," "Full-Time Lover," "Pocket Rocket," "She's Tuff," "Marked Deck," "Walkin' to My Baby," "Rock With Me," "C-Boy's Blues," "Let Me In"), Takoma, 1979.

What's the Word (includes "Runnin' Shoes," "You Ain't Nothin' But Fine," "Low-Down Woman," "Extra Jimmies," "Sugar-Coated Love," "Last Call for Alcohol," "The Crawl," "Jumpin' Bad," "Learn to Treat Me Right," "I'm a Good Man [if You Give Me a Chance]," "Dirty Work," "That's Enough of That Stuff," "Los Fabulosos Thunderbirds"), Takoma, 1980.

Butt Rockin' (includes "I Believe I'm in Love," "One's Too Many," "Give Me All Your Lovin'," "Roll, Roll, Roll," "Cherry Pink and Apple Blossom White," "I Hear You I Knockin'," "Tip On In," "I'm Sorry," "Mathilda," "Tell Me Why," "In Orbit,"), Chrysalis, 1981.

T-Bird Rhythm (includes "Can't Tear It Up Enuff," "How Do You Spell Love," "You're Humbuggin' Me," "My Babe," "'Neighbor' Tend to Your Business," "The Monkey," "Diddy Wah Diddy," "Lover's Crime," "Poor Boy," "Tell Me," "Gotta Have Some/Just Got Some"), Chrysalis, 1982.

Tuff Enuff (includes "Tuff Enuff," "Tell Me," "Look at That, Look at That," "Two Time My Lovin'," "Amnesia," "Wrap It Up," "True Love," "Why Get Up," "I Don't Care," "Down At Antones"), CBS, 1986.

Hot Number (includes "Stand Back," "Hot Number," "Wasted Tears," "It Comes to Me Naturally," "Love in Common," "How Do You Spell Love," "Streets of Gold," "Sofa Circuit," "Don't Bother Tryin' to Steal Her Love," "It Takes a Big Man to Cry"), CBS, 1987.

Sources

down beat, February, 1986.

Guitar Player, June, 1980; July, 1980; July, 1986; August, 1986; September, 1986; December, 1986.

Guitar World, September, 1986; October, 1988.

Los Angeles Times, May 25, 1986.

Oakland Press, August 26, 1988.

USA Today, May 6, 1986.

—Calen D. Stone

Bryan Ferry

Singer, songwriter

"Ferry's artsiness expressed itself so much as style over substance that style itself became substantive," wrote John Rockwell. "As the ultimate self professed lounge lizard, he managed to take pop-rock's hoariest conventions (the love song, even actual oldies on his solo albums) and coat them with witty intimations of unspeakable decadence."

Bryan Ferry was born the son of a miner on September 26, 1945, in County Durham, England. He worked as a teacher and sang in various bands (the Banshees and Gas Board) before forming Roxy Music in 1970. The group was described as "a driving rock band as well as an aesthetically pleasing manifestation of one man's neuroses," by Paul Gambaccini. During their first year, members included Graham Simpson—bass, Dexter Lloyd—drums, Andy MacKay—sax, Brian Eno—keyboards, and David O'List—guitar. By 1971 Paul Thompson and Phil Manzanera had taken over on drums and guitar, respectively. Their first album, entitled *Roxy Music,* was produced by King Crimson lyricist Peter Sinfield and was released in 1972. The LP was a major success in the United Kingdom, yielding a fairly big hit, "Virginia Plain". The album, wrote Robert Christgau, "celebrates the kind of artifice that could come to seem as unhealthy as the sheen on a piece of rotten meat."

With the assistance of Eno on synthesizer, Ferry's vocals and lyrics laid the foundation for a whole school of music known as art-rock (or, as Robert Duncan calls it, chromium-romanticism). This trend towards slick sophistication, as opposed to the traditional raw rebelliousness of rock up to that point, would produce groups as talented as King Crimson and Flock of Seagulls.

Roxy's second album, *For Your Pleasure,* was the only other on which Eno played. The personalities of Ferry and Eno clashed, unfortunately, but on songs like "In Every Dream Home a Heartache" their association is downright eerie. Nevertheless, Eno would move on to carve out his own unique slot in the techno end of pop music. As his replacement, Ferry brought in multi-instrumentalist Eddie Jobson, an addition that would add more of a rock edge to their next two LPs, *Stranded* and *Country Life* (which did manage to crack the American Top 40).

"My musical image in America has been confused, whereas the visual aspect of my work has been quickly defined," Ferry told *Rolling Stone,* "and I think this lack of one total image hurt Roxy." Disappointment from the band's lack of success in the States led Ferry (Manzanera and MacKay, also) to pursue a solo career in 1974. "I think Roxy was too European to go over big in America," said Phil Manzanera. "We weren't raunchy enough."

For the Record. . .

Born September 26, 1945, in Durham, England; son of a miner.

Began singing in various bands, including the Banshees and Gas Board, while working as a teacher; founder and lead singer with rock band Roxy Music, beginning 1970; also solo performer, beginning 1974.

Addresses: *Agent*—E.G. Management Co. Ltd., 63-A Kings Rd. London SW3 4NT, England.

On Ferry's first solo effort, *These Foolish Things,* his interpretation of classics from "It's My Party" to "Sympathy For The Devil" was quite similar in style to David Bowie's *Pinups* LP a year earlier. Especially noteworthy is the reworking of Dylan's "Hard Rain." Robert Christgau wrote, "By transforming Dylan at his most messianic into gripping high camp complete with sound effects, Ferry both undercuts the inflated idealism of the original and reaffirms its essential power." The same year, Ferry would also record *Another Time, Another Place.* While it contains some originals, it too was based on covers with only one real gem in the lot. "The In Crowd."

In 1975 Ferry reassembled Roxy Music for the LP *Siren* and another shot at the American market. "I think of it in terms of pride in my work," Ferry told *Rolling Stone.* "I want to make it here because, after all, rock & roll started here." Ironically, his breakthrough came with a disco song, "Love Is the Drug." Ferry apparently ignored, or was ignorant of, the hatred between followers of rock and those of disco, stating only that "big disco records have better chances to spread."

At the time he was right, but his 1977 solo album, *In Your Mind,* failed in its aim to cash in once again on a disco audience that soon vanished. "What Bryan Ferry sees is a more commercial way to bring a most unconventional pop perspective to a wider audience," wrote John Milward. "If *In Your Mind* doesn't sport the twin-edged blade of prime Roxy Music, that doesn't mean it doesn't bleed." After a while the label rock or disco didn't matter anyway. The key elements of each were borrowed by the other, and eventually drum machines were as prevalent in rock as distorted guitars were in disco. In the previous year, Ferry recorded *Let's Stick Together,* which consisted of flip sides to his singles and reworks of Roxy tunes. Slick L.A. session musicians provided a natural background for Ferry's smoky vocals on his fifth solo album, *The Bride Stripped Bare.*

Ferry had put Roxy on hold after their live 1976 LP, *Viva!*

(a showcase for Paul Thompson's drumming). He has continued alternating between solo albums after regrouping the band in 1979. Probably the finest example of a Ferry/Roxy collaboration yet is the LP *Flesh and Blood.* But, with many of the same musicians appearing on both solo and group albums, it's hard to separate the two. "Ferry, both in and out of Roxy Music, is one of the rank weirdos of rock & roll," wrote Robert Duncan. "In other words, a prize. And, though some choose not to notice, the man's accomplishments are enduring."

Selected discography

Solo Albums

These Foolish Things, Atlantic, 1974.
Another Time, Another Place, Atlantic, 1974.
Let's Stick Together, Atlantic, 1976.
In Your Mind, Atlantic, 1977.
The Bride Stripped Bare, Atlantic, 1978.
Boys And Girls, Warner Bros., 1985.
Bete Noire, Reprise, 1987.

With Roxy Music

Roxy Music, Atco, 1972.
For Your Pleasure, Atco, 1973.
Stranded, Atco, 1974.
Country Life, Atco, 1974.
Siren, Atco, 1975.
Viva! Roxy Music, Atco, 1976.
Manifesto, Atco, 1979.
Flesh and Blood.
Avalon, Warner Bros. 1982.

Sources

Books

Christgau, Robert, *Christgau's Record Guide,* Ticknor & Fields, 1981.
Logan, Nick, and Bob Woffinden, compilers, *The Illustrated Encyclopedia of Rock,* Harmony, 1977.
Miller, Jim, editor, *The Rolling Stone Illustrated History of Rock & Roll,* Random House, 1976.
Rock Revolution, Popular Library, 1976.

Periodicals

Rolling Stone, Decmeber 18, 1975; January 1, 1976; March 11, 1976; September 9, 1976; November 18, 1976; June 2, 1977; August 11, 1977; January 11, 1979; April 5, 1979; May 31, 1979.

Ella Fitzgerald

Singer

"All night long, Ella was taking risks right and left with her scats. In 'God Bless the Child,' she pulled out high operatic hoots, angry belts, even trumpet-like whines woo-wooed with a wa-wa mute. In 'Honeysuckle Rose,' she segued from high little yelps to crazy syllables that tumbled over each other like kids just released from detention." That review by Pamela Bloom might have been written at any time during the 55 years in which Ella Fitzgerald has been delighting critics and audiences. But it was written about her February 11, 1989, sold-out concert at Radio City Music Hall. Ella Fitzgerald, "the first lady of song," is still performing and still taking risks.

Born in Newport News, Virginia, Fitzgerald was raised in Yonkers, New York. Although early publicity biographies refered to her as living and being educated in an orphanage, she has credited an aunt, Virginia Williams, with her upbringing. Fitzgerald's entry into show business came in 1934 when she was discovered in an amateur contest at Harlem's famed Apollo Theater singing "Judy, Object of My Affection." Her voice, which she modelled after Connee Boswell records, caught the attention of conductor Chick Webb who trained it slowly before engaging her to sing with his band. From 1935 until Webb's death in 1939, she performed with him at Levaggi's, the Cotton Club, and other famous night clubs and cabarets. Decca's recording of Webb's band with Fitzgerald singing "Love and Kisses" in 1935 is considered her first single. She did over 230 recordings for Decca in those early years, some of which have been re-issued in an anthology format by MCA as *The Best of Ella Fitzgerald, Ella Swings the Band,* and *Princess of the Savoy.* Their recording of "A-tisket, A-tasket," (1938) became her first of many hit singles. That song also brought Fitzgerald membership into ASCAP in 1940. Fitzgerald led Webb's band until World War II decimated its ranks.

After the War ended, she began a long association with promoter/manager Norman Granz, with whose Jazz at the Philhamonic concerts she performed from 1946 to 1954. Her scatted performances of the pop standards "How High the Moon" and "Oh, Lady Be Good" in 1947 brought her to a wider audience that recognized her as a unique artist, not simply a band singer. She recorded almost exclusively for Granz's label, Verve, after 1955. Her most famous albums for Verve have been the continuing series of "Songbooks" dedicated to the works of America's great composers and lyricists, among them, Cole Porter (1956), Rodgers and Hart (1956), Duke Ellington (1956), George and Ira Gershwin (1958-1959), Irving Berlin (1958), and Harold Arlen (1960). Each contains a mix of well-known and obscure songs. Ira Gershwin is often quoted as saying "I never knew how good our songs were until I heard Ella Fitzgerald sing them." The "Songbooks" are also noted for their superb arrangements by Paul Weston and Nelson Riddle. All of them are being re-issued on CD.

Fitzgerald has recorded almost 150 albums in total. Some were recorded live at jazz festivals in the United States or Europe, among them, the popular *Montreux '77* (on Pablo) with the Tommy Flanagan Trio. Recordings were built around styles like Verve's *Songs in a Mellow Mood* or *Sweet and Hot*. Other albums feature her with specific jazz artists or ensembles, such as Verve's *Ella and Louis* and *Ella and Basie*. Fitzgerald recordings seem to have life spans unlike any other artist's—a re-issue of her 1958 *Live in Rome* was the top-selling jazz album of 1988. Estimates of her total sales range upwards from 25,000,000.

Fitzgerald's career progressed steadily with frequent tours of Europe and the Orient, where she is revered, annual concerts in New York, appearances at the Newport (now Kool and JVC in New York) Jazz Festivals and a constant schedule of recordings. Although almost universally considered the finest solo song stylist in jazz, she has been able to adapt her performances to a surprising variety of bands and combos with different instrumentations and approaches to music. Among the many greats of jazz with whose ensembles she has played are Louis Armstrong, Count Basie,

Duke Ellington, Errol Garner, Earl Hines, and Oscar Peterson. She seldom plays club dates, although in the 1950s, she was often booked into large hotel lounges with the Count Basie Orchestra. A contemporary review described that atmosphere in the usually classy Starlight Roof of the Waldorf-Astoria Hotel during one of their engagements: "The joint was jumpin' last night. Pardon me, I meant to write the performers were received graciously last evening and with considerable enthusiams. . . . But when Ella Fitzgerald sings and Count Basie plays his hot piano, the joint jumps. 'Cause when Ella throbs those blues and the Count picks his way among those 88 keys, something's gotta give. . . . Jazz is jazz and the beat is the beat. Ella Fitzgerald and Count Basie have got both."

Fitzgerald appeared in the 1958 film "Pete Kelly's Blues" and sang "Hard Hearted Hannah" and its title song. She was one of the first black jazz performers to be engaged for a television appearance in the 1950s and has since appeared over 200 times on American and European television.

Difficulties with a detached retina slowed her down briefly in the 1970s, and she now performs with thick glasses that allow her to make contact with the audience. Fitzgerald had open-heart surgery in 1986 but returned to concertizing soon after with a combo that generally includes Paul Smith on piano, Keter Betts on bass, and drummer Jeff Hamilton.

Her approach to the vocal repertory is simple—she maintains classics and continually adds the best songs of each new style of pop. Fitzgerald has always been celebrated for her willingness to experiment with new genres and frequently introduces them to her jazz audiences. Her "Stone Cold Dead in the Market," (with bandleader Louis Jourdan) was mainstream jazz's first Calypso hit. She was among the first to integrate both Bossa Nova and the Beatles into her repertory in the early 1960s. A review of a 1966 engagement with Earl (Fatha) Hines described her performances of jazz standards "Sweet Georgia Brown," "Lover Man," and "Don't Be That Way" and stated that she "changes pace again with the all-out swinging 'Boots are Made for Walking,' a soup-up hit that calls for an encore." As in her "Songbook" recordings, she presents the standards of American love songs, from Arlen to Rodgers but now also adds the music of Kurt Weill and Stevie Wonder, whose "Sunshine of My Life" has become almost her new signature tune. She also celebrates the greats of jazz in her concerts by re-interpreting their signature tunes—in her February 1989 concert, as Bloom wrote, she presented the Billie Holliday classic "God Bless the Child" and Fats Waller/Andy Razaf's "Honeysuckle Rose."

Fitzgerald has won nearly every award imaginable for her live and recorded performances, from 12 Grammys to the Kennedy Center Award to an honorary doctorate in music from Yale University. Her status as a jazz artist and as a singer led to some convoluted Grammy catagorizations. During a four-year stretch from 1958 to 1962, she won Best Vocal Performance (female) for *Ella Fitzgerald Sings the Irving Berlin Songbook* (1958), *But Not For Me* (1959), "Mack the Knife" (1960), *Mack the Knife—Ella in Berlin* (1960), and *Ella Swings Brightly with Nelson Riddle* (1962); and she won Best Jazz Performance awards for *Ella Sings the Duke Ellington Song Book* (1958) and *Ella Sings Lightly* (1959). Fitzgerald was also given the NARAS Trustees Award (The

---

"She's the best singer I ever heard. Absolutely"
—Tony Bennett

Bing Crosby Award) for lifetime achievement in all possible categories in 1967. She holds many records that may never be bested, among them, her 18 consecutive years as best female jazz singer in the *down beat* magazine poll.

Duke Ellington once described Ella Fitzgerald's voice in *Life* magazine: "She captures you somewhere through the facets of your intangibles." Other jazz and pop greats have tried to explain its qualities and her appeal on stage as well. In a February 1989 article in the *New York Post*, Lee Jeske interviewed Tonny Bennett, Mel Torme, and Pegy Lee about Fitzgerald. "She's the best singer I ever heard," said Bennett. "Absolutely." Torme agreed: "When I was looking for somebody to hang my vocal hat on, she was my number one influence. . . . Ella was the absolute epitome of everything that I've

ever believed in or loved as far as popular singing was concerned." And Lee said, "She has a magnificent instrument and she uses it to the best advantage." Jeske concluded that three reactions are most often cited by Fitzgerald's colleagues—"Their awe of her talent, their awe of her as a person (the words 'genuine lady' come up again and again), and their respect for her unabashed love of singing."

Selected discography

Songs in a Mellow Mood, Verve.
Sweet and Hot, Verve.
Ella and Louis, Verve.
Ella and Basie, Verve.
Live in Rome, 1958.
Ella Sings the Duke Ellington Songbook, Verve, 1958.
Ella Fitzgerald Sings the Irving Berlin Songbook, Verve, 1958.
Ella Sings Lightly, 1959.
But Not for Me, 1959.
Mack the Knife—Ella in Berlin, Verve, 1960.
Ella Swings Brightly With Nelson Riddle, 1962.
Montreaux '77, Pablo, 1978.
Princess of the Savoy (1934-39 Decca recordings), MCA, 1988.
Ella Swings the Band (1936-39 Decca recordings), MCA, 1988.
The Best of Ella Fitzgerald (1938-54 Decca recordings), MCA, 1988.

Sources

Life, December 22, 1958.
New York Post, February 9, 1989; February 13, 1989.
New York Times, June 15, 1986; September 5, 1986; June 26, 1987.
New York World, June 5, 1956.
New York World-Journal-Tribune, November 10, 1966.

—Barbara Stratyner

Crystal Gayle

Singer

The svelte and raven-tressed Crystal Gayle is "a country music queen who has captured the pop audience with breakneck speed," to quote *Country Music* contributor Laura Eipper. Having long ago outgrown the image of "Loretta Lynn's younger sister," Gayle today enjoys enormous popularity with country and mainstream audiences alike, in venues as varied as Nashville's Grand Ole Opry and Atlantic City's Trump Plaza. Her repertoire spans an unusually wide range, from straight country tunes to seductive blues ballads to soft pop-rock aimed at Top 40 audiences. Unifying all these elements, however, is Gayle's natural vocal ability, honed over the years without formal training. In *High Fidelity,* Sam Graham praises Gayle's voice: "An often surprisingly big sound for a woman of such diminutive proportions, her instrument is both sultry and ingenuous-sounding, warm and playful. This voice could charm the truth out of Richard Nixon or seduce a eunuch. It could sing the *Congressional Record* in Pig Latin and melt your heart."

Gayle's career includes several notable achievements that even eclipse those of her elder sister. She has been the first female artist to see an album, *We Must Believe in Magic,* go platinum, and she was the first woman entertainer to visit the People's Republic of China after the re-establishment of cordial diplomatic relations. These "firsts" illustrate an essential element of Gayle's success: she has experimented constantly, never contenting herself with a single recognizable sound or image. As Craig Waters notes in the *Saturday Evening Post,* Gayle "has grown from girl to woman, from honky-tonk singer to international star, without sacrificing what she is."

Crystal Gayle was born Brenda Gail Webb in Paintsville, Kentucky, on January 9, 1951. She is the youngest daughter of Melvin Ted and Clara Marie Webb, who raised eight children on a meager coal miner's salary. By the time Gayle was born, her sister Loretta, sixteen years older, had married and moved away. Gayle grew up in Wabash, Indiana, in a community of retired coal miners. The Webb family was somewhat more comfortable during Gayle's childhood than it had been during Loretta Lynn's. Crystal owned a guitar and listened to an eclectic variety of vocal music, including country stars such as Patsy Cline, folk artists Peter, Paul, and Mary, blues singer Billie Holiday, and Broadway show tunes of the period.

Like many other people, Gayle became a fan of her sister's when Lynn began to build her country music career in the 1960s. As early as 1967, while she was still in high school, Gayle began to tour part time with Lynn. Her stage name derives from a "Krystal" chain of hamburger stands in the Nashville area; Lynn coined

you keep the performance as simple as possible, I think it will last longer."

For the Record. . .

Full name, Crystal Gayle Gatzimos; name originally Brenda Gail Webb; born January 9, 1951, in Paintsville, Ky.; daughter of Melvin Ted (a coal miner) and Clara Marie (Ramey) Webb; married Vassilios Gatzimos (an attorney and entertainment manager), June 3, 1971; children: Catherine Claire, Christos James. *Education:* Graduated from high school in Wabash, Ind. *Politics:* Republican.

Toured with her sister Loretta Lynn in the late 1960s; began recording 1970; has toured as a headliner throughout the United States; television appearances include "The Grand Ole Opry," "Country Place," and "Hee Haw," as well as "The Crystal Gayle Special," 1979, "Crystal," 1980, and "Crystal Gayle in Concert," 1982. Spokesperson for American Lung Association, 1982, and Tennessee Department of Health and Environment, 1983-84.

Awards: Named most promising female vocalist by Academy of Country Music, 1975; named outstanding female vocalist by Academy of Country Music, 1977, 1978, and 1980; named best female singer by Country Music Association, 1977 and 1978; Grammy Award for outstanding country female vocalist, 1978; AMOA Jukebox Award, 1978; AMOA Awards, 1979, 1980, and 1986; award for most played country female artist, 1979; named one of America's ten most beautiful women by *Harper's Bazaar,* 1983.

Addresses: *Home*—Nashville, TN. *Agent*—Shefrin Co., 800 South Robertson Blvd., Los Angeles, CA 90035.

With Reynolds's assistance, Gayle became recognized in 1975 as a promising country vocalist, based on the strength of her first two albums, *Crystal Gayle* and *Somebody Loves You.* Then she and Reynolds began to experiment with music outside the realm of pure country, using instrumentation from mainstream and pop sources. The resulting sound caused a surge in Gayle's popularity; in 1978 she recorded her first platinum album, *We Must Believe in Magic,* with its crossover Grammy Award-winning single "Don't It Make My Brown Eyes Blue." Thereafter, Gayle's albums often contained a blend of country, blues, and pop music, sung in a "rich, soothing voice" that seemed "like a cold milkshake made with lots of ice cream," according to Blanche McCrary Boyd in the *Village Voice.*

Throughout the 1980s Gayle has remained in demand for appearances on television and in person. Her singles and albums continue to be well-represented on the country charts, and she is admired for her exceptionally long hair and tastefully-presented beauty. Gayle is unusual in her devotion to home and family—she

> *"This voice could charm the truth out of Richard Nixon or seduce a eunuch."*

gives only 80 to 100 performances per year—and in her outspoken espousal of good health, especially for expectant mothers. A mother of two young children herself, she served as spokesperson for Tennessee's "Healthy Children Initiative" and is credited with expanding prenatal care in that state tenfold. In 1988, Gayle took an active role in politics, stumping on the campaign trail for George Bush throughout the South. Ordinarily, however, she is a quiet and unassuming performer who lives with her family in a modest home near Nashville. Graham writes of her: "One finds no sensationalistic copy in Crystal Gayle, to be sure—none of Patti Smith's pseudo-politic ramblings, Linda Ronstadt's Cub Scout coyness, or Bette Midler's outrageous brazenness. No *National Enquirer* material here. . . . Simply one of the loveliest voices and smoothest styles around. Here is one case where it is truly the music that does the talking."

the name for her, and she liked it. In 1970 Gayle recorded her first single with Decca, her sister's label. The song, "I've Cried the Blue Right Out of My Eyes," climbed to number twenty-three on the *Billboard* country charts. The next year Gayle married her high school sweetheart, Vassilios Gatzimos, who has served as her manager.

Gayle was grateful for her sister's help at the outset of her career, but the young singer soon wanted to set her own direction. She left MCA Records (formerly Decca) in 1973 and signed with United Artists. There she was fortuitiously teamed with producer-songwriter Allen Reynolds, an astute artist who maximized her vocal potential. Reynolds explained his producing strategy in *High Fidelity:* "I've always tried to get a good feeling around [Crystal], whatever will help her perform the song. . . . I like a cleanness and a presence. I don't like to use an excess of limiters and equalization, because I'd rather get that real honest presence, that warmth. . . . If

Selected discography

Crystal Gayle, United Artists, 1975.
Somebody Loves You, United Artists, 1975.
Crystal, United Artists, 1976.
We Must Believe in Magic, United Artists, 1977.
When I Dream, United Artists, 1978.
Classic Crystal, United Artists, 1979.
Miss the Mississippi, Columbia, 1979.
We Should Be Together, Columbia, 1979.
A Woman's Heart, United Artists, 1980.
These Days, Columbia, 1980.
Favorites, Columbia, 1980.
Hollywood, Tennessee, Columbia, 1981.
True Love, Elektra, 1982.
Cage the Songbird, Warner Brothers, 1983.
Nobody Wants to Be Alone, Warner Brothers, 1986.
Straight to the Heart, Warner Brothers, 1986.
Crystal Christmas, Warner Brothers, 1986.
Country Pure, Warner Brothers, 1986.
The Best of Crystal Gayle, Warner Brothers, 1987.
What If We Fall in Love? (with Gary Morris), Warner Brothers, 1987.

Also recorded *Greatest Hits, Musical Jewels,* and, with Tom Waits, *One from the Heart,* 1982.

Sources

Chicago Tribune, August 2, 1981; October 11-13, 1985.
Christian Science Monitor, August 15, 1978.
Country Music, March, 1980.
High Fidelity, November, 1978.
Newsweek, April 17, 1978.
People, June 5, 1978.
Redbook, May, 1980.
Rolling Stone, May 19, 1977.
Saturday Evening Post, May-June, 1985.
Seventeen, March, 1981.
Village Voice, July 24, 1978.
Washington Post, July 19, 1978.

—*Anne Janette Johnson*

Debbie Gibson

Singer, songwriter

At first glance, Debbie Gibson's career looks like a case of Cinderella-like overnight success. Nothing could be further from the truth, however. Gibson possesses persistence, native talent, and a love of music that began in her infancy. The pop music phenomenon of 1987-88, Gibson writes, scores, and sings her own material—tunes that *Los Angeles Times* contributor Dennis Hunt described as "mostly bubbly confections, much like the ones Connie Francis used to sing."

Gibson is not the first teenager to become a pop star, but she is unique in her degree of involvement with the business and creative sides of her output. As Richard Harrington explained in the *Washington Post,* even seasoned professionals have been taken aback by Gibson's level of engineering and songwriting expertise. The result, writes Harrington, is that Gibson has become "not just a singer—the classic role offered women in music—or writer, but also a musician and producer, a total pop package." Amazingly, this "total pop package" has not become sophisticated beyond her years. Gibson's producer Doug Brietbart described her in *Newsday* as "a hundred percent quintessential all-American teenager."

Debbie Gibson was born and raised on Long Island, in the community of Merrick. According to her parents, she was fascinated by music from the time she could walk and talk. She asked for a guitar at age two, but had to settle for a ukelele because it fit into her hands. She was able to pick out tunes on the piano before she went to kindergarten, and she wrote her first song, "Make Sure You Know Your Classroom," about her first experience in school. She was five. Gibson's parents enrolled her in acting, dancing, and piano lessons, all of which she relished.

Gibson's ambitions crystallized at the ripe age of seven, when she saw the Broadway production of *Annie.* "She was seven or eight when 'Annie' hit," Gibson's mother told the *Washington Post.* "That was it; that was when she decided that this was going to be her life. She was going to be Annie one way or another. And she had tremendous determination. She would go to interviews and auditions that would last 10 or 12 hours; she wouldn't care."

Gibson's parents became concerned about her level of ambition, but they decided to support rather than discourage her. "I knew that one way or another, with or without us, she would wind up in the music business and be successful," her mother said. "It was a matter of, do you want to see her stumble and make mistakes, or do you want to offer guidance and encouragement and hopefully see it go the right way?"

For the Record. . .

Born 1970 in Merrick, Long Island, N.Y.; daughter of Joseph and Diane Gibson; *Education:* Graduated (with honors) from Calhoun High School, Merrick, Long Island, N.Y., 1988.

Songwriter, c. 1975—; recording artist, 1987—. Has performed in television commercials for Commodore computers and Wendy's restaurants. Former member of Metropolitian Opera Children's Chorus.

Awards: Won $1,000 in songwriting contest sponsored by local radio station in Long Island area for song "I Come From America," c., 1982.

Addresses: *Home*—Merrick, Long Island, N.Y. *Office*—c/o Atlantic Records, 75 Rockefeller Plaza, New York, N.Y. 10023.

Gibson's parents offered not only encouragement, but an impressive array of musical equipment as well. In effect, they turned the Gibson garage into a miniature production studio, complete with drum machines, microphones, keyboards, mixers, and recorders—all state-of-the-art. As Gibson entered her teens, she began to write and compose songs at an almost incredible rate. She has claimed that most of her tunes take less than a half hour to write, and she rarely revises. A song she wrote at twelve, "I Come from America," won $1,000 in a writing contest sponsored by a local radio station. Then, at thirteen, she represented the state of New York in a national music competition sponsored by the PTA.

Gibson was only fourteen when her parents solicited the help of producer Breitbart, an entertainment lawyer who began to manage and instruct her. Breitbart told *Newsday* that his young protege was "a hundred percent self-motivated. . . . She was eating through people that were in the business fifteen to twenty years longer than she was." Gibson had to endure the usual round of rejections from record companies, and even the television show *Star Search,* but eventually she signed with Atlantic. Her first single, "Only in My Dreams," began as a regional and dance club hit, then slowly climbed the national charts. By the time her first album, *Out of the Blue,* hit the racks, Debbie Gibson was a known entity. The album has sold in excess of two million copies and is still doing business. It was on the charts when Gibson graduated with honors from Calhoun High School in Merrick.

Gibson's music makes no claims to depth of meaning or universal significance. It is pop music pure and simple, with a catchy beat and predominantly cheerful lyrics. A *Newsday* reviewer describes the songs as "the dance-oriented, 1980s extension of the pre-Beatles female pop of the 1960s. Structurally, her songs recall the anxious anthems of the Shangri-Las and Lesley Gore, but the lyrics are bereft of self-doubt. . . . Gibson's teen tunes combine optimism and self-confidence with a walloping rhythmic assault." Hunt assessed Gibson's voice: "While not a budding Streisand, Gibson isn't a bad singer. Her voice has a perky, endearing, little-girl quality, but may yet ripen into one that's full-bodied. But for now it's full of teen-age yearning."

When asked to comment on her music, Gibson told the *Washington Post:* "It's just honest and spontaneous, simple and fun. That's the whole idea of pop music. I don't like to get into, like, social issues, political things. . . . I never want to be writing from some weird point of view." Gibson's many young fans seem perfectly satisfied with her buoyant perspective; their parents appreciate Gibson's clean-cut, family-oriented lifestyle.

> *"Her songs recall the anxious anthems of the Shangri-Las and Lesley Gore, but the lyrics are bereft of self-doubt."*

"There are plenty of Debbiewannabes," notes Harrington. "Like their inspiration, they are clean, wholesome, earnest."

Fame in pop music is notoriously fleeting, especially for teen stars. Gibson's chance for longevity rests in the same forces that brought her to the limelight in the first place: creativity, determination, level-headed business acumen, and a healthy perspective on the pleasures and pitfalls of stardom. According to Harrington, Gibson is the "Steffi Graf of pop music: a prodigious talent identified early, nurtured by family and coaches, developed through years of practice in community theater, commercials, choruses and the like, until finally it's time for center court at Wimbledon, or in this case, the Billboard charts and the concert arenas of the world." Frankie Blue, one of the radio executives who did the most to promote Gibson's "Only in My Dreams," feels that the young star is on her way to a lengthy and lucrative career. "She's with a good record label," Blue told *Newsday*. "I don't think she'll get lost or fade away."

Selected discography

Out of the Blue, Atlantic, 1987.
Electric Youth, Atlantic, 1989.

Sources

Los Angeles Times, August 23, 1987.
Newsday, June 29, 1987; July 7, 1988.
Washington Post, July 10, 1988.

—*Anne Janette Johnson*

Philip Glass

Composer and musician

Today's avant-garde music, if it is successful and accessible, can become the popular music of tomorrow. Philip Glass, whose performance spaces in the late 1960s were limited to lofts and galleries in New York's SoHo district, and whose audiences consisted only of the hip followers of avant-garde, twenty years later had became an accepted and popular musician whose music is heard on radio, television, film scores, and major performance spaces throughout the United States and Europe. His music is often classified with the minimalist movement. And, although he rejects the nomenclature and the placement, his work does have the characteristics of repetition and modular form which are the hallmarks of classical minimalism. However, his use of amplified instruments and tendency toward a loud driving beat give his music its unique appeal to a young audience brought up on rock music.

"Glass's music has its roots in a moment of exhaustion—the period, in the late 1950s and early 1960s, when music seemed to have nowhere to go," explains Annalyn Swan in *New Republic*. "Romanticism appeared irrevocably dead. Serialism, which had begun in the 1920s as a brave new musical language, a welcome antidote to the excess of the late romantics, had in turn composed itself into a corner. Not only were notes subject to rigid mathematical formulas; so too, in the total serialism that followed Schoenberg and Webern, were rhythm and dynamics. Music had become dense, cerebral, and forbidding." Enter minimalism.

Minimalism is often thought to have it's roots in the 1950s with La Mont Young because of his fascination with sustained and repeated tones. Terry Riley's 1964 piece, *In C,* with its steady eight-note pulse, became the model for later minimalist compositions. But while *In C* is a set of rules providing a framework for improvisation by the musicians, Glass's music is strictly composed in standard notation. Another early influence on minimalism was Steve Reich. His experiments with tape loops repeating musical themes that moved in and out of phase, foreshadowed minimalism's use of modular forms interacting to reveal harmonic and rhythmic variety.

Tim Page, in *High Fidelity,* provides an overview of minimalism and, incidentally, an excellent description of Glass's style: "Most immediately striking is the music's incessantly static nature. Minimalism implies fascination with repetition—through either the continual reiteration of brief, elegant melodic modules or the use of extended, drone-like held tones or chords. Compositional material is usually limited to a few elements, which are subjected to transformational processes. One shouldn't expect standard Western musical *events* (sforzandos, diminuendos, etc.) in these scores, rather, the listener is immersed in a sonic weather, in an aural

For the Record. . .

Born January 31, 1937, in Baltimore, Md.; son of Benjamin (owner of a record store) and Ida (Gouline) Glass; married JoAnne Akalaitas (an actress and theater director; divorced); married Luba Burtyk (a physician), October, 1980; children: (first marriage) Juliet, Zachary. *Education:* University of Chicago, B.A., 1956; Juilliard School of Music, M.S. in composition, 1962; studied privately with Nadia Boulanger in Paris.

Began playing piano as a young child, and studied flute beginning at age eight; while attending Juilliard School of Music, composed more than 70 pieces in the traditional classical style; became interested in non-Western styles of music; worked for a time notating the works of Indian sitarist Ravi Shankar; composer and musician with experimental theater group Mabou Mines in the 1960s; composer of operas, including *Einstein on the Beach, Satyagraha,* and *Akhnaten;* composer and musician with Philip Glass Ensemble, 1968—.

Addresses: *Home*—New York City. *Agent*—Performing Artservices, 325 Spring St., New York, NY 10013.

kaleidoscope that slowly turns, revolves, develops and changes."

Glass's joyful and exuberant music can be seen as a reaction against the overintellectualized music of serialism in which the mathematical correctness and inner-consistency of the composition became more important than the effect the music had on the listener—the listener was, in fact, unimportant. Glass saw that the listener is an active participant in the music; the listener completes the piece. Without the listener there is no music. But his music places new demands on those accustomed to conventional music.

As he expressed it in the liner notes to *Music in 12 Parts:* "It may happen that some listeners, missing the usual musical structures (or landmarks) by which they are used to orient themselves may experience some initial difficulties in actually perceiving the music. However, when it becomes apparent that nothing 'happens' in the usual sense, but that, instead, the gradual accretion of musical material can and does serve as the basis of the listener's attention, then he can perhaps discover another mode of listening—one in which neither memory nor anticipation has a part in sustaining the texture, quality, or reality of the musical experience." For Glass, music is not narrative, not intended to conjure up mental pictures. The meaning of the music is the music itself.

Glass's first professional compositions fit the minimalist format. He worked with a few notes, repeating them consistently, with the only variation being intensity and duration. His later work contains much more variety. He began to turn toward traditional melody and harmony although the driving, rock-influenced rhythm continued to be an important trademark of his music.

Glass was raised in Baltimore, where his father owned a record store, His exposure to piano began as he listened to his older brother and sister practice their lessons. At age eight he studied flute at the Peabody Conservatory of Music. An intellectually precocious youth, he entered the University of Chicago at age 15 and studied philosophy and mathematics before beginning his formal music education. He graduated from the prestigious Juilliard School of Music in 1964 with a degree in composition. At Juilliard he was very productive, writing over 70 compositions, although he considers this early work, in the traditional classical style, unremarkable. Then, on a Fulbright grant, he went to Paris to study with the renowned Nadia Boulanger. As he told *Time,* "Boulanger believed that the training we got in America was simply not thorough enough. She was convinced that at age 27 I had to redo completely my musical education."

Although his musical education was extensive, it was not until he took a job notating the music of Indian sitarist Ravi Shankar for director Conrad Rooks's movie "Chappaqua," that he found his own voice. "Ravi and his tabla player, Alla Rahka, kept telling me I was getting it all wrong", he told *Time.* "No matter how I tried to notate the music, they kept shaking their heads. Out of sheer desperation, I just eliminated the bar lines altogether—which, of course, revealed the fact that Indians don't *divide* music, the way Western theory says it must be done. Instead, they *add* to it. That was the closest I'll ever get to a moment when the creative light suddenly kicks on." Later, he traveled extensively in India absorbing more about this music, which his Juilliard training had dismissed as primitive.

While in Paris in the early 1960s Glass became associated with an experimental theater collective for which he was resident musician. Soon the group found that there was not a large enough audience in Paris to support American experimental theater. Most of the group left Paris in 1967 to settle in New York where it has become well established as the Mabou Mines. Glass has written over a dozen scores for the group.

His involvement with theater eventually led him to opera. "I have often said that I became an opera composer by accident," Glass explains in his book, although Robert Wilson, with whom he collaborated on his first opera, told *Time:* "Phil has a keen visual sense and a profound understanding of drama and theater, especially its visual content. Because of him, all kinds of people who thought that opera was something that belonged to the 19th century have come to appreciate it."

Glass's first, and most well received, opera is *Einstein on the Beach,* an almost five-hour work created in collaboration with designer/director Robert Wilson. It was performed throughout Europe before coming to the Metropolitan Opera in November 1976. *High Fidelity* reported that John Rockwell of the *New York Times* declared himself "profoundly—religiously—moved" by the performance. The work redefined the popular notion of opera. The libretto consists of number-counting and solfege syllables (do, re, me). And, instead of an orchestra, the score is performed by amplified ensemble. Although *Einstein* sold out the Metropolitan Opera for two performances and became the most talked-about event of the season, it closed in debt.

> *"Many people recording classical music still try to create the illusion that the listener is in a concert hall. We're trying to create the impression that you're listening to a record."*

His second opera, *Satyagraha,* was commissioned by the city of Rotterdam, Holland, and premiered there in September 1980. It was based on the period of Gandhi's life (1893-1914) that he spent in South Africa evolving his philosophy of nonviolence. The Sanskrit libretto is drawn from the *Bhagavad Gita.* The third opera, *Akhnaten,* about the Egyptian pharaoh completes a trilogy representing, through the lives of three remarkable individuals, the themes of science (Einstein), politics (Gandhi) and religion (Akhnaten). Rothstein, in *New Republic,* explains Glass's approach to opera: "His is not the narrative style of nineteenth-century music, in which a musical idea is subjected to evolutionary analysis and development. Nor is it the style of Romantic operas in which there are rigorous links between personality and music. This music is suited to stagecraft. It evokes without exploring."

Between operas, Glass composes music and plays with the Philip Glass Ensemble. He formed this group in 1968 as an outlet for his unorthodox music. It is an equally unorthodox ensemble consisting of keyboards, saxophones, flute, and a female singer. Their sound engineer is considered an integral member of the group. They embarked on their first American tour in 1972.

Like many contemporary composers and musicians, Glass has used the recording studio almost as another instrument. His approach to making a recording is unorthodox. As he told *down beat:* "Many people recording classical music still try to create the illusion that the listener is in a concert hall. We would never do that. We're trying to create the impression that you're listening to a record." About the recording of *Satyagraha,* for instance, Gregory Sandow remarks in *Saturday Review,* "The orchestral instruments were recorded one by one and then electronically mixed; the result is magically transparent—and, by symphonic standards, utterly unreal."

Since record companies were not eager to back Glass's early works, he released several titles on his own Chatham Square label. However, his most popular work, *Glassworks,* was released by CBS in 1982 and sold over 100,000 copies. His album most oriented toward the popular audience is *Songs from Liquid Days* with lyrics composed by popular musicians Laurie Anderson, David Byrne, Paul Simon and Suzanne Vega. The music is performed by musicians from his ensemble and the Kronos Quartet; Linda Ronstadt, the Roches, and others contribute vocals.

In 1978, Baker's *Biographical Dictionary of Musicians* called Glass an "American composer of the extreme avant-garde." A decade later he had become one of the most successful classical musicians of the post-Romantic era.

Selected discography

Music with Changing Parts, Chatham Square.
Music in Similar Motion/Music in Fifths, Chatham Square.
Solo Music, Shandar.
Music in Twelve Parts—Parts 1 and 2, Caroline.
Strung out for Amplified Violin, Music Observations.
North Star, Virgin.
Mad Rush/Dressed Like an Egg, Soho News.
Einstein on the Beach, CBS Masterworks.

Einstein on the Beach (excerpts), Tomato.
Dance Nos. 1 & 2, Tomato.
Glassworks, CBS.
The Photographer, CBS.
Koyaanisqatsi, Antilles/Island.
Satyagraha, CBS Masterworks.
Mishima, Nonesuch.
Songs from Liquid Days, CBS.
Company, (Kronos Quartet), Elektra/Nonesuch.
*The Official Music of the XXIIIrd Olympiad, Los Angeles 1984:
  The Olympian,* CBS.
Dancepieces, CBS.
Akhnaten, CBS.
Powaqqatsi, Elektra/Nonesuch, 1988.

Sources

Books

Glass, Philip, *Music by Philip Glass,* Harper, 1987.

Periodicals

down beat, December, 1983; February, 1984; April, 1986.
High Fidelity, November, 1981.
Life, August, 1981.
New Republic, December 12, 1983; January 28, 1985.
People, 1980.
Time, June 3, 1985; August 1, 1988.

—*Tim LaBorie*

Marvin Hamlisch

Composer

"I think we can now talk to each other as friends." With those words, Marvin Hamlisch accepted his third Oscar of the night. On April 12, 1974, he won for best score adaptation ("The Sting"), best original score ("The Way We Were") and best song ("The Way We Were," with lyricists Alan and Marilyn Bergman). Recordings of that music were later honored at the Grammy Awards, at which he was also named best new artist. He is the composer of the longest-running musical in the history of Broadway, two other shows, and hundreds of individual songs, and is, thanks to that memorable Oscar evening, one of the best-recognized songwriters of our time.

Hamlisch grew up with melodic songs in New York City, since his father was an accordionist whose band of fellow Austro-Hungarian emigres played Viennese and American popular music. He was trained at the Juilliard School of Music (Pre-College Division) after a successful audition at the age of seven in which he transposed "Goodnight Irene" on the keyboard. He has often credited both Juilliard and Queens College of the City University of New York with both his musical education and his early career, since both were flexible schools that allowed him to work as an accompanist and songwriter. He told the *New York Times* in 1983 that "despite a wild absentee record, . . . the teachers [at Queens] bent over backwards not to make it difficult for me. My first movie score, for 'The Swimmer,' was accepted by my teacher, Gabriel Fontrier, as a class project in place of the required string quartet." Hamlisch's first professional songs were written for Liza Minnelli when they were in high school, and his first major hit, "Sunshine, Lollipops and Rainbows," was recorded by the equally youthful Lesley Gore. He combined his musical education with professional training in arranging and orchestration from the celebrated "Bell Telephone Hour" conductor Donald Vorhees while working for three years as a rehearsal pianist on that NBC show. He later described that experience as "terrific . . . because you're doing different music every week: Lena Horne, Edward Villella, Leontyne Price." At 18, Hamlisch served as assistant to famed vocal arranger Buster Davis for "Fade Out - Fade In" and the Barbra Streisand hit musical comedy "Funny Girl."

Following his score for "The Swimmer" in 1968, Hamlisch relocated to Hollywood and quickly found success in all of the varied jobs of providing music for films. He scored, arranged, orchestrated, or supervised music for many comedies, among them Woody Allen's "Take the Money and Run" (1969) and the contemporary dramas "Save the Tiger" (1973) and "Kotch" (1971). His song from the latter, "Life is What You Make It," with lyrics by Johnny Mercer, earned Hamlisch his first Oscar nomination. Hamlisch created music and orchestrations for his first Broadway show, "Minnie's Boys" (1970), a tribute to the Marx Brothers, and toured as pianist and straight man for Groucho Marx between film assignments.

"The Way We Were" was not only a succesful title song for the Barbra Streisand bittersweet comedy film, it was also a major recording success for Streisand—her first million-selling single. But that song of the year was not Hamlisch's only hit of the year. His arrangements of the rags of turn-of-the-century composer Scott Joplin for the Paul Newman/Robert Redford comedy, "The Sting" (1973), won major awards and had sales of over three million albums. Hamlisch's lush orchestrations of the piano rags has been credited with reviving interest in Joplin's music, which has regained its rightful place in American music and has since been re-published and recorded in its original versions.

These multiple awards were eclipsed in 1975 when "A Chorus Line" won all of the available Tonys and Drama Critics' Circle awards and became only the third musical in history to be granted a Pulitzer Prize. From the first previews at the Public Theatre in May to the Broadway opening the next fall to the audience that saw the still-running show last night, there is no question that "A Chorus Line" is a brilliant combining of text, music, and movement. Clive Barnes, who began his *New York Times* review with "the conservative word for 'A Chorus Line' might be tremendous," described Hamlisch's contribution as "occasionally hummable and often quite cleverly drops into a useful buzz of dramatic recitative." The show, which recreates the audition process through a series of solos and group songs, depends on the "recitatives" that Hamlisch supported with his music. From the exuberant "I Can Do That" to the three concurrent female solos that make up "Everything's Beautiful at the Ballet" to the opening dance routine that begins the show in the middle of a bar, Hamlisch's music was considered perfection. Two songs became popular outside of the show's context. The finale, which presents all of the characters in the show for which they are competing, became succesful as "One Singular Sen-

> *Hamlisch's first professional songs were written for Liza Minnelli when they were in high school.*

sation." The anthem of the show, set as a personal finale for the dancers, "What I Did for Love," became a hit single for Jack Jones, Johnny Mathis, and Andy Williams, among many other pop singers. It is performed as a general lament for the love of a person, although in the show it refers to sacrifices made for love of performance. Ironically, it became the most popular song for auditions for many years. "A Chorus Line" is still running on Broadway, has been seen in over twenty countries on stage, became a motion picture (1985), and has been recorded by Columbia. For many members of the audience, Hamlisch's score represents the Broadway musical.

Hamlisch has created two other musicals for Broadway. "They're Playing Our Song" (1979), loosely based on his relationship with lyricist Carole Bayer Sager, had a succesful run and national tour. It provided stars Robert Klein and Lucie Arnaz with songs created to fit their conversational singing styles, but the title song, in which they, as a composer/lyricist couple, continually interrupt each other's thoughts to draw attention to their successes, won popularity as a jazz and pop instrumental. His third musical, "Smile" (1986), based on the satiric film comedy of that name, was less succesful. As in "A Chorus Line," Hamlisch set himself the difficult task of recreating an unsucessful performance event—in this case the amateurish sounds of a "Young American Miss" state-wide competition in California. He also wrote a muscialized biography of actress Jean Seberg for performance at London's National Theatre in 1983. He compared the risks of that project to "A Chorus Line" in an interview with *New York Times'* Stephen Holden: "A project like 'Jean' seems awfully risky to a producer. . . . I have to keep reminding myself that 'A Chorus Line' was initially considered weird and off the wall. It was 'A Chorus Line' that convinced me that if you give an audience a theatrical moment, whether it's funny or mean or satiric, they'll accpet it as long as it's theatrical. You mustn't underestimate an audience's intelligence." Hamlisch has written often of his desire to continue writing muscials for the stage.

Film continues to be a major focus of Hamlisch's career. In an interview written shortly after the multi-Oscar evening, he told Joyce Wadler that "you work just as hard on a movie that turns out to be a bomb as you do on one that's a hit, and when the movie's over, it's unemployment time. But if you're any kind of artist, money is not your objective; the biggest thrill you can have is to tell people one of your songs and have them be able to hum it." The James Bond thriller, "The Spy Who Loved Me," featured Hamlisch's hummable music and the hit single for Carly Simon, "Nobody Does It Better." His score for the highly acclaimed film "Sophie's Choice" was also a succesful recording in 1985.

Among his many scores for major television projects are settings of two dramatic masterworks—John Osbourne's Americanization of "The Entertainer" for Jack Lemmon in 1976 and Tennessee Williams' "Streetcar Named Desire" for Ann-Margaret in 1985—and the theme for ABC's daily "Good Morning, America." Hamlisch himself has been the subject of television specials by the BBC and the Public Broadcasting Service. He has also written successful individual songs—one, "Break It to Me Gently," became the number one record on the rhythm and blues charts in 1977 as sung by Aretha Franklin.

Hamlisch's third career is as a performer and conductor with orchestras around the country and in Europe, among them the New York Philharmonic, the Minneapolis Symphony, and the Cleveland and Royal Philharmonic orchestras. Appearing most often for charity concerts, he conducts his arrangements of Joplin rags, the overture from "A Chorus Line" and other Broadway shows, and his film scores. He occasionally provides the audiences with what he describes as "the onslaught" of his own voice and provides narrations in his unadulterated New York accent. When he appeared at Carnegie Hall with the New York Pops, conducted by Skitch Henderson, he performed new songs that critic Will Crutchfield thought "brilliant," and "he commenced a series of parody songs that had everyone in stitches."

Hamlisch, who commutes between the coasts, began to teach at Juilliard in 1986, offering an Introduction to American Musical Theatre. Whether creating music for theatre, film, television, or his own voice, Hamlisch has proven his ability to compose songs that everyone can hum on demand.

Selected discography

The Way We Were (soundtrack), Columbia, 1973.
The Sting (soundtrack), MCA, 1974.
A Chorus Line (original cast recording), Columbia, 1975.
Sophie's Choice (soundtrack), Southern Cross, 1985.
A Chorus Line (soundtrack), Casablanca, 1985.

Sources

New York Post, April 6, 1974.
New York Times, May 22, 1975; June 17, 1977; March 16, 1979; May 13, 1983; January 26, 1987.
Village Voice, November 3, 1975.

—Barbara Stratyner

John Hartford

Country and bluegrass performer, songwriter

Whether he's performing "grass-rock," country and western ballads or steamboat narratives, John Hartford has always been a unique figure in twentieth-century popular music. Like his hero Mark Twain, he ran away to work on a steamboat and learned to narrate and sing stories that tell Americans about their own dreams.

Although born in New York City, where his father was completing his medical training, Hartford grew up in St. Louis, Missouri. He worked on a steamboat and as a radio announcer but spent most of his time learning the instruments and musical styles of country music and bluegrass. His first ensembles included the Sourwood Mountain 3 (in high school) and the Iron Mountain Depot, with guitarist Terry Paul, drummer Mac Elsensohn and bassist Colin Cameron. He plays the guitar, banjo, mandolin, and fiddle and has credited Earl Scruggs, Stringbean, and the radio cast of the Grand Ole Opry as his musical mentors. Hartford was one of the first young musicians who performed in the traditional styles of the South and mid-America to win widespread popularity. On albums and in live appearances, he combines his original songs with the classic compositions, strums, and picks of bluegrass playing.

Hartford was a popular performer with a recording contract for RCA when a ballad from his second album became one of the mega-hits of the 1960s. "Gentle on My Mind," as sung by Glen Campbell, has remained one of the most succesful songs of the mid-1960s with memorable performances in jazz, folk, pop, and symphonic arrangements. The status and widespread popularity of the song was reflected in its Grammy credits. It won the 1967 Grammy as best country and western song; Hartford was honored for best folk performance, and Campbell and his record producer (Al DeLory) were given Grammys for best country and western performance. The song brought Campbell and Hartford to national prominence through appearances on the television shows starring and produced by Tom and Dick Smothers.

It was also on "The Smothers Brothers Comedy Hour" and the replacement "Glen Campbell Good-Time Hour" that Hartford was discovered as a straight-faced comic. He played the guitar, banjo, and fiddle with a skill that was unique even in that era when folk music was frequently seen on network broadcasts. Hartford's wry comic songs—and a memorable performance of "Gentle on My Mind" on a banjo filled with water and a live fish—brought him personal recognition unusual for a songwriter. His work on television and in the Smothers Brothers' live appearances was appreciated by fans and critics alike, according to the *New York Times*'s Richard F. Shepard,

For the Record. . .

Born December 30, 1937, in New York, N.Y.; raised in St. Louis, Mo.; son of a physician; divorced; children: one son, one daughter. *Education:* Washington University (St. Louis), B.A. in fine arts, 1959.

Began working as a country and bluegrass performer in high school; plays a number of instruments, including guitar, banjo, mandolin, and fiddle; performed with groups the Sourwood Mountain 3 and the Iron Mountain Depot; comedian and musical performer on several television programs, including "The Smothers Brothers Comedy Hour," "The Smothers Brothers Summer Show," and "The Glen Campbell Good-Time Hour"; has recorded and toured extensively; has written numerous songs for himself and for other artists; in addition to musical career, has worked as a graphic artist, radio announcer, and riverboat pilot.

Addresses: Grammy Award for best folk performance and for best country and western song, both 1967, for "Gentle on My Mind"; Grammy Award for best ethnic or traditional recording, 1977, for *Mark Twang.*

Addresses: *Office*—c/o Flying Fish Records, 1304 West Schubert, Chicago, IL 60614.

who wrote in 1968 that "John Hartford drew voluminous applause with his inventive songs, attractively delivered."

When the Smothers Brothers' shows ran into trouble with the CBS censors in 1969 and the folk boom waned, Hartford returned to writing songs for his own albums and for other performers. He created seven albums for RCA that did well on the country and western, folk, and pop charts. Two albums for Warner Brothers in the early 1970's followed, but in 1976, he switched to a small label, Flying Fish, for his Grammy Award-winning *Mark Twang.* This bluegrass and narrative recording won Hartford his third Grammy—in his third catagory—

since it was awarded best ethnic or traditional recording in 1977.

A fascination with steamboating led Hartford to achieve pilot status on the *Julia Belle,* a paddle-wheeler out of Louisville. His appearances at folk festivals, concerts, and on television, such as the Smothers Brothers' return to CBS prime-time in 1988, are now likely to include songs and narratives about his boat.

Hartford has maintained his commitment to presenting traditional American music as well as original ballads in his self-described "grass-rock" style. He is considered one of the masters of bluegrass strumming and picking on both guitar and banjo. He even accompanies himself with clogging—percussive nineteenth-century "tap" dancing on a wooden stage. It seems that, whatever the current popularity of folk music, bluegrass, talking blues, or country and western songs, John Hartford will continue to present America's past in a form that commands the attention of its present audiences.

Selected discography

John Hartford Looks at Life, RCA, 1967.
Earthworks & Music (includes "Gentle on My Mind"), RCA, 1967.
Housing Project, RCA, 1968.
Gentle on My Mind, RCA, 1968.
Mark Twang, Flying Fish, 1976.
Slumberin' on the Cumberland, Flying Fish, 1979.
Me Oh My How Time Does Fly, Flying Fish, 1987.

Sources

Eye, March, 1968.
Many Worlds of BMI, April, 1971.
New York Times, August 22, 1968; October 9, 1970.
Village Voice, October 21, 1971; February 14, 1977.

—Barbara Stratyner

Heart

Rock group

Heart is one of the few rock groups to feature women—Seattle-born sisters Ann and Nancy Wilson—as lead performers. The band has been working together, with some personnel changes, since the early 1970s, when the members were living in western Canada. Since their first album, *Dreamboat Annie,* went platinum in 1975, the entertainers in Heart have known every extreme that plagues famous rock bands, from the most dizzying heights of success to the most frustrating lulls in appeal.

As Gwenda Blair noted in *Ms.* magazine, however, the Wilson sisters "have always managed to hold up, whether they were facing . . . breakneck superstar tours, or . . . the seemingly endless uphill struggle to break out of . . . obscurity." Blair attributed the group's tenacity to the Wilsons' special bond, "the easy camaraderie of best girlfriends mixed with the special familiarity and sensitivity of sisterhood." The reporter added: "The continuity and companionship provided by that combination have carried the Wilsons a great distance over the years."

For the Record. . .

Group formed in Seattle, Wash., in 1970; originally billed as White Heart; also performed briefly as Hocus-Pocus before adopting name Heart, 1970. Original band members iuncluded **Anne Wilson** (vocals), **Nancy Wilson** (guitar), **Roger Fisher** (guitar), **Howard Leese** (guitar), **Michael Derosier** (drums), and **Steve Fossen** (bass); have subsequently included more than twenty other members.

Addresses: *Office*—Suite 333, 219 First Ave. North, Seattle WA 98109.

Indeed, Heart has enjoyed an impressive level of success throughout most of its two-decade-long existence: four platinum albums, scores of sold-out tours, and number-one hits in the 1970s and 1980s. Blair described the group's draw on its listeners: "Heart's music, with its . . . bouncing-up-and-down-in-your-seat sound is what millions of people like. To some critics Heart's sound may be sheer bubblegum blare fit only for undiscerning and voracious teen appetites. But to Ann and Nancy, escape and fantasy, not heavy messages or avant-garde music, is what rock is all about."

Press coverage of Heart has centered on the Wilson sisters almost since the band began playing together in a one-room house in Vancouver. By all accounts, including their own, Ann and Nancy were ordinary, middle-class young women who grew up in Bellevue, a suburb of Seattle, Washington. They were teens in the 1960s, daughters of parents who embraced the radical causes and experimental lifestyles of that era. "We were pretty normal for the time we grew up in," Ann told *Rolling Stone.* "What we experienced was going on in suburbs all over the country. We weren't that different." On the other hand, high school chum Sue Ennis, who has since written songs for Heart, recalled that the Wilsons were aloof from most of their peers, disdainful of the standard high school popularity contests, and happiest when they were alone in a bedroom, composing or listening to rock music. To quote *Rolling Stone* contributor Daisann McLane, as teenagers Ann and Nancy "played and wrote songs constantly, moody evocations of late-adolescent alienation."

Ann graduated from Sammamish High School in 1968 with one ambition: to sing in a band. She began working with Tex Blaine and the Skyway Ranch Boys, but soon joined a psychedelic rock band called White Heart, staffed by guitarist Roger Fisher and bassist Steve Fossen. After doing a few gigs under the name Hocus-

Pocus, the group members opted to call themselves Heart. Ann began a long romantic relationship with Michael Fisher, Roger's brother, and Nancy eventually became involved with both the band (as a guitarist and flute player) and with Roger Fisher. Blair wrote of the Wilsons: "Two real-life Barbies, they . . . acquired their very own Kens—two handsome brothers who were also members of Heart."

Heart's early existence can hardly be described as a Barbie-and-Ken dream life. The band members moved to Vancouver and subsisted on brown rice and stolen fruit while trying to build a following. Laura Fissinger describes the group's struggle, and ultimate success, in *Rolling Stone:* "In the early Seventies, Heart was just one more club band, doing six nights a week, four sets a night, and letter-perfect carbons of 'Stairway to Heaven.' Guitarist Howard Leese—the only other Heart member still around from the early days—was working for Mushroom records in Vancouver when he was tapped to produce the group's first demo. Leese's employers initially courted Ann as a solo act. When she said no, they took the whole passel."

> "In Ann Wilson, Heart has possibly the greatest female rock and roll singer ever."

That "whole passel" turned out a debut album, *Dreamboat Annie,* that went platinum in seven months despite its obscure Canadian label and minimal promotion budget. The best known song from the album, a mysterious rocker called "Magic Man," is today considered a classic. Heart turned out several more hit albums— *Little Queen* (1977), *Magazine* (1978), *Dog and Butterfly* (1978), and *Bebe Le Strange* (1980)—and had smash singles with "Crazy on You," "Barracuda," and "Dog and Butterfly." McLane noted that the most successful Heart songs "graft heavy-metal musicianship to emotional, image-laden lyrics. This unlikely combination is held together by Ann's powerful, three-octave soprano. She can belt and screech the hardest rock tune, then slide through every delicate nuance of a tender folk ballad."

Nonstop touring also helped to promote Heart as a top rock band. The group's dynamics—two sisters romantically involved with two brothers—made for frenzied press coverage and, at first, energetic live shows. Then problems began to beset Heart. First the group broke its contract with Mushroom and underwent a costly court battle over some unfinished tapes the label wanted to release. Then Ann ended her involvement with Mike Fisher, even though she credited him with the band's success and suffered pangs of anxiety without his support. Nancy followed suit by breaking up with Roger Fisher and then firing him from the band. For a variety of reasons—the loss of Roger's riveting concert presence among them—Heart went into a nosedive in the early 1980s.

The group continued to tour relentlessly, and continued to produce albums, but popular support faded. "Our management had us on the road nonstop," Nancy told *Rolling Stone.* "We surfaced from our exhaustion just long enough to see that we were being mishandled and swept under the carpet." Having taken responsibility for the direction of the band, the Wilsons switched from Epic to Capitol records in 1984. The following year—and on into 1986—Heart experienced a major comeback with their ninth album, *Heart,* and two top-selling singles, "What About Love" and "These Dreams."

Ann and Nancy, whose titillating music videos have occasionally angered censorious critics, admit that their music is "wrong for any given time for what was in"—an observation echoed by some rock writers. The media may be condescending toward Heart's "basic blueprint of heavy metal meets Joni Mitchell," to quote Fissinger, but audiences respond to it warmly. According to Ariel Swartley in *Rolling Stone,* the members of Heart "need no showmanship to carry them: conviction has already been built into the melody, tension embedded in the harmonies." Swartley also concluded that in Ann Wilson, Heart has "possibly the greatest female rock & roll singer ever. . . . And when she's hot . . . the only reserved you're thinking about is your seat for the next show."

Selected discography

Dreamboat Annie, Mushroom, 1976.
Little Queen, Portrait, 1977.
Magazine, Mushroom, 1978.
Dog and Butterfly, Portrait, 1978.
Bebe Le Strange, Epic, 1980.
Greatest Hits Live, Epic, 1980.
Private Audition, Epic, 1982.
Passionworks, Epic, 1983.
Heart, Capitol, 1985.
Bad Animals, Capitol, 1987.

Sources

High Fidelity, February, 1978.
Mademoiselle, June, 1982.
Rolling Stone, November 30, 1978; March 22, 1979; April 24, 1986.

—*Anne Janette Johnson*

Buddy Holly

Singer, songwriter, guitarist

"Even though Buddy Holly never had a Number One single in America, his legacy is immeasurable," stated Chet Flippo in *Rolling Stone*. The composer and recording artist of such early rock megahits as "That'll Be the Day," "Maybe Baby," and "Peggy Sue," Holly, despite a short career tragically ended by his death in a plane crash at the age of twenty-two, is considered one of the founding fathers of rock music. Classified by some as a purveyor of the "Tex-Mex" branch of rock and roll, and by others as falling into the rockabilly category, Holly pioneered many common practices in the recording industry. He was among the first to overdub musical tracks with his own voice and guitar playing, and the first to use classical stringed instruments on rock records—"It Doesn't Matter Any More," written by fellow recording artist Paul Anka, and his own composition, "Raining in My Heart."

In addition to his own hits, Holly's influence is felt in the work of other musicians, including the Beatles (who even named themselves after insects to liken themselves to Holly's backup group, the Crickets) and Bob Dylan. Himself influenced by early rock giant Elvis Presley, Holly nevertheless evolved a distinctive personal style; as Gene Busnar noted in his 1979 book, *It's Rock 'N' Roll:* "His skinny kid with glasses image was in sharp contrast to Elvis's sex appeal. . . . Holly proved that you did not have to be black, tough, or good-looking to be an authentic rock 'n' roll star. Sometimes, talent was enough."

Buddy was born Charles Hardin Holley—dropping the "e" was originally a mistake on the part of a record company talent scout—on September 7, 1936, in Lubbock, Texas. He learned to play the violin and the piano as a child, but soon displayed a preference for the guitar. Contrary to the depiction presented in the popular film version of Holly's life, "The Buddy Holly Story," Holly's parents always supported him in his musical ventures. By the age of thirteen Holly and his friend Bob Montgomery were playing local clubs, specializing in a music they called "western bop," but performing mainstream country tunes as well. They made what Busnar termed "a conventional country album," which met with little attention, but when Holly and Montgomery served as the opening act for pioneer rock group Bill Haley and the Comets at a local rock show a scout for Decca Records signed Holly, without Montgomery, to a contract. Decca cut a few singles featuring Holly, but they were not considered likely to meet with commercial success, and Decca advised the young musician to go back to Lubbock to refine his material.

Holly did so, forming a band called the Crickets with friends Jerry Allison, who played drums, Joe B. Mauldin, who served as bass player, and Niki Sullivan, who provided the rhythm guitar. Holly played guitar and sang lead vocals. The band traveled to Clovis, New Mexico, to record in the studios of Norman Petty, who produced much of their subsequent music. A Petty-produced, livelier version of "That'll Be the Day," a song Holly had already recorded for Decca, brought the Crickets and their leader by circuitous ways back to Decca's attention; a deal was made in which songs released as Buddy Holly and the Crickets would be released on Decca's subsidiary Brunswick label, while records with Holly's solo billing would be on the Coral label.

Holly's unique vocal style, coupled with Allison's drum beat, ensured success. His singing voice has been likened to that of a person with the hiccups; he is remembered for his use of glottal stops and stretched syllables. As Arnold Shaw pointed out in *The Rockin' 50s,* Holly broke with usual practice by singing ballads with "a feeling of nervous excitement." Referring to Holly's first solo hit, "Peggy Sue," an expression of unrequited love taking its title from the name of Allison's girlfriend (and later, wife), Shaw explained: "An older school of singers found this disregard of lyrics rather disconcerting. But Holly's admirers were unconcerned that his performance bore no relation to the woeful words of pleading. What counted was the agitation, tension, and energy of Holly's delivery. . . . His performance was the song. . . . What was amateurville in the eyes of the 'good music' advocates was a new esthetic to teen-agers."

As part of the early rock movement, a cultural innovation many perceived as stemming completely from

rhythm and blues, a field dominated by black artists, Holly and the Crickets were sometimes mistakenly thought to be a black group. Once they were accidentally booked with black singers and musicians to play to a primarily black audience at the Apollo Theater; apparently the audience was shocked to see white musicians on their stage, but Holly and his group performed gamely. As former Cricket Sullivan recounted for Chet Flippo in *Rolling Stone:* "The first two days that we played the Apollo, we were booed. The third day, Buddy said, 'Let's do Bo Diddley,' [a popular rhythm and blues number] and from that moment on we were a hit." Holly's other breakthroughs include helping introduce rock and roll to English audiences. When he and the Crickets toured Great Britain in March of 1958, Holly was enthusiastically received and became even more popular than he was in the United States.

In the summer of 1958 Holly was at the offices of Peer-Southern, his New York City music publishers, when he met Maria Elena Santiago, who was a receptionist

> *Holly, despite a short career tragically ended by his death in a plane crash at the age of twenty-two, is considered one of the founding fathers of rock music.*

there. Two weeks later, he married her. After a honeymoon in Acapulco, the couple returned to Lubbock; at this time Holly broke with Petty, feeling that he and the Crickets could be their own producers. The Crickets disagreed, however, resulting in Holly's splitting with them as well. He and Maria Elena set up housekeeping in New York City.

With new backup musicians, one of whom was future country music star Waylon Jennings, in early 1959 Holly toured with a rock show that also featured stars J. P. Richardson ("The Big Bopper") and Ritchie Valens. They rode in buses from performance to performance; the buses kept breaking down, and finally, after a concert in Clear Lake, Iowa, Holly decided to charter a small four-seater plane to reach the next town in time to rest and do laundry. Jennings gave up his seat to Richardson, who was ill; Holly's other back-up man was persuaded by Valens to do the same for him. Early on the morning of February 3, the plane took off from the nearby Mason City, Iowa, airport and crashed eight miles out, killing the pilot and his famous passengers.

Compositions

Composer of songs, including (with Norman Petty; under name Charles Hardin) "Not Fade Away"; (with Petty) "It's So Easy"; (with Petty) "True Love Ways"; (with Petty and Jerry Allison) "Peggy Sue"; and (with Petty and Allison) "That'll Be the Day."

Selected discography

Single releases; as Buddy Holly and the Crickets

"That'll Be the Day," Brunswick, July 1957.
"Oh Boy!" Brunswick, November 1957.
"Not Fade Away," Brunswick, 1957.
"Every Day," Brunswick, 1957.
"Maybe Baby," Brunswick, February 1958.
"It's So Easy," Brunswick, September 1958.

Solo single releases

"Peggy Sue," Coral, November 1957.
"Rave On," Coral, May 1958.
"Heartbeat," Coral, January 1959.
"It Doesn't Matter Anymore," Coral, February 1959.
"Raining in My Heart," Coral, February 1959.

Anthologies

Buddy Holly Story, Coral, 1959.
Buddy Holly Story II, Coral, 1960.
Best of Buddy Holly, Coral, 1966.
Greatest Hits, Coral, 1967.
Rock 'n' Roll Collection, MCA, 1972.

Sources

Books

Busnar, Gene, *It's Rock 'n' Roll,* Messner, 1979.
Goldrosen, John, *Buddy Holly: His Life and Music,* Popular Press, 1975.
Goldrosen, John, and John Beecher, *Remembering Buddy: The Definitive Biography,* Penguin, 1987.
Laing, Dave, *Buddy Holly,* Macmillan, 1971.
Shaw, Arnold, *The Rockin' 50s,* Hawthorn, 1974.
Ward, Edward, Geoffrey Stokes, and Ken Tucker, *Rock of Ages: The Rolling Stone History of Rock and Roll,* Summit Books, 1986.

Periodicals

New Republic, January 27, 1979.
Rolling Stone, April 20, 1978; September 21, 1978.

—Elizabeth Thomas

John Lee Hooker

Blues singer, guitarist

"First comes the class in the small, crinkled, slightly seedy person of John Lee Hooker, a.k.a. The Hook, Doctor Feelgood, and, by way of formal on-stage introduction, 'The Godfather of the Blues'. . . . The first great recorded practitioner of the electric blues-rock-funk and stream-of-consciousness boogie, he introduced a style to which every white blues band since 1962 must trace at least half its roots." John Lee Hooker was 72 when his 1979 appearence at New York's Lone Star Cafe brought on that tribute from Patrick Carr in the *Village Voice*. Hooker's influence on blues, blues-folk and blues-rock musicians remains vital ten years later.

Born in Clarksdale, Mississippi, he learned his "Delta licks" style of guitar playing from his stepfather, William Moore, and his colleagues James Smith and Coot Harris. He ascribed his style—with, in writer Fred Stuckey's words, "tonal 'bendings' of the third, fifth and seventh degrees of the scale and abrasive two-finger picking"—to them in an interview with Stuckey in *Guitar Player,* stating that "Down in Clarksdale, my stepfather taught me all I know about playing the guitar. . . . After this uprising of fancy music, I never did drop what I learned back then. I'm doin' what the blues singers was doin' back then, and it sounded good. It still sounds good, and I'm always goin' to keep it just the way it is."

Hooker travelled to Memphis, Cincinnati and Detroit where, in the mid-1940s, he made a demo for distributor Bernie Besman. Hooker recorded his first single, "Boogie Chillen" and "Sally Mae," for the Sensation label. As distributed by Modern Records, it became a hit on the blues charts of 1949. He followed this record with "In the Mood for Love" and "Crawling King Snake" for Modern. From 1955 to 1964, he recorded for Vee Jay, making singles and albums for that Chicago-based firm, such as *Travelin'* (1961) and *Big Soul: Best of John Lee Hooker* (1963). He also recorded under a confounding variety of pseudonyms—among them, Delta John, Johnny Lee, and Birmingham Sam and his Magic Guitar—for a large number of companies. Many of these one-time contracted recordings have been collected and re-mastered in recent years.

During the revived interest in traditional guitar music and performance styles prompted by the popularity of folk music in the 1960s, Hooker was "rediscovered" for the first of many times. He performed at the Newport Folk Festival in 1960 and appeared at coffee houses and college campuses. Hooker was also being rediscovered in Great Britain, where he was an important influence on groups that equated blues with rock and roll, such as the Rolling Stones and the Animals, who recorded his "Boom Boom." Hooker performances became as famous for the rock superstars who appeared in the audience as for his own music. In an engagement at Ungano's in 1969, for example, the *Village Voice* reported that "three nights after opening, Eric Clapton, Delaney and Bonnie, Ginger Baker and Chris Wood came down to jam with the Doctor and returned the next night for more. And on Saturday, Richie Havens with his whole band in tow showed up to sing and jam."

In the 1970s, as musical forms fused, he concertized with performers from the rock group Canned Heat (with whom he recorded *Hooker 'n' Heat*) to folk vocalist Bonnie Raitt. He was frequently honored as one of the creators of his genre in joint and group concerts by the long-time greats of blues music. In the Blues Variations concert at Lincoln Center in 1973 he was paired with Muddy Waters and Mose Allison, while in A Night of the Blues at the Brooklyn Academy of Music two years later, he shared the program with Albert King and folk harmonicist Peg Leg Sam.

Hooker plays flexible blues of 10-13 bar phrases punctuated with foot tapping and an electric guitar sound that has been described as "percussive . . . just shy of dissonance and distortion." Each song is a monologue that retells a story of emotional pain that requires a unique verbal pattern. Reviews of Hooker performances, generally by music historian/journalists who are long-term admirers, provide vivid pictures of his unique song structures and performance style. Carmen Moore wrote in 1970 in the *Village Voice* that "in his entire set, John Lee sang only one rhymed song. As usual, he paid little heed to the famed three blues chords: all, it seemed, were present at once. What his guitar did was talk, in snaky lines, in sitar quivers, in sudden shocks, in hilly phrases. . . . Gifted with one of the richest voices in contemporary music, this serious of serene of bassos sat down, the mike at his lips, and shared a few instances from his personal black life." Ian Dove, reviewing the Blues Variations concert, also noted the personal delivery style: "He is a complete,

closed-in performer, who accents the rhythmic drive of his performances by chopping off phrases and choking off the ends of his rhythmic lines. He keeps things simple, rarely straying from a couple of chords, and delivers his autobiographical blues with growing menace and much vibrato." Almost a decade later, Patrick Carr wrote that Hooker "continues to perform and record with the same slow mastery of blue-life imagery, the same spare, quirky, throttled-violence guitar technique, and the same beautifully resonant leather-and-raw-silk vocal genius that were his from the start."

The optimal way to hear Hooker is in live performance, but there are scores of albums featuring his work. He has made over forty albums under various names. Chess Records has recently begun to re-issue tapes and studio cuts in series of albums simply called *The Blues, Volumes 1-3*. Amiga Records also distributes a Hooker anthology, *Blues, Collection 2*.

"Godfather of the blues" or simply one of its greatest practitioners, Hooker has maintained one of the great native art forms of the United States. He described its universal importance and appeal to *Guitar Player:* "Everybody understands the blues now—the young, all races, all over the world. Back then people pretended they didn't know, but now they know. The young people have really brought it out. . . . It's a tremendous thing because it's true. It's the truest music that ever been written. . . . Everything comes right from the blues—spirituals, jazz, rock. The blues is the root of all this."

Selected discography

"Boogie Chillun" (single), Sensation/Modern, 1948.
Travelin', Vee Jay, 1961.
Big Soul: Best of John Lee Hooker, Vee Jay, 1963.
Hooker 'n' Heat, (with Canned Heat), Liberty, 1971.
Boogie Chillun (includes a new version of the title song), Fantasy, 1972.
The Cream, Tomato, 1979.
Blues, Collection 2, Amiga, 1986.
Jealous, Pausa, 1986.
The Blues, Volumes 1-3, Chess Records.

Sources

Guitar Player, March, 1971.
New York Times, July 11, 1970; September 26, 1971; January 7, 1973; April 28, 1975.
Village Voice, July 24, 1969; June 18, 1970; November 16, 1972; August 8, 1979; August 29, 1986.

—*Barbara Stratyner*

Vladimir Horowitz

Pianist

Vladimir Horowitz is recognized as the greatest piano virtuoso of the twentieth century. Possessor of staggering technique, he was, in his prime, probably unequaled for speed and dynamic range, and he remains unequaled in his ability to evoke the Romantic tradition of highly expressive, personalized pianism as practiced by such legendary musicians as Franz Liszt and Sergei Rachmaninoff. As *Time*'s Michael Walsh noted in a 1986 report, "At his peak, Horowitz had it all, heightened and amplified by a daredevil recklessness that infused every performance with an exhilarating, unabashed theatricality." Walsh proceeded to refer to Horowitz as "this most extraordinary of artists."

Horowitz was born in Russia in 1904 and began studying piano with his mother around age three. Within a few years he was studying the instrument seriously. In his youth Horowitz was already a dazzling pianist, but he aspired to composition, and by his late teens he had already composed several songs. But when the Russian Revolution resulted in the decline of his family's fortune, Horowitz turned to the concert stage as a more efficient means of deriving an income. In the early 1920s he gave nearly one hundred performances and earned substantial recognition as an explosive pianist capable of breaking piano strings with his thundering style. As a result of his success, he was allowed to leave the Soviet Union to commence further musical study in Germany. Horowitz, however, had no intention of returning home. Stuffing approximately five thousand dollars worth of Russian rubles into a shoe, he crossed the border as a Soviet guard wished him good fortune in the West.

Once in Berlin, Horowitz immersed himself in the music community, hearing such pianists as Edwin Fischer and Rudolf Serkin and collaborating with such conductors as Bruno Walter and Arturo Toscanini. Even among such great musicians Horowitz stood out as an extraordinary musical force, stunning audiences with overwhelmingly passionate interpretations of works by pianistic masters such as Liszt and Frederic Chopin. After enjoying a few years of great success in Europe, Horowitz traveled to the United States in early 1928.

Horowitz made his American debut playing Tchaikovsky's first piano concerto with conductor Thomas Beecham and the New York Philharmonic. in a performance that strengthened his reputation as an unrivaled virtuoso, Horowitz broke from Beecham's stately tempo and charged to the finale several measures before the orchestra. The result was, at once, vulgar and exhilarating, and Beecham fumed at the podium as the audience shouted their appreciation for Horowitz. Critics, too, overlooked his questionable taste and bestowed wild praise on his spellbinding technique.

By the mid-1930s Horowitz was working at what was, for him, an exhaustive pace of nearly one hundred recitals each year. In addition, he still appeared with orchestras, and in 1933 he gave a memorable performance of Ludwig van Beethoven's *Emperor* with Toscanini and the New York Philharmonic. The strain of Horowitz's schedule eventually overwhelmed him, however, and in 1935 he abruptly ceased performing. "I couldn't take the traveling, five days a week, all those trains, all those towns, no sleep, bad food," he later explained to *Newsweek*'s Hubert Saal.

Horowitz spent his brief retirement recuperating with his family—in 1933 he had married Wanda Toscanini, the conductor's daughter—and studying music. When he resumed playing in the late 1930s, it was with a renewed seriousness towards music. He complimented his largely virtuosic performing repertoire with works by modern composers such as Sergei Prokofiev and Samuel Barber and began drawing greater attention for his interpretive talent as well as his technical skills. During World War II, at which time Horowitz became an American citizen, he also gave many concerts for the American war effort. Out of these patriotic endeavors came what has become one of his most popular compositions, a flamboyant arrangement of John Philip Sousa's "Stars and Stripes Forever."

After the war Horowitz continued to enjoy great success on the concert stage, and in 1953 he celebrated the twenty-fifth anniversary of his American debut by once again performing Tchaikovsky's first piano concerto. Great publicity surrounded the event, and critics generally agreed that Horowitz had matured from mere virtuoso into a provocative artist, one capable of stirring contemplation as well as exhilaration. But after the anniversary performance he once again withdrew from public performance, claiming increasingly problematic health—notably stomach distress and general exhaustion. For the next twelve years Horowitz abstained from public performance, choosing instead to study music and indulge his extracurricular enthusiasms, which ranged from walking to watching baseball games and television programs. His only music output derived from occasional recordings, which ranged from works by masters such as Beethoven and Chopin to those by the more obscure Muzio Dlementi and early modernist Alexander Scriabin.

> *"Horowitz matured from mere virtuoso into a provocative artist, one capable of stirring contemplation as well as exhilaration."*

In the early 1960s, after ending his association with RCA Records and signing a recording contract with Columbia, Horowitz realized considerable success with a recording of works by Chopin, Rachmaninoff, Liszt, and Robert Schumann. This record, which became the top-selling classical work of 1962, earned Horowitz the first of four successive Grammy Awards. But as his recording success ensued, so did his interest in acoustics. Horowitz's first recordings for Columbia had been executed in a church, but he eventually sought a fuller sound, and in 1965 he decided to record at Carnegie Hall, site of some of his greatest recitals. Once seen at the hall, however, Horowitz was plagued by hearsay of his imminent return to the concert stage. He denied the rumors, but when a young journalist showed an unfamiliarity with Horowitz's musicianship, the pianist decided to resume performing.

Horowitz ended his twelve-year absence from the concert stage in May, 1965, with a Carnegie Hall recital that included Schumann's *Fantasy* and various works by Scriabin and Chopin. The performance earned great acclaim, and the subsequent recording of that concert proved immensely successful. The following year Horowitz released another concert recording, this time with works by Haydn and Mozart as well as those of Chopin and Liszt. By the end of the decade Horowitz was once again concertizing regularly. This period, though, was followed by still another withdrawal, and Columbia was compelled to sustain his record output by culling material from both recitals and studio sessions. By this time Horowitz's eccentricities and emotional sways were more generally known and there was speculation that his extreme mood swings—from extreme elation to equally profound despair—had undermined his ability to perform regularly.

By the end of the 1970s, however, Horowitz was yet again touring and recording vigorously. A highlight of this period was a celebration of the fifty-year anniversary of his American debut. For this occasion he performed Rachmaninoff's third piano concerto, a work that its composer—himself an accomplished pianist—had surrendered to Horowitz after hearing him produce a particularly dazzling account of it in the 1930s. This occasion was also special in that it marked Horowitz's first appearance with an orchestra since a recording of Beethoven's *Emperor* concerto in the early 1950s. The anniversary celebration, in collaboration with conductor Eugene Ormandy and the New York Philharmonic, provided Horowitz with still another great success, as did the subsequent recording of that concert—for RCA, to which he had recently returned.

Horowitz has continued to enjoy great acclaim in the 1980s, though he has withdrawn significantly from both performing and recording. Even in recent years, however, he has proven himself unmatched in popularity. His brief return to the Soviet Union resulted in widespread attention from media throughout the world and earned him the cover of *Time,* which reported his return as "triumphal." The recording of his Moscow recital—broadcast the same day by an American news program—brought Horowitz still further recognition as a master musician. Since the Moscow recital, though, he has performed in public only rarely, and it is believed by many that with the passing of Horowitz may go the passing of the entire Romantic tradition. "I am a nineteenth-century romantic," he conceded to *Newsweek*'s Saal in 1978. "I am the last."

Selected discography

Frederic Chopin, *Horowitz Plays Chopin,* Columbia.
Chopin, *New Recordings of Chopin,* Columbia.
Chopin, *My Favorite Chopin,* Columbia.
Chopin, *The Chopin Collection* (three volumes), RCA.
Muzio Clementi, *Horowitz Plays Clementi,* RCA, 1955.
Franz Liszt, *Sonata in B,* RCA.
Wolfgang Amadeus Mozart, *Horowitz Plays Mozart,* Deutsche Grammophon, 1987.
Sergei Rachmaninoff, *Horowitz Plays Rachmaninoff,* Columbia.
Rachmaninoff, *Piano Concerto No. 3 in D,* RCA.
Robert Schumann, *Kreisleriana, Opus 16,* Deutsche Grammophon.
Valdimir Horowitz at Carnegie Hall: An Historic Return, Columbia, 1965.
Valdimir Horowitz at Carnegie Hall, Columbia, 1966.
Valdimir Horowitz at the Met, RCA, 1981.
Horowitz in London, RCA, 1982.
The Studio Recordings, Deutsche Grammophon, 1985.
Horowitz in Moscow, Deutsche Grammophon, 1986.

Sources

Books

Dubal, David, *Reflections From the Keyboard: The World of the Concert Pianist,* Summit Books, 1984.
Plaskin, Glenn, *Horowitz,* Morrow, 1983.

Periodicals

Atlantic, August, 1986.
Commentary, May, 1977.
Horizon, March, 1978.
Newsweek, December 2, 1974; January 23, 1978; April 28, 1986.
New Yorker, January 23, 1978; October 9, 1978.
New York Times Magazine, January 8, 1978.
Stereo Review, December, 1986.
Time, December 2, 1974; January 23, 1978; May 5, 1986.

Michael Jackson

Singer, songwriter, producer

Artfully clad in an outfit featuring his signature white socks, red leather jacket, and single, sequined white glove, Michael Jackson is widely recognized as one of the world's top musical entertainers. In barely two decades he has grown from a five-year-old boy-wonder singing with his brothers to a legendary solo artist who dazzles audiences worldwide with his deftness as songwriter, producer, video pioneer, showman, and vocalist *par excellence*. With a knack for translating tunes from almost any genre—rhythm-and-blues, pop, rock, soul—into success, the prodigy defies all labels. Jackson is "a half-mad and extraordinary talent," marveled Mikal Gilmore in *Rolling Stone,* with the ability to "combine [his] gifts in an electrifying, stunning way . . . that has only been equalled in rock history by Elvis Presley."

Born into a black, working-class family in Gary, Indiana, Jackson was the seventh of nine children, all of whose lives were shaped by their parents' insistence on firm discipline. The Jackson parents, however, were also musical. Joe Jackson, a crane-operator for U.S. Steel, sang and played the guitar with a small-time group known as the Falcons, and Katherine Jackson played the clarinet. Both believed that encouraging their children to pursue their musical interests was a good way to keep them out of trouble.

By the time he was five years old, Michael, together with his four older brothers (Jackie, Tito, Jermaine, and Marlon), had formed a rhythm-and-blues act called the Jackson Five. Initially enlisted to play the bongos, Michael revealed himself as such a little dynamo that he soon became the group's leader, even at a young age able to mesmerize audiences with his singing and dancing. The group won their first talent competition in 1963, gave their first paid performance in 1964, and had proven themselves a popular local act by 1967. Although primarily imitative at this stage, with their work rooted in the tradition of such musical greats as the Temptations, Smokey Robinson, and James Brown, they were good enough to cut a couple of singles for Steeltown Records, an Indiana label.

They were also good enough to compete, in 1968, at Harlem's Apollo Theatre, then the most prestigious venue for launching black musicians. Their riveting performance brought them so many national engagements that Joe Jackson left his job to manage his sons' act. It also captured the attention of Motown Records, in its golden days as the United States's premier black recording label. Before long, the young musicians signed with Motown and moved to California when the label relocated its headquarters there.

Under the strict guidance of the Motown magnates, the Jackson Five propelled themselves into the public eye

Full name, Michael Joseph Jackson; born August 19, 1958, in Gary, Ind; son of Joseph (a crane operator) and Katherine (a homemaker and occasional sales clerk; maiden name, Corse) Jackson. *Education:* Attended schools in Indiana and California. *Religion:* Jehovah's Witness.

Vocalist with the Jackson Five, 1963-76, recording first singles, 1967-68, began performing nationally as opener for other artists, 1968, signed with Motown, c. 1968, released first album, 1969, started appearing on television, 1970, including "The Ed Sullivan Show," "American Bandstand," and the "Andy Williams Show," first worldwide concert tour, 1972; vocalist with the Jacksons, 1976-1981, signed with Epic, recording first album for that label, 1976, made a thirty-six-city tour, 1981; made "Victory" reunion tour with his brothers, 1984; co-organizer of U.S.A. for Africa famine relief effort, 1985.

Solo career, including work as a vocalist, songwriter, producer, video artist, and actor, 1972—, recorded first solo album, *Got to Be There,* 1972, made songwriting debut with "Shake Your Body (Down to the Grave)" on the *Destiny* album, 1978, with later credits including "Beat It," "Billie Jean," and "Wanna Be Startin' Somethin'," co-produced *Thriller* album, 1982, established himself as a significant video artist with the *Thriller* videos, 1983, made first solo concert tour, 1987.

Also appeared in film version of Broadway musical "The Wiz" and involved with the 3-D film fantasy "Captain Eo." Engages in philanthropic work, including efforts to help eliminate world hunger, establishing a burn center in Los Angeles, Calif., and supporting the United Negro College Fund (UNCF) and a camp for children suffering from cancer.

Awards: Winner of numerous awards, including twelve Grammy Awards (eight in 1984); named number one recording artist of 1983 by *Billboard* magazine; winner of eight American Music Association Awards in 1984, winner of two special American Music Association Awards, 1989; *The Guinness Book of World Records* lists *Thriller* as the biggest-selling album of all time.

Addresses: *Home*—4641 Hayvenhurst Ave., Encino, Calif. 91436.

with their first Motown single, "I Want You Back." Released in November, 1969, the recording reached number one on the charts in early 1970 and eventually sold more than one million copies. It was quickly followed by other hit singles like "ABC," the Grammy

Award-winning pop song of 1970, as well as similarly successful albums. Even a "Jackson Five" television cartoon program was created to showcase the group's music. By the time the Jackson Five took their version of "bubblegum soul," as their music was now called, on worldwide tour in 1972, they were a smashing success, especially among the teenybopper set. Indeed Michael, "the little prince of soul," was barely a teenager himself and had become not only a millionaire, but an international sex symbol ready to launch his solo career.

The rising star premiered as a solo artist with the 1972 album *Got To Be There,* earning him a Grammy Award as male vocalist of the year, and followed it with the gold album *Ben,* thus beginning a steady stream of solo recordings. With his first solo tour more than a decade away, however, the young Jackson still directed most of his energy into the group's work. The Jackson Five, in fact, made another breakthrough in 1973 with the single "Dancing Machine." Succeeded by the epynomous album, the sophisticated recording introduced a disco beat that broadened the group's audience.

As members of the Jackson Five matured, so did their music, and they eventually outgrew the agenda Motown had established for them. They were eager for greater artistic control, and when their contract with Motown expired in 1976 they signed with Epic renamed as the Jacksons (Jermaine dropped out of the group while youngest brother, Randy, joined it).

Although frustrated by the creative restrictions placed on their first two albums for the label, the Jacksons were finally given control with *Destiny,* an album marking Michael's songwriting debut. The risk proved fruitful both for the recording company and for the artists. Featuring the "funkier" sound the entertaining brothers favored, the 1978 album went platinum and spun off two hit singles. In 1980 the group duplicated the feat with *Triumph,* written and produced by Michael, Jackie, and Randy, and in the summer of 1981 they embarked on the enormously successful thirty-six city tour that produced *The Jacksons Live,* the group's last album together.

As the Jacksons disbanded to pursue individual interests, Michael exploded onto the music scene as an independent artist, outstripping the success of his own multiaward-winning album of 1979, *Off the Wall,* as well as shattering almost every other record in recording history. His landmark album was *Thriller,* unleashed in 1982. It was a sensation that appealed to almost every imaginable musical taste and established Jackson as one of the world's pre-eminent pop artists. The album went platinum in fifteen countries, gold in four, and garnered eight Grammys; its sales exceeded thirty-eight million copies worldwide, earning it a place in the

Guinness Book of World Records as the largest-selling album in recording history; it spun-off an unprecedented seven hit singles; and it enabled Jackson to claim the spotlight as the first recording artist to simultaneously head both the singles and albums charts for both rhythm-and-blues and pop.

The extraordinary *Thriller* also generated a frenzy among the heartthrob's fans, dubbed Michaelmania by the media, and its remarkable success sealed the musician's reputation as "brilliant" and a "rock phenomenon"; one critic even went beyond "superstar" to call Jackson a "megastar." But success has also brought the artist under intense scrutiny, both by his admirers and the communications industry, and each new achievement—from his innovative video work to his astonishing 1984 reunion "Victory" tour with his brothers to his latest, most startling album, the 1987 *Bad*—has only seemed to fuel the lust for information.

Indeed, for someone who has been in the limelight since the age of five, Jackson has seemingly by magic

---

There are rumors that Jackson has lightened his skin with chemicals and taken female hormones to maintain his falsetto voice . . .

---

kept his private life private. Writing for *Maclean's,* Gillian MacKay reported that he "has astonished his fans by shedding his lively, button-cute image and transforming himself into a mysterious, otherworldly creature perpetually posing behind a mask." So intensely private is this star that he rarely interacts with the media.

His silence, however, has tended to stimulate conjecture, and the tabloids are notorious for speculating about him. One day there are rumors that he has lightened his skin with chemicals and taken female hormones to maintain his falsetto voice quality, while the next day gossip columns question his sexual identity and charge that he has extensively remodeled his body with plastic surgery. He is also infamous for what has been described as a certain "weirdness" or "quirkiness," although many dismiss the charge as nonsense. As Jackson's friend, producer Quincy Jones, was quoted in the star's defense by *People:* "[Michael is] grounded and centered and focused and connected to his creative soul. And he's one of the most normal people I've ever met."

Dissecting the Jackson mystique is a task that even seems to have eluded more serious journalists. Most view him as a paradox. He is both superstar and devout Jehovah's Witness, a man who—as neither drinker, smoker, nor drug experimenter, has eschewed much of the glamorous life for healthy living. Some see him as a man-child living in his own reality—like one of his heroes, Peter Pan, refusing to grow up. Others, like *Newsweek*'s Jim Miller, find him "a stunning live performer, but also a notorious recluse. . . . He's utterly unlike you and me, with a streak of wildfire that unpredictably lights his eyes."

Theories aside, admirers and detractors alike agree, as Gilmore concluded, that Jackson's success is based on his "remarkably intuitive talents as a singer and dancer—talents that are genuine and matchless and not the constructions of mere ambition or hype." It is this talent, coupled with the star's hard work and often touted perfectionism, that has enabled Jackson to cross virtually every music line ever drawn.

Jackson, in fact, has been credited with resuscitating a languishing music industry and with practically eliminating barriers barring blacks from mainstream music venues. More than one critic has imbued him with a chameleon-like capacity for being all things to all people and thus pleasing everyone. In a review for *People,* Gary Smith related the artist's musical conquest to his ability to create "a portable dream," explaining that "in this dream world his androgyny does not threaten the virile, his youth does not threaten the old. His blackness does not threaten the white, for nothing seems quite real and all is softened by fragility and innocence."

Although the music idol himself might be eccentric or enigmatic, his achievements are very real. With the completion of his first solo tour, a long, triumphant venture begun in September, 1987, Michael Jackson seems to be at the peak of his powers, a hero living the American Dream. Indeed, experts who appoint Frank Sinatra as the star of the 1940s, Elvis Presley as the star of the 1950s, and the Beatles as the stars of the 1960s have already named Michael Jackson the star of the 1980s—and speculate that he will claim the 1990s as well.

Selected discography

Single releases for Steeltown Records; With the Jackson Five

"I'm a Big Boy Now," c. 1967.
"You've Changed," c. 1967.
"We Don't Have to Be Over 21 (To Fall in Love)," c. 1968.

"Jam Session," c. 1968.

LPs; With the Jackson Five

Diana Ross Presents the Jackson Five, Motown, 1969.
ABC, Motown, 1970.
Third Album, Motown, 1970.
The Jackson Five Christmas Album, Motown, 1970.
Maybe Tomorrow, Motown, 1971.
Goin' Back to Indiana, Motown, 1971.
The Jackson Five's Greatest Hits, Motown, 1971.
Looking Through the Windows, Motown, 1972.
Skywriter, Motown, 1973.
Get It Together, Motown, 1973.
Dancing Machine, Motown, 1974.
Moving Violation, Motown, 1975.
Joyful Jukebox Music, Motown, 1976.
The Jackson Five Anthology, Motown, 1976.
Boogie, Natural Resources/Motown, 1980.
Farewell My Summer Love (recorded, 1973; previously unreleased), Motown, 1984.

Also released numerous anthologies since 1980.

LPs; With the Jacksons

The Jacksons, Epic, 1976.
Goin' Places, Epic, 1977.
Destiny, Epic, 1978.
Triumph, Epic, 1980.
The Jacksons Live, Epic, 1981.
Victory, Epic, 1984.

LPs; Solo

Got to Be There, Motown, 1972.
Ben, Motown, 1972.
Music and Me, Motown, 1973.
Forever, Michael, Motown, 1975.
The Best of Michael Jackson, Motown, 1975.
Off the Wall, Epic, 1979.
Thriller, Epic, 1982.
Bad, Epic, 1987.

Also narrator for *E.T.: The Extra-Terrestrial Storybook,* MCA, 1982. Other recording credits include the soundtrack to the documentary film *Save the Children;* the soundtrack from the movie *The Wiz,* MCA, 1978; and, in collaboration with an all-star ensemble of the top American recording artists collectively known as U.S.A. for Africa, *We Are the World,* Columbia, 1985.

Videos

(With the Jacksons) *Blame It On the Boogie,* 1978.
Don't Stop 'Til You Get Enough, 1979.

Rock With Me, 1979.
(With the Jacksons) *Triumph,* 1980.
(With Paul and Linda McCartney) *Say, Say, Say,* 1983.
Billie Jean, 1983.
Beat It, 1983.
Thriller, 1983.
Bad, 1987.
Smooth Criminal, 1988.
Moonwalker, 1989.

Compositions

Has written and co-written numerous songs, including "Shake Your Body (Down to the Grave)," 1978, "Beat It," 1983, "Billie Jean," 1983, "Wanna Be Startin' Somethin'," 1983, (with Lionel Richie) "We Are the World," 1985, "Bad," 1987, "I Can't Stop Loving You," 1987, and "The Way You Make Me Feel," 1987.

Writings

Moonwalk (autobiography), Doubleday, 1988.

Sources

Books

Bego, Mark, *Michael,* Pinnacle Books, 1984.
Bego, Mark, *On the Road With Michael,* Pinnacle Books, 1984.
Brown, Geoff, *Michael Jackson: Body and Soul, an Illustrated Biography,* Beaufort Books, 1984.
George, Nelson, *The Michael Jackson Story,* Dell, 1984.
Latham, Caroline, *Michael Jackson: Thrill,* Zebra Books, 1984.
Machlin, Milt, *The Michael Jackson Catalog,* Arbor House, 1984.

Periodicals

Ebony, June, 1988.
Essence, July, 1988.
Jet, May 16, 1988.
Macleans, July 23, 1984.
Newsweek, July 16, 1987.
People, June 11, 1984; July 23, 1984; August 27, 1984; September 14, 1987; October 12, 1987; March 28, 1988.
Rolling Stone, March 15, 1984; September 24, 1987; October 22, 1987; May 19, 1988.
Time, July 16, 1984; September 14, 1987.

—*Nancy H. Evans*

Al Jarreau

Singer, songwriter

Al Jarreau is regarded by many fans as the quintessential jazz vocalist. Schooled in the jazz tradition that produced such scat singers as Billie Holiday and Nat "King" Cole, Jarreau has adapted the style to become one of jazz-fusion's premier voices. His remarkable versatility and orginality have earned the singer/songwriter widespread acclaim, including two Grammy Awards for best male vocalist as well as several European music awards. Dubbed the Acrobat of Scat, Jarreau, for many critics, stands unrivaled by other singers of his generation.

Born in Milwaukee, Wisconsin, Jarreau grew up as part of a musically inclined family. His father, a Seventh-day Adventist minister, was an accomplished singer, and his mother was a church pianist. Some of Jarreau's earliest musical experiences, in fact, involved church music. As he told Robert Palmer in an interview for *Rolling Stone:* "I can remember rocking on my mother's knee in church, hearing music and being transported by it. I think I got transported sometime way back there and never really came back yet; some part of me is still way off out there."

As a youth, however, Jarreau was exposed to more than just church music. He listened to everything from country music to the then-popular tunes of entertainers such as Patti Page, Frankie Lane, and the Four Freshmen, whose harmonizing ability he particularly admired. In addition, Jarreau sang songs from Broadway shows as a high school student, and he fell in love with jazz. Indeed, throughout his college and graduate school years, as well as during his days as a counselor for the handicapped in San Francisco, Jarreau found time for jazz.

Finally, in 1968, the singer decided to give up his counseling career and devote his full attention to music. Although he had been singing in San Francisco night clubs as a sideline to his primary career, even performing with pianist George Duke's jazz trio, the transition to full-time musicianship was a difficult one for Jarreau. He spent nearly a year teamed with Brazilian guitarist Julio Martinez, entertaining at Gatsby's, a jazz club in Sausalito, California, then moved on to Los Angeles and subsequently to New York City. But despite performances in many eminent venues, Jarreau was unable to secure a recording contract. Though this was not considered unusual in the late 1960s, when heavy metal and acid rock were in vogue, Jarreau decided to head back to his hometown, Milwaukee, where he temporarily fronted his own jazz-rock group.

Shortly thereafter, Jarreau returned to Los Angeles, where, still unable to interest the record producers, he continued to develop his repertoire of vocal techniques and began creating his own lyrics. Before long he

For the Record. . .

Full name, Alwyn Lopez Jarreau; born March 12, 1940, in Milwaukee, Wis.; son of Emile (a minister and welder) and Pearl (a pianist) Jarreau; married Phyllis Hall (divorced); married second wife, Susan. *Education:* Ripon College, B.S., 1962; University of Iowa, M.S., 1964.

Worked as a counselor for the handicapped in San Francisco, Calif., 1965-68; jazz vocalist and composer, 1968—; solo recording artist, 1975—. Has appeared on television and in film.

Awards: Named outstanding male vocalist by German Music Academy, 1976; named number one jazz vocalist by *Cashbox* magazine, 1976; Italian Music Critics Award for best foreign vocalist, 1977; winner of *down beat* magazine readers' poll for best male vocalist, 1977-81; Grammy Awards from National Academy of Recording Arts and Sciences, 1978 and 1979, for best male vocalist; Emmy Award nomination from National Academy of Television Arts and Sciences, 1985, for musical theme for television series "Moonlighting"; recipient of Mabel Mercer Award.

Addresses: *Office*—c/o Patrick Rains, 8752 Holloway Dr., Los Angeles, Calif. 90069.

pop, *Look to the Rainbow* was a live recording, and *All Fly Home* combined originals with oldies. Although Jarreau had toured Europe, where he was enormously popular, the artist remained relatively unknown in the United States, despite Grammy Awards for best male jazz vocalist in 1978 and 1979, until the commercial success of *Breakin' Away* in 1981.

Jarreau's very success, however, has given some critics cause for disappointment. There are reviewers, for example, who disparage *Breakin' Away* for relying on formula ballads that please pop fans while neglecting

> *Dubbed the Acrobat of Scat, Jarreau, for many critics, stands unrivaled by other singers of his generation.*

the scat skills that have made Jarreau one of jazz-fusion's top talents. Similar laments have greeted the artist's succeeding albums, with recent releases, like *High Crime* and *L Is for Lover,* regarded by jazz purists as pop-funk style commercial recordings.

Regardless of the criticism accorded his albums, however, Jarreau rarely gives anything but superlative live performances. Indeed, the Acrobat of Scat is a charismatic performer who delights in displaying the full range of his vocal talents—and who refuses to be limited by anyone. As he told *down beat*'s Steve Bloom: "I like to do a lot of music, so I don't intend to be confined by my critics or anybody else. I might want to do some punk rock & roll someday. And I like to sing rhythm & blues, too. I may funk for an album and then do some jazz. Or my next thing might be inspired by some classical piece of music 'cause that's in me too. But you can be sure of one thing—whatever it is I do, it'll always be fine music."

became a popular performer at Studio City's Bla Bla Cafe, and his career was launched after Warner Bros. president, Mo Austin, heard him perform at the Troubador in Hollywood. Austin signed the singer to a contract in 1975, and Warner Bros. released his first album, *We Got By,* that same year.

Comprised mostly of original songs, *We Got By* showcased the versatility and inventiveness that had earned Jarreau such a devoted local following. He is most highly praised for his innovative scat singing. Scat, an improvisational vocal style that evolved with be-bop in the 1940s, uses nonsense words and syllables for vocal effect. Jarreau is credited with both continuing and adapting the tradition of such greats as Billie Holiday, Nat "King" Cole, John Hendricks, and Dave Lambert. Writing for *Rolling Stone,* Robert Palmer observed that "while the scat singers of previous generations imitated saxophones and trumpets with their *shun-diddly-do-wahs* and jazz drummers with their *oop-bop-sh'bams,* Jarreau imitates the electronic and percussive hardware of the Seventies."

After *We Got By,* Jarreau continued to record well-received albums. His next, *Glow,* incorporated some

Selected discography

Released by Warner Bros.

We Got By, 1975.
Glow, 1975.
Look to the Rainbow, 1977.
All Fly Home, 1980.
This Time, 1981.

Breakin' Away, 1981.
Jarreau, 1983.
High Crime, 1984.
Jarreau in London, 1985.
L Is for Lover, 1986.

Sources

Books

Coryell, Julie, and Laura Friedman, *Jazz-Rock Fusion: The People, the Music,* Dell, 1978.

Periodicals

down beat, March 23, 1978; April 19, 1979; February, 1981; February, 1982.
Essence, August, 1979; February, 1982; March, 1985.
Jet, April 8, 1985; August 18, 1986; November 16, 1987.
New York Times, May 8, 1984.
Rolling Stone, January 25, 1979; October 29, 1981.

—Nancy H. Evans

Keith Jarrett

Pianist and composer

In the February 1989 *down beat,* Josef Woodward described the unique artistry and career of Keith Jarrett: "Like an unruly, self-determined river, Keith Jarrett's pursuit of musical truth has taken him in a multiplicity of directions, either coursing a wide swath or branching off into tiny tangential reivulets. Similarly, his audience has been alternately swept up by the current, carried into the sidestreams, or has been left behind on the riverbanks." Celebrated for his virtuosity and eclecticism, the pianist has continued to experiment with the possibilities of the keyboard.

Jarrett was born in Allentown, Pennsylvania, in 1945. He began to play the piano as a child, and started formal composition training at 15. Jarrett spent a year at the Berklee School of Music in Boston but moved to New York to perform. Participation in Monday jam sessions at the Village Vanguard led to his first engagements. He toured with many of the most important ensembles in 1960s jazz, including Art Blakeley's Jazz Messengers and experimental saxophonist Rahsaan Roland Kirk, and became the acoustic pianist for the Charles Lloyd Quartet on its succesful tours of Western and Eastern Europe, the centers of popularity for American jazz.

Jarrett's compositions "Days and Nights Waiting" (1966) and "Sorcery" (1967) were given premieres in Europe by Lloyd's Quartet. His own experimentation in these early years included one album of songs, *Restoration Ruin* (Vortex, 1968), on which he played and overdubbed parts on the soprano saxophone, recorder, harmonica, guitar, piano, organ, electric bass, drums, bongos, tambourine, and sistra. When Lloyd's group disbanded in 1969, Jarrett played with other jazz innovators, most notably Miles Davis, but he also travelled and recorded with his own trio (Ornette Coleman veteran Charlie Haden on bass, and Bill Evans sideman Paul Motian on drums), adding saxophonist Dewey Redman in 1971 for their first album, *Birth.* The quartet's second album, *Expectations,* was awarded the French Grand Prix for Jazz (1971).

Remaining devoted to the acoustic piano, despite the contemporary fashion for the electronic keyboard, Jarrett continued to write music for his own group. He has also composed for larger numbers and has integrated existing classical music ensembles into his works, as he did with the American Brass Quintet and the string section of the Stuttgart Philharmonic on his double album *In the Light* (1976). His association with ECM has continued based on his collaborations with producer Manfred Eicher, and his jazz and classical compositions are released by that label. His most popular ECM albums are the solo piano recordings *Facing You, Solo Concerts,* and *The Koln Concert.* (1975).

Jarrett's reputation grew during the 1970s in Europe and the United States. His honors included a Guggenheim Fellowship for composition and being named *Rolling Stone*'s Jazz Artist of 1973 and *down beat*'s Composer and Pianist of the Year, 1975. *Solo Concerts* (1974) was named record of the year by *down beat, Stereo Review, Jazz Forum, Time* and the *New York Times*. Jarrett began to split his time between his American quartet and the group of Scandinavian musicians (Jan Gabarek, Jo Christensen, and Palle Danieslsson) with whom he recorded *Belonging* (1974). He brought them to New York in 1979 and sold out the venerable jazz club, the Village Vanguard, for five nights.

A return to classical piano performance began in the early 1980s as he performed the solo parts of concerti with orchestras. His repertory included the classics of 20th century composition, such as *Concerti* by Samuel Barber, Bela Bartok (2nd and 3rd) and Igor Stravinsky *(Concerto for Piano and Woodwinds),* as well as commissioned works by Lou Harrison and Peggy Glanville-Hicks. He has also given piano recitals of the classical repertory, favoring Bach, Handel, Scarlatti, and Shostakovich; and has recorded Bach's *Well Tempered Clavier.* Crossover critic John Rockwell wrote of Jarrett's first recital in the *New York Times:* "His interpretations had much to recommend them. . . . He has a venturesome musical mind, eager to embrace new music and new ways of playing familiar music."

In a 1989 *down beat* article, Jarrett analyzed the differences between playing the fully realized Bach compositions and the jazz standards: "In the case of the 'Well Tempered Clavier,' I can see so clearly the process. The logic and motion of these lines makes beautiful sense . . . I'm just more or less following his weave. He's woven this thing and I'm reproducing it by hand. . . . In standards, there's only a sketch, this single line with harmony. So I have to invent the rest of the rug." He described "My Song," which *down beat* called his "most hummable" work, this way: "If somebody can write 'My Song,' then either they have [a] brainstorm and wrote this deceptively simple piece that everybody likes when they hear it, or they know what they're doing."

Jarrett is best known for his improvisatory performances—a musical genre that owes much to Baroque keyboard composers such as Bach and Scarlatti and to the traditions of jazz. In an article by James Lincoln Collier in the *New York Times Magazine,* Jarrett described the depth of his "Tabula-rasa approach to jazz improvising" as "I like to turn off the thought process. I'd like to forget that I even have hands. I'd like to sit down as if I'd never played the piano before." He continues to write music and cites a wind quintet and viola concerto as current projects for 1989.

Selected discography

Restoration Ruin, Vortex, 1968.
Birth, Atlantic, 1971.
Expectations, Columbia, 1972.
Belonging, ECM, 1974.
Solo Concerts (triple-album), ECM, 1974.
The Koln Concert, ECM, 1975.
In the Light, ECM, 1976.
My Song, ECM, 1977.
Facing You, ECM.

Sources

down beat, April 17, 1969; February, 1989.
New York Times, March 26, 1985; March 30, 1987.
New York Times Magazine, January 7, 1979.

—*Barbara Stratyner*

Stanley Jordan

Guitarist, composer

Stanley Jordan grabbed the music world by the ears when he arrived in New York in 1984. Musicians and critics alike were blown away by the guitarist's radical approach to the instrument, which left listeners shaking their heads in disbelief. Jordan's technique of using both hands to tap the fingerboard like a pianist (as opposed to the traditional method of strumming with one hand and fingering with the other) allows him to play chords, melodies, and bass lines simultaneously. Players like Jimmy Webster and Eddie Van Halen had previously used the tapping technique to embellish their solos. But never before had anyone been as innovative with the concept as Jordan, who, according to guitarist Al DiMeola in *Guitar Player* magazine, "has taken tapping into another dimension. He has to be twenty years ahead of his time."

The road to New York began at an early age for Jordan. Born in Chicago and raised in California, he started his musical training with classical piano lessons at age six. A short period with the trumpet a few years later eventually led him to the guitar at a time when guitar heroes were becoming household names. It was during this period that he discovered his biggest influence, Jimi Hendrix, while reading an article at a doctor's office.

"One of the main reasons I got interested in jazz was from listening to [Hendrix]. . . . I came to realize that the sky is the limit, that there's no upper level to the content of the music," Jordan told *Guitar World.* He added that he was led to look for other musical forms, mainly jazz, that were beyond what he knew. "And the only reason I was searching in the first place was because of the inspiration I got from Jimi Hendrix."

Shortly after picking up the guitar, Jordan began playing in soul and rock bands. By age fifteen he was captivated by the sounds of jazz music and his six-string instrument, but he wanted to bring the flexibility of piano to the guitar. Frustrated with having to deal with all the complex fingerings of standard tuning (E,A,D,G,B,E), Jordan began experimenting with alternate tunings. He finally arrived at what is now known as fourths-tuning (E,A,D,G,C,F). The combination opened new doors for the teenager in his effort to simplify the guitar's fretboard. As he told *Guitar World:* "Now I had hundreds of chords with about half as much to learn. And that was really significant. The whole world seemed to open up after that. I could begin to think more about music and less about mechanics."

Just six months after his tuning breakthrough, he began to toy with the idea of tapping. Because he was basically pioneering the field, Jordan had very little information to rely on except for his piano training. That knowledge and coordination helped him to perfect the tap technique, and he soon developed his own theory system to complement it. He calls it the chromatic system (briefly, the system utilizes the chromatic scale as opposed to the major scale for measuring intervals, and starts at zero instead of one when counting intervals).

Enrollment at Princeton University in 1977 yielded some startling news for the young guitarist. Faculty member Milton Babbitt had devised a similar system in the late 1950s. The two began working together, and Babbitt eventually became Jordan's adviser. Besides music theory, Jordan studied computers and their role in music composition, a field in which he continued to break ground even after graduating.

Armed with his degree in music, Jordan set out to conquer the Big Apple. In 1983 he released a self-produced LP entitled *Touch Sensitive.* While it contained all the trademarks of his remarkable style, the all-solo effort did little for advancing his career. He literally resorted to playing in the streets, dues-paying which eventually caught the attention of some of the jazz world's heavyweights. He wound up auditioning for impressario George Wein, which led to an unannounced performance at the 1984 Kool Jazz Festival. That gig was impressive enough to earn Jordan the right to open for Trumpeter Wynton Marsalis at Avery Fisher Hall. Stanley had indeed arrived.

In 1985 the jazz guitarist rose nearer the top with the release of *Magic Touches.* The record, produced by Al DiMeola, sold over 400,000 copies worldwide, an incredible number for an instrumental jazz album. Aspiring guitarists went back to their woodsheds while the critics' praise dispelled any notions that Jordan's tap technique was merely a gimmick. Dan Forte wrote in *Guitar Player,* "His music is valid *regardless* of the fact that he employs exclusively two-handed tapping—*what* he plays is as important as *how* he plays it." In the 20th anniversary issue of *Guitar Player,* Jim Ferguson selected it as one of the twenty essential jazz LP's of all time, stating that it "immediately assured him a prominent place in the annals of guitar history." The success of *Magic Touches* allowed Jordan some time off to delve back into computers, but a restless public necessitated the early release of his follow-up album.

While his first major outing contained three originals, various ensembles and a few punched-in solos, Jordan shifted gears for his next effort. Entitled *Standards, Volume I,* it was recorded live and completely unaccompanied in the studio. *down beat* reviewer Frank-John Hadley complained about poor song selection but still gave it a four-star rating. That in itself is a testament to Jordan's brilliant musicianship. His 1988 release, *Flying Home,* contains only one non-original, which should negate any complaints that might be left over from *Standards.* With eight compositions of his own, Jordan is just beginning to tap his writing skills.

Selected discography

Touch Sensitive, Tangent, 1983.
Magic Touch, Blue Note, 1985.
One Night With Blue Note (with others), Blue Note.
Hideaway (with Stanley Clarke), Epic, 1986.
Standards, Volume I, Blue Note, 1987.
Blind Date (film soundtrack; with others), Rhino, 1987.
Morning Desire (with Kenny Rogers), RCA.
Artists Against Apartheid—Sun City (with others), EMI.
RU Tuff Enough (with Rebee Jackson), Columbia.

Also recorded music for "The Bill Cosby Show."

Sources

down beat, March, 1987.
Guitar Player, September, 1983; July, 1984; May, 1985; October, 1985; December, 1985; February, 1986; January, 1987; February, 1987; December, 1987.
Guitar World, May, 1984; September, 1985; September, 1986; January, 1987; March, 1987; April, 1987.

—Calen D. Stone

B.B. King

"Riley B. King is the world's preeminent blues guitarist," wrote Tom Wheeler in *Guitar Player*. "There is hardly a rock, pop, or blues player anywhere who doesn't owe him something." B.B. King was born in 1925 in the area between Itta Bena and Indianola, Mississippi. When he was four his parents separated, and his mother took him to the hills near Kilmichael to be with her family. She died when King was nine. After he turned thirteen his father found him, and together they went to Lexington, Mississippi, to live. They stayed together for only a few years before King ran away back to Indianola.

Until he was inducted into the Army in 1943, King had spent his entire childhood as a laborer on farms, where he was first exposed to the blues. "I guess the earliest sound of blues that I can remember was in the fields while people would be pickin' cotton or choppin' or somethin', " he told *Living Blues*. "When I sing and play now I can hear those same sounds that I used to hear then as a kid."

His first musical influence, however, came through religion. A member of the Church of God In Christ, he was forbidden to play blues at home. He sang in spiritual groups like the Elkhorn Singers and Saint John's Gospel Singers. A relative who was a guitarist and a preacher showed King his first chords on the instrument. As a teenager he began playing streetcorners for coins, combining gospel songs with the blues. When he started making more money playing in one night than he would in a week on the farm, he decided to head to Memphis. After a few years, King went back to Indianola to work and repay some debts, eventually returning to Memphis to stay.

He moved in with his cousin Booker (Bukka) White, the famous slide guitarist. In an attempt to duplicate the stinging sound of the steel slide, King developed the trilling vibrato which has since become his trademark. With the help of the late Sonny Boy Williamson he began singing radio commercials on station WDIA, which led to a three-and-a-half year stint as a disc jockey. He was known as "the blues boy from Beale Street," later shortened to B.B. The records he spun on his show would come to have a great impact on his own playing. Artists as diverse as Frank Sinatra, Roy Brown, Louis Jordan, Nat Cole, Django Reinhardt, and especially T-Bone Walker, were absorbed, interpreted and presented in the polished sound now known as the "B.B. King style of blues".

"Technically, harmoncially, conceptually far in advance of his postwar contemporaries, B.B. King developed the single most satisfying, popular and influential of all modern blues approaches," wrote *Guitar World*'s Pete Welding. Many critics have cited King's wide range of

Full name, Riley B. King; born September 16, 1925, near Indianola, Miss.; son of Albert and Nora Ella (Pully) King; married twice; children: eight.

As a child, worked as a farmhand, began singing in spiritual groups, and learned to play guitar; as a teenager, played for money on streetcorners; sang on radio commercials; disc jockey, 1949-53; began recording while working as a disc jockey; played in small clubs from the mid-1950s until the mid-1960s; began playing larger venues in the mid-1960s; has toured extensively throughout the United States and around the world, appearing in concerts, at blues festivals, on television, and in films. Co-founder of Foundation for the Advancement of Inmate Rehabilitation and Recreation (FAIRR); has made more than 40 concert appearances at San Quentin prison. Columist for *Guitar Player* magazine, 1983. *Military service:* U.S. Army, 1943.

Awards: Golden Mike Award, National Association of Television and Radio Artists, 1969 and 1974; Academie du Jazz award (France), 1969; Grammy Award for best rhythm & blues vocal, male, 1970, for "The Thrill Is Gone"; a "Day of Blues" was established in his honor by the city of Memphis, Tenn., 1971; presented with key to city of Cleveland, Ohio, 1971; "B.B. King Day" was established by the governor of Mississippi, 1972; honorary doctorate from Tongaloo College, 1973; Humanitarian Award, B'nai B'rith Music and Performance Lodge of New York, 1973; NAACP Image Award, 1975; "B.B. King Day" was established in city of Berkeley, Calif., 1976; honorary doctor of music, Yale University, 1977, and Berkley College of Music, 1985; Grammy Award for best traditional blues recording, 1986, for "My Guitar Sings the Blues"; Lifetime Achievement Award, National Academy of Recording Arts and Sciences, 1987; has received awards from numerous magazine reader polls.

Addresses: *Office*—c/o MCA Records, 100 University City Plaza, North Hollywood, CA 91608.

influences, from jazz to gospel to country blues, as the main reason for his widespread popularity.

While at WDIA King recorded four sides for the Bullet record company. He was starting to gather a small following, but it wasn't until the 1951 release of "Three O'Clock Blues" that things started to really happen. The single was a number one hit, staying on the charts for over four months. Like many of King's hits, he did not write it. It was penned by Lowell Fulson, as was "Every-day I Have the Blues," another hit for King. In fact, many of the songs that have become synonymous with King were non-originals, but all contained his stylistic stamp: "How Blue Can You Get" by Louis Jordan, "Rock Me Mama" by Arthur Crudup and Lil Son Jackson, "Sweet Little Angel" by Tampa Red, and "Sweet Sixteen" by Big Joe Turner.

King recorded for the Bihari brothers' Modern label (and its subsidiaries—RPM, Kent, and Crown) from 1950 to 1961 and settled finally with ABC (MCA). In 1964 he released the blues benchmark album "Live at the Regal." In *Guitar Player* Dan Forte called it *The classic album of urban blues. . . . The master works the throng into a frenzy, like an evangelist at a tent revival."*

Until 1965, King played the chitlin' circuit almost endlessly, averaging well over 300 nights per year. His early popularity had died down, but the blues revival of the sixties gave his career a second wind. Musicians like Eric Clapton and Mike Bloomfield praised King's guitarmanship and influence and acknowledged their debt to him. White audiences rediscovered the "King of the Blues" as he started performing in larger concert halls and Las Vegas clubs. In 1969 he scored his first and only Top 20 pop hit with "The Thrill is Gone."

> *"Riley B. King is the world's preeminent blues guitarist. There is hardly a rock, pop, or blues player anywhere who doesn't owe him something."*

King has continued touring and recording albums (over 50 to date). His late seventies efforts, produced by the Crusaders, may have disappointed traditional blues fans but showed that he was still trying to expand his audience. The early eighties saw him scoring music for the film "Into the Night." Throughout his quest to sanctify the blues, B.B. King has fought sterotypes and forged new musical styles, all the while remaining true to his roots.

In a *Rolling Stone* interview King stated: "I was almost afraid to say that I was a blues singer. Because it looked like people kind of looked down on you a lot of times when you mention the word blues. But I thank God today I can stick out my chest and say, yeah, I'm a blues singer!"

Selected discography

LPs

Anthology of the Blues, Kent.
Better Than Ever, Kent.
Boss of the Blues, Kent.
Doing My Thing, Lord, Kent.
From the Beginning, Kent.
Incredible Soul of B.B. King, Kent.
The Jungle, Kent.
Greatest Hits of B.B. King, Kent.
Let Me Love You, Kent.
Live, B.B. King on Stage, Kent.
Original "Sweet Sixteen," Kent.
Pure Soul, Kent.
Rock & Roll Festival, Vol. 1, Kent.
Turn On With B.B. King, Kent.
Super Rhythm & Blues Hits, Kent.
Underground Blues, Kent.
Live at the Regal, MCA, 1965.
Electric B.B. King, MCA, 1969.
Completely Well, MCA, 1970.
Indianola Mississippi Seeds, ABC, 1970.
Live and Well, MCA, 1970.
Live in Cook County Jail, MCA, 1971.
Back in the Alley, MCA, 1973.
Best of B.B. King, MCA.
Guitar Player, MCA.
Love Me Tender, MCA, 1982.

Take It Home, MCA.
Rhythm & Blues Christmas, United Artists.
Midnight Believer, MCA, 1984.

Sources

Books

Dalton, David, and Lenny Kaye, *Rock 100*, Grosset & Dunlap, 1977.
Evans, Tom, and Mary Anne Evans, *Guitars from Renaissance to Rock*, Facts on File, 1982.
Guralnick, Peter, *The Listener's Guide to the Blues*, Facts on File, 1982.
Miller, Jim, editor, *The Rolling Stone Illustrated History of Rock & Roll*, Random House, 1976, revised edition, 1980.
The Rolling Stone Interviews, St. Martin's, 1981.

Periodicals

down beat, October, 1987.
Guitar Player, September, 1980; November, 1982; February, 1983; March, 1983; May, 1984; August, 1984; August 1985; May, 1986; September, 1986; January, 1987; December, 1987.
Guitar World, September, 1988.
Living Blues, May-June, 1988.

—*Calen D. Stone*

Kitaro

New Age musician and composer

Surrounded by banks of synthesizer keyboards, Kitaro eases out a seamless thread of flowing, melodic sounds. Is it enhanced elevator music or the harkening sound of the new age? The category New Age came along after 1977, when Kitaro began releasing his long list of successful solo albums. But he embraces the philosophy that this new style of music reaches to our hearts, that it can uplift us to a spiritual peace, that music can heal.

As he told John Diliberto in *down beat:* "The sound has a power for humans, for nature. I took two speakers and in front of each I placed a flower. On one side came loud music, on the other side came my music. After one week, the flower in front of my music is bending towards the speaker, the other one is dead. I think it is the same thing for humans." No innocent humility here. But as Diliberto expresses it: "The problem is, he *is* innocent. Kitaro has a childlike demeanor that is disarming. I looked for guile and found utter guilessness."

New Age music has been as much maligned as praised. Most musicians who fit the mold despise the term because they feel it fails to include their individual expression of this new musical style. But Kitaro does not seem to object to the categorization. He has sold millions of albums in Japan, and after a long period as a cult figure in the United States has emerged as a premier New Age star.

Kitaro was born in Japan in 1953. His given name is Masanori Takahashi, but he has taken the stage name Kitaro, which means "man of joy and love." His first instrument was acoustic guitar, and he lists the Beatles and British progressive rock bands like Pink Floyd and King Crimson among his influences. His introduction to the synthesizer came in 1970 when he worked with the Far East Family Band. German synthesizer wizard Klaus Schulze produced two albums by the group: *Nipponjin* and *Parallel World.* "I feel that the music [the Far East Family Band] pursued was more inwardly directed," Kitaro told *down beat.* "It was a more personal expression. When the time came for me to go solo, it wasn't a dramatic change or departure, but rather a natural progression of the expression of the deep inner self."

In the mid-1970s Kitaro lived at the ashram of free-love guru Bhagwan Shree Rajneesh. Although he took on the trappings of conversion, he claims that his main purpose was to learn chanting and music for meditation. He gives credit for his creations to a power beyond himself. "This music is not from my mind," he told *Rolling Stone.* "It is from heaven, going through my body and out my fingers through composing. Sometimes I wonder. I never practice. I don't read or write music, but my fingers move. I wonder 'Whose song is this?' I write my songs, but they are not my songs."

In 1977 he released his first solo album, *Ten Kai-Astral Trip.* Ten years and about a dozen albums later, the United States was ready for Kitaro. His first American tour, which began in the fall of 1987, attracted listeners of all ages and lifestyles. The touring band consisted of seven musicians, with Kitaro matching his banks of synthesizers against two other keyboardists and a guitarist, violinist, drummer, and percussionist. A light show added dramatic flair. *USA Today* reported that the bank recreated what Kitaro calls "impressionistic music" or "sound pictures." At times his show, like his records, is cosmic, almost like a science fiction soundtrack, with high-decibel sparkling tones. Other times, it sounds like music from terra firma, an electronic flute singing to the cascading waves of the ocean.

Kitaro's albums, originally only available as expensive Japanese imports, have all been released on the German Kuckuck label and in the United States on Gramavision. Geffen Records also offers Kitaro releases, although some are compilations or are confusingly retitled. *Audio* described the 1986 Geffen release, *Asia,* this way: "It surely is excellent music to zone out with."

For the Record. . .

Real name, Masanori Takahashi; born 1953, in Japan. Began playing acoustic guitar; played keyboard synthesizers with Far East Family Band, beginning 1970; began recording solo albums, 1977; has toured throughout the Far East and North America.

Addresses: *Office*—Geffen Records, 9130 Sunset Blvd., Los Angeles, CA 90069.

Relaxing music with a spiritual flair is what many listeners turn to New Age music for, but there is a danger if the artist does not evidence some level of progression. A 1987 *Audio* review of the album *Tenku* stated: "Now, more than a dozen albums later, Kitaro is still doing it. Taken on it's own, *Tenku* is magnificent. Kitaro bends synthesizer technology in strangely delicate ways, obtaining a nuance of expression that few can match. His Asian melodies bolstered by thickly layered harmonies, are tinged with melancholy. However, among the romantic cosmic feelings that Kitaro evokes is a sense of *deja vu.* I've heard it all before."

Perhaps Kitaro's best-known and most representative work is contained in the *Silk Road* albums which were drawn from the sound track music for a long-running Japanese television series. A *down beat* review said that "*Silk Road* is seductive and intoxicating, forming a musical veil with the translucency of Japanese rice paper" but criticized compositional weaknesses. *Rolling Stone* described the album's music as "serene, seductively melodic electronic compositions that, at their best, evoke the fragile tension of Japanese traditional music and, at their worst, veer sharply into middle-of-the-road."

Kitaro's music is unique to the ear of most Western listeners. Many will find it pleasant, relaxing, even mystical. Some will find it too nebulous to be really satisfying. It is unlikely that Kitaro will be bothered or inspired by any critical ruminations—he'll just go on producing his own best creations as he hears them. *USA Today* characterized him this way: "He is more than just another Japanese musician seeking worldwide recognition. Kitaro's compositions *are* mystical and they are enhancing legions of listeners. In fact, the more one learns about him, his lifestyle, and his history, the more incredible he becomes."

Selected discography

Solo Albums

Astral Voyage, Geffen.
From the Full Moon Story, Geffen, 1985.
Oasis, Gramavision.
Silk Road Volumes 1 & 2, Gramavision, 1982.
In Person Digital, Gramavision.
Tunhuang, Gramavision.
Ki, Gramavision.
Millenia, Geffen, 1985.
Asia, Geffen, 1986.
India, Geffen.
Toward the West, Geffen, 1986.
Silver Cloud, Geffen, 1985.
Tenku, Geffen, 1986.
The Light of the Spirit, Geffen 1988.

With the Far East Family Band

Parallel World, Mu Land.
Nipponjin, Vertigo.

Sources

Audio, September, 1986; January, 1987; July, 1988.
down beat, September, 1982; January, 1988.
Rolling Stone, December 18, 1986.
USA Today, January, 1988.

—*Tim LaBorie*

Gladys Knight

Singer

"Of all the voices in the pop pantheon, one of the richest, warmest and most comforting belongs to Gladys Knight. . . . Knight's husky, raw honey vocals are full of heat and miles deep. From the beginning, Knight's was a strikingly seasoned voice, dark and smokey, intense but contained, more glowing than explosive." Vince Aletti's praise for the vocal power of Gladys Knight is only one of the many such descriptions that she has received over her more than thirty years of performing and recording with the Pips. Together, Gladys Knight and the Pips are one of the classic R&B and crossover groups whose sound has grown in popularity from the heyday of Motown in the early 1960s to the present day.

Born in Alabama in 1944, Gladys Knight was a gospel singer from childhood. Her debut was made at the Mount Mariah Baptist Church in Atlanta at the age of four. She was a prize winner on the Ted Mack "Amateur Hour" in 1952, singing popular solos. The Pips were invented when she joined with her bother Merald ("Bubba") and cousin William Guest to perform at a family party. Knight told the *New York Times* that their first professional engagement was singing "Canadian Summer" and "In the Still of the Night" at a Y.M.C.A. tea. They performed pop music as the Pips, opening for such soul stars are Sam Cooke, and maintained the gospel audience by singing as the Fontaineers. Their first single, "Whistle My Love," was released by Brunswick in 1957. Their first hit, "Every Beat of My Heart," although reaching the Top 20 Rhythm and Blues chart, was pirated and earned them no money.

Knight told *Ebony* that her status as lead vocalist developed by accident, but theirs was a contemporary sound in the early 1960s, when male and female close harmony groups were popular. The creative dance routines and exquisite harmonies of the Pips evolved in time, along with Knight's own voice, influenced by the song stylists whom she heard on recordings. In a 1983 interview in the *New York Times,* she defended the unified sound of the group: "Throughout our career, people have tried to break us up. Because my voice is out front most of the time, they tend to want to separate that personality. But we know differently. People don't know why the picture is being painted so beautifully. One reason is that the background voices—the 'oohs and ahs' against the powerful lines I'm singing—work on the subconscious. They make the picture complete."

In 1965, Gladys Knight and the Pips (by now Merald Knight, William Guest, and their cousin Edward Patten) joined Motown Records, home of the black close harmony sound. They soon began a string of successes for the R&B and crossover markets with such songs as "Just Walk in My Shoes," "I Heard It Through the

For the Record. . .

Full name, Gladys Maria Knight; born May 28, 1944, in Atlanta, Ga.; daughter of Merald, Sr., and Elizabeth (Woods) Knight; married Barry Hankerson, October, 1984; children: (previous marriage) Kenya, James; (second marriage) Shanga. *Education:* Graduated from high school.

Made singing debut at age four at Mt. Mariah Baptist Church, Atlanta, Ga.; toured with Morris Brown Choir, 1950-53, and performed at numerous recitals at local churches and schools; member of vocal group Gladys Knight and the Pips (originally known as just the Pips), 1953—; began recording 1957; has toured throughout the world, and has made a number of television appearances.

Awards: Two Grammy Awards; NAACP Image Award; numerous awards from magazine readers polls.

Addresses: *Office*—c/o MCA Records, 445 Park Ave., New York, NY 10022. *Agent*—Sidney A. Seidenberg, 1414 Avenue of the Americas, New York, NY 10019.

Grapevine," and "The End of the Road." Touring with the Motown Revue, along with television appearances, helped bring the unique performance style of Knight and the Pips to the general audience.

Unhappy with their status at Motown (which then featured the Supremes, the Temptations, and Marvin Gaye), they switched to Buddah records at the conclusion of their contract. Ironically, their final Motown recording, "Neither One of Us," became their first number-one crossover hit single. The mid-1970s was a period of personal triumphs for the group, which had a hit album, *Imagination,* four gold singles, "Midnight Train to Georgia" (1973's number 1), "Imagination," "On and On," and "Best Thing That Ever Happened to Me." They won Grammy awards for "Neither One of Us" (Best Pop Vocal) and "Midnight Train" (Best R&B Vocal Performance). *I Feel a Song,* although not as succesful as *Imagination,* featured a performance of the Oscar- and Grammy-winning Marvin Hamlisch song, "The Way We Were," putting Knight in direct competition with Barbra Streisand. Knight's version reached number 11, despite the tremendous publicity campaign for Streisand's single and the soundtrack album. The group was featured on a television special on NBC in the summer of 1975.

Contractual problems between Buddah and Columbia Records forced Knight and the Pips to record separately in the late 1970s, although they continued to perform together in person. Their "reunion" albums, *About Love* (1980), *Touch* (1982), and *Visions* (1983), produced a new string of hit singles, among them "Landlord," "Save the Overtime for Me," and "You're Number One." They currently record for MCA, which released their album *All Our Love* and most recent hit single, "Love Overboard."

Knight has acted in films, such as "Pipe Dreams" (1976), and on television, including a season as Flip Wilson's wife on the comedy series "Charlie and Company" (CBS, 1985-1986). She has also produced television musical specials, among them the highly acclaimed "Sisters in the Name of Love" (HBO, 1986), which featured the voices of Patti LaBelle and Dionne Warwick.

The continuity of the Pips is unique as both a back-up group and a close-harmony trio. Their voices mesh perfectly, and the rhythm that they maintain on stage with their dance routines is perceptible even on record-

> *Gladys Knight was a gospel singer from childhood. Her debut was made at the Mount Mariah Baptist Church in Atlanta at the age of four.*

ings. Although Knight and the Pips record music by a variety of artists, many of their songs have lyrics by Pip William Guest. He told *Ebony* his feelings about the group's image: "We dig being funky, but we will never exploit that to the point of lewd bumps and grinds. Our roots are in our culture, so that's where our future lies."

The group tours constantly in the United States and Europe. Despite their unquestioned popularity around the world, Gladys Knight and the Pips have always been considered an act that was unable to reach its full professional potential. An article in *Rolling Stone,* for example, asked in its sub-head "Why can't [Gladys Knight] score with a mainstream audience?" The recordings she made with the Pips that were in direct competition with other artists' seem to bear out her claim that they were not allowed to cross over as did Marvin Gaye's "Heard It Through the Grapevine." Their continuing success, however, makes their fans hope that they, at least, will be able to continue buying records—no matter how they are marketed.

Selected discography

"I Heard It Through the Grapevine" (single), Motown, 1967.

"Neither One of Us [Wants to be the First to Say Goodbye]" (single), Motown, 1973.

Imagination (includes "Midnight Train to Georgia," "Imagination," and "Best Thing That Ever Happened to Me"), Buddah, 1973.

I Feel a Song (includes "The Way We Were"), Buddah, 1975.

About Love (includes "Landlord"), Columbia, 1980.

Visions (includes "Save the Overtime for Me" and "You're Number One"), Columbia, 1983.

All Our Love (includes "Love Overboard"), MCA, 1988.

Sources

Ebony, June 1973; November 1980.

New York Times, October 7, 1983; April 29, 1978.

Rolling Stone, June 30, 1988.

—Barbara Stratyner

Ladysmith Black Mambazo

South African a capella group

"Humanity's first instrument was the human voice." This is the basic philosophy behind much of post-modern experimental performance. It is also the truth behind the music that a Zulu choir has brought out of South Africa into recording and concert prominence in the United States in recent years. The ten members of Ladysmith Black Mambazo were the best-selling group in the Union of South Africa. Now, thanks to their participation in Paul Simon's *Graceland* album and tour, they have become popular recording artists in the United States as well.

The group, led by Joseph Shabalala, present a Zulu harmonic and variation style known as *mbube*. Stefan Grossman, distributor of the group's albums on Shanachie Records and a major figure in the rise of knowledgable audiences for African music in America, has described their style as "a timeless beauty that transcends culture, language and all other artificial barriers dividing humanity." American audiences, as attracted by the beat as the shifting harmonies, have purchased Ladysmith Black Mambazo's own four albums, *Induku Zethu,*

For the Record. . .

Founded by leader **Joseph Shabalala**; other members include **Abednigo Mazibuko, Albert Mazibuko, Geophrey Mdletshe, Russel Methembu, Jabulane Mwelase, Inos Phungula, Ben Shabalala, Headman Shabalala,** and **Jockey Shabalala**; very popular in South Africa, the group came to prominence in the United States after performing on the Paul Simon album *Graceland*, 1986; toured with Simon, 1987, and appeared on his television special; has also toured the United States independently and appeared on television series "Saturday Night Live."

Awards: Shared Grammy Award with Paul Simon, for *Graceland*.

Addresses: *Office*—c/o Shanachie Record Corp., P.O. Box 208, Newton, NJ 07860. *Agent*—Triad, 10100 Santa Monica Blvd., 16th Floor, Los Angeles, CA 90067.

Umthombo Wamanzi, Ulwande Olungwele, and *Inala,* in greater and greater numbers.

But it is still as a part of the *Graceland* album, tour, and television special that most North Americans know Ladysmith Black Mambazo. Paul Simon heard the group when he was considering which of the many African musical ensembles to include in his album (which was recorded in London). He selected the group, along with Tao Ea Matsekha, the Boyoyo Boys and others, as examples of the "mbaqanga" sound (roughly translatable as "township jive") which has political connotations within Africa and, as Simon recognized, an internationally attractive beat. Their cuts on the *Graceland* album, "Diamonds on the Soles of her Shoes" and "Homeless" (by Simon and Shabalala), were trememdously succesful, but it was the promotional performances with Simon on NBC's "Saturday Night Live" and their participation in the Graceland concerts that won over America.

New York critics were fervent in their praise of Ladysmith Black Mambazo's sound and show. Commenting on the first set of Graceland performances at the Radio City Music Hall in late April 1987, David Hinckley wrote in the *New York Daily News* that they "won the crowd most easily with amazingly rich 10-part harmony whose elements ranged from call-and-response gospel to rhythm and blues and human beat box." Don Aquilante wrote in the *New York Post* that "the real show-stoppers of the evening were Ladysmith Black Mambazo. . . . I have no idea what [Shabalala] called out in Zulu or what the gentlemen in his band responded, but it was fantastic, joyous, heartfelt, and big. These performers under-

stand music performance is more than sound. They danced, mimed and interacted with one another, breaking any language barrier." The call-and-response mode also caught the attention of Jon Pareles, writing in the *New York Times:* "In a tradition of competitive singing called *iscanthamiya,* Zulu choruses do dance routines while they harmonize, and Ladysmith Black Mambazo, led by Joseph Shabalala, has great moves. Ladysmith's own unaccompanied selections, in Zulu, call for singing and pointing and soft-shoeing."

Critical and audience acclaim was just as positive when the *Graceland* tour returned to New York in July for appearances at Madison Square Garden. Even in that 19,000-seat sports arena, Aquilante wrote in the *New York Post,* "this 10-man Zulu choir has an amazing rapport with the audience." This rapport was also evident in the television special "Graceland: The African Concert," taped in Zimbabwe for Showtime Entertainment and broadcast on the cable network in May 1987. Vince Aletti wrote in the *Village Voice* that, in their performances of "Nonathema" and "Hello to My Baby," "the vivacious Ladysmith Black Mambazo, a 10-man a capella choir that fills the stage with concentrated energy, begins to pivot, kick and bounce in unison."

When *Graceland* was awarded the Grammy as record of the year, many in the audience believed that the National Academy of Recording Arts and Sciences was recognizing more than a single album, star, group, or production. *Graceland* brought New African popular music out of the boycott/embargo that apartheid and its foes had erected around it. In the years since, the music forms, as represented by Ladysmith Black Mambazo, have quickly become among the most popular for both listening and dancing, with a growing audience throughout the world.

Selected discography

Graceland (includes Ladysmith Black Mambazo performing "Diamonds on the Soles of her Shoes" and "Homeless"), Warner Brothers, 1986.
Induku Zethu, Shanachie Records, c. 1987.
Umthombo Wamanzi, Shanachie Records, c. 1987.
Ulwande Olungwele, Shanachie Records, c. 1987.
Inala, Shanachie Records, c. 1988.

Sources

New York Daily News, April 27, 1987.
New York Post, April 27, 1987; July 4, 1987.
New York Times, April 27, 1987.
Village Voice, May 12, 1987.

—*Barbara Stratyner*

Led Zeppelin

British rock group

Guitarist Jimmy Page enjoyed moderate success with his first group, Neil Christian and the Crusaders, a Chuck Berry/Bo Diddley-styled British group. After a continuous battle with bad health problems, Page quit in 1961 to attend art school in Sutton. By then he had converted the front room of his parents' house into a makeshift studio to jam with friends. Word of the guitarist's abilities spread, and soon English producers were using Page for session work on records by the Who, the Kinks, and even Tom Jones.

Meanwhile, the Yardbirds' manager, Giorgio Gomelsky, wanted Page to replace Eric Clapton on guitar. But, with the money he was making on sessions, Page could hardly afford to leave, and instead he recommended Jeff Beck for the position. Page also began producing for Immediate Records and experimenting with his bow/guitar technique.

In mid-1966 Yardbirds' bassist Paul Samwell-Smith quit, and Page was offered the spot. By then he was burned out from studio work and accepted. "I remember one particular occasion when I hadn't played a solo

For the Record. . .

Founded 1968, by guitarist **Jimmy Page** (full name, James Patrick Page; born January 9, 1944); other members included **John Paul Jones** (name originally John Baldwin; born January 3, 1946) on bass and keyboards, **Robert Plant** (full name, Robert Anthony Plant; born August 20, 1948) on vocals, and **John Bonham** (full name, John Henry Bonham; born May 31, 1948; died September 24, 1980) on drums;

Began recording October, 1968; first toured United States, 1968-69; recorded and toured extensively throughout the world, 1968-80; re-formed for Live Aid benefit concert, 1985, with drummer Tony Thompson; also performed at Atlantic Records' fortieth anniversary celebration, 1988, with Bonham's son, Jason, on drums.

Addresses: *Office*—c/o Swan Song, Atlantic Records, 75 Rockefeller Plaza, New York, NY 10019.

for, quite literally, a couple of months. And I was asked to play a solo on a rock & roll thing," he told Cameron Crowe. "I played it and felt that what I'd done was absolute crap. I was so disgusted with myself that I made my mind up that I had to get out of it. It was messing me right up."

On one particular night Beck was too ill to perform, so Page substituted on guitar. His flashy technique was so impressive that the band moved Chris Dreja over to bass and continued with the dual lead guitars of Page and Beck. When they were in sync with each other, the two would sound like nothing before. But, more often than not, Beck's ego would take over, and he eventually dropped out in the middle of a U.S. tour.

The group continued on with Peter Grant replacing Mickie Most as manager, but their future was very uncertain. By the spring of 1968 all remaining members except Page decided to call it quits. Two members of the Who, Keith Moon and John Entwistle, talked about forming a group with Page and Steve Winwood. "We'll call it Lead Zeppelin," joked Entwistle, "cause it'll go over like a lead balloon."

With Clapton's Cream and the Jeff Beck Group blazing new paths for the blues rock genre, Page knew what type of band he wanted to form. His first acquisition would be bassist John Paul Jones. A veteran of early sixties sessions like Page, Jones was also an arranger—highly influenced by jazz—and equally competent on keyboards. "I jumped at the chance of getting him,"

Page told Stephen Davis, author of *Hammer of the Gods*.

Next in order would be a vocalist and finally, a drummer. Page was informed of a singer named Robert Plant who performed with the group Hobbstweedle. Formerly an apprentice accountant, Plant quit at age sixteen to become a bluesman, singing with Sounds of Blue, Crawling King Snakes, Tennessee Teens, Listen, and Band of Joy. Just one listen convinced Page that he had his man. "I just couldn't understand why, after he told me he'd been singing for years already, he hadn't become a big name yet," he told Davis.

Plant told Page of a drummer he had worked with previously in two other bands who would be perfect for them. John Bonham was a ham-fisted pounder who was heavily influenced by Keith Moon and Ginger Baker. With much persuasion, Page was able to pry 'Bonzo' away from the Tim Rose band, and the New Yardbirds were now complete.

Davis reported Jones's initial reaction the first time the four played together: "the room just exploded." And Plant told Cameron Crowe, "I've never been so turned on in my life." With such a unique sound, they decided they needed a different name and chose Led Zeppelin (instead of Lead to prevent any mispronunciations). They first recorded in October of 1968, and Peter Grant took the tapes to Atlantic Records where reaction was so enthusiastic that the group was given a $200,000 advance and total artistic control.

Unable to secure proper gigs in England, the group came to America, where they ended up touring for a year and a half. Their first album ripped into the Top 10 within five months after its release despite a poor review in *Rolling Stone*. Their reworkings of blues classics without crediting the original composers would not earn them much respect either ("Dazed and Confused" and "How Many More Years"). Their tour also earned the band a very well-deserved reputation of debauchery.

Led Zeppelin II was written and recorded on the road and and had a 400,000 copy advance order. Within two months it had bumped the Beatles' *Abbey Road* from its No. 1 American spot. It too was slammed by *Rolling Stone* even though it contained a new anthem for rockers, "Whole Lotta Love." Once again, Zep failed to acknowledge the songwriter, this time Willie Dixon, who won a lawsuit against the band. Tour manager Richard Cole defended Zep's "unusual" road habits, which were becoming legendary. "There's nothing immoral in it. It's just that most people wouldn't *dream* of doing it. That's the whole story of Led Zeppelin right there," he told Davis.

The heavy-metal rampage continued on *Led Zeppelin III* with "Immigrant Song," but Page and Plant were heavily influenced by the California folkies during their stay in the States. Critics said the group was going acoustic when actually they had been doing so on *I* and *II*. There was no mistaking their live shows however. "With their epic explosions of sound and light, Led Zeppelin seemed to be a sublimation for the din of battle. A wargasm experience for its audience," wrote Davis.

For their fourth album, Page gave no mention of the band just to see if the music alone would stand up. He was more than right as IV produced gems like "Rock & Roll," "When the Leavee Breaks," and "Black Dog". But, it was "Stairway to Heaven" that would come to be recognized as Zep's signature tune and one of the all-time rock classics. It started off with a beautiful 12-string intro before slowly building up to a near-perfect solo by Page and then back down. "It had everything there and showed the band at its best," Page said in *Hammer*.

Their follow-up LP, *Houses of the Holy*, included more of Jones's keyboards and also went to No. 1 in America. The ensuing tour broke all attendance records in the States with a live show that included fog, cannons, and smoke bombs (eventual staples of hard-rock concerts).

In 1974, Led Zeppelin resigned with Atlantic, which gave the band their own label to work with, Swan Song. It proved to be a very successful venture, with bands like Bad Company, the Pretty Things, Dave Edmunds, and Detective all signed to their label. Zep's 1975 *Physical Graffiti*, a double album *tour de force*, went No. 1 and, with their previous LPs and the stable of Swan Song albums, they had nine albums on the charts simultaneously.

Things were not all roses, however, as Plant was seriously injured in a car accident, and Page became addicted to heroin. Bonham became known as The Beast, with a temper like a monster and the maturity of a five-year-old. He lost control when he learned that he had finished behind drummer Karen Carpenter in a *Playboy* poll. Still, Led Zeppelin ruled the rock world. "It's not just that we think we're the best group in the world, it's just that we think we're so much better than whoever is Number Two," Plant told Lisa Robinson.

In 1976 they would release two albums. The first, *The Song Remains the Same*, was a double live soundtrack from their movie of 1973 concert footage. As usual, it was belittled by critics, and even die-hard fans were a little dismayed. "A few bars from one piece convince the listener he's hearing the greatest of rock & roll, then the very next few place him in a nightmarish 1970 movie

about deranged hippies," *Rolling Stone* reported. Expectations for their studio LP, *Presence*, were high, though, due to a one million-copy advance. Although it contains some quality cuts, like "Achilles Last Stand," the record eventually wound up in the bargain bins.

The band was on hold for nearly three years as Plant recovered from the mysterious death of his son Karac. Rumours were spreading that Page's dabbling in black magic had brought bad karma on the band. He was already living in the late occultist Aleister Crowley's Loch Ness mansion in Scotland, and things were looking suspicious.

In 1980 they entered the studios to record *In Through the Out Door*. With the exception of Page's guitar on the cut "In The Evening," the LP was basically a keyboard album, composed mainly by Jones. It did give a slumping record industry a much needed boost, and the band hit the road to promote it. Tragically, on September 24, 1980, John Bonham died in his sleep after an all-day drinking binge. On December 4, 1980, Led Zeppelin officially disbanded.

Besides the 1982 *Coda*, an LP of Zep outtakes, Page continued to work, recording soundtracks for "Death Wish" I and II. At the 1983 ARMS benefit concerts for Ronnie Lane, Page, now off heroin, jammed with Clapton and Beck and proved the magic was still there. He later teamed with Paul Rodgers to form the Firm, and in 1988 he released his solo album, *Outrider*. Plant has also recorded several fine solo albums himself, quite different in sound from Zeppelin.

In 1985, with Tony Thompson on drums, Led Zeppelin regrouped for the Live-Aid concert in Philadelphia. Word was that Zep was back together, but, alas, it was just a one-shot deal. Then, on May 14, 1988, at Atlantic Records' fortieth anniversary celebration at Madison Square Garden, Led Zeppelin tore into five rockers. On drums sat Jason Bonham, John's son, sounding remarkably like his father. "It was really Jason's night. The atmosphere was fabulous and I made a few mistakes, but that doesn't make any difference," Page told *Guitar World*. As for any future projects, it remains uncertain. Regardless, Led Zeppelin has proved to be one of the most memorable rock acts ever.

Selected discography

Led Zeppelin

Led Zeppelin, Atlantic, 1968.
Led Zeppelin II, Atlantic, 1969.
Led Zeppelin III, Atlantic, 1970.
Led Zeppelin IV, Atlantic, 1971.

Houses of the Holy, Atlantic, 1971.
Physical Graffiti, Swan Song, 1975.
Presence, Swang Song, 1976.
The Song Remains the Same, Swan Song, 1976.
In Through the Out Door, Swan Song, 1976.
Coda, Swan Song, 1982.

Other

Death Wish II (Jimmy Page; soundtrack), Swan Song.
Pictures At Eleven, (Robert Plant), Swan Song.
The Principle of Moments, (Plant), Atlantic.
The Honeydrippers Volume One, (Page and Plant), Es Peranza.
The Firm, (Page with group the Firm), Atlantic.
Shaken 'n' Stirred, (Plant), Es Peranza.
Mean Business, (Page, with the Firm), Atlantic.

Sources

Books

Christgau, Robert, *Christgau's Record Guide,* Ticknor & Fields, 1981.

Dalton, David, and Lenny Kaye, *Rock 100,* Grosset & Dunlap, 1977.
Davis, Stephen, *Hammer of the Gods,* Ballantine, 1985.
Fong-Torres, Ben, editor, *What's That Sound?,* Anchor Books, 1976.
The Guitar Player Book, Grove Press, 1979.
Kozinn, Allan, and others, *The Guitar,* Quill Press, 1984.
Logan, Nick, compiler, *The Illustrated Encyclopedia of Rock,* Harmony Books, 1977.
Marsh, Dave, with John Swenson, *The Rolling Stone Record Guide,* Random House, 1979.
Miller, Jim, editor, *The Rolling Stone Illustrated History of Rock & Roll,* Random House, 1976.
Rock Revolution, Popular Library, 1976.

Periodicals

Guitar Player, January, 1987.
Guitar World, July, 1986; October, 1988; September, 1988.
Rolling Stone, May 20, 1976; December 2, 1976; October 4, 1979; October 18, 1979.

Little Richard

Singer, songwriter, pianist

Little Richard Penniman is a rock and roll pioneer in every sense of the word. Rock's first certified zany, he brought outlandish clothes and hairstyles to the national stage for the first time, astonishing 1950s audiences with his brazen homosexual campiness. Mere stage appeal does not account for Richard's wide cross-racial appeal, however. As Arnold Shaw notes in *The Rockin' '50s,* the artist "sang with an intensity and frenzy and commitment that marked the outer limits of rock 'n' roll. . . . He was excitement in motion, a whirling dervish at the keyboard, showmanship royale in eye-dazzling costumes topped by a high, slick pompadour of hair."

From the scat-singing prologue of "Tutti-Frutti" to his favorite expression, "Ooh, my soul!," Richard brought a new level of intensity—an unlikely pastiche of gospel and sexual innuendo—to popular music. A *People* magazine contributor wrote: "No performer deserves more credit for the metamorphosis of black rhythm and blues into rock 'n' roll." In *The Dave Given Rock 'n' Roll Stars Handbook,* author Given claims that Richard "gave R&R its meaning, its depth, and in so doing he inspired the careers of other great artists that followed: James Brown, Elvis, Gene Vincent, Jerry Lee Lewis, and Joe Tex, just to name a few."

Nor did Richard's influence end with the first generation of rockers. Many groups of the British Invasion, including the Beatles and the Rolling Stones, also looked to him as a mentor. According to Jay Cocks in *Time,* Richard "let blast with rock of such demented power, . . . that he seemed possessed of darkling forces. . . . Songs that sounded like nonsense . . . but whose beat seemed to hint of unearthly pleasures centered somewhere between the gut and the gutter."

Richard Wayne Penniman was born in Macon, Georgia, in 1932 (some sources say 1935). He was the third of twelve children, and the only child in his family with a physical defect—his right leg is shorter than his left. From earliest childhood he was marked as "different" by his effeminacy, as he explained in a *Rolling Stone* interview: "The boys would want to fight me because I didn't like to be with them. I wanted to play with the girls. See, I *felt* like a girl." In the hope of curing his physical ailment—and curbing his behavior—Richard's mother enrolled him in a charismatic Baptist church in Macon. There, at the age of ten, he started a gospel group called the Tiny Tots Quartet. This experience filled him with the desire to be a professional gospel singer like his hero, Brother Joe May, the "Thunderbolt of the Midwest."

Richard's religious fervor was not lasting, however. He dropped out of school in the ninth grade and joined a travelling medicine show. Then he hired on with Sugarfoot

Sam, a minstrel show, where he occasionally donned a dress and danced with the chorus girls. It was during this period that he met Billy Wright, a popular postwar black performer. "Billy was an entertainer who wore very loud-colored clothing, and he wore his hair curled," Richard told *Rolling Stone*. "I thought he was the most fantastic entertainer I had ever seen."

As early as 1951 Richard cut his first recordings, having won a rhythm and blues talent contest at Atlanta's Eighty One Theatre. The songs, "Get Rich Quick," "Why Did You Leave Me," "Every Hour," and "Thinkin' 'bout My Mother," did not sell. Optimistically, Richard cut four more sides of the same blues/boogie-type material, and it likewise failed. He returned to Macon with his band, the Upsetters, and half-heartedly sent a demo tape to Art Rupe of Specialty Records in Los Angeles. That tape languished at Specialty for almost a year, during which time Richard garnished his live act with various outrageous spectacles.

Rupe, it turned out, was looking for another black singer with a Ray Charles sound, and eventually Richard's tape came to him for review. He invited the young rocker to cut some songs in New Orleans. At first Richard began taping the same kind of blues-oriented songs he had been recording, but during a break he launched into a raucous song of his own invention, "Tutti Frutti," that contained the memorable line "A-Wop-Bop-A-Loo-Bop, A-Lop-Bam-Boom." Rupe was captivated. He ordered new lyrics (to replace Richard's frankly sexual ones), and released the song

just before Christmas in 1955. It was resting at number 21 on the charts by the end of December.

"Many white kids had never heard a black man singing with the 'brakes off'," writes Stuart Colman in *They Kept On Rockin'*. "But when *Tutti Frutti* was released, . . . several white stations thought the time was right and showed no hesitation in programming the disc. . . . From that point on there began a hit trail of some of the classiest, black rock 'n' roll records that America and the world would ever see." Even though Richard sometimes had to watch other performers (like Pat Boone) score with his material, he did not lack for top hits himself.

Backed by the best studio musicians and his own inimitably vigorous piano playing, Richard soon had chart-toppers with "Long Tall Sally," "Rip It Up," "Slippin' and Slidin'," "Lucille," "The Girl Can't Help It," "Jenny, Jenny," and "Good Golly, Miss Molly." *Rolling Stone* corespondent Gerri Hirshey noted that onstage and in the movies, Richard "was compelled to invent his par-

> *Little Richard "gave rock and roll its meaning, its depth, and in so doing he inspired the careers of other great artists that followed."*

ticular brand of majesty. This was Little Richard, 'Handsomest Man in Rock & Roll.' His image was an immaculate conception, a fantasy born of years in travelling medicine shows, drag-queen revues, churches and clubs. . . . But in Fifties America, this made for a terrible mess. He was black and gay, talented and loud, and worse—much worse—absolutely sure of himself."

Teens of both races loved the audacious Richard. No one was prepared, therefore, for his sudden abandonment of fame and fortune to study the Bible at a Seventh-day Adventist seminary. In 1957 Richard vowed never to sing rock 'n' roll again—some say an airplane malfunction frightened him into a conversion; another story has it that he interpreted the Soviet launching of *Sputnik* as a sign that rock and roll was evil and that he should quit performing. The Bible studies did not occupy Richard too long, though. By the early 1960s he was back on tour, this time in England with an unknown group called the Beatles. By his account in *Rolling Stone,* Richard not only taught his musical British admirers some of his falsetto voice stunts and riffs, he also had an opportunity to buy a 50 percent share of the group. He was a musician, not a businessman, so he passed on the Beatles' offer and returned to America to launch his own comeback.

For roughly twelve years Richard performed his old hits and—less successfully—new material to audiences hungry for classic rock. Then, in the mid-1970s, the lifestyle again began taking its toll. Richard told *Rolling Stone:* "I was getting deeper and deeper into drugs. All I wanted to do was to have sex with beautiful women and get high. I spent thousands of dollars getting high." He missed engagements, or performed poorly, and eventually was overcome by the conflicts of his bisexual personality. Once again he turned to the church, becoming an evangelist preacher and Bible salesman.

Little Richard renounced his strict religion early in 1988 and began to perform again, in a more subdued manner. He has had no trouble lining up engagements, even though he no longer decks himself in mirror-studded jackets, eyeliner, and tie-dyed headbands. Had he never taken the stage again, he would still have enjoyed a prominent place in the pantheon of rock 'n' roll legends. Hirshey sums up his career: "Little Richard bent gender, upset segregationist fault lines and founded a tradition of rock dadaists devoted to the art of self-creation. But unlike the studied incarnations, . . . Richard never seemed to think about it. He went, with the inspiration of the moment, be it divine or hormonal, and caromed like a shiny, cracked pinball between God, sex and rock & roll."

Selected discography

Major single releases

"Tutti-Fruitti," Specialty, December, 1955.
"Long Tall Sally," Specialty, March, 1956.
"Slippin' and Slidin'," Specialty, March, 1956.
"Rip It Up," Specialty, June, 1956.
"The Girl Can't Help It," Specialty, January, 1957.
"Lucille," Specialty, March, 1957.
"Jenny, Jenny," Specialty, June, 1957.
"Keep a Knockin'," Specialty, September, 1957.
"Good Golly, Miss Molly," Specialty, January, 1958.

LPs

Here's Little Richard, Specialty, 1958.
Little Richard 2, Specialty, 1958.

The Fabulous Little Richard, Specialty, 1959.
Well Alright, Specialty, 1959.
Little Richard's Greatest Hits, Joy, 1964.
Coming Home, Coral, 1964.
Little Richard Sings Freedom Songs, Crown, 1964.
King of Gospel Songs, Mercury, 1965.
Wild & Frantic, Modern, 1965.
Greatest Hits, Live, Okeh, 1967.
The Explosive Little Richard, Okeh, 1967.
Every Hour with Little Richard, RCA, 1970.
The Rill Thing, Reprise, 1971.
King of Rock n Roll, Reprise, 1971.
Second Coming, Reprise, 1971.
Little Richard's Greatest Hits, Trip, 1972.
The Very Best of Little Richard, United Artists, 1975.
Lifetime Friend, Warner Brothers, 1987.
22 Classic Cuts, Ace, 1987.
(With Billy Wright) *Hey Baby, Don't You Want a Man Like Me?,* Ace, 1987.
Shut Up!: A Collection of Rare Tracks, 1951-1964, Rhino, 1988.

Also recorded *Biggest Hits,* Specialty; *Greatest Hits,* Specialty; *Little Richard Is Back,* Vee Jay; *Mr. Big,* Joy; *Rip It Up,* Joy; *Slippin' & Slidin',* Joy; *The Little Richard Story,* Joy; *Little Richard Sings,* Twentieth Century; *Little Richard,* Kama Sutra; *Best of Little Richard,* Scepter; *Little Richard Sings Spirituals,* United; *Right Now,* United; *Keep a Knockin',* Rhapsody; *King of Gospel Singers,* Wing; *Clap Your Hands,* Spinorama; *Little Richard Rocks,* RCA; *Little Richard,* Camden; *Grooviest 17 Original Hits,* Specialty; *Rock King,* JEM Classic Series; and *Talkin' 'Bout Soul,* Vee Jay.

Sources

Books

Colman, Stuart, *They Kept On Rockin',* Blandford, 1982.
Given, Dave, *The Dave Given Rock 'n' Roll Handbook,* Exposition, 1980.
Shaw, Arnold, *The Rockin' '50s,* Hawthorne, 1974.
Shaw, Arnold, *Black Popular Music in America,* Schirmer, 1986.
Stambler, Irwin, *The Encyclopedia of Pop, Rock, and Soul,* St. Martin's, 1974.

Periodicals

People, January 8, 1979.
Rolling Stone, July 19-August 2, 1984.

—*Anne Janette Johnson*

Henry Mancini

Composer

"Whatever style you have comes out of years of synthesizing your *own* mind. In your daily work, certain harmonies, certain intervals, certain colors in orchestration come back because they express *you*. Whatever came into your ear comes out of the hand in some way or another. That's what I like about movies. The canvas is always empty when you start and you can always go in any direction you want." The number of films that Henry Mancini has scored—more than 70—attests to the statement of individual creativity that he made to *Filmmusic Notebook* in 1978.

Born in Cleveland, Ohio, on April 16, 1924, Mancini was raised in the industrial town of Aliquippa, Pennsylvania, where his father was a steelworker. His introduction to music came from his father's avocation, playing flute and piccolo in the local Sons of Italy band. Mancini, who learned his father's instruments, has credited that amateur band with sparking his interest in both classical and new music and wrote a tribute to it in his orchestral work, *Beaver Valley '37*. In the Pittsburgh Symphony program for its premiere in May 1970, he described "our weekly ration of Puccini, Rossini, Leoncavallo and Verdi . . . Sunday morning at about eleven o'clock. 'The William Tell Overture' was my big feature number." He became expert enough to be named first flute in the All-State Band and taught himself piano by imitating a neighbor's player piano rolls. Mancini's formal training in orchestration and arranging began at 14 when he studied with Max Adkins, then the leader of the pit band at the Stanley Theatre in Pittsburgh. He attended the Carnegie Institute of Technology and Juilliard briefly before he was drafted into the Air Force.

As well as Adkins, Mancini credits formal studies with composers Ernst Krenek and Mario Castelnuovo-Tedesco and an apprenticeship with Universal's orchestrator David Tamke. He has written a highly acclaimed textbook himself—*Sounds and Scores: A Practical Guide to Professional Orchestration*.

On Glenn Miller's recommendation, Mancini joined the Army Air Forces band. Following the end of World War II, during which Miller had been killed, he began to perform and arrange with the Miller Orchestra, now led by Tex Beneke. With his wife, Ginny O'Connor (then a vocalist with the MelloLarks), he moved to Hollywood. Radio scoring from 1947 to 1952 taught him the "craft of writing for dramatic shows," as he later told *Filmmusic Notebook*. His wife's recording job with Jimmy Dorsey's Orchestra in 1952 led him to Universal Studios, where he soon became a staff composer and arranger. He has estimated that he worked on several hundred films before his first complete scoring assignments on the jazz-oriented movies "The Glenn Miller Story" (for which he received his first Oscar nomination in 1954) and "The Benny Goodman Story" (1956). He came to public attention with his atmospheric score for the Orson Welles thriller "Touch of Evil" in 1958. In the trade magazine *Action,* Mancini described that film's unique challenge: *"Touch of Evil"* was one of the first pictures to take advantage of what we call 'Source' music (that means music coming from a source such as a radio). In this film, we used horns outside of all the bars in a Mexican border town."

In 1959, Mancini's theme for the Blake Edwards television series "Peter Gunn," which was set in a jazz club, became a top-selling record and earned him Grammy Awards for Album of the Year and Best Arrangement. "The Theme from Peter Gunn" is considered the first television title music to stand on its own as a single. Mancini wrote in *Action* that Edwards "challenged me weekly with long scenes without any dialogue—already hearing the musical score in his mind's eye. Blake regarded the music as a vital voice in the total picture."

Many of Mancini's complete film scores included theme or title songs that went on to success as singles with lyrics by Johnny Mercer. "Moon River" was played in "Breakfast at Tiffany's" (1961) on an amplified harmonica to represent the main character's past, but it soon became a standard pop ballad that won the Best Song

Oscar and Grammy for 1961. It has been recorded by scores of male and female vocalists and was a top-seller and signature tune for Andy Williams.

The themes from "Charade" (1963), "Dear Heart" (1964) and "Days of Wine and Roses" also became award-winning pop standards with added lyrics. All were nominated for Oscars—"Days of Wine and Roses" (with lyrics by Mercer) won Best Song in 1962. It also won 1963 Grammy awards for Song of the Year, Record of the Year, and Best Background Arrangement. The 1962 Grammy for Best Instrumental Arrangement went to Mancini for the novelty, "Baby Elephant Walk," from "Hatari" (1962). Mancini described the process of creating it for *Filmmusic Notebook:* "[Director Howard Hawks] said, 'The girl's going down to take a bath with the elephants, you know, that's cute'. . . . So he said, 'Write Something.' I looked at the thing several times and . . . thought of an old Will Bradley-Freddie Slack record called 'Down the Road Apiece.' And it was as simple as that. The elephants were walking down the road and I could hear 'Down the Road Apiece.' It was a

> *Mancini's formal training in orchestration and arranging began at 14 when he studied with Max Adkins.*

boogie-woogie piece, with the eight top the bar, and that was the clue. It was the funny gait that the elephants had."

Mancini's most famous film theme is probably the lurking vamp that he wrote to go under the animated credits in Blake Edwards' "The Pink Panther" (1964). Like "Inspector Clouseau," the bumbling hero of the series, the animated animal (complete with theme song) had a long and prosperous life in six films, a cartoon series, and advertisements. The theme won 1964 Grammy awards for Best Instrumental Arrangement, Best Instrumental Composition, and Best Instrumental Performance in the non-jazz categories. Among his many other Edwards collaborations have been the backstage musicals "Darling Lili" (1970) and "Victor-Victoria." (1982), for which he won the 1983 Best Song Score Oscar. Plans were announced to create a Broadway musical based on "Victor/Victoria" in 1985. Alan Warner described the score for the former film in *Film and Filming:* "Mancini weaves in some suprises including a delightful short melody sing by small children's chorus. Also worked into the score are a couple of

World War One 'hits,' namely 'Tipperary' and 'Pack Up Your Troubles.' The film closes with [Julie] Andrews singing probably the best *Lili* number, 'Whistling Away the Dark.'"

Having, as he told the *New York Sunday News* in 1964, "put music on everybody's minds far as TV is concerned," Mancini continued to write for the medium. A second private eye show with a jazz background, "Mr. Lucky," (1960) also spawned a top-selling record. "How Soon," the theme from the 1963 "Richard Boone Show" was popular in the United States and in England, when it was shown on the BBC. He composed themes for NBC News and NBC election coverage. Among his recent projects have been the jazzy theme for "Remington Steele," the romantic background for the mini-series "The Thorn Birds," and the lyrical "travelogue" music for "Newhart."

Mancini has also won Grammy awards for Best Instrumental Arrangements of film themes by other composers, among them "Love Theme from Romeo and Juliet" by Nino Rota and "Theme from Z and other Film Music" by Mikis Theodorakis. He records for London/Poly-Gram and RCA with his own studio orchestra or, as a guest conductor, symphony orchestras around the world, among them, the Pittsburgh Symphony, the Milwaukee Symphony, and the Boston Pops. His music is also played by many soloists, especially the flutist James Galway. There are over 60 Mancini albums currently available and hundreds of recorded versions of Mancini songs.

"In most cases," Mancini told *Electronic Age* (a television trade magazine), "a composer must not approach the score as though he is the star of the show. He has to know when to hold back, when not to blast the audi-ence, when not to intrude on the dialogue." Although every filmgoer and television watcher can hum a Mancini tune, he has become most celebrated for obeying his own dictum. As a composer, arranger, orchestrator and film scorer, he creates atmosphere but does not intrude on the product on the screen.

Selected discography

Music from Peter Gunn, RCA, 1958.
Music from Mr. Lucky, RCA, 1959.
Sarah Vaughan Sings the Henry Mancini Songbook, Mercury, 1965.
Victor/Victoria, Polygram, 1986.
The Hollywood Musicals (vocals by Johnny Mathis), Columbia, 1986.

Writings

Sounds and Scores: A Practical Guide to Professional Orchestration, Northridge, 1973.

Sources

Action, November-December, 1971.
Electronic Age, autumn, 1968.
Filmmusic Notebook, winter, 1978.
Films and Filming, November, 1970.
New York Sunday News, April 5, 1964.
Pittsburgh Symphony Program Magazine, May, 1970.

—Barbara Stratyner

Dean Martin

Singer

Singer Dean Martin has achieved show-business success with an unlikely combination—romantic crooning and low-key comedy. A headliner in both television and movies for thirty years, Martin is admired today for his deep and easy baritone renditions of such favorites as "That's Amore" and "Everybody Loves Somebody." A *Look* magazine contributor explains that Martin has appealed to millions of fans in America and abroad because "they see him as a very fine person touched only by a few glamorous faults—that is, the reputation of a drinker, a woman chaser, a swinger—and nobody will say a word against him."

That so-called "reputation" is more fantasy than fact; Martin long ago developed an onstage act of semi-drunkenness as a comic routine, and his personal life is less sensational than many of his fellow crooners. In *Newsweek,* a reviewer notes that whatever his private style, Martin's "not-give-a-damn attitude in public is probably the quality that endears him to most fans." Fellow actor Anthony Quinn offered a similar observation in *Time.* "All of us seem to be plagued by responsibility, hemmed in by convention," Quinn said. "Dean is the symbol of the guy who can go on, get drunk, have no responsibilities."

Martin was born Dino Crocetti on June 17, 1917. His father was an immigrant from the Abruzzi region of Italy who came to live with his brothers in Steubenville, Ohio. Martin grew up in Steubenville in what he describes in *Look* as a good measure of comfort. "These emigrated Italians were not skilled workers like pharmacists or lawyers, but they knew how to work hard," he said. "My father did too. He worked hard as a barber, and he got his own barbershop. . . . He gave us a beautiful home, and a car, and good food, and good Christmases, and we never were poor, my brother and I."

Martin was enthralled by Hollywood from an early age, and he spent most of his free afternoons at Steubenville's movie theatres. He was particularly influenced by Bing Crosby, as he remembered in *Look:* "When a Bing Crosby movie ever came to Steubenville, I would stay there all day and watch. And that's how I learned to sing, cause it's true I don't read a note. I don't. I learned from Crosby, and so did [Frank] Sinatra, and Perry Como. We all started imitatin' him; he was the teacher for all of us."

Martin dropped out of school in tenth grade and drifted through a series of odd jobs in the Midwest. He earned the most money by dealing cards in gambling houses, but he also did stints as an amateur boxer, a steel mill worker, and a singer with the Ernie McKay Band in Cleveland. He adopted Dino Martini as a stage name at first, then changed it to the more American Dean Martin—for many of the early years of his career he was

For the Record. . .

Real name, Dino Crocetti; born June 17, 1917, in Steubenville, Ohio; son of Guy (a barber) and Angela Crocetti; married Elizabeth Ann MaDonald, 1940 (divorced, 1949); married Jeanne Bieggers, 1949 (divorced); married Cathy Hawn, 1973; children: (first marriage) Craig, Claudia, Gail, Deanna; (second marriage) Dino (deceased), Ricci, Gina.

Singer, 1940—; during 1940s also worked in a steel mill, as a croupier, and as a welterweight boxer; performed in comedy-musical team with Jerry Lewis, 1946-56; actor in numerous feature films, including "My Friend Irma Goes West," 1949, "At War With the Army," 1950, "Jumpin' Jacks," 1953, "The Caddy," 1953, "Rio Bravo," 1959, "Some Came Running," 1959, "Robin and the Seven Hoods," 1964, "The Sons of Katie Elder," 1965, "The Silencers," 1966, "Airport," 1970, "Cannonball Run," 1981, and "Cannonball Run II"; star of television variety show, "The Dean Martin Show," NBC, 1966-70; star of television specials, "The Dean Martin Celebrity Roast," 1976-78.

Awards: Academy Award nomination for best song, "That's Amore," 1963; Golden Globe Award, 1967, for "The Dean Martin Show"; holder of numerous gold records.

Addresses: *Home*—2002 Loma Vista Dr., Beverly Hills CA 90210. *Office*—c/o Mort Viner, International Creative Management, 8899 Beverly Blvd., Los Angeles CA 90048.

sensitive about his ethnic background. Martin moved to New York in the early 1940s to seek work as a club singer. He had several lean years during which he had to drive a cab to support his growing family.

Finally, in 1946, he earned a regular spot at the Rio Bamba club. In the summer of that same year he appeared at the Club 500 in Atlantic City, on the same bill with a young comedian named Jerry Lewis. After-hours, Martin and Lewis began to socialize. "We started horsing around with each other's acts," he told the *Saturday Evening Post*. "That's how the team of Martin and Lewis started. We'd do anything that came to our minds." Martin and Lewis tried out their new act on the customers at Club 500. They were a hit, so much so that they were invited to the prestigious Copacabana in New York, where they soon garnered top billing and salaries of $5000 per week.

Martin and Lewis went west to Hollywood as established stars. They signed a long-term movie deal with Paramount Pictures and subsequently made sixteen films for the company. Their film work reflected the same pattern as their stage show—while Martin played the suave, straight crooner, Lewis perpetrated noisy and disruptive antics. Inevitably both men looked like buffoons, but Martin was the partner who suffered most. "I sang a song and never got to finish the song," Martin told *Look*. "The camera would go over [Lewis] doin' funny things, then it would come back to me when I'd finished. Everythin' was Jerry Lewis, Jerry Lewis, and I was the straight man. I was an idiot in every picture. And I was makin' a lot of money, you know, but money isn't all, is it, and I knew I could do so much better. And I proved it. Not to the public, not to the country or the world. To myself."

Martin's first solo film, "Ten Thousand Bedrooms," was a critical failure. *New York Times* critic Bosley Crowther commented that, without Lewis, Martin was "just another nice-looking crooner. . . . Together, the two made a mutually complementary team. Apart, Mr. Martin is a fellow with little humor and a modicum of charm." The ensuing years would prove Crowther's judgment wrong. Martin's film career blossomed in the 1960s, with major

---

Martin's so-called "reputation" is more fantasy than fact.

---

roles in works like "Rio Bravo," "Some Came Running," "Bells Are Ringing," and the drama "Toys in the Attic." By 1970 he was awarded the coveted role of the captain in the first "Airport" movie, one of the biggest films released that year.

Martin further confounded the critics by becoming one of the most popular television stars of the 1960s. His weekly variety hour, "The Dean Martin Show," led the ratings from 1966 until the early 1970s. On that show, unencumbered by Lewis, Martin was able to sing—several songs each week—as well as pursue his affable drunk routine to comic perfection. A *Time* reviewer called "The Dean Martin Show" the "closest thing on the air to the free and easy spontaneity of old-fashioned live television."

Martin was best known in the 1970s for his celebrity roasts, television specials in which a selected star would endure a string of good-natured insults from his or her peers. He also aired a series of Christmas specials, some of which featured his seven children. More recently Martin has returned to club work in

California and Las Vegas; his films of the 1980s include "Cannonball Run" and "Cannonball Run II." Tragedy struck Martin in 1987 when his son, Dean Paul, was killed in an airplane crash; the singer has kept a lower profile since that event.

Where once Martin was somewhat ashamed of being Italian—and ashamed of his poor command of English—he has come to value his heritage as it relates especially to his singing. "Italians are so talented," he told *Look*. "Just take the singers here; 90 percent are Italian. . . . Cause they sing from here, from the heart, the stomach, not the throat. Anybody can sing from the throat, but then you just say words." No one has ever accused Martin of singing from the throat—his rolling baritone seems to slide from beneath his ribs. Reflecting on his many years as a superstar of screen and stage, Martin told *Newsweek:* "I never have cared what New York or Hollywood or Las Vegas want. I always plays to de common folk. I guess it's just that I seem to have a good time, and I do, and they'd like to do what I'm doing."

Selected discography

That's Amore, Capitol, 1953.
Everybody Loves Somebody, Reprise, 1964.
The Best of Dean Martin, Capitol, 1966.
Dreams and Memories, 1986.
Dino, Capitol.

Also recorded *Memories Are Made of This.*

Sources

Life, December 22, 1958.
Look, November 8, 1960; December 26, 1967.
Newsweek, March 20, 1967.
New York Post Magazine, June 5, 1960.
New York Times, April 4, 1957.
Saturday Evening Post, April 29, 1961.
Time, March 11, 1966.

—Anne Janette Johnson

Meredith Monk

Vocalist, composer, choreographer

"The center is the voice, and the center is the music. I use center in the largest sense of the word, because I feel that when I do a theater piece now, I'm an orchestrator of music and image and movement," Meredith Monk explained to *OPERA America* in October 1984. "I have tried, in my music, to go back to the beginnings of the voice and deal with it as an instrument in the most direct way possible. Some of the things I've discovered I came upon by simply working with my own voice." Vocalist, composer, and choreographer Meredith Monk has often been described as a Renaissance woman of the arts.

Born in Lima, Peru, where her vocalist mother was concertizing, Monk was raised in New York City and Connecticut. She received formal training in piano, ballet, modern dance, and eurhythmics from an early age. Monk has credited her years at Sarah Lawrence College, and classes with modern dance choreographers Bessie Schonberg and Judith Dunn, with releasing her creativity. In a profile in *Music Journal* (1979), she reminisced that "I was encouraged to work with a feeling [and] let the medium and form find itself. It seemed that finally I was able to combine movement with music and words, all coming fom a single source."

Monk was introduced to the choreographers who became the leaders of the post-modern dance movement by Dunn. She joined the Judson Dance Theater, a loosely organized experimental group that sprung from classes by Robert Dunn at the Merce Cunningham Studio in 1964. The Judson dancers gave concerts of short works at the Judson Memorial Church in New York's Greenwich Village and in other locations. Her best known works from the Judson concerts were mixed-media pieces, such as *16mm Earrings,* which she performed with projections at the Billy Rose Theatre Festival of the Avant-Garde in 1969.

Monk experimented with the limitations created by specific locations in many early works created for her own troupe, The House. *Juice: A Theatre Cantata in 3 Installments* (1969), for example, was created for performance at three different locations—from the ramps of the Guggenheim Museum to The House's Soho loft. Her more recent works do not depend on externals, however. Her 1973 *Education of the Girlchild* is a pure performance tour de force as Monk takes 45 minutes to regress from an elderly woman to a young child using movements and vocal sounds.

Music became more important in Monk's work as she assembled her troupe and taught them her vocal repertory. *Quarry* (1976) was the first of many works to be described as an "opera" since the abstract images of World War II were presented in a score that included solos, duets, small groups, and a large chorus, as well

For the Record. . .

Born November 20, 1942, in Lima, Peru (where her mother was performing); daughter of Theodore Glenn Monk and Audrey Zellman (a vocalist). *Education:* Sarah Lawrence College, B.A., 1964.

Studied piano, ballet, and modern dance as a child; member of experimental Judson Dance Theater in the 1960s; founder of her own dance troupe, The House, 1969; has presented experimental dance performances and mixed-media operas; has also given solo and ensemble vocal concerts.

Awards: Obie and Bessie Awards for sustained achievement; six medals for composition from American Society of Composers, Authors, and Publishers (ASCAP); has received fellowships from Guggenheim Foundation and National Endowment for the Arts.

Addresses: *Home*—New York, NY. *Office*—The House Foundation for the Arts, 325 Spring St., New York, NY 10013.

as dance sequences and a scale-manipulating film. *Recent Ruins* (1979), another mixed-media opera, depicted archeologists from the future unearthing New York. Its film sequence, *Ellis Island,* was broadcast separately on the Public Broadcasting System and on European television and was awarded the CINE Golden Eagle in 1982. Based on Walt Whitman's Civil War writings, *Specimen Days* (1981) presented a look at the past, focusing again on civilians in war. *The Games,* created with Ping Chong in 1983, was an alternative view of the Olympics of the future commissioned by a West Berlin theater group and presented in the United States at the Brooklyn Academy of Music's Next Wave Festival.

Its large chorus and massed movements were in sharp contrast to the smaller scale of *Turtle Dreams (Cabaret)* (1983). The latter work, with its five soloists performing isolated Cha-Cha dances, was described by *Newsweek* as "the precise sensation of being a foreigner, wholly cut off from the activities that consitute ordinary life around us." The magazine quoted her as demanding "the constant shift of perceptions, the shifting of balance, the multidimensional experience—that's what I want in my theatre. It has mobility."

Monk's feature-length film, "Book of Days" (Tatgo-Lasseur Productions in association with TV Sept [France], 1989) uses the fourteenth century as a metaphor for the present world. The work, to be given its United States premiere on the Public Broadcasting System series "Alive from Off-Center," is, as she described it in The House literature, "a film about time—future and past—an abstract treatment of the sadness and joy of daily life."

Monk's concerts and recordings have been focused on the voice. At a May 1981 "music concert with film," she screened excerpts from *Ellis Island* and presented a solo version of *Education of the Girlchild.* She has given recitals for solo voice accompanied only by her finger rubbing a water glass, a chilling effect that she used on the recording *Our Lady of Late* (1973). As L.K. Telberg described it in *Music Journal,* "it is set, quite ingeniously, against the bourbon pitches heard as Monk rubs her finger against the rim of a glass goblet in which the water is gradually descreased (and the pitch lowered) by sipping. "Monk analyzed it in an unpublished memo, "Notes on the Voice," as "the naked voice, the female voice in all its aspects; gradations of feeling, nuance, rhythm, quality, each section another voice ('character, persona'), each section a particular musical problem, area of investigation."

Her *Songs from the Hill* (1976) is a trio for women, premiered with House members Andrea Goodman and Monica Solen. In a 1976 review, John Rockwell wrote in the *New York Times* that she had "perfected her own technique to emit amazing varieties of sounds rarely heard from a Western throat, full of wordless cries and moans, a lexicon of vocal coloration, glottal attacks and microtonal waverings that lie at the heart of all musical culture." In *Dolmen Music* (1979), Monk added three male voices and a cello for the 40 minute work. As recorded, it was given the German Music Critics' award for Best record of 1981. *Fayum Music,* originally the score of a film about Egyptian Fayum portraits, was composed for vernacular instruments—the voice, hammered dulcimer, and double ocarina.

Monk now performs and records with pianist and keyboard artist Nurit Tilles. She discussed their recital in December 1988 with Stephen Holden in his "The Pop Life" column in the *New York Times:* "I'm working with a much more delicate palette, using the voice as a transparent kind of instrument. Some of the songs, I call 'click songs,' because they have percussion and melody going on at the same time." She is developing a work for the Minnesota Opera's New Music-Theater Ensemble and is composing a score for the Jose Limon Dance Company.

Monk has received both an Obie (from the Off and Off-Off Broadway critics) and a Bessie (from dance critics) for sustained achievement, as well as fellowships from the Guggenheim Foundation and the National Endowment for the Arts. Her music has received six ASCAP awards for Composition.

When *OPERA America* paired Monk with Leonard Bernstein and Stephen Sondheim in the first issue of its newsletter, *Opera for the 80's and Beyond*, it was recognizing her importance in music and music-theater. The newsletter quotes her on her own definitions of the art forms: [Her aim is to create] "an art that is inclusive rather than exclusive; that is expansive, whole, human, multi-dimensional. An art which seeks to re-establish the unity that exists in music, theater and dance. . . . I want an art which reaches towards emotion that we have no words for, that we barely remember—an art that affirms the world of feeling in a time and society where feelings are being systematically eliminated." Monk has found that her voice and her art forms, in live performance, film or recordings, can create the world she envisions.

Selected discography

Our Lady of Late, Wergo, 1973; re-released 1986.
Key: An Album of Invisible Theatre, Lovely Music, 1977.
Songs from the Hill, Wergo, 1979.
Dolmen Music, ECM, 1980.
Turtle Dreams, ECM, 1983.

Sources

Music Journal, September-October 1979.
New York Times, March 28, 1976; December 7, 1988.
Newsweek, October 29, 1984.
OPERA America, October, 1984.

—Barbara Stratyner

Bill Monroe

Singer, mandolin player

Bill Monroe is affectionately known as the "father of bluegrass music," the architect of a unique new brand of American sound. The whole genre of bluegrass is named after Monroe's band, the Blue Grass Boys, because that band—and especially Monroe—originated the particular blend of vocal harmonies and instrumental riffs that have come to characterize traditional bluegrass. In *The Encyclopedia of Country and Western Music,* Rick Marschall writes of Monroe's groundbreaking group: "All of a sudden America had a new music. It had evolved, yes, and its roots were easily traceable. But Bill Monroe's [Blue Grass Boys] were playing something new. It was driven, intense music. It exploded with brilliant solos. It was an integrated ensemble of string instruments that had never actually been combined heretofore. The singing was bluesy, the instrumentation was jazzy, and the name was Bluegrass. The development of bluegrass was logical, but its synthesis was by no means inevitable; it took Bill Monroe's taste and vision to bring it into being."

Bill C. Malone, the author of *Country Music U.S.A.,* also feels that Monroe has been the primary force behind the creation of the bluegrass genre. Malone calls Monroe "a man of rugged independence and intense, almost stubborn pride" whose "quiet resolve to be unique, coupled with brilliant musicianship, made him one of the most respected and influential performers in country music history."

Monroe's "rugged independence" began in early childhood. He was born near Rosine, Kentucky, in 1911, the youngest son of a hardworking farmer. Plagued by poor eyesight and considerably younger than his eight siblings, he grew up reclusive, taciturn, and serious. In *The Stars of Country Music,* Ralph Rinzler comments: "The musics Bill heard in early childhood were important formative forces, but equally significant was the work ethic he absorbed from his parents. . . . 'Thrawn,' the Scots would say—set, determined, obstinate, thriving on hard work." Monroe actually enjoyed driving a plow or engaging in other solitary tasks that would give him an opportunity to practice singing out of earshot of his family. When he was ten he began to play the guitar and mandolin, following with interest the stringband and square dance music of his region.

Monroe had several strong influences on his playing and singing style. The first was his uncle Pendleton Vandiver, a fiddler much in demand for local dances and socials. Monroe told Rinzler: "Maybe if I hadn't of heard him, I'd have never learned anything about music at all. Learning his numbers gave me something to start on. One thing that he learnt me how to do was to keep time, and the shuffle that he had on the bow was the most perfect time that you ever heard. I give him credit for all of my timing."

Another influence was Arnold Shultz, a black musician who played both country and blues guitar. Monroe wanted his own music to have a blues sound, so he imitated the runs Shultz played and applied them to traditional Appalachian melodies in innovative ways. Vocally, Monroe was at least in part indebted to shape-note singing—a type of gospel music dependent upon spare, strident harmonies done in full voice. Monroe sang in both the Methodist and Baptist churches in Rosine, memorizing his parts because he could not see to read the notes. By the age of thirteen he was accompanying his uncle Pen, Arnold Shultz, or his older brothers as they made their dance band rounds. He settled on the mandolin primarily because it was the instrument his brothers did not play.

In 1929 Monroe went north to Indiana to join his brothers in an automobile manufacturing plant. The three Monroes performed together in their off-hours for several years, and in 1934 Bill and Charlie decided to make music their full-time profession. As The Monroe Brothers, the two men landed a contract with Texas Crystals and eventually settled into radio shows in the Carolinas. Malone notes that as a duet team, "The Monroe Brothers set a standard of performing excellence that is still remembered by older country fans. . . . The harmony of their music performances, however,

was not always matched by a similar consonance in their brotherly relations. They fought both physically and verbally, and their musical partnership was therefore terminated in 1938." Each brother went his own way and formed his own band. Bill's, the Blue Grass Boys, began performing on the "Crossroad Follies" in Atlanta. In 1939 the group auditioned successfully for the Grand Ole Opry. The Opry's founder, George D. Hay, was particularly delighted with Monroe's clear, high tenor and spirited arrangements. Monroe has been a regular on the Grand Ole Opry since then—half a century and counting.

Malone writes: "Until 1945 the Blue Grass Boys gave the surface appearance of being merely a string band. . . . They were a string band, however, with a crucial difference: Bill Monroe. The listener was always aware that, despite the particular vocal or instrumental style conveyed, Monroe was the driving cog and all other musicians revolved around him. With his mandolin setting the beat and rhythm for the band, Monroe

> *By the early 1950s so many bands were performing in Monroe's style that disc jockeys and fans began asking for "that blue grass music."*

also did most of the singing, taking most of the solo parts and generally sweeping up to a high tenor harmony on the choruses. Monroe's tenor singing—now often described as the 'high, lonesome sound'—set a standard for which most bluegrass musicians have striven."

Monroe's band began its major stylistic moves in the mid-1940s. First Monroe added a finger-picking banjo player to the group, even though the banjo was traditionally considered a comic instrument. Then he withdrew from the limelight somewhat, allowing other band members to do solo riffs and help with the singing. When the Blue Grass Boys greeted postwar America with a combination of fiddle, banjo, mandolin, guitar, and bass—and a rousing blend of traditional, blues, and instrumental tunes—the dynamic sound known as bluegrass was born.

The personnel of the Blue Grass Boys changed almost constantly, and it reads like a "Who's Who" of the genre: Earl Scruggs, Lester Flatt, Vassar Clements, Mac Wiseman, and Jimmy Martin were only a few of the musicians who worked with Monroe. Likewise, the list of songs Monroe either wrote or performed contains numerous bluegrass favorites, including "Blue Moon of Kentucky," "Little Georgia Rose," "Footprints in the Snow," "Orange Blossom Special," "Muleskinner Blues," "Rawhide," and "Panhandle Country."

Imitation is said to be the sincerest form of flattery, and Monroe's music soon drew legions of imitators—some of whom became temporarily more popular than their mentor. By the early 1950s so many bands were performing in Monroe's style that disc jockeys and fans began asking for "that blue grass music." The name was combined and used to describe a sound that was no longer identifiable as country or string band, although it seemed more traditional than either. Monroe himself experienced a lull in popularity in the late 1950s, watching in frustration as his proteges Flatt and Scruggs took center stage.

Monroe was rediscovered, however, as part of the folk revival of the 1960s and has been nearly worshipped ever since. Bluegrass itself has diverged dramatically from country-western music; Monroe's sound has become a favorite in the Northern industrial states, among college students and professionals as well as descendents of hill country folk. It is often performed outdoors at festivals, and one of the biggest is the yearly Bean Blossom Festival near Monroe's home, where the entertainer offers advice and encouragement to would-be pickers.

Malone notes that over the years Monroe "has mellowed significantly, becoming more open with interviewers and accepting his role as the patriarch of bluegrass." Never one to analyze his style or success, Monroe is quoted in *The Best of the Music Makers* as saying of his work: "If a man listening will let it, bluegrass will transmit right into your heart. If you love music and you listen close, it will come right into you. . . . If you really love bluegrass music it will dig in a long ways. If you take time to listen close to the words and the melody, it will do something for you."

Selected discography

Knee Deep in Blue Grass, Decca, 1958.
I Saw the Light, Decca, 1958.
Mr. Blue Grass, Decca, 1961.
The Great Bill Monroe, Harmony, 1961.

The Father of Bluegrass Music, Camden, 1962.
Blue Grass Ramble, Decca, 1962, reissued, MCA, 1980.
My All Time Country Favorites, Decca, 1962.
Blue Grass Special, Decca, 1963.
Bill Monroe—Songs with the Blue Grass Boys, Vocation, 1964.
I'll Meet You in Church Sunday Morning, Decca, 1964.
The Best of Bill Monroe, Harmony, 1964, reissued, MCA, 1980.
Bluegrass Instrumentals, Decca, 1965, reissued, MCA, 1980.
The High Lonesome Sound, Decca, 1966; reissued as *The High and Lonesome Sound of Bill Monroe and His Blue Grass Boys,* MCA, 1980.
Bill Monroe's Greatest Hits, Decca, 1968.
Early Blue Grass, RCA, 1969.
Bill Monroe and Charlie Monroe, Decca, 1969.
A Voice from on High, Decca, 1969, reissued, MCA, 1980.
Kentucky Blue Grass, Decca, 1970.
Sixteen All-Time Greatest Hits, Columbia, 1970.
Bill Monroe's Country Music Hall of Fame, Decca, 1971.
Bill Monroe's Uncle Pen, Decca, 1972.
Bill Monroe and James Monroe: Father & Son, MCA, 1973.
Bean Blossom, MCA, 1973.
Blue Grass Time, MCA, 1973.
Bill Monroe Sings Country Songs, MCA, 1973.
Bluegrass for Collectors, RCA, 1974.
Road of Life, MCA, 1974.
Weary Traveler, MCA, 1976.
Bill Monroe Sings Bluegrass Body and Soul, MCA, 1977.
Bill and James Monroe: Together Again, MCA, 1978.
Bean Blossom '79, MCA, 1979.
Blue Grass Style, MCA, 1980.
Master of Bluegrass, MCA, 1981.
Bill Monroe and Friends, MCA, 1983.
Bill Monroe, Columbia Historic Editions, 1984.
Classic Bluegrass Instrumentals, Rebel [Canada], 1985.
Bill Monroe and the Stars of the Bluegrass Hall of Fame, MCA, 1985.
Bluegrass '87, MCA, 1987.
Southern Flavor, MCA, 1988.

Sources

Books

Malone, Bill C. and Judith McCullogh, editors, *The Stars of Country Music,* University of Illinois Press, 1975.
Malone, Bill C., *Country Music U.S.A.,* revised edition, University of Texas Press, 1985.
Marschall, Rick, *The Encyclopedia of Country and Western Music,* Exeter, 1985.
Rooney, James, *Bossmen: Bill Monroe & Muddy Waters,* Dial Press, 1971.
Rosenberg, Neil V., *Bill Monroe and His Blue Grass Boys: An Illustrated Discography,* Country Music Foundation Press, 1974.

Simon, George T., *The Best of the Music Makers,* Doubleday, 1979.

Periodicals

Journal of American Folklore, July-September, 1965; April-June, 1967.
New York Times Magazine, September 13, 1970.

—*Anne Janette Johnson*

Mötley Crüe

Heavy metal rock group

Mötley Crüe's loud, irreverent, and hard-driving heavy metal music has drawn sneers from rock critics and nothing short of adulation from millions of teenaged fans. The songs, both in sound and substance, are precisely calculated to echo the aggressions and sexual fantasies of alienated younger Americans—and are just as precisely calculated to disturb parents and other adult authority figures. The members of Mötley Crüe do more than just preach a musical ethic of parties, fast women, and immediate self-satisfaction, they live those values from day to day, a phenomenon that is no small part of their appeal.

As David Handelman noted in *Rolling Stone,* heavy metal of the Mötley Crüe variety "has caught on as a sort of Lite punk: it smells and tastes like rebellion but without that political aftertaste. Its main selling points are that adults find it unlistenable, preachers call it blasphemous, and Tipper Gore blushes reading the lyrics. Fans at Crüe concerts say they like the group because the music is hard and fast, but they also like the band's reckless hedonism, which they read about in the metal fanzines."

For the Record. . .

Band formed in California during the early 1980s; original members include **Tommy Lee** (full name, Tommy Lee Bass; born c. 1963) on drums; **Mick Mars** (real name, Bob Deal; born c. 1956) guitar, vocals; **Vince Neil** (full name, Vince Neil Wharton; born c. 1961) lead singer; and **Nikki Sixx** (real name, Frank Carlton Serafino Ferranno; born c. 1959). Tommy Lee married Heather Locklear (an actress), May 10, 1986; Nikki Sixx married Vanity (a singer and actress); Mick Mars is twice divorced; Vince Neil was divorced in 1986. All band members are high school dropouts.

Addresses: c/o Elektra Asylum Nonesuch Records, 962 N. La Cienega Blvd., Los Angeles CA 90069.

That hedonism has become legend in less than six years: two Crüe members, Tommy Lee and Nikki Sixx have married starlets, singer Vince Neil was convicted of felony manslaughter for a drunk driving accident, and Sixx was a heroin addict during much of the band's early days. Handelman claims that the four rockers in Mötley Crüe "have continued to indulge in every conceivable rock & roll vice," and have celebrated their lifestyles in ear-splitting concerts with fireworks and other dazzling pyrotechnics. "I've always thought of us as the psychiatrists of rock & roll," Sixx told *Rolling Stone,* "because the kids come to see us get all this anxiety and pent-up aggression out. That hour and a half is theirs. No one can take it away. No parent can tell them to turn it down."

All four members of Mötley Crüe are high school dropouts who displayed rebellious tendencies in early youth. They met in California in the early 1980s after each had worked some time in various heavy metal club bands. Nikki Sixx was the founder of the group, originally called Christmas, but the band's name comes from the imagination of guitarist Mick Mars. Handelman recounts that Sixx and Tommy Lee recruited Mars after seeing his ad: "LOUD, RUDE, AGGRESSIVE GUITARIST AVAILABLE." Handelman quotes Lee as saying, "We didn't even have to hear him play. We went, 'This is the guy—he's disgusting.'" The band was rounded out with singer Vince Neil, whose onstage theatrics were more valuable than his vocal prowess.

By 1983 Mötley Crüe was a favorite new band among the heavy metal aficionados. Handelman notes that Crüe "has consumed more than 750 bottles of Jack Daniel's in its quest for musical excellence." In 1983 Sixx was quoted as saying: "We could just fall apart tomorrow or go straight to the top, because we're such extremists as personalities. It's like riding a roller coaster twenty-four hours a day. Every time you turn around, somebody's in jail or 100,000 kids are buying our album."

As with many heavy metal bands of the 1980s, Mötley Crüe was helped immensely by the advent of MTV (Music Television). The band's graphic music videos delighted teens and enraged would-be adult censors such as Tipper Gore, wife of congressman Albert Gore. The adult antipathy to Crüe's style only intensified the appeal for some teens; what surprised Crüe, and many other observers, was the age of the audience. Fan letters from ten- and eleven-year-olds were not uncommon, and the average age of a Mötley Crüe fan was fifteen—albeit a rather sophisticated fifteen.

"We play and write for the kids," Sixx told *Rolling Stone.* "We've never had peer acceptance. They couldn't see past the costumes. . . . Kid's don't buy Whitney Hous-

> *"Heavy metal of the Mötley Crüe variety has caught on as a sort of Lite punk: it smells and tastes like rebellion without that political aftertaste."*

ton. People that buy one record a year buy that. In the golden age of rock it was all kids playing for kids. Now it's that again." Neil added: "We don't write songs to be messages. . . . When I was younger, even now, I don't listen to the words. If I like the melody, I like the song." Sixx claimed: "I'm not a parent. I don't want to tell kids what to do."

Admittedly, Mötley Crüe music is not strong on lyrics. Most songs deal with the band, touring, male exploits with buddies or women, and parties. The tunes are classic hard rock, with insistent drum beat and catchy guitar riffs. What has made Mötley Crüe famous, however, is its road show—ninety minutes of special effects, racy leather clothing, and macho antics, all delivered at the peak of amplification. "We try to go overboard with the stage show," Neil told *Rolling Stone,* "so the kids get their money's worth. I'd be bummed if I went to a concert and they just stood there and played. That's not my idea of show business." Handelman comments that the music "stirs the kids up only to dump them back in the malls, as exhausted and aimless as ever."

Mötley Crüe has managed to maintain its original personnel despite occasional run-ins with the law and infrequent stays in substance abuse rehabilitation clinics. Marriages and drinking or drug problems are kept somewhat quiet, as they're seen to conflict with the band's wild and hedonistic image. In *Esquire* magazine, Bob Greene polled some Crüe fans for ideas on the source of the group's attraction. One nineteen-year-old girl replied: "I think they're all gorgeous. When I see them, I just naturally think of leather and whips and chains. I think that means that they're aggressive. I happen to love that image; it's a neat image. I think it's that kind of aggressiveness that a woman is always looking for." A thirteen-year-old female fan put it even more succinctly. "They're really good-looking," she said. "Good and mean. They just look like guys who are out to party and have a good time."

Selected discography

Mötley Crüe, Elektra, 1982.
Too Fast for Love, Elektra, 1982.
Shout at the Devil, Elektra, 1983.
Theatre of Pain, Elektra, 1985.
Girls, Girls, Girls, Elektra, 1987.

Sources

Esquire, May, 1984.
Rolling Stone, August 13, 1987.

—*Anne Janette Johnson*

Holly Near

Singer, songwriter; record company executive

Many of America's native art forms, from folk songs to pop ballads, relate the emotional life of women. Holly Near is becoming famous for bringing her feminist perspective to the full range of American sounds as she becomes one of the most widely known representatives of "women's music." Raised in northern California, Near was active in politically percieved performance of the early 1970s, from the rock musical "Hair" to Jane Fonda's Free the Army tour of Vietnam. She became a popular folksinger in the 1970s, writing both music and lyrics to her songs. Near chose to establish her own label, Redwood Records, rather than follow a major recording contract into pop or rock. Through women's music catalogues, such as Ladyslipper, sales at performances, and word-of-mouth, Redwood has managed to achieve success and stability. *Imagine My Surprise,* although considered Near's most women-identified recording by Ladyslipper, sold so well that it was named 1979 Album of the Year by the National Association of Independent Record Distributors.

Although best known as a solo vocal stylist, she has recorded with ensembles that represent the performance and/or political mode appropriate for specific songs, among them the reggae band Afrikan Dreamland (in "Unity" on *Speed of Light),* the Chilean group Inti-Illimani (on *Sing to Me This Dream),* and the Appalachian instrumental quartet Trapezoid (on *Watch Out).* Near's most famous coliaborations have been with the celebrated veteran of folk music, Ronnie Gilbert. They first worked together in 1980, when Near taught Gilbert her "Hay Una Mujer Desparecida," a process that was included in *Wasn't That a Time,* a film about the reunion concert of Gilbert and The Weavers. They sang together on two albums—*Singing with You* and *Lifeline*—and made a successful 11-city tour in 1983.

Near told Jennifer Dunning of the *New York Times* why she believed that the duets with Gilbert were so succesful: "I remember as a child seeing the Weavers perform and there was this woman who just stood there, threw back her head and sang. . . . So I went home and threw back my head for the next while. Ronnie has a huge voice and so do I. We can sing at the top of our lungs and not hold each other back and also understand that's not always appropriate." A critic for the *New York Times* described the atmosphere as "as much like a revival meeting as a pop concert."

In 1985 Near joined Gilbert, fellow Weaver Pete Seeger and Arlo Guthrie for a concert tour and recording both titled *Harp,* singing Weavers songs and her own "Foolish Notion." She can also be heard on three anthology albums—the soundtrack of *Woody Guthrie: Hard Travelin'* (singing "Pastures of Plenty" with Gilbert), *Bullets and Guitars* (songs for Central America), and *Reagonomics Blues* (singing "I Got Troubles").

Her solo concerts are almost always benefits for political or environmental causes. She performs a wide variety of music, ranging from her own songs and narratives to the classic ballads of the 1940s, including "Stormy Weather" and "Come Rain or Come Shine." Near frequently brings a new perspective to those songs, as Stephen Holden thought when he reviewed a 1985 concert: "She led the audience in a rendition of 'I Can't Give You Anything but Love' that treated the song as a folk anthem rather than a Tin Pan Alley standard." Her voice and vocal control are often admired in reviews, as Robert Palmer did in a 1979 *New York Times* review: "An engaging singer, with excellent control of texture and dynamics from the top to the bottom of her broad range . . . she can be enjoyed for her purely musical qualities and her ability to transmit the depth of her feelings without resorting to stridency."

Selected discography

Hang in There, Redwood, 1973.
Imagine My Surprise, Redwood, 1979.
Lifeline, Redwood, 1983.
Sing to Me the Dream, Redwood, 1984.
HARP, Redwood, 1985.
Singing with You, Redwood, 1986.
Don't Hold Back, Redwood, 1987.

Sources

New York Times, December 16, 1979; June 13, 1982; October 2, 1983; October 13, 1983; December 15, 1985.
Village Voice, April 26, 1983.

—Barbara Stratyner

Willie Nelson

Singer, songwriter, guitarist

robably no country singer has generated more warmth from a more diverse group of fans than Willie Nelson, the "outlaw" superstar from Texas. Nelson's unusual voice, eclectic musical tastes, down-home personality, and songwriting talents have combined to produce an engaging performer whose "fast living and hard-won wisdom . . . stirs even the most well-guarded emotions, "wrote an *Esquire* reviewer. In *Superstars of Country Music,* Gene Busnar wrote: "Who would ever guess that this gritty-looking . . . man is one of America's most important stars. A singer whose records cross all boundaries of audience appeal; an actor with a natural presence who is as comfortable on a movie set as he is on the concert stage; a personality so magnetic that a clothes designer has even started marketing jeans with his name on them. . . . In an era that favors glitter and glamour, Willie comes across as the kind of guy with whom you could sit down and swap stories rather than some distant pop star who lives in his own world."

Rolling Stone contributor Stephen Holden feels that it is Nelson's music, more than his casual rural persona, that attracts listeners. "What makes Nelson contemporary is the way his singing lets in the darkness—fear, loneliness, despair—so that the lyrics emerge as statements of truth rather than as soothing homilies," Holden maintains. "Willie Nelson has a touch of the preacher in him. He can stand back, look outside himself and turn pop tunes into parables that have a universal as well as a personal meaning." Frank McConnell speaks even more highly of Nelson in a *Commonweal* essay. According to McConnell, Nelson, "God help him, seems to have turned himself into a living repository of the tradition of American popular song."

Nelson himself might be taken aback by the praise heaped upon him. His origins were extremely modest, and he spent many years behind the Nashville scenes as a songwriter for others before America's taste in music caught up with his innovative style. Nelson was born in tiny Abbott, Texas, on April 30, 1933, the only son of Ira and Myrtle Nelson. When he was only two his parents separated, so he and his sister Bobbie (who still performs with his band) were raised by their grandparents.

Like most youngsters of his era, Nelson enjoyed listening to the radio; he heard broadcasts of the Grand Ole Opry and the pop standards of the Depression era, and these were offset by the live singing he heard in church and out in the cotton fields. Busnar quotes Nelson: "I first heard the blues picking cotton in a field full of black people. One would sing a line at this end of the field, another one at that end. I realized they knew more

For the Record. . .

Born April 30, 1933, in Abbott, Tex.; son of Ira D. (a pool hall owner) and Myrtle Nelson; married Martha Matthews (a barmaid) c. 1951 (divorced, c. 1960); married Shirley Collie (a singer), c. 1962 (divorced, 1969); married Connie Koepke (a lab technician), 1972; children: (first marriage) Lana, Billy, Susie; (third marriage) Paula Carlene, Amy Lee; (with Ann-Marie D'Angelo) Lucas Nelson. *Education:* Attended Baylor University. *Military service:* Served in U.S. Air Force.

Songwriter and performer, 1946—. Worked as door-to-door salesman and radio announcer, c. 1952-59; bass player in Ray Price band, Nashville, Tenn., 1960-62; formed his own band, 1962; regular cast member of Grand Ole Opry, 1964-69.

Actor in motion pictures, including "Electric Horseman," 1979, "Honeysuckle Rose," 1980 (also released as "On the Road Again," 1982), "Thief," 1981, "Barbarosa," 1982, "Red-Headed Stranger," 1986, and "Stagecoach" (made-for-TV), 1986; has also appeared in guest roles on television, including "Miami Vice."

Awards: Named to Nashville Songwriters Association Hall of Fame, 1973; winner of five Grammy Awards, five Country Music Association Awards, and one Academy Award nomination (for best song, 1980, for "On the Road Again").

Addresses: *Residence*—Colorado. *Business*—Mark Rothbaum & Associates, P.O. Box 2689, Danbury, CT 06813. *Other*—6600 Baseline Rd., Little Rock AR 72209.

about music, soul, and feeling than I did. Plus they could pick more cotton."

Nelson got his first guitar at the age of nine, learned some chords from his grandfather, and was soon performing in John Ray's Polka Band, a favorite of the Polish and Czech immigrants in the area. By his freshman year of high school he had joined a family band led by his father and his sister, Bobbie. This was a standard country/swing band and it soon became popular enough to perform regularly in honky tonks and local radio spots. On the side Nelson wrote songs—both lyrics and music. He wanted to be a career musician, but the obstacles seemed insurmountable to a rural Texas boy.

After a brief stint in the Air Force (he was discharged after a back injury), Nelson married Martha Matthews, a waitress, and took whatever work he could find. He soon had three children to support. For a time he sold encyclopedias and Bibles door-to-door, worked as a janitor, a plumber's helper, and a disc jockey, while continuing his nightly performing in bars and clubs. Busnar notes that some of Nelson's performing venues "were so rough that chicken-wire fences were put up to protect the band from bottles and chairs that were thrown around."

Nelson might have lost hope in these lean years if some of his songs hadn't attracted attention. In 1959 he sold the rights to "Family Bible," an early effort, for $50—just to feed his family. The next year, Claude Gray recorded the song, and it became a top ten country hit—without earning Nelson another dime. Still, Nelson had earned a name as a songwriter, so he decided to risk his fortune in Nashville. He sold the rights to another tune, "Night Life," for $150, bought a used car, and moved to Tennessee. Ironically, "Night Life" became a country classic, recorded by more than seventy artists, and selling an estimated 30 million copies. But since Nelson had sold the rights, he did not earn any royalties for it.

Nelson lived a hard-drinking and brawling life in Nashville, but his songwriting and singing careers took off nevertheless. His first wife left him, and the money he earned for his tunes "either went for booze or lawyers," he said in Busnar's account. He married a second time, to singer Shirley Collie, and performed his own music at Tootsie's Bar, a proving ground for young Nashville hopefuls. There he met Ray Price, who had had a major hit with "Night Life." Price invited Nelson to join his band, and for several years Nelson played bass with the group.

During those years Nelson wrote hits for Patsy Kline ("Crazy") and Faron Young ("Hello Walls"), and saw one of his pieces, "Funny How Time Slips Away," recorded more than eighty times. Nelson was still dissatisfied, however. He wanted to sing his own songs, in his own style. Nashville's conservative producers fought him every step of the way, convinced that his voice needed slick background instrumentation to cover its "defects." Nelson had one country hit, "Touch Me," in 1962, and a popular duet with his wife, "Willingly," but his overproduced albums failed to sell. However, he was invited to join the regular cast of the Grand Ole Opry in 1964, and he appeared regularly there for five years.

A chance house fire proved the final catalyst to a daring career change for Nelson in 1969. When his Nashville home suddenly went up in flames—all he saved was his beloved guitar—he decided to head home for Texas and perform the way he wanted to perform. At that time Austin had become a minor music center and was known as a refuge for disenchanted country-western bands. When Nelson returned to his home state, "he immediately became the center of the Austin scene, and therefore became the focus around which the attempted mating of country and rock would take place," wrote to Bill C. Malone and Judith McCulloh in *The Stars of Country Music.*

Nelson and his pals Kris Kristofferson, Leon Russell, and Waylon Jennings became the nucleus of the celebrated "Outlaws" of country music, a group of performers who dared to integrate rock, blues, and pop into their music and their images. The Outlaws were more than mere country/rock singers however—they simply rebelled against Nashville's well-groomed sound and returned in style and substance to the foot-pounding dance hall music favored by so called "rednecks" and cowboys.

Interestingly enough, the Outlaw sound did indeed appeal to the rural rowdies, many of whom shared Nelson's disillusionment with glitzy Nashville, but it also found an audience among the urban young of the counterculture. Nelson had finally found his stride as a performer. His 1971 album *Shotgun Willie* sold more copies than all his previous albums combined, and two subsequent works, *Phases and Stages* and *Red Head-*

"His singing lets in the darkness—fear, loneliness, despair—so that the lyrics emerge as statements of the truth rather than as soothing homilies."

---

ed Stranger, did even better. In 1976 Nelson and Jennings recorded *Wanted: The Outlaws,* an effort that won the Country Music Association's "album of the year" and "single of the year " awards.

Ironically, as Nelson's performing career accelerated, his writing career slowed. He turned out less original work and began to record more and more tunes written by other people, especially Kristofferson. This creative slowdown did not diminish Nelson's significance, however, because he experimented constantly with fresh arrangements of older material. McConnell calls Nelson's music "a *reclamation* and rediscovery of songs we thought we had already heard too often. Like Billie Holiday—the one singer to whom he can be seriously compared—Willie brings pristine intelligence to the cliche-ridden lyrics among which we live our lives. And is this not the central act of intelligence altogether?"

Intelligent or simply moving, Nelson has not lacked for hits old and new in the years since 1975. He has won Grammies for "Blue Eyes Crying in the Rain" and "Georgia on My Mind," two often-recorded classics, and has had top ten hits with "Mamas, Don't Let Your Babies Grow up To Be Cowboys," "On the Road Again," and "You Were Always on My Mind." He has been equally at home with roaring country dance tunes and wistful melodies like "Somewhere over the Rainbow," and has consequently attracted fans of many different tastes.

In a final wry twist, the critics have begun to praise Nelson for the very trait that almost stymied his career—his unusual voice. Holden contends that Nelson "seizes the emotional kernels of songs, wrings out the words in a keening baritone, then shucks off the filler like chaff." McConnell simply states that Nelson's is "a voice that may be one of the true marvels of twentieth-century song."

Whatever the ups and downs of Nelson's personal life may be—and they are many—he tries to keep in touch with his true fans, the devotees of decades as well as the more sophisticated newcomers. McConnell writes: "Even at this stage of his legend, he will still show up in a packed auditorium redolent of corn dogs and draft beer as readily as in a room smelling of expensive grass and Beefeater martinis." Nelson most enjoys outdoors concerts such as his now-famous Fourth of July "picnics" and the benefit "Farm Aid" performances. Busnar concludes that the "former country outlaw" has become "a primary reason why country music grew from a regional music form to one that now has devoted followers in all parts of America. . . . If there is anything aspiring vocalists can learn from him, it would be to absorb as much music as possible and sing it as honestly as one can."

Selected discography

And Then I Wrote, Liberty, 1962.
Here's Willie Nelson, Liberty, 1963.
Country Willie—His Own Songs, RCA, 1965.
Country Favorites—Willie Nelson Style, RCA, 1966.
Hello Walls, Sunset, 1966.
Country Music Concert—Willie Nelson, RCA, 1966.
Make Way for Willie Nelson, RCA, 1967.
The Party's Over, RCA, 1967.
Texas in My Soul, RCA, 1968.
Good Ol' Country Singin', CAL, 1968.
Good Times, RCA, 1968.
My Own Peculiar Way, RCA, 1969.
Both Sides Now, RCA, 1970.
Laying My Burdens Down, RCA, 1970.

Columbus Stockade Blues, Camden, 1970.
Willie Nelson and Family, RCA, 1971.
Yesterday's Wine, RCA, 1971.
The Words Don't Fit the Pictures, RCA, 1972.
The Willie Way, RCA, 1972.
The Best of Willie Nelson, United Artists, 1973.
Country Winners by Willie, Camden, 1973.
Shotgun Willie, Atlantic, 1973.
Spotlight on Willie Nelson, Camden, 1974.
Phases and Stages, Atlantic, 1974.
Red-Headed Stranger, Columbia, 1975.
Willie Nelson and His Friends, Plantation, 1975.
What Can You Do to Me, RCA, 1975.
Country Willie, United Artists, 1975.
Famous Country, RCA, 1975.
The Sound in Your Mind, Columbia, 1976.
The Troublemaker, Columbia, 1976.
(With Waylon Jennings) *Wanted: The Outlaws,* RCA, 1976.
Columbus Stockade Blues and Other Country Favorites, Camden, 1976.
Willie Nelson Live, RCA, 1976.
Texas Country, United Artists, 1976.
Willie Before His Time, RCA, 1977.
To Lefty from Willie, Columbia, 1977.
Willie Nelson—1961, Shotgun, 1977.
(With Jennings) *Waylon and Willie,* RCA, 1978.
Stardust, Columbia, 1978.
Face of a Fighter, Lonestar, 1978.
There'll Be No Teardrops Tonight, United Artists, 1978.
Willie and Family Live, Columbia, 1978.
(With Leon Russell) *Pretty Paper,* CBS, 1979.
Help Me Make It Through the Night, Columbia, 1979.
Sweet Memories, RCA, 1979.
(With Russell) *One for the Road,* Columbia, 1979.
Willie Nelson Sings Kristofferson, Columbia, 1979.
The Electric Horseman, Columbia, 1979.
(With Ray Price) *San Antonio Rose,* Columbia, 1980.
(With the Nashville Brass) *Danny Davis and Willie Nelson,* RCA, 1980.
Honeysuckle Rose, Columbia, 1980.
(With Davis, Price, and the Nashville Brass) *Family Bible,* Songbird, 1980.
Minstrel Man, RCA, 1981.
Somewhere over the Rainbow, Columbia, 1981.
Greatest Hits and Some That Be, Columbia, 1981.
Always on My Mind, Columbia, 1982.
The Best of Willie, RCA, 1982.
(With Jennings) *W.W. II,* RCA, 1982.
(With Kris Kristofferson, Dolly Parton, and Brenda Lee) *Kris, Willie, Dolly and Brenda: The Winning Hand,* Monument, 1982.
(With Merle Haggard) *Poncho and Lefty,* Columbia, 1983.
Tougher than Leather, Columbia, 1983.

Without a Song, CBS, 1983.
(With Jennings) *Take It to the Limit,* Columbia, 1983.
Portrait in Music, Columbia, 1984.
City of New Orleans, Columbia, 1984.
(With Jackie King) *Angel Eyes,* Columbia, 1985.
Collector's Series, Columbia, 1985.
Partners, Columbia, 1986.
The Promiseland, Columbia, 1986.
Island in the Sea, Columbia, 1987.

Also recorded *City of Dreams,* Columbia; *Don't You Ever Get Tired of Hurting Me,* RCA; *My Own Way,* RCA; (with Hank Snow) *Brand on My Heart;* and (with Faron Young) *Funny How Time Slips Away.*

Compositions

Composer of numerous songs, including "Night Life," "Crazy," "Hello Walls," "Funny How Time Slips Away," "Family Bible," "I Just Can't Let You Say Goodbye," "One Day at a Time," "The Party's Over," "Touch Me," "Pretty Paper," "Half a Man," "What Can You Do to Me Now," "Shotgun Willie," "So Much To Do," "I Still Can't Believe You're Gone," (with Waylon Jennings) "Good Hearted Woman," "Angel Flying Too Close to the Ground," "On the Road Again," and "Forgiving You Was Easy."

Sources

Books

Busnar, Gene, *Superstars of Country Music,* J. Messner, 1979.
Malone, Bill C. and Judith McCulloh, *Stars of Country Music,* University of Illinois Press, 1975.
Marschall, Rick, *The Encyclopedia of Country and Western Music,* Exeter, 1985.
Nelson, Willie, *Willie: An Autobiography,* Simon & Schuser, 1988.
The Rolling Stone Record Guide, Random House, 1979.

Periodicals

Commonweal, October 4, 1985.
Country Music, January, 1974.
Esquire, March, 1985.
High Fidelity, March, 1981.
Life, August, 1986.
Newsweek, August 14, 1978.
New York Times Magazine, March 26, 1978.
Rolling Stone, June 11, 1981.
Time, September 19, 1977; September 23, 1985.

—Anne Janette Johnson

Mark O'Connor

Violinist, guitarist

Mark O'Connor is a true musical prodigy. He began playing guitar at age six, moved on to violin at 11 and was winning national fiddle championships by age 12. He won the National Junior Fiddle Championship four years running from 1974 to 1977. During almost the same period (1973 to 1976) he won the National Old Time Fiddle Championship. He moved on to win more prestigious titles and captured the Grand National Fiddle Championship three years in a row (1979 to 1981). Then he exited the contest circuit and began touring with David Grisman's band.

Grisman was a bluegrass pioneer who helped shake country music loose from its rural roots. He wrote music for the traditional bluegrass quartet (fiddle, mandolin, guitar and bass) that was closer to jazz and classical chamber music than down-home country. O'Connor joined Grisman's group in the early 1980s but primarily played guitar while the group featured violinists Stephane Grappelli and Darol Anger. He departed the group after a skiing accident resulted in a broken arm.

In an interview in *down beat* O'Connor said: "Breaking my arm was like fate. I lay in the hospital bed and knew someone was trying to tell me something. I'd been a little unhappy in the Grisman band because . . . I knew I

could be better known as a violin player because it's my natural instrument." In his tenure in the Grisman band, he had learned about the new directions the country violin was taking and the new realms into which country music could be pushed. His next outings moved him into the world of rock.

When O'Connor joined the Dregs they had simplified their name from the Dixie Dregs to help dispel their image as just another southern country-rock band. The Dregs' music can best be described as jazz-rock, or "fusion"—a term that indicates the influence of jazz improvisation, classical motifs, and a variety of ethnic rhythms. O'Connor loved playing in an electric band with the added kick of drums and the punch of electric bass. Although the Dregs' music allowed a lot of room for improvisation, most of it was orchestrated. O'Connor, who never learned to read music, learned the orchestrated parts by ear. The Dregs' 1982 release, *Industry Standard,* with O'Connor playing violin, may be one of the band's most successful albums.

O'Connor's earliest solo albums are steeped in bluegrass and country music and showcase his violin virtuosity. The 1979 release *Markology* is for the guitar aficionado—O'Connor's innovative flatpicking style can be heard along with guest guitarists Tony Rice and Dan Crary. Reviewing the album, *Guitar Player* said: "Mark O'Connor flatpicks bluegrass music in a clear, rippling style punctuated with unexpected chromatic flurries, effective syncopation, and blues bends. . . . [His] maturity and his musical intuition are even more remarkable than his dazzling technique."

On the Rampage (1981) mirrors the fusion influences of his tenure with Grisman and the Dregs, but his still-youthful enthusiasm is reflected in this quote from the album jacket: "Thanks to the obsession I had with skateboarding during my 17th year, this music was able to flow out from me. As you listen, picture me catching air off a vertical wall. I'm still going for it."

With the releases of *Meanings of* and *False Dawn* we see the emergence of O'Connor's personal style, one that incorporates the many different influences in his career. He demonstrates that he can compose and arrange music and play almost any instrument with strings. The albums are self-produced and he overdubs his playing on violin, viola, mandolin, cello, dulcimer, bass, and a variety of acoustic, classical, and electric guitars. *Meanings of,* his first album for Warner Brothers, got mixed reviews. It was praised for O'Connor's inventiveness and mastery of his instruments but was also called "cluttered and claustrophobic" *(Washington Post)* and marked by "instrumental pyrotechnics and run-wild egotism" *(down beat).*

But his pyrotechnics are not egoistic. They just show his youthful delight at discovering new sounds with his instruments. His early violin playing was grounded in the strict traditional styles which were required to win fiddle contests. His approach to the guitar evolved when he played with the Grisman band and is strongly influenced by his violin techniques. He says that when he played guitar with country musicians he surprised them by inventing new chords. Later, as he played with a broader range of musicians, he discovered that his chords were well known in jazz circles.

He also has a remarkable pair of hands. *Guitar Player* noted that he has a reach of seven frets: "He has extremely long, thin left-hand fingers that can actually stretch between 1/4 and 3/8 [of an inch] out of their sockets. His joints even allow him to bend his fingers to touch the back of his hand." O'Connor attributes this physical dexterity to a long history of playing during his youth while his hands were still developing.

Success at a young age has not been easy. As he told *Guitar Player:* "When you're around drunken Texans and drugged-out rock and rollers and you're young, you've got to keep control. I was really strong about that and nobody could budge me. I just told myself what was happening and let all my emotions and feelings out through the music." Now a much in-demand Nashville session player, he regularly appears in recording studios with the likes of Dolly Parton, Chet Atkins, Leon Redbone and the Nitty Gritty Dirt Band. With his eclectic solo releases he is earning a reputation as a musician of the New Age. Although he started young, his musical career is still just beginning.

Selected discography

Four-Time National Junior Fiddle Champion, Rounder, 1974.
Pickin' in the Wind, Rounder, 1976.
Texas Jam Session, OMAC.
In Concert, OMAC.
Markology, Rounder, 1979.
On the Rampage, Rounder, 1981.
Soppin' the Gravy, Rounder.
False Dawn, Rounder, 1984.
Meanings of, Warner Bros., 1986.
Stone from Which the Arch Was Made, Warner Bros., 1987.

With David Grisman Band

Quintet '80, Warner Bros., 1980.
Mondo Mando, Warner Bros., 1981.
Stephane Grappelli/David Grisman, Warner Bros.

With the Dregs

Industry Standard, Arista, 1982.

Sources

Audio, June, 1986; October, 1987.
Country Music, May-June, 1986.
down beat, June, 1982; May, 1984; July, 1986.
Esquire, December, 1985.
Guitar Player, May, 1980; April, 1981; July, 1982; March, 1984; April, 1987.
People, February, 1986.
Stereo Review, September, 1984; February, 1987.
Washington Post, August 15, 1981.

—Tim LaBorie

Luciano Pavarotti

Singer

Luciano Pavarotti is considered by many to be the greatest male singer since Enrico Caruso, and in his prime—the mid-1970s—he was probably the century's best lyric tenor. He is known for his extraordinary vocal capacity, earning the nickname "King of the High Cs" after executing the string of high notes in Gaetano Donizetti's fiendishly difficult *La Fille du regiment.* His voice, at once capable of sweetness and immense volume, is considered the ideal medium for Italian opera's celebrated *bel canto* works, those works calling for purity of tone and articulation even in the upper register. Pavarotti has embraced such works gleefully, and with both his extraordinary voice and his endearing, puckish personality, he is largely perceived as the opera performer who best recalls previous greats such as Caruso and Jussi Bjoerling. As Hubert Saal noted in a 1976 *Newsweek,* "More than any other tenor today, Luciano Pavarotti . . . summons up the legendary golden age of singing."

Born in Modena, Italy, in 1935, Pavarotti sang from early childhood. At home, he was often exposed to recordings by Caruso, Bjoerling, and Benaimino Gigli. Though an impressive singer, Pavarotti aspired in his youth to a career as a professional soccer player. His mother, however, urged him to pursue a more realistic career, and in the 1950s he trained as a teacher. He subsequently taught at an elementary school for two years, but with his father's encouragement he continued to train his voice. Pavarotti's efforts proved successful in 1961 when he won a music contest and secured the role of Rodolfo in Giacomo Puccini's *La Boheme* in nearby Regia Emilia. His success in Puccini's great opera led to further roles in such works as Donizetti's dramatic masterwork *Lucia di Lammermoor.*

Throughout the early 1960s, Pavarotti continued to distinguish himself in the *bel canto* repertoire, enjoying particular success with celebrated soprano Joan Sutherland in Donizetti operas, including *L'Elisir d'amore* and the aforementioned *Lucia di Lammermoor.* In still another Donizetti work, *La Fille du regiment,* he awed audiences by soaring through the difficult string of high Cs that mark the opera's highlight. Word soon spread through the opera world of Pavarotti's extraordinary capacity for sustained vocal purity, and in 1967 he made his American debut as Rodolfo in a San Francisco Opera production of *La Boheme.* The following year he reprised the role at the Metropolitan Opera, whereupon he won great praise for his supremely beautiful singing. By the end of the decade Pavarotti was recognized as a supreme force in *bel canto* opera, distinguishing himself further with his performances on recordings of *La Fill du regiment* and Bellini's *Beatrice di Tenda.*

Aside from mastering the *bel canto* repertoire, Pavarotti also earned distinction with his performances in works by Giuseppe Verdi, who is often considered Italy's master opera composer. Among Pavarotti's greatest Verdi roles at this time was the duke in *Rigoletto,* in which capacity he inevitably astounded audiences with his rendition of the well-known "Donna e mobile." As his voice grew in richness and depth, Pavarotti broadened his own repertoire to include other Verdi operas, notably *Il Trovatore,* where his rousing interpretation of Manrico's call to war often inspired wild enthusiasm from opera lovers. Other roles Pavarotti assumed at this time include Cavaradossi in Puccini's *Tosca* and the Calaf—though on recording only—in Puccini's *Turandot.* "Nessun dorma," the tenor centerpiece of this work, has become a mainstay of Pavarotti's solo performances.

In the 1980s, Pavarotti has strengthened his status as one of the opera world's leading figures. Since his first appearance on the Metropolitan Opera's stage, Pavarotti has expanded his repertoire with considerable success, assaying works ranging from Wolfgang Amadeus Mozart's *Idomeneo* to Verdi's *Aida,* while continuing to appear in those works—notably *La Boheme, Lucia di Lammermoor,* and *Rigoletto,* which helped established him as one of the century's great tenors. Televised performances of Pavarotti in many of his greatest roles have enabled him to not only sustain his status but to considerably broaden his appeal, reaching millions of viewers each time one of his opera performances and solo concerts or recitals is broadcast. He has also shown increasing flexibility as a recording artist. While he continues to appear on recordings of complete operas—with *Idomeneo* and Bellini's *Norma* among his most impressive records from the 1980s—he has also released collections of Italian folk songs and even an album of compositions by Henry Mancini.

Pavarotti seems comfortable with his vast popularity. Although mobbed in public and worshipped in the opera house, he stays committed to serving his art. Unabashed in proclaiming his own pursuit of fame and acclaim—"I want to be famous everywhere," he told *Newsweek*'s Saal—he greatly reciprocates his fans' dedication and shows a marked appreciation for the attention he is accorded by music lovers everywhere. "I tell you," he confided to Saal, "the time spent signing autographs is never long enough."

Selected discography

Collections and concert recordings

Best of Pavarotti (four-record set), London.
Bravo Pavarotti (two-record set), London.
Great Pavarotti, London.
Pavarotti's Greatest Hits (two-record set), London.
Pavarotti in Concert, London.
Mamma, London.
O Solo Mio-Neopolitan Songs, London.
Passione, London.
Verismo Arias, London.
Volare, London.
World's Favorite Tenor Arias, London.
Yes, Giorgio (motion picture soundtrack), London.

Opera recordings

Bellini, Vicenzo, *Norma,* London.
Bellini, *I Puritani,* London.
Donizetti, Gaetano, *La Fille du regimente,* London.
Donizetti, *La Favorita,* London.
Donizetti, *Lucia di Lammermoor,* London.
Donizetti, *L'Elisir d'amore,* London.
Mozart, Wolfgang Amadeus, *Idomeneo,* London.
Puccini, Giacamo, *La Boheme,* London.
Puccini, *Madama Butterfly,* London.
Puccini, *Turandot,* London.
Puccini, *Tosca,* London.

Verdi, Giuseppe, *Aida*, London.
Verdi, *Un Ballo in maschera*, London.
Verdi, *Rigoletto*, London.
Verdi, *La Traviata*, London.
Verdi, *Il Trovatore*, London.

Writings

(with William Wright) *Pavarotti: My Own Story* (autobiography),
   Warner Books, 1982.

Sources

Books

Hines, Jerome, *Great Singers on Great Singing*, Doubleday,
   1982.

Matheopoulos, Helena, *Divo: Great Tenors, Baritones, and
   Basses Discuss Their Roles*, Harper, 1986.
Mayer, Martin, and Gerald Fitzgerald, *Grandissimo Pavarotti*,
   Doubleday, 1986.
Pavarotti, Luciano, and William Wright, *Pavarotti: My Own Story*,
   Doubleday, 1981.
Schoenberg, Harold, *The Glorious Ones: Classical Music's
   Legendary Performers*, Times Books, 1985.
Tenors, edited by Herbert H. Breslin, Macmillan, 1974.

Periodicals

Esquire, June 5, 1979.
Newsweek, March 15, 1976.
New York, May 18, 1981, January 27, 1986.
New Yorker, October 15, 1973.
Opera News, December 10, 1983, March 29, 1986.
Time, October 25, 1976.

Iggy Pop

Singer, songwriter, drummer

"Iggy had gone beyond performance—to the point where it really was some kind of psychodrama," said John Sinclair. "I'd just watch him and I'd think, 'Wow, this guy will stop at nothing. This isn't just a show—he's out of his mind.'"

Indeed, that's the exact reaction Iggy Pop hoped to get out of his audiences as they witnessed a show by his band, The Psychedelic Stooges. Resembling the freak show in a circus, Iggy often reverted to tactics such as smearing peanut butter and feces on himself, rolling around on stage in broken glass and even diving head first into the crowd. All of this a good seven years before the punk movement and about 1,000 light years away from the Pat Boone school of rock and roll.

Born James Osterberg in 1947 in Ypsilanti, Michigan, he first became musically involved in high school, playing in a local band, the Iguanas. He left them for a rival band, the Prime Movers, before he took off to Chicago to play blues drums. Upon moving back to the Ann Arbor area, he switched his name to Iggy Pop and formed The Psychedelic Stooges. With Dave Alexander on bass and brothers Ron and Scott Ashton on guitar and drums respectively, Iggy held down the vocals and insanity positions. They played their first gig on March 3, 1968, opening for Blood Sweat & Tears at Detroit's Grande Ballroom.

The music in Michigan at that time was quite different from what was popular on the national scene. The Motown sound was dying down but bands like the MC5, Frost, and the Amboy Dukes were highpowered and revolutionary. By 1969 Elektra records realized the potential and signed both the Stooges and MC5 to contracts. Former Velvet Underground member John Cale produced their first album, *The Stooges*. With songs like "No Fun" and "I Wanna Be Your Dog" it was obvious the band was about as far from flower-power as one could get.

The Stooges continued to play around the Midwest, and in 1970 they entered the studio to record their follow-up LP, *Funhouse*. Robert Christgau's review in his *Record Guide* noted: "Now I regret all the times I've used words like 'power' and 'energy' to describe rock and roll, because this is what such rhetoric should have been saved for. Shall I compare it to an atom bomb? a wrecker's ball? a hydro electric plant? Language wasn't designed for the job."

The live show was beyond pathetic by now; later, in 1979, Iggy would reflect in *Rolling Stone,* "I hated the audience, at times, for things they made you do. Why did they come see me?" A band cannot survive for long playing with such abandon and, sure enough, the Stooges collapsed shortly after. Their last performance was at the Goose Lake [Michigan] Festival before 100,000 fans. Iggy took a year off to kick a heroin habit, enduring three weeks of cold turkey in the process. "Iggy's power and Iggy's curse," wrote Chris Holdenfield in *Rolling Stone,* "is that he has always lived out his show, unlike those who make a production out of the pose, Alice Cooper, Kiss . . . or Bowie."

In 1972 British pop star David Bowie regrouped the Stooges, with James Williamson now on guitar and Ron Ashton moving to bass. Bowie took the band to London to produce, or overproduce, their third LP, *Raw Power.* Even with Bowie mixing the sound as thin as possible, "It's a toss-up as to whether this disc or the earlier *Funhouse* takes the throne as Highest Energy Album Ever Made," wrote the editors of *Rock Revolution,* "but there's absolutely no competition. All other Heavy Metal was and is farina next to them."

Again the band burnt out, this time for good. A posthumously released album (recorded on a cassette), *Metallic K.O.,* captured the Stooges last performance ever (at the Michigan Palace). It's obvious from listening that Iggy was completely losing it by that time. The back of the album jacket blatantly states in hugh quotes "OPEN UP AND BLEED." Iggy badgers the audience with the foulest language and songs like "Cock in My Pocket".

Iggy spent the next two years wandering around the streets of Los Angeles. Under his mother's insurance he was checked into the UCLA mental hospital for treatment. He was visited by Bowie, the only member of the music community to do so. Bowie made a deal with Iggy to clean up his act so he could join him on his upcoming tour, *Station To Station.* "I saw David entertaining and running his life," Iggy told Charles Young in *Rolling Stone.* "I thought, 'Now there's a man. I can do it too.'" He moved to Berlin in the spring of 1976, shortly after Bowie.

The two collaborated on Iggy's comeback effort, 1977's *The Idiot.* Bowie co-wrote the songs and played keyboards on the ensuing tour (along with Hunt Sales-drums, Tony Sales-bass and Ricky Gardiner-guitar). The sound was a far cry from the Stooges'. It was stripped down and hauntingly different from anything else. "*The Idiot* is the most savage indictment of rock posturing ever recorded," John Swenson wrote, reflecting on Iggy winning the 1977 *Rolling Stone* Critics' Poll Comeback of the Year Award ("But back from where?").

With basically the same band (with the addition of Carlos Alomar) Iggy quickly followed up with *Lust For*

> *"Iggy is bizarre enough to attract those inclined toward something different but safe enough not to scare them away."*

Life, again recorded in Berlin and styled after *The Idiot.* The live performances showed a healthier Iggy, more in control, but "like Lou Reed," wrote Billy Altman, "Iggy is most likely headed on a course just left of center, bizarre enough to attract those inclined toward something different but safe enough not to scare them away."

Iggy has released six more solo albums, all with his trademark deadpan vocals, moans, and shrieks, but nothing as powerful as the Stooges. He continues to provide entertaining concerts and to influence younger musicians, but as Sid Vicious might have testified, the Ig was a hard act to follow. He's a "willful, bratty child, a cruelly shrewd man and a total ham—in short, a classic American hero," according to Kristine McKenna in *Rolling Stone,* ". . . right up there with Abraham Lincoln." High praise for a man who used to wear his Skippy.

Selected discography

With the Stooges

The Stooges, Elektra, 1969.
Funhouse, Elektra, 1970.
Raw Power, Columbia, 1973.
Metallic K.O., Skydog, 1976.

Solo albums

The Idiot, RCA, 1977.
Lust for Life, RCA, 1977.
T.V. Eye, RCA, 1978.
New Values, Arista, 1979.
Soldier, Arista, 1980.
Zombie Birdhouse, Animal, 1982.
Blah-Blah-Blah, A&M, 1986.
Instinct, A&M, 1988.

Sources

Books

Christgau, Robert, *Christgau's Record Guide,* Ticknor & Fields, 1981.
Dalton, David, and Lenny Kaye, *Rock 100,* Grosset & Dunlap, 1977.
The Illustrated Encyclopedia of Rock, Harmony, 1977.
Nilsen, Per, and Dorothy Sherman, *The Wild One: The True Story of Iggy Pop,* Omnibus Press, 1988.
Rock Revolution, by the editors of *Creem* magazine, Popular Library, 1976.
The Rolling Stone Record Guide, edited by Dave Marsh and John Swenson, Randon House/Rolling Stone Press, 1979.

Periodicals

Fun, November, 1988.
Rolling Stone, May 5, 1977; May 19, 1977; December 29, 1977; January 12, 1978; October 4, 1979; May 27, 1980.

—*Calen D. Stone*

Elvis Presley

Singer, songwriter, guitarist

Admired as one of the most successful recording artists of all time, American singer and guitarist Elvis Presley exploded onto the music scene in the mid-1950s. With a sound rooted in rockabilly and rhythm-and-blues, a daringly sexual performing style, and a magnetic charm, the pioneer rock 'n' roller became an idol for an entire generation of music enthusiasts. Adoring fans remember him as The Father of Rock 'n' Roll, The King, and Elvis the Pelvis, and he is widely credited with introducing a new era in popular culture. Writing for *Newsweek,* Jim Miller reported that Presley himself has become ''a complex figure of American myth: as improbably successful as a Horatio Alger hero, as endearing as Mickey Mouse, as tragically self-destructive as Marilyn Monroe.''

Indeed, neither critics nor biographers can find much in the Mississippi-born star's background to presage his rise to fame. The boy spent his earliest years in his hometown of Tupelo, where he and his family shared a two-room house, and as a teen he lived in Memphis, Tennessee, where his family relocated when he was in the eighth grade. Shortly after finishing high school in 1953, the unknown artist began driving a delivery truck for the Crown Electric Company. He fooled around with the guitar in his free time.

The year he graduated, however, the young hopeful also made an amateur recording at the Memphis Recording Studio. He followed it with a second in 1954 and captured the attention of Sam Phillips at Sun Records. As a result, Presley created the now-legendary Sun recordings, hailed by many as among his finest. With a musical career in the offing, the future star quit his truck-driving job in 1954 and began performing professionally, mostly in rural areas where he was billed as The Hillbilly Cat. He also saw his first Sun recording, ''That's All Right Mama,'' rise to number three on the Memphis country-and-western charts. Thus, despite some disappointments, including discouraging words from the Grand Ole Opry and rejection by New York City's Arthur Godfrey Talent Scouts, Presley persisted. By the end of 1955, after making a six-state Southern tour with Hank Snow's Jamboree that piqued considerable interest, the up-and-comer had negotiated the agreement with RCA that would bring him stardom.

Presley's very first RCA single, ''Heartbreak Hotel'' (co-written by Presley, Tommy Durden, and Mae Boren Axton, mother of country star Hoyt Axton), was wildly succesful and became his first Gold Record. ''From the opening notes of the song,'' opined Miller in another *Newsweek* review, ''the air is electric.'' The air remained electric as the singer scored hit after hit with such tunes as ''Don't Be Cruel,'' ''Hound Dog,'' ''Blue Suede Shoes,'' and ''Love Me Tender.'' His sound, which evolved from his roots in the deep South and combined elements of

in the *New York Times,* "defined the style and gave it an indelible image."

Voice alone did not comprise the star's appeal. He was also a remarkable showman. Advised by Colonel Tom Parker, whom he signed as his manager early in 1956, Presley began making films, appearing on television, and otherwise keeping himself in the public eye. Though reportedly shy and disinclined to be interviewed, the upstart musician gave performances that drove audiences mad. His captivating smile, coupled with the pelvic "bump-and-grind" rhythm that earned him the appellation Elvis the Pelvis, projected an exciting sexuality that was unprecedented in the music world. He prompted moral outrage from the older generation and hero worship from the younger to become, in Rockwell's words, an entertainer "parents abhorred, young women adored and young men instantly imitated."

Presley was already a legend by the time he was drafted into the U.S. Army in 1958, and during his two-year hitch, most of it spent in West Germany, his recordings continued to sell well. But by the time he returned from his tour of duty, the music climate in the United States had changed. There was a notable downturn in his career, and The King of Rock and Roll devoted most of the 1960s to making movies that were entertaining but undistinguished. In 1968 the rocker staged a successful, if short-lived, comeback, and during the seventies he concentrated on playing nightclubs.

At approximately 2:30 p.m. on August 16, 1977, Presley's body was found in the bathroom at Graceland, his Memphis, Tennessee, home. Although the medical examiner reported that Presley died of heart failure, rumors of the star's amphetamine use flourished. For a number of years prior to his death, in fact, Presley looked as if he had passed his prime. Apparently, though neither a drinker nor a smoker, The King was known as a junk-food addict (reputed to favor fried peanut butter and banana sandwiches) and had gained considerable weight. He also had a history of mild hypertension. As Miller summed it up, Presley, formerly "an icon of glowing youth . . . died tallow-faced and tubby, the victim of too many Dreamsicles and Nutty Buddies, too much Dexedrine, Dilaudid, Demerol, Quaalude, [and] Percodan."

Despite the circumstances, The King continued to grow in stature after his death. Indeed, in a piece for the *Saturday Evening Post,* Jay Stuller even suggested that death "lent [him] a tragic aura." Whatever the reasons, grief-stricken fans remained fiercely devoted and scrambled to preserve their idol's memory. In the process, they spawned an entire industry. More than ten years later, memorabilia abounds and hundreds of new prod-

country-and-western, rhythm-and-blues, and gospel, was new, and it was instantly popular. Though not the inventor of rock and roll, Presley, reflected John Rockwell

ucts pay tribute to the Presley legend—everything from slippers and shampoo to porcelain dolls and grandfather clocks. There are some two hundred-odd active Elvis fan clubs, the city of Memphis hosts an annual Elvis Week, and at one time a bill was put before the U.S. Congress that advocated making the recording giant's birthday a national holiday.

The King's achievement has yet to be duplicated. He racked up more than one hundred Top Forty hits as well

---

"Presley, formerly an icon of glowing youth . . . died tallow-faced and tubby, the victim of too many Dreamsicles and Nutty Buddies, too much Dexedrine, Dilaudid, Demerol, Quaalude, [and] Percodan."

---

as more than forty Gold Records, and sales of his recordings exceed one billion copies. He also influenced an entire generation of rock musicians, including Bob Dylan, John Lennon, and Bruce Springsteen. Trying to unravel the mystique, Stuller quoted Graceland Enterprises marketing director, Ken Brixey: "I guess the best answer is that he was a blue-collar worker who in spirit never tried to rise above his roots. He's the epitome of a man who started out with nothing, became something and never lost his attraction to the masses. He's a true folk hero."

Compositions

Composer and co-composer of songs, including "All Shook Up," "Don't Be Cruel (To a Heart That's True)," "Heartbreak Hotel," and "Love Me Tender."

Selected discography

45 & 78 RPM Recordings; Released by Sun

That's All Right Mama, 1954.
Blue Moon of Kentucky, 1954.
Good Rockin' Tonight, 1954.
You're a Heartbreaker, 1954.
Baby, Let's Play House, 1955.
I'm Left, You're Right, She's Gone, 1955.

Mystery Train, 1955.
I Forgot to Remember to Forget, 1955.

Major hit singles; Released by RCA

"Heartbreak Hotel," February, 1956.
"Blue Suede Shoes," March, 1956.
"I Want You, I Need You, I Love You," May, 1956.
"Hound Dog," July, 1956.
"Don't Be Cruel," July, 1956.
"Love Me Tender," October, 1956.
"All Shook Up," March, 1957.
"Let Me Be Your Teddy Bear," June, 1957.
"Jailhouse Rock," October, 1957.
"Wear My Ring Around Your Neck," April, 1958.
"Hard Headed Woman," June, 1958.
"Stuck On You," April, 1960.
"It's Now or Never," July, 1960.
"Are You Lonesome Tonight?," November, 1960.
"Surrender," February, 1961.
"Can't Help Falling In Love," December, 1961.
"Return To Sender," October, 1962.
"(You're the) Devil In Disguise," June, 1963.
"Crying In the Chapel," April, 1965.
"In the Ghetto," May, 1969.
"Suspicious Minds," September, 1969.
"Burning Love," August, 1972.

LP Albums; Released by RCA

Elvis Presley, 1956.
Elvis, 1956.
Loving You, 1957.
Elvis's Christmas Album, 1957.
Elvis's Golden Record, 1958.
King Creole, 1958.
For LP Fans Only, 1959.
A Date With Elvis, 1959.
50,000,000 Fans Can't Be Wrong, 1959.
Elvis Is Back, 1960.
G.I. Blues, 1960.
His Hand in Mine, 1960.
Something for Everybody, 1961.
Blue Hawaii, 1961.
Pot Luck, 1962.
Girls, Girls, Girls, 1962.
It Happened at the World's Fair, 1963.
Fun in Acapulco, 1963.
Kissin' Cousins, 1964.
Roustabout, 1964.
Girl Happy, 1965.
Elvis for Everyone, 1965.
Harum Scarum, 1965.
Frankie and Johnnie, 1966.
Paradise Hawaiian Style, 1966.
Spinout, 1966.
How Great Thou Art, 1967.

Special Palm Sunday Programming, 1967.
Double Trouble, 1967.
Clambake, 1967.
Elvis's Gold Records, Volume 4, 1968.
Speedway, 1968.
Elvis Sings Flaming Star and Others, 1968.
Elvis: TV Special, 1968.
From Elvis in Memphis, 1969.
From Elvis to Vegas/Vegas to Memphis, 1969.
On Stage, February 1970, 1970.
Worldwide Fifty Gold Award Hits, 1970.
Elvis in Person at the International Hotel, 1970.
Elvis: Back in Memphis, 1970.
Elvis: That's the Way it Is, 1970.
Elvis Country, 1971.
Love Letters From Elvis, 1971.
Worldwide Fifty Gold Award Hits, Volume 2: Elvis The Other Sides, 1971.
Elvis Sings the Wonderful World of Christmas, 1971.
Elvis Now, 1972.
He Touched Me, 1972.
Elvis Recorded Live at Madison Square Garden, 1972.
Elvis: Aloha From Hawaii Via Satellite, 1973.
Elvis, 1973.
Raised on Rock, 1973.
Elvis, Volume 1: A Legendary Performer, 1974.
Elvis Forever, 1974.
Good Times, 1974.
Elvis Recorded Live on Stage in Memphis, 1974.
Having Fun With Elvis on Stage, 1974.
Promised Land, 1975.
Pure Gold, 1975.
Elvis Today, 1975.
Elvis, Volume 2: A Legendary Performer, 1976.
The Sun Sessions, 1976.
From Elvis Presley Boulevard, Memphis, Tennessee, 1976.
Elvis in Hollywood, 1976.
Welcome to My World, 1977.
Moody Blue, 1977.

RCA Victor also released more than thirty Elvis EPs between 1956 and 1973.

Albums; Released by Camden

Let's Be Friends, 1970.
Almost in Love, 1970.
Elvis's Christmas Album, 1970.
You'll Never Walk Alone, 1971.
C'mon Everybody, 1971.
I Got Lucky, 1971.
Elvis Sings Hits From His Movies, Volume 1, 1972.
Burning Love and Hits From His Movies, Volume 2, 1972.
Separate Ways, 1973.
Almost in Love, 1973.
Double Dynamite, 1975.
Frankie & Johnny, 1976.

Posthumously released albums

RCA has issued numerous Elvis recordings since his death, including the six-record set *Elvis Presley: A Golden Celebration,* commemorating what would have been his fiftieth birthday.

Films

"Love Me Tender," Twentieth Century Fox, 1956.
"Loving You," Paramount, 1957.
"Jailhouse Rock," MGM, 1957.
"King Creole," Paramount, 1958.
"G.I. Blues," Paramount, 1960.
"Flaming Star," Paramount, 1960.
"Wild in the Country," Twentieth Century Fox, 1961.
"Blue Hawaii," Paramount, 1961.
"Follow That Dream," United Artists, 1962.
"Kid Galahad," United Artists, 1962.
"Girls, Girls, Girls," Paramount, 1962.
"It Happened at the World's Fair," MGM, 1963.
"Fun in Acapulco," Paramount, 1963.
"Kissin' Cousins," MGM, 1964.
"Viva Las Vegas," MGM, 1964.
"Roustabout," Paramount, 1964.
"Girl Happy," MGM, 1965.
"Tickle Me," Allied Artists, 1965.
"Harum Scarum," MGM, 1965.
"Frankie & Johnny," United Artists, 1966.
"Paradise, Hawaiian Style," Paramount, 1966.
"Spinout," MGM, 1966.
"Easy Come, Easy Go," Paramount, 1966.
"Double Trouble," MGM, 1967.
"Clambake," United Artists, 1967.
"Stay Away, Joe," MGM, 1968.
"Speedway," MGM, 1968.
"Live a Little, Love a Little," MGM, 1968.
"Charro," National General Pictures, 1969.
"The Trouble With Girls," MGM, 1969.
"Change of Habit," NBC/Universal, 1970.
"Elvis, That's the Way it Is," MGM, 1970.
"Elvis on Tour," MGM, 1972.

Sources

Books

Dunleavy, Steve, Red West, Sonny West, and Dave Hebler, *Elvis, What Happened?,* (expose) Ballantine Books, 1977.
Escott, Colin and Martin Hawkins, *Catalyst: The Sun Records Story,* Aquarius Books, 1975.
Goldman, Albert, *Elvis* (expose), Avon Books, 1981.
Gregory, Neal, and Janice Gregory, *When Elvis Died,* Communications Press, 1980.

Hammontree, Patsy Guy, *Elvis Presley: A Bio-Bibliography,* Greenwood Press, 1985.

Hemphill, Paul, *The Nashville Sound: Bright Lights and Country Music,* Simon & Schuster, 1970.

Hopkins, Jerry, *Elvis: A Biography,* Warner Books, 1971.

Hopkins, Jerry, *Elvis: The Final Years,* Playboy Publishers, 1981.

Marcus, Greil, *Mystery Train: Images of America in Rock 'N' Roll,* Dutton, 1976.

Marsh, Dave, *Elvis* (photo essay), Rolling Stone Press, 1982.

Parish, James Robert, *The Elvis Presley Scrapbook,* Ballantine Books, 1975.

Pleasants, Henry, *The Great American Popular Singers,* Simon & Schuster, 1974.

Presley, Priscilla Beaulieu with Sandra Harmon, *Elvis and Me,* Putnam's 1985.

Tharpe, Jac L., editor, *Elvis: Images and Fancies,* University Press of Mississippi, 1979.

Periodicals

Esquire, December, 1987.

New York Times, August 17, 1977.

Newsweek, November 12, 1984; August 3, 1987; June 6, 1988.

Saturday Evening Post, July-August, 1985.

People, March 4, 1985; January 14, 1985; August 17, 1987.

Time, July 20, 1987.

—*Nancy H. Evans*

Prince

Singer, songwriter, musician, producer

When a gifted musician becomes a symbol of social behavior, his songs become documents of his time. Prince, the composer, lyricist, instrumentalist, and singer who brought the Minneapolis sound into mainstream rock, has become such a performer. Although his techno-funk sound remains one of the most danceable of the 1980 s fusion, he is more generally judged as a barometer of sexual morality based on his lyrics, stage performance and album cover art.

Prince has manipulated his own biography and has allowed it to be altered by others, but it is generally agreed that he was born in Minneapolis, Minnesota, on June 7, 1958. He was named Prince Rogers Nelson for his parents' jazz ensemble, the Prince Rogers Trio, in which his mother, Mattie Shaw, was vocalist and his father, John Nelson, was pianist. Since it was impossible for a progressive jazz band to find enough high-paying jobs in the Minneapolis area, Nelson also worked for the Honeywell electronics plant. Prince, who has used only his first name professionally, became an expert pianist, keyboard player, guitarist and drummer while in junior high school and formed his first group, Grand Central, with longtime friend Andre Anderson. He spent his later adolescence living with Anderson's family.

In 1976, Prince, who had mastered reed instruments as well as keyboards and strings, made his first demo, playing all the parts. He was 18, but his then-manager, Owen Husney, subtracted years from his age and described him as "a new Little Stevie Wonder." Warner Bros. liked the demo and gave him a contract which allowed him to produce his own first album. That record, *For You* (1978), received high praise from critics, as did his second, *Prince* (1979). A single, "I Wanna Be Your Lover," from the latter became a top seller on the Soul charts and pushed *Prince* to gold-record status.

Dirty Mind (1980) and *Controversy* (1981) institutionalized Prince's status as a social rebel. Its songs were overtly sexual in message and title, among them, "Head," "Soft and Wet" and "Do Me, Baby." He also added some political messages to the fourth album, such as "Ronnie, Talk to Russia," about international accords. Prince's fusion sound brought him a crossover success that spanned the black and white radio stations, and music columnists, such as the *New York Times*'s Robert Palmer, saw in his music a chance to achieve "true biracialism" in popular music. "*Controversy* is a perfectly realized fusion of black and white pop idioms, alternating stretches of taut dance-floor funk with a more melodic, songlike refrain," Palmer wrote in 1981. "It transcends racial stereotyping because it's almost all Prince."

But Palmer, and Warner Bros., underestimated the

effect of the album's warning stickers ("contains language which may be unsuitable for some listeners") or overestimated America's readiness for biracial rock. Prince's reputatution, titles and lyrics made some FM stations ban many of his songs and even complete Prince albums.

Prince's image led to nationwide publicity, including a column in *Newsweek* in December 1981, in which Jim Miller called him "The naughty Prince of Rock. . . . On stage he's a punk scarecrow bringing the passion of soul to rock and roll burlesque. In the studio, he's a self-taught prodigy, composing, arranging and producing a mongrel mix of creamy ballads and brittle funk, blazing rock played with rude-boy spunk. He's a prophet of sexual anarchy."

1999 (1982) and *Purple Rain* (1984), however, brought Prince the crossover success that his antithesis, Michael Jackson, had earned with *Thriller* in 1982. *1999,* which went triple-platinum, included three hit singles—the title song, "International Lover," and "Little Red Corvette." Named number 17 in *Rolling Stone*'s 1988 listing of the Top 100 singles, "Little Red Corvette" was "his tightest metaphor, getting double duty out of a clever horse and Trojan imagery to craft an ode to a speedy, gas-guzzling, 'love machine.' The sexual motif is reinforced by the song's rhythmic structure which builds from a mellow, pulsing synthesizer opening, then chugs into a power-driven sing-along chorus." It

broke through from the black radio stations to pop charts by working through the theme of car adoration that had been a part of rock since long before the Beach Boys.

Purple Rain, the soundtrack from his 1984 film, sold over 17,000,000 copies and won an Oscar for best original sound score. Prince also won three Grammys and three American Music Awards for the album and songs. Its hit single, "When Doves Cry," became the ultimate symbol of a crossover success when it reached number one on the pop, soul, and dance charts. Videos of film clips integrated with Prince in "live" performance, shown on cable and network television shows, helped to push other singles up the charts, among them, the title song, "I Would Die 4 U," "Take Me with You," and "Let's Go Crazy," which was considered by many the best dance recording of the year. *Purple Rain* also spawned a five-month concert tour that set attendence records in theaters, auditoriums, and sports arenas. *Billboard,* the trade paper of the recording industry, honored Prince's achievements in film, recordings and live performance when it gave him the Trendsetter Award for 1984 for "unprecedented multi-media success."

Prince's next two albums, *Around the World in a Day* (1985) and *Parade* (1986), a preview of the soundtrack for his second film, *Under the Cherry Moon,* were less successful and received harsh criticism from some reviewers for their softer sound and fuzzy message. *Musician,* in a November 1988 retrospective, called them "claustrophobic, self-obsessed, sometimes downright creepy." The film, a stylized, black-and-white 1920's melodrama, was also denounced by critics.

His next album, *Sign o' the Times* (1987), had the opposite problem. It was well-received by critics (as *Musician* stated—"fun and free and unselfconscious") but sold only decently. Mark Rowland in *ASCAP in Action* described the album as moving "from gospel to flower pop to avant-garde funk with remarkable elasticity, sometimes, as on "U Got the Look" and "The Cross," melding two or more idioms in a single song." In this album Prince returned to his origins as the soloist, playing and overdubbing instrumental parts—here, everything but the horn section, except in the live recording of "It's Gonna Be a Beautiful Night."

Prince followed with two albums—*LoveSexy* and *The Black Album,* which was withdrawn by Warner Bros. that year but remained an open secret that seems to be readily available on the black market. Even *Variety,* which as an entertainment industry trade paper abhors the existence of bootleg recordings, reviewed it and printed an article on its availability. Jon Pareles of the *New York Times* was one of many critics to publish joint reviews of *LoveSexy* and *The Black Album*. He ascribed the title to Prince's committment in the latter to "black" music styles, such as blues and rap, since "for Prince, clearly, 'black' music means music that relies on rhythm above all." "*LoveSexy*," he continued, "purveys melodies the way *The Black Album* knocks out rhythms. In fact, there's so much melody that Prince gets away with extraordinary liberties in his harmonies: long stretches of the album qualify as polytonal, with the rhythm section in one key and horns, keyboards and voices in others."

In an ironic move that seems typical of Prince's career, the covers of both records led to the banning of the "official" album by the 1100-store Walmart chain, according to the *Village Voice*. *The Black Album*'s cover is, of course entirely black, in what some critics see as a reference to the Beatles' classic *White Album*. And the *LoveSexy* cover presents Prince, as *Essence* described it, "looking like Adam before the creation of fig leaves, delicately perched on a white orchid while purple dahlias sprout like wings from his shoulders. Legs shaved; right hand pressed against his heart as if pledging allegiance to the unseen forces of the universe." The *LoveSexy* tour's opening in Paris was reviewed by Steve Perry in *Musician* as "the Exploding Purple Inevitable." "No one has ever conceived an arena rock show with this much audacious theatricality . . . this kind of explosive kinetic energy or this musical dynamism." And *Rolling Stone* described Prince's entrance "in a white 1967 Thunderbird rigged up to take a quick spin around the tri-level, seventy-by-eighty stage—complete with swing set and basketball hoop."

Contradictions about Prince's life and work abound, at least in part because he has promoted them. He has been quoted in *Essence* and elsewhere as having said that "I used to tease a lot of journalists [about my racial background] early on because I wanted them to concentrate on the music." He often creates imaginary characters for his album notes and assigns to them his creative and professional decisions, as he did in the *LoveSexy* tour book, in which he named "Spooky Electric," as creator of *The Black Album*. The incident which most threatened his reputation was, ironically, not at all related to his self-described "sexy" nature. He recieved negative press when he decided to donate a cut to the *USA for Africa* benefit album, rather than participating in the all-star recording session that created its title song, "We are the World."

Prince's influence on the music scene in the Minneapolis area has been enormous. As Bonnie Allen wrote in *Essence*, "he has given Minneapolis, a city many East and West Coasters didn't realize even had a Black population, the same mystical musical aura of Motown in the sixties." He has sponsored bands and ensembles from Minneapolis in his live performances. Among those which have gone on to their own successes are his original band The Revolution, Mazarati, The Family, Shiela E. (headed by percussionist Shiela E.), Cat and Apollonia 6, which has spun off the careers of vocalists Vanity and Apollonia. Prince records his own music and produces other bands at the 65,000-square foot Paisley Park Studio, in a Minneapolis suburb.

Prince songs have also been recorded by other artists, among them "When You Were Mine" by Mitch Ryder. *ASCAP in Action* cited a John Cougar Mellencamp concert in which that celebrated songwriter played a tape of Prince's "Little Red Corvette" to his audience. Peter Watrous, reviewing a sold-out concert at Madison Square Garden in October 1988 for the *New York Times*, assessed Prince's impact on contemporary popular music in this way: "[He] projects one of the most confusing, enigmatic images in pop music, mixing erotic love with religion, irony and humor with seriousness. It is these contradictions that separate him from straightforward, bland, mainstream performers and ultimately make him more interesting than they are."

Selected discography

For You, Warner Bros., 1978.
Dirty Mind, Warner Bros., 1979.
Controversy, Warner Bros., 1981.
1999, Warner Bros., 1983.
Purple Rain, Warner Bros., 1984.
Around the World in a Day, Warner Bros., 1985.
Parade, Paisley Park/Warner Bros., 1986.
Sign O' the Times, Paisley Park/Warner Bros., 1987.
LoveSexy, Paisley Park/Warner Bros., 1988.

Sources

ASCAP in Action, winter, 1988.
Essence, November, 1988.
Musician, November, 1988.
New York Times, December 2, 1981; March 30, 1986; April 12, 1987; October 4, 1988.
Newsweek, December 21, 1981.
Rolling Stone, September 12, 1985; August 25, 1988; September 8, 1988.
Variety, June 8, 1988.
Village Voice, May 24, 1988.

—*Barbara Stratyner*

Jean
Redpath

Singer

"In her purity of line, precision of intonation and control of pitch, the Scottish traditional singer Jean Redpath is an unequaled vocal technician among contemporary folk interpreters." With this description, Stephen Holden of the *New York Times* explained the international appeal of this unique artist. From Scotland to Lake Wobegon to Lincoln Center, Jean Redpath has presented the gems of her chosen repertoire to appreciative audiences. She is recognized as the foremost interpreter of traditional Scottish music, which she described in 1986 as "a brew of pure flavor and pure emotion." The purity of her voice and *a capella* performance have brought her an international following far from her roots in Scotland.

Redpath grew up in a musical family in the country of Fife, near Edinburgh, Scotland. Her father played the hammered dulcimer. Redpath also continues a maternal tradition of music. "My mother's family were all musical, without any kind of formal background at all," she told Jennifer Dunning in the *New York Times* in 1988. "And most of the women were keepers of the song tradition, with incredible memories. When my mother would say, 'Ooh, I've just remembered a song but I can't remember the verses, 'there were four sisters

to go ask. We could reassemble almost anything among them." As a student in the School of Scottish Studies at Edinburgh University, she combined this oral tradition with scientific studies in folk ethnography. A specialist in "reassembling" as well as performing traditional Scottish ballads and composed songs, she has served on the faculties of Stirling University (Scotland, since 1979) and Weslyan University (Connecticut) and has lectured extensively at universities in Great Britain, Canada and the United States.

Through program notes and performance commentary, Redpath has also educated her audience in concerts from Greenwich Village folk houses to Lincoln Center's Mostly Mozart Festival. Her first engagements in the United States, at Gerde's Folk City, were as a star of the folk and traditional music revival of the 1960s. Her solo debut, at the New School of Social Research, July 19, 1963, featured selections from her repertory that even then numbered over 400 songs. These appearances led to recordings by Elektra—at the time a leader in traditional and ethnic music.

Live concerts continue to be an important part of Redpath's career. She selects her programs with great care to include 500 years of traditional ballads, credited songs by Scottish poets and composers, contemporary music and "Scottish-style" songs by the great composers of the classics. A typical recital, as reviewed by Stephen Holden of the *New York Times* in 1984, "offered selections from [her albums of Robert Burns songs] along with traditional ballads, some of which date back more than five centuries. These were augmented by a smattering of contemporary tunes and an adaptation of a Tchaikovsky melody that the singer inbued with a strong Celtic feel." One of her most memorable appearances in recent years was as a recitalist in the "Haydn Marathon," presented by the Mostly Mozart Festival of Lincoln Center for the Performing Arts in New York City. In a promotional article in the *New York Times* and in her presentation at the concerts, Redpath was pleasantly ironic about Haydn's brief "adoption" of Scottish nationalism: "Basically it was hack work. . . . There was a trend at the end of the 18th century . . . to 'improve' Scottish music by rendering it more English and more classical. The end result is meant to be Scottish enough to be recognized but not so Scottish that one needs to be embarassed about it . . . publishers invited the well-known Europen composers to set the songs—thereby, of course, improving their worth immeasurably. . . . My involvement came because I like to remove the walls between pigeonholes."

Redpath joined Philo Records in Vermont in 1975. She has created one of the largest discographies in the folk and traditional music catalogues, with over three dozen

For the Record. . .

Born April 28, 1937, in Edinburgh, Scotland; came to United States, 1961; daughter of James Redpath. *Education:* Attended Edinburgh University, School of Scottish Studies.

Concert performer specializing in *a capella* renditions of traditional Scottish folk music, 1960—; has made numerous appearances on television and radio programs, including "A Prairie Home Companion" (National Public Radio), 1974-87. Lecturer at Weslyan University and Stirling University, Scotland.

Addresses: *Office*—c/o Steorra, 243 West End Ave., New York NY 10023. *Record company*—Phil Records, 70 Ct. Street, Middlebury VT 05753.

invidual albums. Among her many on-going recording projects are a complete cycle of songs by the Scottish poet Robert Burns. Six of the estimated 20 volumes have been released by Philo, as of 1988. She has also recorded the Scottish songs of Joseph Haydn for Philo and, with Lisa Neustadt, Scot-derived songs of American Appalachia. A continuing series of albums featuring the Scottish songs of identified woman composers for Philo has produced *Lady Nairne* (the works of Caroline Oliphant) and recordings of songs by Lady John Scott, Violet Jacob, and Helen Cruikshank on *A Fine Song for Singing.*

The broadcast media have become "classrooms" for Redpath as well. She appears frequently as a performer and folklorist on radio and television in Great Britain and the United States. Selections from her BBC-TV series, "BalladFolk," have been released on the album of the same name. In the United States, she has been a frequent visitor on many of the foremost classical radio stations, among them, WQXR in New York and the "Morning Pro Musica" broadcasts of Robert Lurtsema on WGBH in Boston. Redpath has become famous with a new audience from her performances on Garrison Keillor's "A Prairie Home Companion" over the American Public Radio network, from 1974 to 1987. Although she was originally engaged to perform her traditional folk form (just as Keillor presented bluegrass, klezmerim, and Scandinavian choirs), she also participated in the advertising campaigns for many of his imaginary sponsors in the town of Lake Wobegon.

The range of her repertory, the scholarship, and the commitment to her selected genre are all justly celebrated, but it is Redpath's voice that has continued to attract fans and critical acclaim. Holden, writing in 1984 and 1986, described its qualities vividly. "[Her] voice is more than merely pretty. Her sweetness is backed by a fiber and quiet detemination that lend everything she sings a deep, lived-in quality. With her arching sense of melody and plain, unsyncopated phrasing, she is able to imbue everything she touches with a mysterious, slightly mournful quality that is the quintessence of a certain kind of folk classicism. . . . Redpath possesses a mezzo-soprano that most classically trained art singers might envy. Through not large, her voice projects a mixture of resilience and tenderness with a smooth, subtle, humming vibrato."

Redpath is generally described as an *a capella* vocalist, but, in fact, she often performs with instrumentation. She accompanies herself on the acoustic guitar, "strumming it delicately to produce a subdued harp-like effect." She also frequently performs and records with cellist Abby Newton, most notably on the Philo albums *Lady Nairne, Song of the Seals,* and *Jean Redpath.* Among her other occasional collaborators are violinist John Graham, fiddler Pamela Swing, and, on the aptly titled Greenhays album *The Most Dulcimer,* Mike Seeger and Diane Hamilton.

Selected discography

Skipping Barefoot Through the Heather, Prestige/International, 1962.
Scottish Ballad Book, Elektra, 1962.
The Songs of Robert Burns, Philo, 1980—(volume 6 is most recent release).
Lady Nairne, Philo, 1986.
A Fine Song for Singing, Philo, 1987.

Sources

New York Times, November 15, 1961; November 12, 1984; April 21, 1986; August 19, 1988.
Stereo Review, June, 1981.

—Barbara Stratyner

Lou
Reed

Singer, songwriter, guitarist

Lou Reed gained limited notoriety in the late 1960's as the songwriter and guitarist of the Velvet Underground. Unfortunately the group lasted only four years, breaking up in 1970 with the release of their fourth album. Their impact, however, continues as artists like David Bowie and Iggy Pop, virtually the entire punk movement, and many heavy metal bands reflect the Velvet Underground's influence.

After attending Syracuse University in New York, Reed began writing songs for the Long Island-based Pickwick Records, where he met fellow musician (bass and viola) John Cale; together they formed the Warlocks in 1965. With the addition of guitarist-bassist Sterling Morrison and drummer Maureen Tucker, the group changed their name to the Primitives and later the Falling Spikes. In 1966 they settled on the Velvet Underground a name taken from the title of a pornographic novel. The Group was signed by Verve records and artist Andy Warhol was assigned to produce their first album. Warhol brought in German-born singer Nico to round out the vocals. After recording the album the group toured with Warhol's multi-media project, The Exploding Plastic Inevitable. Their music was stark in contrast to the hippie-style love songs of the west coast. With subject matter like sadomasochism, drugs and street life played at deafening volumes, the Velvet Underground shocked its audiences.

Warhol and Nico left in 1967 before the group's second album, *White Light/White Heat,* which featured the heavy metal sound almost two years before the so-called fathers of the genre, Led Zeppelin, had even formed. The album became a favorite among avant-garde music fans, but was ignored by the general public. Meanwhile, Cale left before the third LP, *The Velvet Underground,* and was replaced by Doug Yule. Even though their sound mellowed slightly, they were still trapped under the "cult-favorites" category. Ironically, their final studio effort, *Loaded,* which produced classics like "Sweet Jane" and "Rock and Roll", sold reasonably well, but Reed had decided to quit the band even before the album was released. Two subsequent live albums were issued after the Velvet Underground's breakup; of these, *1969* captured an excellent performance in a small Texas club.

After leaving the Velvet Underground, Reed worked for a time with his father's accounting firm in Long Island, but in 1971 RCA signed him to a solo contract and Reed was off to London to record his self-titled debut LP. Backed by British session musicians, Reed's work was again ignored by radio stations, but it featured some outstanding writing and depictions of inner-city life. Reed stayed in England and eventually met Bowie, who openly expressed his admiration for Reed's talents

In the spring of 1975 Reed unleashed *Metal Machine Music* on the world. This album was Reed's powerful commentary on the music industry—four album sides (16:01 each) of what he described in *Rolling Stone* as "the all-time feedback guitar solo unrestricted by key or tempo." Needless to say, reviews of the album were extremely positive, but once again Reed seemed to be his own worse enemy, lashing out at anyone who doubted the enormous chip on his shoulder. His verbal battles with the press (who tended to believe Reed's songs were mostly autobiographical) were by now legendary. In 1976 he told *Rolling Stone*'s Tim Ferris, "If only they (critics) knew that not only am I such a worthless churl as to write songs about these things, but on top of that, I stole it all. Stole it from people."

In 1976 Reed ended a short-lived marriage, changed managers and released a new album, *Coney Island Baby.* With Reed on guitar and piano, it was a mixture of bitter ballads, twisted love songs and restrained rock-

and even offered to produce his next record, *Transformer,* which featured Reed's well-known song, "Walk on the Wild Side". *Transformer* helped to re-establish Reed in the music world and placed him in the public eye, where the dark side of his personality began to emerge. According to *The Illustrated Encyclopedia of Rock,* "after *Transformer* he hooked himself firmly into his role as Elder Statesman of Ersatz Decadence and deteriorated at a rapid pace. This was a sobering sight for aficionados: Reed in eye-liner and phantom drag, aping Bowie the disciple of Reed."

A collage of sex, drugs and death, Reed's third album, *Berlin,* sold poorly despite a tour and heavy promotion. Oddly enough, this record, which did so much to harm Reed commercially, also contributed to his ensuing comeback. The 1973 tour to promote *Berlin* included one of the finest bands ever assembled. With the dual guitars of Steve Hunter and Dick Wagner weaving in and around Reed's poetry, the tour produced one of the most powerful live albums ever, *Rock 'n' Roll Animal.* Another album from the same tour, *Lou Reed Live,* concentrated on ballads and was released a year later in 1975. Sandwiched between the two live LPs was *Sally Can't Dance,* which stereotyped Reed as the "street-poet of rock." The song "Kill Your Sons" chronicled Reed's experience during high school when his parents submitted him to electroshock therapy. Although the album climbed to number ten on the charts, it is not regarded by Reed or his fans as one of his better efforts.

> *"I call [Rock and Roll Heart] a full-fledged attack, a seething assault. I think of it as Clearasil on the face of the nation. Jim Morrison would have said that if he was smart, but he's dead."*

ers. After a switch from the RCA label to Arista, Reed released his seventh studio LP, the directionless and enigmatic *Rock and Roll Heart.* Playing against a background of television sets, Reed called the *Rock and Roll Heart* tour a "full-fledged attack, a seething assault. I call it germ warfare. I think of it as the Clearasil on the face of the nation. Jim Morrison would have said that if he was smart, but he's dead."

In 1978 Reed released his most honest album up to that point, *Street Hassle. Rolling Stone*'s Tom Carson wrote, "the recognition of his own self-destruction has been made integral to *Street Hassle*'s concept, and the effect is double edged; as we respond to the album's excellence, we are never allowed to forget just how much it cost." The public was finally starting to see the true Lou Reed.

Things would get even better on his 1979 album, *The Bells,* which contained three songs co-written by guitarist Nils Lofgren. The late critic Lester Bangs compared *The Bells* to Van Morrison's *Astral Weeks* and the

Rolling Stones' *Exile on Main Street,* calling it "great art." In the next four years Reed released three more fine albums, *Growing Up In Public, The Blue Mask,* and *Legendary Hearts.* He summed this trio up as ". . . the absolute end of everything from the Velvet Underground up." He began to take a brighter outlook on life and his next two albums, *New Sensations* and *Mistrial,* contained up-tempo songs and a happier Lou Reed.

Reed played all six dates on the 1986 Amnesty International tour and was also a contributor to the Artists Against Apartheid *Sun City* record. It seems as if Reed has finally come clean (he even did ads for Honda scooters) but with such a complex personality, it's hard to tell where he'll be next. As *Rolling Stone*'s Billy Altman wrote, "One's opinion of Reed's solo work changes constantly, because his constant shifts of stance and style continually confound any sense of perspective."

Selected discography

Lou Reed, RCA, 1972.
Transformer, RCA, 1972.
Berlin, RCA, 1973.
Rock 'N' Roll Animal, RCA, 1974.
Sally Can't Dance, RCA, 1974.
Lou Reed Live, RCA, 1975.
Metal Machine Music, RCA, 1975.
Coney Island Baby, RCA, 1976.
Rock and Roll Heart, Arista, 1976.
Take No Prisoners—Lou Reed Live, Arista, 1978.
Street Hassle, Arista, 1978.

The Bells, Arista, 1979.
Growing Up In Public, Arista, 1980.
The Blue Mask, Arista, 1982.
Legendary Hearts, Arista, 1983.
New Sensations, RCA, 1984.
Mistrial, RCA, 1984.
New York, Warner Bros., 1988.

Also appeared on several recordings with the Velvet Underground, including:
The Velvet Underground and Nico, Verve, 1967.
The Velvet Underground, MGM, 1969.
Loaded, Cotillion, 1970.

Sources

Books

Christgau, Robert, *Christgau's Record Guide,* Ticknor & Fields, 1981.
Dalton, David and Kaye, Lenny, *Rock 100,* Grosset & Dunlap, 1977.
The Illustrated Encyclopedia of Rock, Harmony, 1977.
The Rolling Stone Record Guide, edited by Dave Marsh and John Swenson, Random House/Rolling Stone Press, 1979.

Periodicals

Rolling Stone, March 25, 1976; April 8, 1976; September 23, 1976; December 2, 1976; April 6, 1978; February 6, 1979; March 22, 1979; June 14, 1979; August 23, 1979; September 25, 1986.

—Calen D. Stone

Smokey Robinson

Singer, songwriter, record company executive

Smokey Robinson, the "poet laureate of soul music," has been composing and singing rhythm and blues hits for three decades. As the lead singer of The Miracles, Robinson helped to put Detroit and its Motown Records on the music map; more recently, his solo performances have netted Grammy Awards and praise from pundits who usually shun the pop genre. *People* magazine contributor Gail Buchalter calls Robinson "one of the smoothest tenors in soul music," a romantic idol whose 60 million-plus in record sales "helped turn Motown into the largest black-owned corporation in the world."

According to Jay Cocks in *Time,* Robinson has written, produced, and performed "some of the most enduring rhythm and blues ever made. The church kept easy company with the street corner in his rich melodies, and his lyrics had a shimmering, reflective grace that, at his pleasure, could challenge or seduce. With the Miracles, Smokey helped make a kind of soul music that balanced ghetto pride and middle-class ambition. Some of the group's best tunes . . . stayed true to the R & B roots even as they beckoned, and found, a larger pop audience." In *Rolling Stone,* Steve Pond concluded that Robinson has written "some 4000 songs and recorded hundreds that have made him a true poet of the soul—and a voice of the soul, too."

William "Smokey Joe" Robinson, Jr. not only rose from obscurity, he brought along a number of other now-famous black recording stars when he began to find success. He was born and raised in Detroit, in the rough Brewster ghetto, where, as he told *People,* "you were either in a [music] group or a gang—or both." Young Smokey grew up listening to his mother's records, including the works of B. B. King, Muddy Waters, John Lee Hooker, Sarah Vaughan, and Billy Eckstine. He told *Rolling Stone* that these black artists were "the first inspirational thing I had." When Robinson was ten, his mother died, and his sister Geraldine took him to raise along with her ten children. The family was poor but close-knit, and Robinson spent his youth writing songs and singing in local bands.

Robinson would not consider a professional career until he graduated from high school, and even then he tried barber school and courses in dentistry before giving his full attention to music. In 1954 he formed a rhythm & blues group called The Matadors; the name was changed to The Miracles three years later to accomodate a female singer, Claudette Rogers, who married Robinson in 1959. At first The Miracles found the music business difficult, even with the five-dollars-per-week salaries granted them by their energetic young agent, Berry Gordy. "For a while," Claudette Robinson told *Essence,* "we lived basically in one bedroom. But we didn't stay in that house very long. Fortunately, the music started to happen."

Robinson was lucky to have encountered Berry Gordy during an audition for another agent; Gordy, then a fledgling music producer on a shoestring budget, was equally fortunate to have found Robinson. Gordy began to produce The Miracles' singles in 1958, collaborating with Robinson on lyrics and tunes. Their first release, "Got a Job" (an answer to The Silhouettes' number one hit "Get a Job"), hit number 93 on the nationwide *Billboard* Top 100. The debut was encouraging, but nothing prepared Gordy and Robinson for the limelight they would attain in 1960. Late in that year they released an upbeat single, "Shop Around," that became a chart-topping million seller. The Miracles became a national phenomenon, and Gordy was able to launch Motown Records, a landmark production company that introduced such talents as Diana Ross and the Supremes, Stevie Wonder, Marvin Gaye, and the Temptations.

Robinson and The Miracles were Gordy's first star-quality group, and they continued their association with Motown as the company gained prestige. Indeed, Robinson wrote hit songs not only for his group but for other Motown headliners as well. He explained the Motown philosophy in *Rolling Stone:* "We set out to . . . make music for people of all races and nationalities. Not to make *black* music—we just wanted to make good music that would be acceptable in all circles. . . . All we were doing, man, was just putting good songs on good tracks, songs that anybody could relate to. . . . We had good, solid songs that would fit your particular life situation if you were white or Oriental or Chicano or whatever you happened to be. And that made a world of difference."

Throughout the 1960s, especially in the latter half of the decade, the Motown Sound competed with the British Invasion as the most popular new music for the young. Robinson and The Miracles were favorites among the Motown personnel, earning more than a half doz-

> "Smokey helped make a kind of soul music that balanced ghetto pride and middle-class ambition."

en gold records with hits including "The Tracks of My Tears," "You've Really Got a Hold on Me," "I Second That Emotion," and "Ooo Baby Baby." Still, Robinson was on the verge of quitting the group in 1968 when his son Berry was born. He reconsidered almost immediately, however, when a Miracles single, "The Tears of a Clown," became a number one hit, first in England and then in the United States. Robinson told *Rolling Stone* that "The Tears of a Clown" became "the biggest record we ever had. It catapulted us into another financial echelon as far as what we made on dates, and I felt that the band was entitled to reap the benefits." The Miracles endured, a model group in terms of road behavior, until 1972, when Robinson quit.

For a time after leaving The Miracles, Robinson concentrated on business duties as vice-president of Motown Records. He soon returned to recording, however, this time as a solo artist. Robinson's solo albums are, on the whole, more reflective and mellow than his work with The Miracles. All of them highlight the singer's particular talent—the creation and performance of meaningful love songs in a day when many erstwhile romantics have become jaded cynics. Stephen Holden analyzed Robinson's music in *Rolling Stone:* "Smokey Robinson is that rare pop singer whose rhapsodic lyricism hasn't diminished with approaching middle age. Indeed, time has added a metaphysical depth to his art. The postadolescent Romeo who created 'The Tracks of My Tears' and 'Ooh, Baby Baby' exudes the same sweetness today he did fifteen years ago, but his tenor and falsetto have shaded into a single dusky croon. . . . Smokey Robinson's faith in the redemptive power of erotic love continues unabated. In Robinson's musical world, sexual happiness isn't the product of spiritual equilibrium but its source. . . . Don't think, however, that Robinson's songs aren't filled with sex. They are. But in this man's art, sex isn't a fast roll in the hay, it's sweet manna shared during a leisurely stroll into paradise. Smokey Robinson creates that paradise every time he opens his mouth to sing." Recent Robinson hits include "Cruisin'," "Just to See Her," and "Being with You," all rendered in a voice *Essence* contributor Jack Slater described as "a hypnotic, airy aphrodisiac that puts tens of thousands in the mood for love." In the *Chicago Tribune,* Lynn Van Matre notes that when Robinson is singing, he "is among the most appealing of soul men, sexy in a low-key, warm way that generates a far greater amount of genuine heat than all the contrived posturings of the 'giddy-up gonads' group currently doing the old synthetic sex soft shoe."

Robinson plans to keep writing songs, singing, and producing music indefinitely. He told *Time* that he still loves to perform for live audiences. "If I don't remember all the words to some of the old songs, I'll sing what I remember," he said. "We all have a great time. I can be down in the dumps and really feeling bad. But when I go onstage, it's like wow." Nor does Robinson plan to discontinue writing love songs, the appeals to romance, and the laments on separation that have made him famous. "Love is basically what we're all about, man," he told *Rolling Stone.* "We're about our business, the nine-to-five trip, but our basic thing in life is love. It's the most powerful force. It's never passe, it's not a fad. It's *always.*"

Compositions

Has written and co-written numerous songs, 1954—, including "Ain't That Peculiar?," "Don't Mess With Bill," "Going to a Go-Go," "I Second That Emotion," "It's Growing," "More Love," "My Girl," "The Tracks of My Tears," "You Beat Me to the Punch,"

"You've Really Got a Hold on Me," "Here I Am Baby," "I'll Be Doggone," "The Love I Saw in You Was Just a Mirage," "Ooo Baby Baby," "Two Lovers," "Cruisin'," "First I Look at the Purse," and "The Tears of a Clown."

Selected discography

Major single releases; with The Miracles; all released by Tamla

"Got a Job," March, 1958.
"Shop Around," November, 1960.
"What's So Good About Goodbye?," January, 1962.
"I'll Try Something New," May, 1962.
"You've Really Got a Hold on Me," December, 1962.
"Mickey's Monkey," August, 1963.
"I Gotta Dance to Keep From Crying," November, 1963.
"Ooo Baby Baby," April, 1965.
"The Tracks of My Tears," July, 1965.
"Going to a Go-Go," January, 1966.
"The Love I Saw in You Was Just a Mirage," March, 1967.
"More Love," June, 1967.
"I Second That Emotion," November, 1967.
"The Tears of a Clown," December, 1970.

Major single releases; solo

"Cruisin'," 1979.
"Just to See You," 1987.
"Being with You."

LPs; with The Miracles

Hi, We're the Miracles, Motown, 1961.
Shop Around, Motown, 1962.
Doin' Mickey's Monkey, Motown, 1963.
The Fabulous Miracles, Motown, 1964.
The Miracles on Stage, Motown, 1964.
Going to a Go Go, Motown, 1964.
The Miracles from the Beginning, Motown, 1965.
Away We Go, Motown, 1965.
Make It Happen, Motown, 1968.
Greatest Hits Volume 2, Motown, 1968, reissued, 1987.
The Miracles Live, Motown, 1969.
Special Occasion, Motown, 1969.
Time Out, Motown, 1970.
Four in Blue, Motown, 1970.
What Love Has Joined Together, Motown, 1970.
Smokey and the Miracles, Motown, 1971.
1957-1972, Motown, 1973.
Anthology, Motown, 1974.
The Miracles, CBS, 1977.
Compact Command Performances, Volume 2, Tamla, 1986.
Going to a Go Go/The Tears of a Clown, Tamla, 1986.

Also recorded *Cookin' with the Miracles, Christmas with the Miracles, Tears of a Clown, I Like It Like That, Greatest Hits,*

Pocketful of Miracles, One Dozen Roses, The Season for Miracles, Compact Command Performances, Greatest Hits from the Beginning, and *Flying High Together,* all with Motown.

LPs; solo

Renaissance, Motown, 1973.
Smokey, Motown, 1973.
Pure Smokey, Motown, 1974.
Do It, Baby, Motown, 1974.
A Quiet Storm, Motown, 1974.
City of Angels, Motown, 1974.
Love Machine, Motown, 1975.
Smokey's Family Robinson, Motown, 1975.
Power of the Music, Motown, 1977.
Deep in My Soul, Motown, 1977.
Big Time (motion picture soundtrack), Motown, 1977.
Love Crazy, CBS, 1977.
Smokey's World, Motown, 1978.
Love Breeze, Motown, 1978.
Smokin', Motown, 1978.
Where There's Smokey, Motown, 1979.
Warm Thoughts, Motown, 1980.
Being with You, Motown, 1981.

Yes It's You, Lady, Motown, 1981.
Pure Smokey, Motown, 1982.
Touch the Sky, Motown, 1983.
Great Songs and Performances, Motown, 1983.
Essar, Motown, 1984.

Sources

Books

Given, Dave, *The Dave Given Rock 'n' Roll Stars Handbook,* Exposition Press, 1980.
The Rolling Stone Record Guide, Random House, 1979.

Periodicals

Ebony, October, 1971, October, 1982.
Essence, February, 1982.
People, March 10, 1980.
Rolling Stone, April 16, 1981, September 17, 1981, November 5-December 10, 1987.

—*Anne Janette Johnson*

Kenny Rogers

Singer

Kenny Rogers has been described in *McCall*'s as "the silver-haired singer with the voice that's turned dozens of songs to gold." Rogers, an astute thirty-year veteran of the music business, is a rarity, indeed: he's a crossover artist who moved *from* pop *to* country, rather than vice versa. His story ballads and love songs have found a wide mainstream audience and have been phenomenal successes, earning him eleven platinum and eighteen gold albums in a ten-year span.

"There are many flashes in the pan in popular music, people who have a hit record or two and then disappear from the spotlight," observes Gene Busnar in *Superstars of Country Music*. "But Kenny Rogers, who had his first hit as a teenager, worked hard and kept at it for twenty years before reaching true superstardom. In that time, he played in jazz combos, folksinging groups, and rock bands. Better musicians with better voices took their bow in the spotlight and faded from glory as the musical trend they were part of was replaced by something new. But Kenny kept growing and changing with the times until he finally carved out a permanent spot as a superstar."

Few would argue that Rogers is one of the best-known singers in America, but his contribution to his industry is more substantial than mere personal popularity. Rogers is a pioneer of mainstream country music—a style that appeals to a far wider group than standard country fans. He told the *Chicago Tribune* that he views his fusion of rock, folk, pop, and country as a positive force that has "brought a lot of people into the fold who wouldn't have listened to country music otherwise. It used to be you either liked country music or you didn't, because it all sounded alike. Now it's no longer one-dimensional, and I think that's great."

Kenneth Ray Rogers was born and raised in Houston, Texas, one of seven siblings. He grew up in a federal housing project that he has described in *People* magazine as "a tenement." The Rogers family was very poor, and Rogers's father had a drinking problem, but still Kenny remembers his family fondly. By ninth grade the young Rogers had decided to become a professional musician. He bought himself a guitar with money earned as a restaurant busboy and formed a band, The Scholars, with several friends from school. Thanks to his brother Lelan, who worked for a Houston record distributor, The Scholars actually got to record some music. A few of their songs became regional hits, and the band earned money doing live performances.

In 1957 Rogers recorded several solo singles, and one of them, "That Crazy Feeling," became a million-selling hit. Rogers appeared on "American Bandstand" and became prematurely convinced that he was headed for

For the Record. . .

Full name, Kenneth Ray Rogers; born August 21, 1938, in Houston, Tex.; son of Edward Floyd (a carpenter) and Lucille (Hester) Rogers; married fourth wife, Marianne Gordon (an actress), October 2, 1977; children: (first marriage) Carole Lynn; (third marriage) Kenneth Ray, Jr.; (fourth marriage) Christopher Cody. *Education:* Attended University of Houston, c. 1958.

Pop-rock singer, 1957-76; country-pop singer, 1976—. Formed group The Scholars, 1957; member of The Bobby Doyle Trio, 1959-66; member of The New Christy Minstrels, 1966-67; founding member (with Mike Settle, Terry Williams, and Thelma Camacho) of The First Edition, 1967, name changed to Kenny Rogers and The First Edition, 1969-76; solo artist, 1976—. Star of numerous motion pictures and television shows.

Awards: Named "crossover artist of the year" by *Billboard* magazine, 1977; Grammy Award for best male country vocal performance, 1977, for "Lucille"; Academy of Country Music awards for best single and for best song, 1977, for "Lucille"; Country Music Association citation for song of the year, 1977, for "Lucille"; received best male vocalist awards from Academy of Country Music, 1977 and 1979; recipient of Country Music Association Awards, 1978 and 1979. Named top male vocalist by *People* magazine, 1979 and 1980; Grammy Award for best male country performance, 1980, for "The Gambler"; American Music Awards for best male country vocalist and for best country album, 1984; recipient of United Nations Peace Award, 1984; received Most Awarded Artist Award from Recording Industry Association of America (RIAA), 1984; recipient of Roy Acuff Award, 1985; American Music Awards for best male country vocalist and for best country album, 1985; Grammy Award (with Ronnie Milsap) for best country vocal duet, 1987. Holder of eleven platinum and eighteen gold records.

Addresses: *Home*—Athens, Ga; and Los Angeles, Calif. *Manager*—Kragen & Co., 1112 North Sherbourne Dr., Los Angeles, CA 90069.

permanent stardom. Many lean years lay ahead of him, however. Lacking a good song to follow his first success, and a professional band to back him, Rogers could not duplicate his first hit. Instead he went to college for one term and then joined a jazz group, The Bobby Doyle Trio. The trio attracted the attention of Kirby Stone, a star of that era. Stone invited the group to tour with him, and under that tutelage, Rogers learned how to conduct himself in the music business.

In 1966 Rogers was playing with a jazz combo called The Lively Ones when Stone's manager offered him a position in The New Christy Minstrels. The Minstrels were a pop-folk group that had had several hits and were planning a national tour. Rogers joined the group even though he had to take a cut in pay—he thought the national exposure would advance his career. According to Busnar, The Minstrels "were making a nice living playing the safe kind of folk music that much of middle America still wanted to hear. But Kenny and some of his cohorts wanted to become part of the more exciting and potentially more rewarding new folk rock."

Rogers and three associates left the Minstrels in 1967 to form their own group, The First Edition. Adopting the long-haired look of the times, the band released folk songs with rock overtones, and within six months it had a hit, "Just Dropped in (To See What Condition My Condition Was In). The First Edition had to wait two years for another hit, but when it came it was a major one. With Rogers singing lead, "Ruby, Don't Take Your Love to Town" topped the 1969 charts. That same year the group changed its name to "Kenny Rogers and the First Edition," recognizing that the charming but driven lead singer was the main attraction.

The First Edition fell into a slump in the mid-1970s, finally disbanding in debt in 1976. Rogers describes that period as the low point of his career. "For five or six months I just sat around and thought," he told *People.* He also said that he came to realize that "there's a new hit rock group or singer every five minutes, but with country music, you have one hit and those people love you forever." Rogers headed for Nashville, changed his stage image, and began recording country music. "Emotionally," he said, "it was like coming home."

In 1977 he had four top-ten country hits and one crossover million-seller, the mock-tragic "Lucille," about a broken marriage. "Lucille" won numerous awards for Rogers, including a Grammy and citations from both the Academy of Country Music and the Country Music Association. "For Kenny Rogers and his manager Ken Kragen," writes Busnar, "it was only the beginning." Rogers promoted himself tirelessly and carefully, with an eye on his business affairs and an ear on potential recording material.

Before long he was churning out a string of platinum albums and top-ten singles that rode both the country and pop charts. Just a few of these hit singles include story ballads such as "The Gambler" and "The Coward of the County," the love songs "Lady," "You Decorated My Life," and "She Believes in Me," and the duet

"Islands in the Stream." By 1980 Rogers was one of the best-paid performers in the country, and he and his fourth wife Marianne Gordon were breaking records with extravagant expenditures on homes in Los Angeles and Georgia.

Despite his success, Rogers retains an element of insecurity, based on his poverty-stricken youth and his off-years as an adult. The insecurity has had positive repercussions, however. Rogers has never been content with a comfortable niche—he is constantly experimenting with other performance options. "How long can I go on singing *Ruby, Don't Take Your Love to Town* and *Lady?*" he asked in *People.* "Can I still do this when I'm 55? Movies will allow me to carry on for a few years after the music is over."

With his rugged but regular features and characteristic growling voice, Rogers has indeed found film roles in both features and made-for-TV vehicles, some of which have been based on his story songs. He is also

> *"It used to be you either liked country music or you didn't, because it all sounded alike. Now it's no longer one-dimensional, and I think that's great."*

entering the competitive daytime talk-variety show market with a syndicated program for television. Rogers told *McCall's:* "A lot of people in this business devote ninety-five percent of their lives to music. When the music goes, there goes ninety-five percent of their lives. I can express my creativity in different ways." Rogers insists he does not plan to give up singing—he simply is engaged in diversifying his talents among acting, hosting television, photography, and writing.

Not every critic has been charitable about Roger's music. *Esquire* reviewer Mark Jacobson contended that Rogers "can barely sing. His middle range isn't that awful. . . . But down low he croaks bad. Upward, he's so pinched as to recall a trapped, furry thing. For a country artist, he is without down-homeness; as a rocker, he ignites nothing." New York *Daily News* contributor William Carlton offered a different view of the popular entertainer. According to Carlton, Rogers "sings in a warm, supple, romantic, tender voice with a surprisingly wide range. His story songs are always fresh, tasteful, honest and intelligent, well-crafted and inter-

esting. The man and his music are as welcome as old friends and family."

Rogers and his wife divide their time between Los Angeles and a farm near Athens, Georgia, where they raise horses. Rogers has admitted that his early quest for success ruined his three previous marriages and alienated him from his oldest two children, now grown adults. He has sought to make amends by spending more time with his families, including his youngest son, Christopher. Still, Rogers is intense about his career and almost singleminded in his pursuit of prestige. His manager Ken Kragen told *McCall's:* "Part of Kenny never really slows down. He wears out the people who travel with him."

The years have given Rogers a perspective on success, however. He told *McCall's:* "Being onstage, getting immediate feedback from an audience, is absolutely addictive. It's worse than heroin. I'm lucky because other things in my life give me the same sort of high." In *People,* Rogers concluded: "I'm enjoying my rise from the ashes. I just hope I can spread some of the happiness that's been coming my way."

Selected discography

With the First Edition

The First Edition, Reprise, 1968.
The First Edition's Second, Reprise, 1968.
Ruby Don't Take Your Love to Town, Reprise, 1969.
Something's Burning, Reprise, 1970.
Tell It All, Brother, Reprise, 1970.
Fools, Reprise, 1971.
Kenny Rogers and the First Edition's Greatest Hits, Reprise, 1971.
Transitions, Reprise, 1971.
The Ballad of Callico, Reprise, 1972.
Back Roads, Jolly Rogers, 1972.
Monumental, Jolly Rogers, 1973.
Rollin', Jolly Rogers, 1973.
Kenny Rogers and the First Edition, Warner Brothers, 1979.
Hits and Pieces, MCA, 1985.
60s Revisited, MCA, 1985.
(With The New Editions) *15 Greatest Hits,* MCA, 1987.

Solo albums

Love Lifted Me, United Artists, 1976.
Lucille, United Artists, 1977.
Daytime Friends, United Artists, 1977.
Ten Years of Gold, United Artists, 1977; reissued, 1986.
(With Dottie West) *Every Time Two Fools Collide,* United Artists, 1978.
Love or Something Like It, United Artists, 1978.

Convoy (soundtrack), United Artists, 1978.
The Gambler, United Artists, 1978.
(With West) *Classics,* United Artists, 1979.
Kenny, United Artists, 1979.
Singles Album, United Artists, 1979.
Shine Out, Radar, 1980.
Gideon, United Artists, 1980.
Kenny Rogers's Greatest Hits, Liberty, 1980.
Share Your Love, Liberty, 1981.
Lady, Liberty, 1981.
Kenny Rogers Christmas, Liberty, 1982.
Love Will Turn You Around, Liberty, 1982.
We've Got Tonight, Liberty, 1983.
Eyes That See in the Dark, RCA, 1983.
The Best of Kenny Rogers, Breakaway, 1984.
(With West) *Something's Burning,* MCA, 1984.
What About Me?, RCA, 1984.
The Heart of the Matter, RCA, 1985.
They Don't Make Them Like They Used To, RCA, 1986.
Duets, Capitol, 1987.
I Prefer the Moonlight, RCA, 1987.
Love Is What We Make It, Liberty, 1987.
Short Stories, Liberty, 1987.
There Lies the Difference, 1989.

Also recorded *20 Greatest Hits,* Liberty, *25 Greatest Hits,* and, with Dolly Parton, *Once Upon a Christmas.*

Writings

Author of photo books *Kenny Rogers's America,* 1986, and *Your Friends and Mine,* 1987.

Sources

Books

Busnar, Gene, *Superstars of Country Music,* J. Messner, 1984.

Periodicals

Chicago Tribune, August 12, 1979.
Country Music, October, 1977.
Daily News (New York), March 26, 1979.
Esquire, March, 1986.
McCall's, November, 1988.
People, January 9, 1978; December 10, 1979; March 29, 1982.
Stereo Review, April, 1980.

—*Anne Janette Johnson*

Diana Ross

Singer

When Diana Ross returned to Motown Records as a vocalist and partial owner in February 1989, it was announced on the front page of the *New York Times* business section as "the Queen returning home." One of the most popular recording artists of the last 30 years, Diana Ross, with and without The Supremes, "virtually defined the Motown sound." Her rise to fame, starting with the discovery of The Supremes, has become one of the primal myths of American popular music. She was born in Detroit, Michigan, on March 26, 1944, and raised in the Brewster-Douglass housing project there. She sang in the Olivet Baptist Church choir while studying design at Cass Technical High School. The Supremes originated when Ross and two friends, Mary Wilson and Florence Ballard, formed The Primettes as a "sister" group to Eddie Kendricks's The Primes.

Berry Gordy, Jr., founder and long-time president of Motown Records, based the popularity of his company's product on a steady danceable beat performed by close-harmony groups. He signed The Primes (renamed The Temptations) and hired The Primettes as one of many "girl groups" to back up Motown recording stars, including Marvin Gaye and Mary Wells. Recognizing their potential, he renamed them The Supremes and turned them over to his "charm school," the Artists Development Department. When they graduated from high school, they were sent on the road with other Motown groups. Ross told Andy Warhol in an October 1981 *Interview* cover story that the tours were designed to bring them to the attention of not just the record-buying teen-age public, but also the media powers: "Our first tour was a Motown revue and then we went on a Dick Clark tour. Dick Clark was very helpful, as was Ed Sullivan. Then the Murray the K [radio] Show was here in town." Between their training in social ettiquette and their exposure in live and television performances as a package deal with The Temptations, Marvin Gaye, and Stevie Wonder, The Supremes had everything but a unique sound.

Although Ross ascribed the group's success to the lessons of the "charm school," rock music historians consider Gordy's assignment of the writing team of Eddie Holland, Lamont Dozier, and Brian Holland to be a much greater contribution. The trio of voices combined with the three songwriters to produce a string of six consecutive Gold Records that truly defined the sound of The Supremes. The overlay of Ross's voice over the back-up sound of Wilson and Ballard repeating "Baby baby" made million sellers of "Where Did Our Love Go?," "Baby Love," "Come See About Me," "Stop! in the Name of Love," "Back in My Arms Again," and "I Hear a Symphony." The Supremes never had a

For the Record. . .

Born March 26, 1944, in Detroit, Mich.; daughter of James (a factory worker) and Ernestine (Earle) Ross; married Robert Silberstein (a manager of popular musicians), January 1971 (divorced, 1976); married Arne Naess (a shipping magnate), October 23, 1985; children: (first marriage) Rhonda Suzanne, Tracee Joy, Chudney (daughter); (second marriage) Ross Arne. *Education:* Graduated from Cass Technical High School, Detroit, Mich., 1962.

Singer, c. 1960—. Member of vocal group The Primettes (later named The Supremes), c. 1960-68, (renamed Diana Ross and the Supremes, 1969); solo performer, 1970—. Actress in motion pictures, including "Lady Sings the Blues," 1972, "Mahogany," 1975, and "The Wiz," 1978. President of Diana Ross Enterprises (fashion merchandising), Anaid Film Productions, RTC Management Corp. (artists management), Chondee Inc., and Rosstown and Rossville music publishing companies. Part-owner of Motown Records, 1989—.

Awards: Grammy Award for best female vocalist, 1970; *Billboard, Cash Box,* and *Record World* awards for best female vocalist, 1970; named female entertainer of the year, 1970, by National Association for the Advancement of Colored People (NAACP); Academy Award nomination for best actress, 1972, for "Lady Sings the Blues"; Cue Award for entertainer of the year, 1972; Antoinette Perry (Tony) Award, 1977; inducted into Rock and Roll Hall of Fame, 1988.

Addresses: *Home*—Norway; New York, NY; and Beverly Hills, CA; *Office*—RTC Management, P.O. Box 1683, New York, NY 10185; and c/o Shelly Berger, 6255 Sunset Blvd., Los Angeles, CA 90028.

bluesy sound or a heavy beat—just enough to dance to.

Novelist Jamaica Kincaid reminisced about the group's sound in a 1975 article in the *Village Voice:* "I heard 'Baby Love' and that was the greatest. Because just the way Diana Ross sounds on that particular record was just the way I wanted to be. It was so cool, so sexy, so sweet, so pretty, all of those things for two-and-a-half minutes." *Rolling Stone* was more analytical as it named "Stop! in the Name of Love" to number 10 on its 1988 list of Top 100 singles: "[Holland, Dozier, and Holland's] grasp of the pop-music form enabled them to produce three-minute symphonies: simultaneously simple and intricate, ephemeral and yet enduring." *Rolling Stone* quoted Dozier about Berry Gordy's input on the final mix-down: "[It] was done through a radio speaker,

since Gordy was ever mindful of how most of the audience would hear the music. We had to mix low and soft . . . Berry would say, 'What are you guys mixing so loud for? If you can hear things down low and soft, that's what you're going to hear on the radio.'"

Their hits continued through 1969 as they reflected contemporary trends by adapting the basic Motown sound to ballads, country and western, and psychedelic rock in "My World Is Empty without You" (1966), "The Happening" (1967), and "Love Child" (1968). *Rolling Stone* recently described their fifteen singles after 1964 as "almost a perfect song cycle, progressing steadily from the wide-eyed simpicity and sexy venerability of the first hit to the world-weary complexity of the last." Their album titles reflect the ability of the Motown producers to spread them throughout the market— *Meet the Supremes, At the Copa* (including standards), *Country Western and Bop, Supremes a Go-Go,* and their Beatles album *A Bit of Liverpool.*

Ross's departure from The Supremes was spread over six months. Ballard was replaced by Cindy Birdsong (of Patti LaBelle's Bluebelle backup group) in 1969, and the act was renamed Diana Ross and the Supremes to recognize her role as lead singer. Her final departure came in a farewell performance at the Frontier Hotel in Las Vegas, January 1970. Their final recording as a trio, "Someday We'll Be Together," was a success. The changes in the group's structure from its founding to Ross's departure have been the focus of much speculation and many conflicting reports. Among many fictionalized accounts of the proceedings are *roman a clef* novels and the multi-award-winning Broadway musical "Dreamgirls."

The solo career of Diana Ross began in night-clubs and proceeded into concert tours during the 1970s. Berry Gordy was quoted in *Ebony,* claiming that "Diana's success is almost built in. . . . She's not taking a big chance because people are buying her like mad. Vegas is buying her. Miami is buying her, the Waldorf [Astoria Hotel] in New York. She's a super-star and everybody is trying to buy her; like the stock market, she's up now because everything she's done has been a total success." Ross did jazz-oriented concerts at first, including a well-received appearance at Radio City Music Hall to end the 1974 Newport [now New York] Jazz Festival. As Harry Stathos described it in the *New York Daily News,* "Surrounded by some of jazzdom's finest musicians, she then proceeded to show why she is considered one of the nation's top singers with soulful renditions of well-known jazz standards made famous by Lady Day [Billie Holiday. . . "Good Morning Heartache," "God Bless the Child," and "He's My Man."

Ross's commitment to jazz performances waned and she returned to pop and Motown ballads. Program listings included the Rodgers and Hart standard "The Lady is a Tramp," Lennon/McCartney songs "Yesterday" and "Michelle," and a medley of show tunes from "Thoroughly Modern Millie" and "Mame," as well as the ever-present Supremes medley. As Robert Palmer put it in the New York Times in 1977, "in stage shows, she is perfectly at home with contemporary middle-of-the-road material. On records, she continues to be convincing as a rhythm-and-blues singer, performing in an updated disco-style idiom."

Her appearances, with gowns by Bob Mackie and staging by Joe Layton, grew in complexity and were often accused of overemphasizing production values. Frequently cited was the opening of "An Evening with Diana Ross," reviewed by Clive Barnes in the New York Times during a 1976 engagement at Broadway's vaudeville pinnacle, the Palace Theater: "The overture starts with the theme from her No. 1 hit, 'Mahagony.' Miss Ross enters in a white flared gown. Her hands are slightly nervous—tense against this special moment. She is suddenly flanked by a couple of mimes, one wearing white makeup on white, the other wearing black makeup on black, and both un morceau du Marceau. The skirt is pulled out to form a screen and on the screen, while [she] sings, are projected images of her singing."

Marie Moore, in the New York Amsterdam News, reviewed the finale of a live 1978 concert as "as emotionally devastating as her opening. Singing into the mike in her hand and perched in the up-stretched hands of her four male dancers, the dynamic Diana Ross was whisked up the same staircase whence she had come. As she was devoured by the screen and dissolved into the celluloid, she was as she had started out—a two dimensional figure in a film ascending the stairs." She generally included a tribute to blues greats Josephine Baker, Ethel Waters, and Bessie Smith in her live and televised acts. Ross backed up her extravaganzas with a list of personal recording hits—Ashford and Simpson's "Reach Out and Touch [Somebody's Hand]"; "Ain't No Mountain High Enough," her new signature theme; "Last Time I Saw Him"; "Remember Me"; "Touch Me in the Morning"; "Believe in Yourself"; "Home," from "The Wiz"; and, ironically, "We are Family," from "Dreamgirls."

Ross's television specials have been filmed live appearances or made-for-television shows designed and produced by Layton, as are her stage shows. A New York Times review of "An Evening with Diana Ross" (NBC-TV, 1977) criticized the "'special material' that keeps getting in the way" and the overly-done make-up that diminished her tribute to Baker, Smith,

and Waters, but stated that "when she's allowed simply to perform, the program bursts into theatrical life."

Her film career has been controversial. She had appeared with The Supremes on television and in films as a singing group/novelty on "Tarzan" and the film "Beach Ball" (1965), but had no formal training. Ross chose to make her "official" film debut portraying the jazz great Billie Holiday in "Lady Sings the Blues" (1972), produced by Gordy. Her personal reviews were favorable, but the film was generally considered a disappointment. Ross's second film, "Mahagony" (1975), was a melodrama about a fashion designer who finds unhappiness in Paris couture and returns to her home. Ross's own popularity and that of her co-star in both films, Billy Dee Williams, made them into box office successes. "The Wiz" (1978) has become a cult favorite for its production design by Tony Walton and its co-stars, Richard Pryor, Ted Ross, Lena Horne, Nipsy Russell, and Michael Jackson. Diana Ross, who purchased the rights to the Broadway musical based on

---

One of the most popular recording artists of the last 30 years, Diana Ross, with and without The Supremes, "virtually defined the Motown sound."

---

the Frank Baum stories, was criticized for playing the role of Dorothy. But Ross adapted the script so that the character, instead of being a young girl, was a shy adult nervous about functioning away from her family. The soundtracks to the first two films were successfully released by Motown and produced hit singles for the title songs.

Ross still presents concerts and personal appearances although she has cut down on long concert tours since her second marriage and the birth of young sons. The most publicized of her recent concerts was in New York City's Central Park. Originally planned as a benefit for playground construction, it was plagued by problems. The first evening was rained out amid damage to the park caused by the crowd of more than 350,000 fans. The second evening went as planned and was taped for broadcast on the cable network Showtime. Ross and her production company received criticism when it was announced that no profit was made on the concerts, especially after New York magazine analyzed the accounting for the events. Ross diffused the criticism by making a personal donation for the construction of a playground.

Ross has become a superstar with an international following—perhaps the first truly non-racial performer. She has been named to the Best Dressed list often in the last fifteen years. Her private life is covered by the press in detail and she has been the subject of at least six biographies. Her return to Motown as its superstar and investor will provide a new chapter in the continuing Diana Ross saga.

Selected discography

Major single releases; with The Supremes; released by Motown

"Where Did Our Love Go?," July 1964.
"Baby Love," October 1964.
"Come See About Me," November 1964.
"Stop! in the Name of Love!," February 1965.
"Back in My Arms Again," May 1965.
"Nothing But Heartaches," July 1965.
"I Hear a Symphony," October 1965.
"My World Is Empty Without You," January 1966.
"Love Is Like an Itching in My Heart," April 1966.
"You Can't Hurry Love," August 1966.
"You Keep Me Hangin' On," October 1966.
"Love Is Here and Now You're Gone," January 1967.
"The Happening," April 1967.
"Reflections," August 1967.
"In and Out of Love," November 1967.
"Love Child," October 1968.
"Someday We'll Be Together," November 1969.

LPs; with The Supremes; released by Motown

Meet the Supremes, 1964.
Live at the Apollo, 1964.
A Bit of Liverpool, 1965.
Where Did Our Love Go?, 1965.
Country Western and Bop, 1965.
Hits, 1965.
More Hits, 1965.
We Remember Sam Cooke, 1965.

Merry Christmas, 1965.
I Hear a Symphony, 1966.
Ago Go, 1966.
The Supremes Sing Motown, 1967.
The Supremes Sing Holland Dozier Holland, 1967.
The Supremes Sing Rodgers and Hart, 1967.
Greatest Hits, 1968.
Live at the Talk of the Town, 1968.
Reflections, 1968.
Love Child, 1969.
The Supremes Join the Temptations, 1969.
TCB, 1969.
Let the Sun Shine In, 1969.

LPs; solo

Diana Ross, Motown, 1970.
Everything Is Everything, Motown, 1971.
Touch Me in the Morning, Motown, 1973.
Lady Sings the Blues, Motown, 1973.
(With Marvin Gaye) Diana and Marvin, Motown, 1974.
Live at Caesars Palace, Motown, 1974.
Last Time I Saw Him, Motown, 1974.
Mahogany, Motown, 1975.
Greatest Hits, Motown, 1976.
Baby It's Me, Motown, 1977.
Ross, Motown, 1978.
Why Do Fools Fall in Love?, Capitol, 1981.
Silk Electrics, RCA, 1982.

Sources

Ebony, February, 1970.
Interview, October, 1981.
New York Amsterdam News, October 14, 1978.
New York Daily News, July 9, 1974.
New York Times, July 15, 1976; March 4, 1977; July 25, 1977; February 19, 1989.
Rolling Stone, November 23, 1972; September 8, 1988.
Village Voice, June 28, 1976.

—Barbara Stratyner

David Lee Roth

Singer, songwriter

Infamous as the lead vocalist and colorful frontman for Van Halen, one of America's most popular hard-rock bands, David Lee Roth turned solo artist in 1985. Indeed, after the enormous success of his extended play album *Crazy From the Heat,* Roth, in a decision that stunned Van Halen fans, decided to leave the group permanently. Although many of Van Halen's followers feared that neither he nor the band would survive the split, each has continued to dazzle rock and roll devotees. Roth, flamboyant as ever, has managed to keep his talents in the public eye with masterful videos and such albums as *Eat 'em and Smile* and *Skyscraper.*

Born in Bloomington, Indiana, the rock star remembers being introduced to music fairly early in life. His father, an ophthalmologist, presented him, at age seven, with recordings by jazz artist Al Jolson—still one of Roth's heroes—and at age eight he began listening to Ray Charles sing on the radio. Summer visits to his Uncle Manny, who operated the famed Greenwich Village Cafe Wha, were also influential, enabling him to view a variety of performers. By the time he was a teenager the aspiring musician, then living with his family in California, was singing solo as well as with a group called the Red Ball Jets.

Another Los Angeles area group, Mammoth—comprised of a bass player and the two Dutch-immigrant Van Halen brothers, Alex on drums and Edward singing and playing lead guitar—occasionally rented the Red Ball Jets' PA system. They were impressed with Roth and soon invited him to join them as lead vocalist (later joking that all they really wanted was his amplification equipment), and the group was eventually completed with the permanent addition of Mike Anthony on bass. Around 1974, after discovering that another group already owned the copyright to the name Mammoth, the group renamed itself Van Halen and began its struggle for fame and fortune.

The fledgling band seized the opportunity to play wherever and whenever it could, with its members doing everything for themselves, from securing engagements to promotional work. Performing both original songs and established tunes, Van Halen eventually became a local success and began to routinely open for such established acts as UFO and Santana; they also became a regular feature at the Starwood Club, the West Coast venue to fame. It was during their four-month stint there, in fact, that they were "discovered." First, Gene Simmons, bass player for the rock band Kiss, helped the group produce their first demo tape, then Warner Brothers' Ted Templeman came to the Starwood, heard the group, and signed them to a contract with his label.

Released in 1978, the band's first album, *Van Halen,* brought the group national attention. The album was a smashing success with more than two million copies sold, and the original members of Van Halen went on to release five more successful albums over the next seven years. Unlike many up-and-coming groups, the increasingly popular Van Halen never lacked press coverage, which was generated by its members' wild lifestyles as often as by its music.

More than any other band member, Roth is credited with promoting Van Halen's image as the quintessential rock band, one devoted to a lifestyle described by David Fricke in *Rolling Stone* as "a nonstop booze-and-babes party train." An on-stage rowdy, Roth became an expert at sexist slapstick who, in the opinion of Carl Arrington, writing for *People,* "helped gild the groups' head-banger image . . . with mock-macho stage posturing and costumes that looked like they were ripped off the backs of passing lions." But if, as Arrington suggested, Roth has fostered the image of himself as a "renaissance rocker," the critic also found him "less a fraud than most good actors or successful politicians." According to Arrington, Roth has played the part so long that "his concert persona and offstage personality [are] closer than most of his peers."

Sometimes referred to as "the bad boy of rock and roll" and "Mr. Bigmouth," Roth, in fact, is just as famous for his off-stage antics. Reports abound of the rocker's antipathy toward marriage, his refusal to permit other band members' wives to go on tour with the group, and of nude girls dancing on tabletops backstage as well as of his party-till-you-drop philosophy. Interviewing the star for *Rolling Stone,* Nancy Collins asked if the Van Halen backstage scene was really "akin to a bacchanalian feast." Roth, a student of karate, responded: "It's excessive. In terms of the fringe benefits you're supposed to get from rock & roll, I'd say we're black belts."

Despite his propensity for debauchery, Roth has earned applause for his abilities as a lyricist and singer. With a friend at the wheel of his 1951 Mercury convertible, Roth pens his words while cruising around the Los Angeles canyons. The generally simple lyrics work in harmony with the musical scores composed by Edward Van Halen to create the band's trademark tunes, tunes that helped transform Van Halen, in Fricke's words, into "the monster rock action squad that ruled the charts and the airwaves for seven years."

In 1985, after some much publicized squabbling, Roth decided to leave Van Halen and try his luck as an independent artist. With his first solo album, *Crazy From the Heat,* already a best-seller and a movie contract in the offing, Roth became the focus of even

> *With a friend at the wheel of his 1951 Mercury convertible, Roth pens his words while cruising around the Los Angeles canyons.*

more rumors than usual, most speculating that he had simply become too egotistical to continue working with the group. But after the initial furor subsided, Van Halen and Roth set about proving that each could survive in the music world without the other.

Although Roth's movie career never materialized, he has continued his ingenious video work as well as recorded new albums. The star's 1986 *Eat 'em and Smile* has sold more than two million copies, and in 1988 he released *Skyscraper.* What's most important to Roth, however, whether alone or with a group, whether involved in showmanship, writing lyrics, or singing, is to be *"rockin'."* That, he told Collins, is "all I ever really wanted to do."

Selected discography

With Van Halen

Van Halen, Warner Brothers, 1978.
Van Halen II, Warner Brothers, 1979.
Women and Children First, Warner Brothers, 1980.
Fair Warning, Warner Brothers, 1981.
Diver Down, Warner Brothers, 1982.
1984, Warner Brothers, 1984.

Solo Albums

Crazy From the Heat (EP), Warner Brothers, 1985.
Eat 'em and Smile, Warner Brothers, 1986.
Skyscraper, Warner Brothers, 1988.

Sources

Books

Kaye, Annene, *Van Halen,* J. Messner, 1985.
Matthews, Gordon, *Van Halen,* Ballantine Books, 1984.

Periodicals

Musician, February, 1986.
People, February 11, 1985; June 23, 1986; September 29, 1986.
Rolling Stone, June 21, 1984; April 11, 1985; August 15, 1985;
   July 3, 1986.

—Nancy H. Evans

David Sanborn

Saxophonist

An alto saxophonist with a signature squeal, David Sanborn is a musician at the height of his career. Indeed, after spending years developing his own sound, the artist now finds that other saxophonists are trying to imitate him. "A cursory twirl of the radio dial or channel selector might suggest that every commercial musician and would-be alto star out there is aping Sanborn's sound," observed Bill Milkowski in the introduction to his interview with the star for *down beat.* The Sanborn of the eighties, however—busy juggling live performing with studio playing as well as scoring films and hosting a radio show—has little time to worry about copycats.

The St. Louis native's struggle to the top began during the 1960s, when he played with rhythm and blues bands in the midwest. After sharpening his skills with Albert King and Little Milton, he headed for San Francisco, where he joined the Paul Butterfield Blues Band around 1967. By the early seventies he was gaining visibility for his work with such stars as David Bowie, Stevie Wonder, and Bruce Springsteen, and in 1975 he cut his first solo album, *Taking Off.* Since 1981, when he received a Grammy Award for best rhythm and blues instrumental performance for *Voyeur,* Sanborn has found his career on a stellar trajectory.

Although his playing is rooted in rhythm and blues, the saxman has made a splash in jazz circles, with a number of his albums securing top spots on the jazz charts. Sanborn, however, denies that he is a jazz musician. When *down beat* interviewer Gene Kalbacher noted that Sanborn used "a certain amount of improvisation and jazz phrasing and swing, which are essential ingredients or components of jazz," the musician agreed but qualified Kalbacher's remarks, explaining: "I don't see myself in a direct line in the tradition of jazz. I didn't come out of that tradition. . . . Most of the contexts I've played in have been either blues-based or r&b or straight-out rock & roll. What experience I've had in playing jazz has been pretty sporadic. . . . And I'm not trying to distance myself from jazz in any way. I'm just trying to clarify how I think of myself. See, I don't want to misrepresent myself, and I don't want to misrepresent the music."

Disinclined to be limited by any label, Sanborn has devoted himself to developing an individual style, and many critics and fans have credited him with success. But he has also eschewed his acclaim as an innovator, telling Milkowski that he sees himself not as an original so much as a synthesizer. "I'm not doing anything new," he remarked. "I was just distilling a lot of my influences. You know, I was always trying to sound like Cannonball or Phil Woods or Jackie McLean or Hank Crawford or other people I greatly admired."

Regardless of his tactics and his disclaimers, Sanborn

For the Record. . .

Born in St. Louis, Mo. (?), in 1945. *Education:* Attended Northwestern University and University of Iowa.

Saxophonist and composer. Began playing in rhythm-and-blues bands in St. Louis, including time with Albert King and Little Milton; started performing in the San Francisco area in 1967, including work with the Paul Butterfield Blues Band; has worked with many other artists, among them Stevie Wonder, 1970-72, as well as such vocalists as James Taylor, Paul Simon, and Rickie Lee Jones; solo recording artist, 1975—; tours with own band; has scored several films, including "Soul Man" and the unreleased "Stelle Sulla Citta"; host and co-producer of NBC-radio's "The Jazz Show," 1986—; regularly accompanies The World's Most Dangerous Band on NBC-TV's "Late Night With David Letterman."

Awards: Grammy Award from Academy of Recording Arts and Sciences, for best rhythm and blues instrumental performance, 1981, for *Voyeur,* and for best pop instrumental, 1989, for *Close Up.*

Addresses: *Home*—New York, NY. *Office*—c/o 9034 Sunset Blvd. #250, Los Angeles CA 90069.

some of the little grace notes—the mannerisms of my playing that I hear a lot of other people imitating when they're trying to sound like me. Those little 'da-de-aa-da,' those turns and stuff."

Indeed, because Sanborn's sound is perceived as both original and commercially successful, it has spawned many copiers. But Sanborn, who lived through many impoverished years before finding financial success, believes that it's fruitless to adopt a particular musical approach strictly for commercial purposes. "Because when you do that, you die inside," he reflected in his conversation with Milkowski. He continued: "The ironic thing is if you die musically then you die commercially too. I believe that. Maybe I'm naive in that regard. But I really believe that the true sense of being commercial in the long run is to be yourself and hope that people will buy *that.* But if you go into it thinking about trying to calculate what people are going to like and trying to figure out what they might buy and then you go and do that, then you're screwed."

> *"I don't see myself in a direct line in the tradition of jazz. I didn't come out of that tradition."*

The saxophonist, who defines success in terms of opportunities to make music rather than in economic terms, confessed to Tolleson that for him, even becoming a musician was a calling rather than a conscious choice. "I don't feel like I really chose to be a musician. I feel like it just happened, and that it almost chose me. It was part destiny, part free choice. Music became what I had to do. It was never something I thought about, nor did I have any goals or aspirations in that area. It was just my means of expression, my way of expressing how I felt about the world. It just became my voice."

Finding that voice has opened the door to many opportunities for the saxman. From his early days as a studio musician and member of rhythm and blues bands Sanborn has gone on to tour with his own band, score films, and host his own radio program, "The Jazz Show." But above all he has earned a reputation, in Kalbacher's words, for "rhythmic directness," for becoming "the alto saxman whose semisweet-yet-masculine tone and rhapsodic rhythm & blues drive have endeared him to the doyens of rock and pop."

is generally regarded as a saxophonist who has managed to create his own singular sound. "He goes for the heart," assessed *down beat* interviewer Robin Tolleson, adding that "a Sanborn contribution to an album may only be three minutes long, but always conjures up a range of feelings, and always leaves a mark." Similarly, Albert de Genova, also writing for *down beat,* commented that Sanborn has the ability to communicate "intense musical emotion to a capacity crowd . . . with every scream, with every honk, with every crying blue note" he strengthens "the empathy between musician and listener."

Discussing his technique with Tolleson, the artist explained that he enjoys experimenting with dynamics—gradations of volume—in his soloing not only because it's "another element of music and improvising, and melodic creativity" but because he believes "you shape a line using dynamics—in terms of attack and crescendo, decrescendo, and phrasing, legato, and staccato." In this respect, the saxophonist revealed that he has learned the most from Stevie Wonder, with whom he worked in the early seventies. "I picked up a lot of his little turns, and mordents, and appoggiaturas, and all that—things that he did on harmonica. And I think probably Stevie more than anybody else influenced

Selected discography

Taking Off, 1975.
Sanborn, 1976.
Promise Me the Moon, 1977.
Heart to Heart, 1978.
Hideaway, 1980.
Voyeur, 1981.
As We Speak, 1982.
Backstreet, 1983.
Straight to the Heart, 1984.

Sanborn has also performed with many other musicians on a variety of albums, including *Double Vision* and *Heads* with Bob James, *Undercover* with the Rolling Stones, *In My Own Dream, Keep on Moving,* and *The Resurrection of Pigboy Crabshaw* with Paul Butterfield, *Talking Book* with Stevie Wonder, *Gorilla* with James Taylor, *Young Americans* with David Bowie, *Svengali* with Gil Evans, *Electric Outlet* with John Scofield, *Pirates* with Rickie Lee Jones, and *Gaucho* with Steely Dan.

Sources

down beat, March, 1983; August, 1984; August, 1986; August, 1988.

—Nancy H. Evans

Carlos Santana

Guitarist and bandleader

"Carlos Santana's own spiritual committment, his natural love of the festival and of dance have made for a fabulous melting pot of a rock band, not the greatest rock band in the world but the greatest world band in rock," John Piccarella wrote in 1979 in a *Village Voice* column entitled "Santana's Indegenous Internationalism." In the ten years that followed, rock music was redefined almost monthly, but the world music of Carlos Santana and his ensembles has remained popular around the world.

Santana was born in Autlan de Navarro, Mexico, on July 20, 1947. His father, a mariachi violinist, taught him the violin and guitar. After the family moved to Tijuana, he began to learn and copy American blues from recordings of B.B. King and Chuck Berry, later adding T-Bone Walker and Saunders King to his list of influences. Santana moved to San Francisco, where his parents had relocated, and discovered jazz. According to Mark Rowland in the liner notes for the album *Viva Santana!,* Santana also discovered "the salsa giants like Tito Puente, Ray Baretto and Eddie Palmieri." Santana explained to Rowland that salsa was "a serious music, proud. A positive side, a dignifying side of Africa through Cuba and Puerto Rico."

The band Santana was formed in 1966 around the talents of bass guitarist David Brown and keyboard player Gregg Rolie. The band's improvisational sessions rooted in Latin American rhythms quickly became popular with jazz enthusiasts who recognized its creativity in combining salsa and blues riffs. The music of Santana also had a large audience among the Mexican-American, Puerto Rican, and Latin American communities in the United States, as well as among those who enjoyed dancing to the band's rhythmic beat.

Santana made its breakthrough to the mainstream audience at the Woodstock festival, via San Francisco's Fillmore Theatre and its manager Bill Graham. Although they were still unrecorded, they were included in a festival line-up that featured Janis Joplin, Jimi Hendrix, and Joan Baez. Their set, ending with "Soul Sacrifice," was documented in the film "Woodstock" (1970), which reached an audience that did not listen to jazz or Latin stations. Santana, now made up of Carlos Santana on guitar, Rolie, Brown, percussionist Michael Carabello (on drums, congo drums and tambourine) and timbalist/percusionist Chepito Areas, had a string of gold and platinum albums for Columbia—*Santana, Abraxas,* and *Santana III*—testifying to their crossover success. The first single, "Jingo," was given frequent playings on FM and Spanish-language AM stations on either coast. Two hit singles, "Evil Ways" and Peter Green's "Black Magic Woman" were popular on dance lists across the country. Later gold albums included

Caravanserai (1972) and *Welcome* (1972). Among the other instrumentalists who have appeared with Santana are congoist Armando Peraza, Ndugu Chancler, and jazz saxophonist Wayne Shorter. Carlos Santana has also performed as a jazz musician.

The spiritual conversion of Carlos Santana to Sri Chinmoy affected his music and the group's. As Devadip [Eye of God] Santana, he performed and recorded with fellow believers John Coltrane, Turiya Alice Coltrane, and Mahavishnu John McLaughlin. Frank Rose, reviewing a collaborative concert of Santana, Contrane, and McLaughlin in 1974 for the *Village Voice,* described Santana as "flourishing in the double shadow of Coltrane's genius and McLaughlin's spiritualism," partially because, as Rose wrote, "Santana's piecing quitar slashed through it like a lightning bolt." The fusion period of the early and mid-1970s brought such experimental albums as *Love, Devotion, Surrender* (1973) in collaboration with McLaughlin. Most of Santana's interviews in this period concentrated on his conversion and on the changes that it had brought to his band's collaborative functioning. It also brought Santana back to Woodstock, this time for an outdoor concert dedicated to Sri Chinmoy's music.

Latin-based rock returned as Santana's principal genre with the album *Amigos* (1976) and *Zebop* (1982). His personal fusion of rock and salsa was not always appreciated by the audience, according to John Storm Roberts of the *Village Voice.* "Despite everything, Carlos Santana's musical achievement seems to me under-

rated," he wrote in a review of a May 1976 concert. "His music is an uncommonly equal yoke of salsa and rock and his musicians can sear steak. The strength of this fusion is fully grasped neither by his rock audience, which certainly doesn't understand the richness of his Afro-Latin references, nor by older Latins, who often talk as through he was trying to play salsa, and not quite making it."

By 1979, Santana had split his musical identity into his work with the band, which still played fusion Latin-rock and his solo albums, which were more overtly religious. In John Rockwell's *New York Times* column, "The Pop Life," in March 1979, he described the difference between Santana's two new releases. *Inner Secrets* [the band album] is a typically appealing Santana grab bag with a couple of overt extensions into disco that don't represent any real alteration at all. The songs are more concise and pop oriented than ever, yet Mr. Santana's strong, lyrical guitar solos and the percussion build a bridge to his past. . . . Now, Santana is more willing to confine his overt religiousity to such projects as *Oneness* [the solo album] and to let his spiritual mesage be more indirectly conveyed at Santana concerts." Santana credited Bill Graham with his return to his musical roots, according to an interview Graham gave Robert Jasinski in the *New York Daily News* in 1982. "I told Devadip Santana that people wanted to hear the street sound that made them dance and sweat and that they associated with the band," said Graham.

Santana has also conveyed his message of spiritual awareness at a variety of political and socially conscious benefits. The band was one of only four acts to appear at both Woodstock and LiveAid. They can be seen and heard on *Musicourt* the United Cerebral Palsy benefit jam sessions recorded on video in 1981. Santana joined with Run-D.M.C at a Crack-Down concert (for Artists for Crack Education) in November 1986 that featured a collaboration among its members, West African percussionist Babtunde Olatunji, and second-generation salsa-fusionist Reuben Blades.

Santana's annual summertime concert in New York City, held either at Forest Hills Stadium, Pier 84, or at an outdoor location, gives the band an opportunity to collaborate with other fusion groups. In 1987, for example, they performed with the New Orleans-based Neville Brothers, with results that Dan Aquilante of the *New York Post* described as "spellbinding." "If the Santana repertory was a pack of 52, then each time he snapped a song off the top of the deck it was an ace." A reunion concert in 1988 brought Santana together with Rolie and Michael Shrieve for "a tough jamming band that favored long improvisations," as Peter Watrous described it in a *New York Times* review. "The loose song forms give Mr. Santana room to toss out some of the musical ideas on his mind; throughout the night, acting like a jazz musician, he quoted from other songs. . . . But more than anything, it is an instrumental band and it was over a steaming, raunchy blues boogie that both Mr. Santana and Mr. Rolie . . . found their highest moments."

Viva Santana! is both a re-issuing of old material and a reunion of early collaborators. Although the band's family tree is so complex that it is printed over two double-page spreads, it is apparent from the sounds on the double album that Santana's fusion still holds and is capable of continuous evolution. Santana has often been described as "America's premiere rock and roll ambassador to the world" because it accepts the musical heritage of the entire world as valid and worthy of experimentation within its improvisatory borders.

Selected discography

With group Santana; released by Columbia

Santana, 1968.
Abraxas, 1970.
Santana III, 1972.
Caravanserai, 1972.
Welcome, 1973.
Greatest Hits, 1974.
Borboletta, 1974.
Lotus, 1975.
Amigos, 1976.
Festival, 1977.
Moonflower, 1977.
Inner Secrets, 1979.
Marathon, 1979.

Swing of Delight, 1980.
Zebop, 1981.
Shango, 1982.
Havana Moon, 1983.
Beyond Appearances, 1985.
Freedom, 1987.
Viva Santana! (compilation), 1989.

Solo albums

Devadip Carlos—Oneness: Silver Dreams, Golden Reality, Columbia, 1979.
Blues For Salvador, Columbia, 1987.

With others

With Buddy Miles, Columbia, 1971.
(With John McLaughlin) *Love Devotion Surrender*, Columbia, 1973.
(With Alice Coltrane) *Illuminations*, Columbia, 1974.

Has appeared as guest artist on numerous albums, including on Gato Barbieri's *Tropico*, 1978; Mike Bloomfield's *Live Adventures*, 1969; Papa John Creach's *Papa John Creach*, 1971; Bob Dylan's *Real Live*, 1984; Herbie Hancock's *Monster*, 1980; and Boz Scaggs's *Middleman*, 1980.

Sources

New York Daily News, August 6, 1982.
New York Post, July 20, 1987.
New York Times, May 9, 1976; March 9, 1979; November 2, 1986; September 17, 1988.
Rolling Stone, December 7, 1972; May 6, 1976.
Villiage Voice, March 14, 1974; May 17, 1976; March 26, 1979.

—Barbara Stratyner

Doc Severinsen

Trumpet player, bandleader, songwriter

By virtue of his two-decade association with "The Tonight Show," Doc Severinsen is probably the best-known trumpeter in the nation. The flamboyantly dressed entertainer has been playing in bands since the mid-1940s, but it is his long association with Johnny Carson that has made his fame. Severinsen earns in excess of a half million dollars a year for 200 "Tonight Show" tapings; on his days off he may appear with his own band, Xebron, the Phoenix Pops, or any one of a number of classical orchestras in the United States.

Zan Stewart observed in *down beat* that the best accompanists for Severinsen's work "spotlight the trumpeter's masterful ability to produce clear, powerful tones throughout the range of his horn and over an assortment of rhythmic and harmonic foundations." If Seversinsen gets little opportunity to display the full range of his talent on "The Tonight Show," he is nonetheless respected by his peers in the music business—especially those involved with jazz and big bands. "I have not known a musician who is as talented as Doc and who works as hard as he does to stay there," fellow "Tonight Show" band member Tommy Newsom told *People* magazine. "Doc has always been the world's greatest trumpet player, and his crazy clothes just helped to make people aware of it."

The nickname "Doc" has been with Severinsen since birth. He was born Carl Hilding Severinsen in tiny Arlington, Oregon, on July 7, 1927. The nickname came from his father, a dentist, who was also known as Doc Severinsen. The elder Doc was the only dentist in town and an avid amateur musician. Severinsen reminisced about his youth in *down beat*. "I was born in a cow town," he said. "Really, they had cattle drives down the main street, and you had to close your doors so the animals didn't come into your house. My dad was the dentist and he played a little violin, so he started me on a junior-sized model. But I wanted to play trombone, so I refused to have anything to do with the violin. There weren't any music stores in Arlington, and thus no trombones, but a guy down the street had a cornet for sale, so that became my instrument."

At first the young Severinsen hated to practice his horn as well, but gradually he began to apply himself. At thirteen he was named the youngest member of an all-star band from four western states, and by his junior year of high school he had formed a band, "The Blue Notes," that performed at local dances and parties. As early as 1940—at age fourteen—Severinsen auditioned for the Tommy Dorsey Orchestra in Portland. He did not win a spot in the prestigious band at that time, but he did learn a great deal from the experience of associating with Dorsey's musicians.

Severinsen joined the Ted Fio Rito Band during his

For the Record. . .

Full name, Carl Hilding Severinsen; born July 7, 1927, in Arlington, Ore.; son of Carl Severin (a dentist) and Minnie Mae Severinsen; married third wife, Emily Marshall, 1980; children (first marriage) Nancy, Judy, Cindy; (second marriage) Robbin, Allen. *Education:* Finished high school by correspondence course, c.1944.

Formed band The Blue Notes, c. 1944; member of Ted Fio Rito Band, 1945; member of Charlie Barnet Band, 1947-49; also played with the bands of Tommy Dorsey, Benny Goodman, Norro Morales, and Vaughn Monroe during late 1940s and early 1950s; member of and soloist in network band for "The Steve Allen Show," NBC TV, 1954-55; member of NBC Orchestra for "The Tonight Show", 1962—, musical director, bandleader, and soloist, 1967—. Bandleader, member, and featured soloist in Xebron; resident conductor of Phoenix Pops Orchestra. Vice-president of C. G. Conn Company (musical instrument manufacturer).

Awards: Voted top instrumentalist in *Playboy* magazine music poll for ten straight years.

Addresses: *Office*—c/o NBC Press Dept., 30 Rockefeller Plaza, New York, N.Y. 10020.

senior year of high school, finishing his studies by correspondence course. Even during his compulsory stint in the army he won a spot in the Special Services band. When he was discharged at the age of twenty, Severinsen was a polished professional performer, ready to try his luck with the numerous big bands that were so popular at the time. For two years he played in a mixed-race be-bop band led by Charlie Barnet. Then, in 1949, he finally landed a regular job with Tommy Dorsey—a position he has described as "a dream come true."

Severinsen told *down beat:* "Tommy was such a great musician that you couldn't help but play great with him. His sound was one of the finest I've ever heard, but he was a little old-fashioned." From Dorsey's band Severinsen moved on to Benny Goodman's, and from there to the NBC staff orchestra in New York City. As television began its ascent in popularity Severinsen found himself a member and soloist of the band on "The Steve Allen Show." He also did steady moonlighting gigs and studio sessions with a wide variety of jazz, classical, and popular musicians.

In 1962 Severinsen joined "The Tonight Show" at the

same time the show got a new host, the affable comic Johnny Carson. Severinsen merely played in the "Tonight Show" band for the first five years, but when the band's leader Skitch Henderson retired in 1967, Severinsen took over as director. He has had the position ever since, with "his pick of the crop of L.A. studio and jazz players" behind him, to quote Stewart. Nor does Severinsen express any impatience with his job, similar as it is from night to night. "Let's face it," he told *People.* "I owe my career to Johnny."

Severinsen is more than just a standard backup band trumpet player, however. He is wildly experimental, culling material from rock, jazz, blues, and classical sources—and he even co-wrote the country hit "Stop and Smell the Roses." In his numerous nightclub appearances, he told *down beat,* he might even sing "something by Elvis or B.B. King or a new tune, maybe one I've heard on MTV that I've had arranged for my style. As in all my appearances, I just play music that appeals to me, you know, good music with melody." In *People* he put it another way: "What I want people to know is that Doc Severinsen plays many different things."

Severinsen is a recovered alcoholic who lives with his third wife in California. He enjoys exercising and raising animals, especially dogs and race horses. An interest in arresting clothing dates back to his early days in Arlington, when he dressed for the local rodeos. Now his clothes excite regular comment from Carson and have become an established part of his persona. Severinsen told *down beat* that as vice-president of the C. G. Conn musical instrument company he helps to design new horns for sale. "It's important to have a good horn and mouthpiece," the noted trumpeter said. "But the basic requirement to be a good player is not equipment, but practice, practice, practice."

Selected discography

Brass Roots, RCA, 1971.
The Best of Doc Severinsen, MCA.
I Feel Good, Juno.
(With Gerry Mulligan) *A Concert in Jazz,* Verve.
(With Mulligan) *Concert Jazz Band '63,* Verve.
(With Henry Mancini) *Brass on Ivory,* RCA

Sources

down beat, November, 1985.
People, July 13, 1981.

—*Anne Janette Johnson*

Paul Simon

Singer, songwriter, guitarist

"Paul Simon has emerged in the 1980s as a rocker for all ages, one figure from the '60s entering midlife not as a jejune nostalgia act but thriving both financially and artistically," wrote Jim Jerome in *People* magazine. Simon, one of the most successful folk-rockers of the 1960s, has indeed been able to sustain his success through two ensuing decades and through a number of fleeting pop music fads. As a member of Simon and Garfunkel, and later a solo performer, the singer/songwriter seems to have stayed in style precisely because he *creates* the style—from folk-influenced rock ballads to rollicking gospel and rhythm & blues numbers to jazz- and reggae-fueled tunes.

A *New Yorker* contributor noted that Simon's collected body of works "form one of the most original and moving bodies of pop music in America." Addressing himself to the lyrics Simon has written, *Saturday Review* essayist Bruce Pollock claimed: "Simon's songs mirrored the alienation, malaise, and despair of the [1960s] era, but did so melodiously, with a good beat, so you could dance to them. . . . Like the rest of us, Paul Simon has finally passed through adolescence, long considered a terminal condition not only of rock 'n' roll but also of the generation that came to majority in the Sixties. That generation became hooked on rock music as a way of receiving its essential data. And today these same listeners, older and somewhat wiser, continue to respond to Simon [who has] arrived at a more mature perspective and [is] able to mirror in [his] works something beyond pop platitudes."

Simon grew up in the Forest Hills section of Queens, New York. The son of two schoolteachers, he describes himself as a happy child who was very interested in sports. He found popular music at the same moment that rock and roll was finding itself—in the early 1950s. At the same time he became friends with a gangly youth just his age, Art Garfunkel, who lived in his neighborhood. Together the boys would listen to the radio for hours, fascinated by Elvis Presley and Bill Haley and The Comets. They also began singing together, accompanied by Simon's simple guitar chords. Even before they turned sixteen, Simon and Garfunkel were performing together at local sock hops; a producer from Big Records heard them and offered them a recording contract.

At the tender age of fifteen, Simon and Garfunkel, then called "Tom and Jerry," had their first success—a single called "Hey! Schoolgirl." They were invited to sing on "American Bandstand" and several other rock and roll television shows of the time. Simon remembers those days with mixed feelings. "I must have been very angry, probably about not growing [tall]," he told *Peo-*

For the Record. . .

Born October 13, 1941, in Newark, N.J.; son of Louis (a college professor) and Belle (a schoolteacher) Simon; married Peggy Harper, 1969 (divorced, 1975); married Carrie Fisher (an actress), 1983 (divorced, 1983); children: (first marriage) Harper (son). *Education:* Received B.A. from Queens College; attended Brooklyn Law School.

Singer and songwriter, 1956—. Performed with Art Garfunkel as Tom and Jerry, 1957-59; performed with Garfunkel as Simon and Garfunkel, 1964-71; solo performer, 1971—. Has appeared in numerous cable television concerts and in several commercial television specials, including "Simon and Garfunkel," CBS-TV, 1969, and "Paul Simon," NBC-TV, 1977. Producer of and actor in film "One Trick Pony," 1980.

Awards: Winner of Grammy Awards, including (with Garfunkel) for best album, 1969, for *The Graduate;* (with Garfunkel) for best performance by a pop vocal group, 1969; (with Garfunkel) for best album, 1970, for *Bridge Over Troubled Water;* (with Garfunkel) for best single, 1970, for "Bridge Over Troubled Water"; (with Garfunkel) for best performance by a pop vocal group, 1970, for "Bridge Over Troubled Water"; for best album, 1975, for *Still Crazy After All These Years;* and for best album, 1987, for *Graceland;* winner of Emmy Award, 1977, for musical special, "Paul Simon." Holder of nine platinum and fourteen gold records.

Addresses: *Home*—88 Central Park West, New York NY 10022. *Office*—c/o Warner Bros. Records, 3300 Warner Blvd., Burbank CA 91510.

ple. "I was doing well. When I was fifteen Artie and I played on *American Bandstand.* I batted first on the baseball team. I had a school jacket with letters and everything on it. I was popular. But I was a real angry guy. I spent a lot of time by myself playing guitar."

Tom and Jerry did not follow up their first hit song with others. Instead, Simon and Garfunkel went their separate ways, Simon to studies at Queen's College and Garfunkel to Columbia University. They were reunited in the early 1960s, while Simon was unenthusiastically reading law at Brooklyn Law School. Simon had never given up music entirely; in fact, he had been working as a backup player and producer in several New York recording studios. He and Garfunkel began to perform original folk tunes at outdoor concerts and small clubs, and soon they had attracted a regional following. In 1964 they earned a recording contract with the Columbia label.

Their first album, *Wednesday Morning, 3 A.M.,* attracted little attention. In late 1965, more than a year after the album's debut, Columbia—without Simon's knowledge—overdubbed a rock accompanyment to one of the album's songs, "The Sounds of Silence." Released as a single, the remixed version of the song shot to the number one spot on the *Billboard* Top 100 chart. A string of hits followed for the duo, including "I Am a Rock," "Mrs. Robinson," "Scarborough Fair/Canticle," and "The 59th Street Bridge Song (Feelin' Groovy)," most of which are still staples of "classic rock" radio stations.

According to Dave Marsh in the *Rolling Stone Record Guide,* Simon and Garfunkel's "socially relevant but gentle folk rock . . . quietly bridged the Sixties generation gap." Marsh adds that Simon's "elliptical, imagistic writing soon became very big on the rock-lyrics-are-poetry circuit, but he was really an expert popular-song craftsman, influenced by both folk and rock but owing allegiance to neither." Simon was largely responsible for the duo's songs, providing the lyrics and most of the music, but it was Garfunkel—whose clear tenor voice and gentle appearance charmed audiences—who frequently received credit for the group's success. This conundrum became painfully clear when Simon and Garfunkel released their best-known hit, "Bridge over Troubled Water," in 1970. The song and album of the same title sold more than nine million copies in two years, but even that level of achievement failed to save the relationship. After many years of heated arguments, Simon and Garfunkel split in 1971 to pursue solo careers.

Critics issued dire predictions about Simon's viability as a solo performer, underestimating his talent for incorporating various musical styles into his repertory while continuing to issue his poetic and introspective lyrics. His first solo album, *Paul Simon,* included a hit single, "Mother and Child Reunion," that carried a reggae beat and an unusually optimistic message. Every Simon album since then has had at least one memorable single, and all show Simon's enthusiasm for experimentation. His solo hits include the gospel-sounding "Love Me Like a Rock," the calypso "Late in the Evening," "Fifty Ways To Leave Your Lover," "One Trick Pony," "American Tune," and "Call Me Al." Almost thirty years to the day after his first recorded hit, Simon released the album *Graceland,* a frankly experimental collage of music featuring performers from South Africa and a spirited African beat. The album won Simon another Grammy Award and was one of the best sellers of 1987. Marsh finds Simon's solo albums in general "among the greatest popular music anyone in the current era has attempted."

No one shows more facility at assessing Paul Simon's

music than the artist himself. He explained how he works in *Rolling Stone:* "What I feel is, you take basic rock & roll as your primary vocabulary. . . . I don't mean heavy metal, I mean the Fifties—doo-wop, Presley, Chuck Berry, Buddy Holly, the Drifters, that kind of urban R & B and rockabilly. Now, from there I expand to other textures and rhythms. I expand the harmonic concept [to include Brazilian music and modern jazz]—that harmonic way of approaching things, and also the use of different time signatures. So, I'll take the basic rock thing and expand it into different areas musically, and then I'll contract it back to the rock thing. Always coming back to the basics—to either gospel, or rock—but goin' away so it doesn't sound like everything. . . .

"Lyrically, what I do is in a sense parallel to the music. I try to combine ordinary speech patterns—a vernacular way of speaking— . . . with poetic imagery. . . . I try to balance that between striking visual images and ordinary speech. And ordinary speech can be used with the extended harmonic thing to create a sense of irony or contrast, while I can use a strong visual or poetic image with a basic rock & roll thing to undercut." Simon

---

"Part of my personality keeps pushing at what hurts, what hurts."

---

has also never apologized for the somber tone of his lyrics—noticeable since his earliest songs. "I'm investigating . . . all the time, asking what is the problem, what is it. . . ." he told *Esquire.* "Part of my personality keeps pushing at what hurts, what hurts."

Simon's personal life has often offered fuel for his introspective lyrics. Twice married and divorced, he admits to having difficulties sustaining close relationships. He has reconciled with Garfunkel to the extent that they occasionally play and record together (they shared a late 1970s hit "My Little Town," for instance), but he prefers solitude or the company of his teenaged son, Harper. Simon lives in New York City, and, since he has retained rights to all of his songs, is very wealthy. He told *People:* "Entertainers are paid disproportionately high sums of money for their contribution to society. I used to feel guilty, but now I accept that gratefully. When someone tells me, 'You've given me a lot of pleasure in my life,' it all seems like a gratifying, very pure way of earning money." Undaunted by the fact that he will soon turn fifty, Simon plans to continue composing and performing music as long as he has an audience who wants to hear him. "If I'm healthy," he told *People,* "I'll still be doing what I've done since I was 13—writing songs. It's as exhilarating now as ever. I get a very satisfied feeling that I never get in any other part of my life."

Selected discography:

Simon and Garfunkel albums

Wednesday Morning, 3 A.M., Columbia, 1966.
The Sounds of Silence, Columbia, 1966.
Parsley Sage Rosemary & Thyme, Columbia, 1966.
Bookends, Columbia, 1968.
The Graduate (soundtrack), Columbia, 1968.
Bridge over Troubled Waters, Columbia, 1970.
Simon and Garfunkel's Greatest Hits, Columbia, 1972.
Concert in Central Park, Warner Brothers, 1981.

Solo albums

Paul Simon, Columbia, 1972; reissued, Warner Bros., 1988.
There Goes Rhymin' Simon, Columbia, 1973; reissed, Warner Bros., 1988.
Live Rhymin': Paul Simon in Concert, Columbia, 1974; reissued, Warner Bros., 1988.
Still Crazy after All These Years, Columbia, 1975.
One Trick Pony, WEA, 1980.
Hearts and Bones, Warner Bros., 1983.
Graceland, Warner Bros., 1986.

Sources

Books

The Rolling Stone Record Guide, edited by Dave Marsh, Random House/Rolling Stone Press, 1979.
Simon, George T., *The Best of the Music Makers,* Doubleday, 1979.

Periodicals

Esquire, June, 1987.
High Fidelity, May, 1982.
New Yorker, September 2, 1967; April 29, 1972.
New York Post, May 26, 1973.
New York Times, February 27, 1972.
New York Times Magazine, October 13, 1968.
People, September 5, 1983; November 3, 1980; October 6, 1986.
Rolling Stone, May 28, 1970; October 30, 1980; July 2, 1987.
Saturday Review, June 12, 1976.
Time, January 31, 1972.

—Anne Janette Johnson

Frank Sinatra

Singer

Frank Sinatra was born in Hoboken, New Jersey, on December 12, 1915, and even though his tender father, Marty, helped to raise him, it was his mother, Dolly, who would have the most influence on his character. She was a powerful figure in the local community who ran a saloon and, allegedly, an illegal abortion service. She had an extremely short temper and the ability to walk over anyone who got in her way; traits that would also be attributed to her son. A poor student in school, Sinatra decided he wanted to be a singer during his teens. "He didn't have a job at the time, but he loved hanging around musicians," said a friend of Sinatra's, Maria Brush Schrieber, "so I suggested that he get an orchestra together for our Wednesday night school dances. He'd just started singing [in public] a little bit [at about age 17] and in exchange for hiring the musicians he'd get to sing a few numbers with the band," Schrieber told Kitty Kelley, author of the controversial *His Way: The Unauthorized Biography of Frank Sinatra*.

Sinatra has said he always knew he would be a successful singer, bigger than Bing Crosby one day. His first real group was The Three Flashes, a singing and dancing trio which later became The Hoboken Four. "I always liked to sing and I liked to be around bands and to have a part of the band glamour. I couldn't play an instrument and I didn't care about learning to play one. . . . While I wasn't the best singer in the world, they weren't the best bands in the country either," he is quoted in *His Way*.

After taking some vocal lessons, his mother pulled some strings with the musicians' union and got him a job singing at the Rustic Cabin for $15 a week. Trumpeter Harry James had just left the Benny Goodman band and was looking for a singer for the band he was forming when he heard Sinatra on the radio. James went to the Rustic and in June of 1939 hired Sinatra to sing with his Music Makers for $75 a month. Reviews of Sinatra's singing were not overwhelmingly favorable, and the band was even thrown out of Victor Hugo's during one gig. After just seven months of a two-year contract, Sinatra quit the band to join Tommy Dorsey's orchestra.

"I learned about dynamics and phrasing and style from the way he played his horn, and I enjoyed my work because he sees to it that a singer is always given a perfect setting," Sinatra told *Metronome*. His career began to blossom with Dorsey and he worked hard at developing his own unique style of slurring the vocals just enough to drive the young girls crazy. One tale has it that Sinatra's agent, George Evans, planted screaming teenage girls in the front rows as a ploy to create a sensation. Regardless, their single, "I'll Never Smile

Again", went to number 1 and by 1941 Sinatra had dethroned Crosby in the *down beat* poll for Top Band Vocalist. In January of 1942, Sinatra recorded four solo songs and was on the verge of leaving Dorsey's band. The two had become very close; Dorsey was even godfather to Sinatra's daughter. When Sinatra left the band in September, it would be the end of their friendship.

In December of that year Sinatra sang with Benny Goodman's band, the hottest at the time, at New York's Paramount, earning $1,250 a week. He also appeared in the movie "Higher and Higher," but began receiving criticism for not serving in the armed forces during World War II. With things rolling along so well, Sinatra was not about to upset the flow. "I've planned my career. From the first minute I walked on a stage I determined to get exactly where I am," he said in *His Way*. In 1946 he signed a five-year contract with MGM for $260,000 annually to make movies at a time when he was at the top of the music polls.

Because of Sinatra's movie career, his singing was more or less put on hold. By 1949 he had sunk to number 49 in the top 50 in record sales, after selling more than ten million records just three years prior. His films were not taking off like he had planned and his marriage was also shaky. In 1951 he divorced Nancy and married actress Ava Gardner, beginning a stormy relationship that would end five years later. She was able to help Sinatra revive his acting career when she helped to secure his role in "From Here To Eternity." He had desparately wanted the part and eventually earned an Oscar for best supporting actor.

Gardner also had a profound effect on his singing, according to veteran music arranger Nelson Riddle. "It was Ava who did that, who taught him how to sing a torch song. That's how he learned. She was the greatest love of his life and he lost her," he told Kelley. Sinatra's collaboration with Riddle began when he left the Columbia label in 1952 and signed with Capitol. They teamed him with Riddle and the two worked together on such hits as: "My One and Only Love," "A Foggy Day," "My Funny Valentine," and 1954's *Billboard* top single, the million-disc seller, "Young at Heart."

After nearly ten years, Sinatra was back on top in the music world during the late 1950s. His string of million-sellers would continue: "Love and Marriage," "Learnin' the Blues," "The Tender Trap," "All the Way," "Witchcraft," and "Hey, Jealous Lover". After his divorce from Gardner, he courted a seemingly endless row of entertainment beauties, including Liz Taylor, Judy Garland, Lauren Bacall, and Juliet Prowse. His film career continued with the likes of "The Manchurian Candidate" and "The Man With the Golden Arm." All totaled, Sinatra has appeared in over 60 movies.

His affiliations with reputed mobsters have caused him much grief. He has been questioned numerous times about his involvement in the Las Vegas casino world, and after a fight there in 1970, he vowed to never play Vegas again (but he was back at Caesars Palace in 1974.

His 1965 album, *September of My Years,* won a Grammy Award, but in just six years he would announce his retirement from the recording studio at a farewell show at L.A.'s Music Center. But, that too, was short-lived, and Sinatra was back with a television special and a new album, *Ol' Blues Eyes is Back,* in 1973. Although his personal life may raise some eyebrows, as a professional, Sinatra is regarded in the music world as the consummate artist. Quincy Jones, who produced Sinatra's 1984 release, *L.A. Is My Lady,* described the session for *down beat:* "Sinatra came into the office here, and started with a list of things he wanted to do. I had two or three suggestions. He came in at 2 p.m., and in less than two hours we had rehearsed, had keys and routines on 10 songs. That's the way he's always recorded. . . . Frank is one take, that's it. If the band's not in shape, he leaves them behind . . . he came in at 7, and at 8:20, baby, we went home. None of that three month stuff."

Although he was criticized for performing in Sun City, South Africa, in the early 1980s, Sinatra has spent a good deal of time fighting racism and performing community services. He has received numerous awards, including the Philadelphia Freedom Medal and the Presidential Medal of Freedom, accolades that help to quell the publicity focused on the more controversial aspects of his character. After his movies, marriages, reported mobster ties, awards, and bad press have been analyzed and attempts to separate popular myth from fact have been abandoned, there is only one true element by which to judge Frank Sinatra: the voice.

"It was Ava [Gardner] who did that, who taught [Sinatra] how to sing a torch song. That's how he learned. She was the greatest love of his life and he lost her."
—Nelson Riddle

"There can be little doubt that Sinatra is the single greatest interpreter of American popular song we have had the pleasure of hearing," wrote *down beat's* Pete Welding, "the one performer who has raised what he deprecatingly refers to as 'saloon singing' to a high art

and who, over a long and distinguished career, has enriched American music with countless superior recordings of many of the idiom's finest songs."

Selected discography

Albums; released by Capitol

Songs For Young Lovers, 1954.
Swing Easy, 1954.
In the Wee Small Hours, 1955.
Songs for Swingin' Lovers, 1956.
Close to You, 1957.
A Swingin' Affair, 1957.
Where Are You?, 1957
A Jolly Christmas from Frank Sinatra, 1957.
Come Fly With Me, 1958.
Only the Lonely, 1958.
Come Dance With Me, 1959.
Look to Your Heart, 1959.
No One Cares, 1959.
Nice 'n' Easy, 1960.
Sinatra's Swingin' Session, 1961.
All the Way, 1961.
Come Swing with Me, 1961.
Point of No Return, 1962.
Sinatra Sings of Love and Things, 1962.

Released by Reprise

Ring-A-Ding-Ding, 1961.
Sinatra Swings, 1961.
I Remember Tommy, 1961.
Sinatra and Strings, 1962.
Sinatra and Swingin' Brass, 1962.
All Alone, 1962.
Sinatra-Basie, 1963.
The Concert Sinatra, 1963.
Sinatra's Sinatra, 1963.
Frank Sinatra Sings Days of Wine and Roses, Moon River and other Academy Award Winners, 1964.
Sinatra-Basie: It Might as Well be Swing, 1964.
Softly, As I Leave You, 1964.
Sinatra '65, 1965.
September of My Years, 1965.
A Man and His Music, 1965
My Kind of Broadway, 1965.
Moonlight Sinatra, 1966.
Strangers in the Night, 1966.
Sinatra-Basie: Sinatra at the Sands, 1966.
That's Life, 1966.
Francis Albert Sinatra & Antonio Carlos Jobim, 1967.
Frank Sinatra and Frank & Nancy, 1967.
Francis A. & Edward K., 1968.
Cycles, 1968.

My Way, 1969.
A Man Alone, 1969.
Watertown, 1970.
Sinatra & Company, 1971.
Ol' Blue Eyes Is Back, 1973.
Some Nice Things I've Missed, 1974.
The Main Event/Live from Madison Square Garden, 1974.
Trilogy (three-record album), 1980.
She Shot Me Down, 1981.

Released by QWest

L.A. Is My Lady, 1984.

Also featured vocalist on numerous hit songs, including "Night and Day," 1943, "Nancy," 1945, "Young at Heart," 1954, "Love and Marriage," 1955, "How Little We Know," 1956, "Chicago," 1957, "All the Way," 1957, "High Hopes," 1959, "It Was a Very Good Year," 1965, "Softly, As I Leave You," 1964, "Strangers In the Night," 1966, (with daughter, Nancy Sinatra) "Somethin' Stupid," 1969, and "My Way," 1969.

Sources

Books

Ewen, David, *All the Years of American Popular Music,* Prentice-Hall, 1977.
Kelley, Kitty, *His Way: The Unauthorized Biography of Frank Sinatra,* Bantam 1986.
The Rolling Stone Record Guide, edited by Dave Marsh with John Swenson, Random House/Rolling Stone Press, 1979.
Simon, George T., *The Big Bands,* Schirmer Books, 1967.

Periodicals

down beat, March, 1985; April, 1985.
Rolling Stone, June 12, 1980; September 18, 1980.

Patti Smith

Singer, songwriter

atti Smith grew up in Pitman, a lower-class, melting-pot town in New Jersey. Until she saw the Rolling Stones on an Ed Sullivan show, she was totally into the popular black groups of the early sixties. "I was just one of a million girls who could sing Ronettes records 'almost as good as the Ronettes," she told *Rolling Stone.* After high school she began working in a factory around the same time she discovered the poetry of the French symbolist Arthur Rimbaud. While in junior college, Smith became pregnant and gave up the child for adoption. She moved to New York for a brief period and eventually took off for Paris with her sister to study art. In France she began to have premonitions of Rolling Stones guitarist Brian Jones's death just days before he actually died.

She moved back to New York, living at the Chelsea Hotel, a veritable hotbed of musicians, writers, actors and artists during the early seventies. She began working at a local bookstore where she befriended rock-historian/guitarist Lenny Kaye. She also started writing for magazines like *Rolling Stone, Rock,* and *Creem,* offering poetry and critical essays. By 1973, three of her poetry books had been published: *Seventh Heaven, Kodak* and *Witt.* Friends persuaded her to read her works in public, and, with the accompaniment of Kaye on guitar, she could be heard at New York clubs like Max's and CBGB's, opening for bands like the New York Dolls. After the addition of Richard Sohl on piano, the trio even performed at San Francisco's Winterland.

Clive Davis of Arista Records signed Smith to a recording contract and in 1975 she entered the studio to record her debut LP, *Horses.* She personally picked the producer, ex-Velvet Underground member, John Cale. "All I was really looking for was a technical person," Smith told *Rolling Stone*'s Dave Marsh. "Instead, I got a total maniac artist." Cale pushed Smith and her band (Kaye and Ivan Kral—guitars and bass, Jay Dee Daugherty—drums, and Sohl—piano) to their artistic limits. *Horses* is a compilation of all Smith's referential influences. The surrealism of Rimbaud, the violent prose of William Burroughs, and the simple, yet masterful, rhythms of the Velvets are all in some way represented on the album.

Horses features six songs co-written by Smith, her band, Blue Oyster Cult guitarist Alan Lanier (her boyfriend at the time), and Television's Tom Verlaine. The other two songs are reworkings of the Chris Kenner hit, "Land of a Thousand Dances," and the old Them/Van Morrison tune, "Gloria"; both restructured around Smith's poetic vision. Smith became the darling of the in-crowd from coast to coast. Complimentary reviews appeared in *Time,* Knight newspapers, *Mademoiselle,* and even *Rolling Stone,* in which Smith told of another premonition she once had. "I've known I was gonna be a big shot since I was four. I just didn't know it had anything to do with my throat."

Smith charged back into the studio after a triumphant tour of the States to make her follow-up LP, *Radio Ethiopia.* Unfortunately, the album ended up sounding more like a showcase for a garage band than for Smith's poetry: Her voice was nearly drowned out in the mayhem of heavy metal support offered by a group who did not seem to recognize their own musical limitations. As Charles M. Young observed in *Rolling Stone,* "The punks present their instrumental incompetence in the spirit of farce and satire. The Patti Smith Group presents it as a holy sacrament."

The album was a financial flop and the band members were forced to find other means to support themselves. Tragically, during the tour to support *Radio Ethiopia,* Smith fell off the stage in Tampa, Florida, on January 23, 1977, and broke her neck. She spent the following year wearing a neck brace and undergoing physical therapy. She was, however, able to complete another book of poetry, *Babel,* during the time off.

Smith was back in 1978 and determined to make her music more communicative (i.e. commercial) this time around. Her third album, *Easter,* contained her only Top 20 hit, "Because The Night", co-written by fellow New Jersey rocker Bruce Springsteen. In his *Rolling Stone* review, Dave Marsh wrote, *"Easter* makes good on Patti Smith's biggest boast—that she is one of the great figures of Seventies rock & roll. More importantly perhaps, it focuses her mystical and musical visions in a way that makes her the most profoundly religious American popular performer since Jim Morrison."

Smith released her fourth album, *Wave,* in 1979, but the magic seemed to be gone. It was a directionless effort with only one real gem, the song "Dancing Barefoot." The rest of the album, according to Robert Christgau in Christgau's *Record Guide* was "as listenable as *Radio Ethiopia.*" Her creative well appeared to have dried up

and, after her marriage to former MC5 guitarist Fred "Sonic" Smith, she went into retirement for nine years to raise a family.

In 1988 Smith decided to make a comeback, and she recorded the album *Dream of Life.* "Sonic" provided guitar layers and co-produced the album with Jimmy Iovine; former band members Daugherty and Sohl also appeared. In the age of MTV and record executives pushing everything off as 'the next big thing,' Robert Palmer observed in *Rolling Stone:* "What may be most striking about *Dream Of Life* is that there is no product here at all, only music."

Writings

Poetry

Witt: A Book of Poems, Gotham, 1972.
Seventh Heaven, Telegraph, 1973.
Ha! Ha! Houdini, Gotham, 1977.
Babel, Putnam, 1978.

Also author of *Kodak.*

Selected discography

Horses, Arista, 1975.
Radio Ethiopia, Arista, 1976.
Easter, Arista, 1978.
Wave, Arista, 1979.
Dream of Life, Arista, 1988.

Sources

Books

Christgau, Robert, *Christgau's Record Guide,* Ticknor & Fields, 1981.
The Illustrated Encyclopedia of Rock, compiled by Nick Logan and Bob Woffinden, Harmony Books, 1977.
Rock Revolution, by the editors of *Creem* magazine, Popular Library, 1976.
The Rolling Stone Illustrated History of Rock & Roll, edited by Jim Miller, Random House/Rolling Stone Press, 1976.
The Rolling Stone Record Guide, edited by Dave Marsh with Jim Swenson, Random House/Rolling Stone Press, 1979.
What's That Sound?, edited by Ben Fong-Torres, Anchor Press, 1976.

Periodicals

Rolling Stone, February 12, 1976; January 13, 1977; July 28, 1977; April 20, 1978; July 27, 1978; August 25, 1988.

Sweet Honey in the Rock

Gospel group

"**P**art community sing, part singing community," as Jon Pareles described them in the *New York Times,* Sweet Honey in the Rock has become one of the most popular vocal groups in concert and on recordings. Five women integrating their voices into soaring harmonies with exhilerating rhythms, Sweet Honey in the Rock is a "girl's group" as reinterpreted for the politically aware, feminist 1980s. The quintet was formed by Bernice Johnson Reagon in 1973. A long-time civil rights activist from Albany, Georgia, she was serving as vocal director for the highly acclaimed D.C. Black Repertory Theater in Washington. A workshop that she led for unaccompanied voices developed into the present group when only four women appeared at the first rehearsal. As Reagon said in an article in *Scholastic Scope,* "the sound fell into place."

Over twenty women have appeared with Sweet Honey in the Rock over the last fifteen years. Currently, the members are Reagon, Evelyn Harris (who joined in 1974), health care profession Ysaye Maria Barnwell (bass line maintainer since 1979), choreographer Aisha Kahlil (since 1981) and Nitanju Bolade, trained in African-based folklore. Sweet Honey in the Rock performs with a non-singing signer for deaf members of the audience, Shirley Childres Johnson. The vocalists provide their own percussion accompaniment on tambourines, rattles and hand-held drums. The audience's rhythmic clapping adds to the pulsating beat.

Sweet Honey in the Rock continues to perform *a capella.* The group's ability to create a full sound without back-up instrumentalists—a choice that has become more popular with a variety of musical groups over the past decade—still astonishes audiences and critics alike. Although a London reviewer for *The Observer* titled his article "Disturbing discords," American critics, more used to the harmonies of Gospel, West African music, and minimalists, defend the sound as "luminous, virtuosic, ingenious and luxuriant." As Doris Worsham described them in the *Oakland Tribune* in 1985, "Sweet Honey pours forth harmonies of the world."

The political activism and Black-conciousness of Reagon's past is very much present in the Sweet Honey in the Rock concerts and recordings. Reagon's own lyrics are influenced by the writings of black novelists and poets June Jordan, Alice Walder, and Ralph Ellison, whose philsophy "The choice is to live with music or to die with noise," she cited in the *Scholastic Scope* article. The group was chosen to perform at the 1985 United Nations Decade for Women conference in Nairobi, Kenya, and has presented its stirring music at concerts and rallies dedicated to disarmament, African liberation, safe energy, and PUSH.

The range of music performed in each concert and recording has given Sweet Honey in the Rock a unique feel. The group derives its title, and part of its repertory, from the Southern gospel songs that Reagon learned as a child. They have championed the authored hymns of Reverend Charles Albert Tindley and William Herbert Brewster, as well as American protest music of the 1930s, by Woodie Guthrie and Leadbelly. Their annual Carnegie Hall concert in 1988, for example, included Leadbelly,'s "Sylvie," a Georgia White blues lament from the 1930s, the ageless hymn "Let Your Little Light Shine," a reggae number, "Rivers of Babylon," and a new song by Reagon, "Ode to the International Debt."

Sweet Honey in the Rock has also toured extensively in the United States and Canada, with appearences on college campuses, folk clubs, Baptist and AME churches and festivals, and folk and women's music. Their performances have been cheered at the Smithsonian Institution's Festival of American Folk Life on the Mall in their native District of Columbia, at the 1984 Lincoln Center Out-of-Doors in New York City, and at the Edinburgh Festival in Scotland. A Public Broadcasting Service (PBS) profile of the group has brought their music and message to millions more who have not seen them in person.

For the Record. . .

Formed as *a capella* gospel quintet in 1973 by **Bernice Johnson Reagon;** current members include Reagon, **Evelyn Harris** (1974—), **Ysaye Maria Barnwell** (1979—), **Aisha Kahlil** (1981—), and **Nitanju Bolade** (1985—); group performs with non-singing signer for deaf members of the audience, **Shirley Childres Johnson.**

Awards: *B'lieve I'll Run On . . . See What the End's Gonna Be* named best women's album, 1979, by National Association of Independent Record Distributors.

Addresses: *Office*—Roadwork, Inc. 1475 Harvard St. NW, Washington, DC 20009. *Record company*—Flying Fish Records, 1304 West Schubert, Chicago, IL 60614.

received individual praise are the group's version of "[Ain't Gonna] Study War No More," Woody Guthrie's "Deportees," and "Mandiacapella," improvised from West African drum rhythms.

Selected discography

Sweet Honey in the Rock, Flying Fish, 1976.
B'lieve I'll Run On . . . See What the End's Gonna Be, Redwood Records, 1978.
Good News, Flying Fish, 1982.
We All . . . Everyone of Us, Flying Fish, 1983.
Feel Something Drawing Me On, Flying Fish, 1985.
The Other Side, Flying Fish, 1985.
Sweet Honey in the Rock at Carnegie Hall, Flying Fish, 1988.
Breaths (anthology), Flying Fish, 1988 [released only on compact disc].

Recordings for the Flying Fish and Redwood labels also display the diversity of the group in live performance and in studios. The 1985 *Feel Something Drawing Me On* included only sacred music—from Southern gospel to "Meyango," a West African funeral song. Their other six albums, however, include a full range of Sweet Honey songs. *B'lieve I'll Run On . . . See What the End's Gonna Be* (1978) was named best women's album by the National Association of Independent Record Distributors for 1979. Among the cuts that have

Sources

New York Times, October 26, 1988.
Oakland Tribune, October 18, 1985.
The Observer (London), March 27, 1983.
Scholastic Scope, Media Focus section, March 21, 1985.
Washington Post Weekend, November 15, 1985.

—*Barbara Stratyner*

Talking Heads

American new wave/pop group

The band Talking Heads has it roots at the Rhode Island School of Design, where David Byrne, the son of immigrant Scottish parents, was enrolled for two semesters and "hung out" for a few more. There Byrne met drummer Chris Frantz and formed a five-member band called the Artistics. They were popular on campus but were jokingly called the Autistics because of Byrne's bizarre stage antics and the band's quirky performances. The group dissolved when its members graduated. Byrne, Frantz, and Frantz's girlfriend Tina Weymouth (who had not been a member of the band) moved to New York City in 1974. Deciding to form a new band, they auditioned unsuccessfully for a bassist. Finally, Byrne taught Weymouth to play bass—she already played guitar—and Talking Heads was born. They first appeared at CBGB's, a New Music venue in New York's Bowery, in June 1975. A year later they recorded their first single, "Love Goes to a Building on Fire" and toured Europe with the Ramones.

The popular music scene at the time was split between the glitter and banality of disco and the raw energy and

For the Record. . .

Group formed in New York City in 1974; original lineup included **David Byrne** (vocals and guitar), **Chris Frantz** (drums), **Tina Weymouth** (bass), and **Jerry Harrison** (keyboards and guitar); Byrne and Harrison have also appeared and recorded as solo artists since 1981; Frantz and Weymouth additionally formed, appeared, and recorded with group Tom Tom Club, 1981—.

Addresses: *Office*—c/o Sire Records, 3300 Warner Blvd., Burbank CA 91510. *David Byrne*—Indey Music, c/o Overland, 1775 Broadway, New York NY 10019.

rebellion of punk music. Talking Heads took a new approach. Their music was straight-forward rock but offered an intelligent message; and, while other bands had exhausted the drive to appear wild and different, Talking Heads dressed in suits, white shirts, and trousers. *Stereo Review* noted: "Talking Heads have always defied trends by keeping one step ahead of them or by ignoring them." Even *New Republic* took note of the band: "Minimalist in their musical arrangements, the Talking Heads stripped away the accretions of drum and guitar solos and the phallocentric gestures of a corrupted rock 'n' roll. What remained were bare, almost jarring chords and tight structures. The music was less a revolt than a strategy for survival in a world in which the television is never switched off."

By the time Talking Heads was ready to record their first album, *Talking Heads 77,* they were joined by keyboard player Jerry Harrison. They achieved cult status, but it would be a few years before popular success arrived. Their next few albums were produced with the guidance of studio wizard Brian Eno. "Take Me to the River," from the album *More Songs About Music and Food* (1978), was their first song to reach the Top 40.

Byrne has been the most prominent member of the group—front-man, guitarist, singer, and composer of most of the band's songs. He is academically inclined and his lyrics have a seriousness that distinguished the music of Talking Heads from punk music. Set against the easy rocking movements of the band, it is Byrne's quirky performance, his strange jerky stage movements, that make the band fun to watch. He once told *Time:* "People talk about how strange I am. Of course, being inside myself, not having the perspective, I don't think I'm odd at all. I can see that what I'm doing is not exactly what everyone else is doing, but I don't think of it as strange."

In 1981 Byrne found himself involved in personal projects that separated him from the band. With Eno he produced the album *My Life in a Bush of Ghosts,* which drew on exotic Eastern rhythms and used taped radio broadcasts for lyrics. He also became involved in theatrical productions, writing the score for Twyla Tharp's dance production *The Catherine Wheel* in 1981; and in 1985, parts of the score for Robert Wilson's production "The CIVIL warS." The album from *The Catherine Wheel* garnered rave reviews.

Amid insecurities about the breakup of the group, Frantz and Weymouth started a project of their own: Tom Tom Club. Their first album, released in 1981, with the help of Weymouth's sisters and some Jamaican percussion artists, surprised everyone by selling nearly twice as many copies as any Talking Heads album to date. Weymouth and Frantz—who had married—had their first child in 1982; on tour, Weymouth nursed the

> *"Talking Heads have always defied trends by keeping one step ahead of them or by ignoring them completely."*

boy between acts. Jerry Harrison also released his first solo album, *The Red and the Black.*

In 1982 Talking Heads released a double live album, *The Name of This Band Is Talking Heads,* that illustrates the evolution of their music. One disc, featuring songs recorded at shows in 1977 and 1979, features the original quartet; the second, drawn from shows in 1980 and 1981, features an expanded lineup of up to nine musicians who toured with the band during that period, including guitarist Adrian Belew, funk bassist Busta Jones, and percussionist Steve Scales. The band's performance documentary movie "Stop Making Sense," released in 1984, equally demonstrates the band's range. At this time Talking Heads began to make commercial breakthroughs and had already produced two revolutionary (by MTV standards) rock videos on the songs "Once in a Lifetime" and "Burning Down the House."

The movie "True Stories" was released in 1986. It was directed, scored, and partially scripted by Byrne with music performed by Talking Heads and a variety of ethnic groups. *Time* called "True Stories" the "most joyous and inventive rock movie-musical since the Beatles scrambled through *Help*." By this time, the group had come full circle. They had started out with a message that disparaged a culture driven by television and the mediocrity of news weeklies; then, ten years later, they were celebrating the ordinariness and banality of the American way.

"True Stories" takes place in an imaginary town populated by characters whose stories are drawn from tabloid headlines. *Stereo Review* carried this description: "In the film Byrne narrates slices of the lives of peculiar Texas townsfolk with names like Lying Woman and Computer Guy. They wear tacky outfits and tacky hairstyles and live in a tacky but friendly environment, a panorama of shopping malls and other consumer monuments separated by vast empty landscapes."

The soundtrack album features the original Talking Heads quartet playing pop songs based on a range of American music styles. *New Republic* observed that "instead of synthesizing Western and non-Western elements, the band moved in wholesale appropriations of American popular music . . ." and that "Byrne's voice had been purged of its trademark anxiety; instead of his controlled hysteria, he was actually crooning his lyrics." But Talking Heads refused to stand still or limit the direction or their music. By 1988 they had been to Paris and recorded *Naked* with a host of African musicians.

Talking Heads found their own unique voice amid the screams of the new wave rock revolution. Their sound has evolved to one with great appeal to listeners in search of inventive music. As *Rolling Stone* observed: "If the essence of rock & roll is white kids trying to be as cool a black kids, then Talking Heads effected the most rarefied cultural synthesis of the Seventies, a fusion of git-down street rhythms and collegiate sensibilities heady enough to spawn a generation of imitators on both sides of the Atlantic."

Selected discography

All released by Sire Records

Talking Heads

Talking Heads, 1977.
More Songs about Music and Food, 1978.
Fear of Music, 1979.
Remain in Light, 1980.
The Name of This Band is Talking Heads, 1982.
Speaking in Tongues, 1983.
Stop Making Sense, 1984.
Little Creatures, 1985.
True Stories, 1986.
Naked, 1988.

David Byrne

My Life in a Bush of Ghosts, 1981.
The Complete Score from the Broadway Production of "The Catherine Wheel, 1981.
Music for "The Knee Plays" (music from Robert Wilson's "The CIVIL warS," 1985.

Tom Tom Club

Tom Tom Club, 1981.
Close to the Bone, 1983.

Jerry Harrison

The Red and the Black, 1981.
Casual Gods, 1988.

Sources

Books

Reese, Krista, *The Name of This Book Is Talking Heads*, Proteus, 1982.

Periodicals

Guitar Player, March 1984.
New Republic, March 23, 1987.
Rolling Stone, October 27, 1983; April 21, 1988.
Stereo Review, November 1986.
Time, September 2, 1985; October 27, 1986.

—*Tim LaBorie*

Pete Townshend

Singer, songwriter, guitarist

Pete Townshend, The Who's principal songwriter and lead guitarist, is a respected seminal figure in modern rock 'n' roll. As a raging young rocker in the late 1960s, Townshend made concert history by smashing his guitar in frenzied moments onstage; his music both mocked and mirrored the anger and alienation of a whole generation. Townshend is practically canonized for the songs he wrote for and performed with The Who, including the rock operas *Tommy* and *Quadrophenia*, and the driving singles "Won't Get Fooled Again," "My Generation," "Behind Blue Eyes," "Who Are You," and "You Better You Bet."

According to a *Rolling Stone Record Guide* contributor, Townshend and The Who were initially considered "much better in live performance than on record," but today the group's albums "transcend their flaws" and rank among "the most influential rock albums ever released." Speaking directly to Townshend's contribution to modern music, the critic adds: "Using a few standard . . . chord progressions as motifs, Townshend constructed a virtual theory of essential rock forms, running each progression through its possibilities." Now well into his forties, Townshend continues to write and record as a solo performer. His more recent work deals with "the problems faced by an aging rocker who wonders if he can still keep it together," to quote the *Rolling Stone Record Guide,* as well as the political and social malaise of the late 1980s.

Peter Townshend was born in London on May 19, 1945. His parents were both professional musicians, and as a child he accompanied them on dance band tours. By the age of twelve Townshend was experimenting with a guitar; he was quite taken with rock 'n' roll, especially Bill Haley and the Comets. A shy teenager, he spent hours by himself practicing the guitar, and later the banjo, which he performed in a Dixieland-style band founded by his friend John Entwhistle. Initially Townshend preferred jazz to rock, but his high school friends—Entwhistle and a maverick named Roger Daltrey—were gravitating toward rock and incorporating elements of rhythm & blues in their music. Soon after graduating from high school, Townshend, Entwhistle, and Daltrey formed a band called The Detours. They held daytime jobs while performing in small London clubs at night.

England's youth scene in the early 1960s featured sometimes bloody clashes between "Mods," dandyish middle-class teens, and the rowdier "Rockers," or "skinheads." The manager of Townshend's group decided to direct his musicians toward the Mod audience. Soon The Detours were known as The High Numbers and were playing in Soho in the Wardour Street clubs. During this time the group picked up its fourth member,

For the Record. . .

Full name, Peter Dennis Blandford Townshend; born May 19, 1945, in London, England; son of Clifford (a musician) and Betty (a singer; maiden name, Dennis) Townshend; married Karen Astley, 1968; children: Emma, Aminta. *Education:* Attended Ealing Art College, England.

Professional musician, 1960—; with John Entwhistle and Roger Daltrey, formed band The Detours, 1962; added drummer Keith Moon, changed band name to The High Number, 1963, and The Who, 1964; member of The Who, 1964-84; solo contract with Atlantic Records, 1979—; owner, Eel Pie Recording Ltd. 1972—; established Eel Pie (book publishing company), 1976; composed and appeared in motion pictures "Tommy" (rock opera) and "Quadrophenia" (rock opera); author of *Horse's Neck: Lyrical Prose,* 1985.

Awards: With The Who, numerous gold and platinum records; Academy award nomination for soundtrack to movie "Tommy," 1975.

Addresses: *Home*—The Boathouse, Ranelagh Drive, Twickenham, TW1 1QZ, England. *Office*—Entertainment Corporation of America, 99 Park Avenue, 16th Floor, New York, N.Y. 10016-1502.

fourteen, fifteen, sixteen, never stop being fans. The Who don't necessarily captivate the whole teenage generation—as each batch comes up every year—but we certainly hit a percentage of them, and we *hold* them." Fans were fascinated first by the sheer physical catharsis of the live performances, then by the albums featuring Townshend's melodic hard rock and emotionally-charged lyrics. As with many rock groups, however, problems beset the band almost from day one. Moon died of a drug overdose, Townshend had several close calls with drugs himself, and in 1979 eleven people were trampled to death at a Who concert. Those events, coupled with the onset of middle age, forced Townshend into what he describes in *Rolling Stone* as a "two year binge" of cocaine, tranquilizer, and alcohol abuse, from which he emerged, more introspective than ever, in 1983.

"I ultimately had to stop using [The Who] as a vehicle for my songwriting," Townshend told *Rolling Stone.* "In a way, I've got the punk explosion to thank for making

> *"Commercially, leaving the Who was the dumbest thing I've ever done in my life. But artistically, it was undeniably the most logical thing for me to do."*

that decision. Commercially, leaving the Who was the dumbest thing I've ever done in my life. But artistically, it was undeniably the most logical thing for me to do. It was the most important thing I've ever done for me—to allow me to have a new beginning, to actually grow." Certainly Townshend's solo albums have not generated the sales that his Who albums did, but critics have praised them as a step in the evolution of a mature artist. A reviewer in the *Rolling Stone Encyclopedia of Rock 'n' Roll* argues that Townshend, "now a generation older than the fans he had initially spoken for," has begun to "agonize over his role as an elder statesman of rock." This is not to suggest that Townshend's work has lost its bite, however. His recent single "Give Blood" is an angry denunciation of violence in all its forms—state-supported and otherwise. Having sworn off drugs and alcohol, and having somewhat regretfully ended his tenure with The Who, Townshend plans to continue making music on his own. He is also becoming better known as a prose writer, contributing essays and short stories to periodicals in England and America.

drummer Keith Moon. Fortunately for The High Numbers, their contract was bought out by new management, Kit Lambert and Chris Stamp. Townshend in particular benefitted from the management transition; Lambert introduced the young artist to traditional musical forms and state-of-the-art recording techniques. Lambert also allowed the group to change its name to The Who, and he promoted his charges tirelessly. By 1965 the band had an enormous following in England, especially among the Mods. The Who also broke through in America with two songs, "Can't Explain" and "My Generation." Some critics feel that in the latter song, with its stuttered phrases, hard beat, and defiant "hope I die before I get old," Townshend and The Who created nothing less than an anthem for the times.

The Who's first tour of America was in 1967. The last was late in 1982. Throughout that fifteen-year period the group reigned as a premier rock attraction—even though none of its songs ever went to number one on the *Billboard* charts. Analyzing his band's constant popularity, Townshend told *Rolling Stone:* "Always, *always,* there is a very, very strong *grab*—a deep, instant grab—which lasts . . . forever. It's not like a fad. People who get into The Who when they're thirteen,

Townshend reflected on his singular career in *Rolling Stone:* "At [one] time, rock & roll to me was another word for 'life.' . . . What I was experiencing in rock then was a great introduction to what might have been a closeted and isolated, protected view of life, but one that I wouldn't have swapped for all the world. . . . I still feel I hold that key. I am one of those characters who, like a teenager, sits at home with a guitar in front of a full-length mirror, and I do it. And I can do it now just as well as I did it then. And it gives me just as much pleasure as it did then. . . . Once you're in, you're in."

Selected discography

With The Who

My Generation, Decca, 1966.
Happy Jack, MCA, 1966.
The Who Sell Out, Decca, 1967.
Magic Bus, Decca, 1968.
Tommy, Decca, 1969.
Live at Leeds, Decca, 1970.
Meaty, Beaty, Big and Bouncy, Decca, 1971.
Who's Next, Decca, 1971.
Quadrophenia, MCA, 1973.
Odds and Sods, MCA, 1974.
The Who by Numbers, MCA, 1975.
Who Are You, MCA, 1978.
The Kids Are Alright (soundtrack), Polydor, 1979.
Hooligans, MCA, 1981.
Face Dances, Warner Brothers, 1982.
It's Hard, Polydor, 1982.
Who's Missing, MCA, 1986.
Two's Missing, MCA, 1987j.

Also recorded *Greatest Hits,* MCA.

Solo albums

Who Came First, MCA, 1972.
Rough Mix (with Ronnie Lane), MCA, 1977.
Empty Glass, Atco, 1980.
All the Best Cowboys Have Chinese Eyes, Atco, 1982.
Scoop, Atco, 1983.
Another Scoop, Atco, 1986.
White City: A Novel (soundtrack), Atco, 1986.
Deep End Live, Atco, 1987.

Sources

Books

Barnes, Richard, *The Who: Maximum R & B,* 1982.
Herman, Gary, *The Who,* November Books, 1971.
Marsh, Dave, *Before I Get Old: The Story of The Who,* 1983.
Simon, George T., *The Best of the Music Makers,* Doubleday, 1979.
Stambler, Irwin, *The Encyclopedia of Pop, Rock, and Soul,* St. Martin's, 1974.
The Rolling Stone Encyclopedia of Rock 'n' Roll, Summit Books, 1983.
The Rolling Stone Record Guide, Random House, 1979.

Periodicals

Chicago Tribune, October 3, 1982.
Newsday, October 24, 1982.
People, May 12, 1980.
Rolling Stone, November 17, 1977; June 26, 1980; June 24, 1982; November 5, 1987.

—Anne Janette Johnson

Tina Turner

Singer

"'Tell me, who sounds like Tina Turner?' asks the lady herself. 'Nobody. It's a strange little gutsy kind of voice, isn't it? I never liked how it sounded but I always felt good when I was singing. And I always kept doing it in spite of not liking how I looked or how I sounded; I knew it was all I had. When it's all you have, whatever it is, you keep on opening doors with it.'" Tina Turner may be the only person on earth who does not like her distinct sound, a sound that engenders respect, admiration, and soul from an audience.

Tina Turner's life, details of which have been published in her autobiography, *I, Tina,* began as Anna Mae Bullock in Nutbush, Tennessee. She spent her adolescence in St. Louis, where, in 1956, she first met Ike Turner, then performing with his band, The Kings of Rhythm, at the Club Manhattan. She sang with them as "Little Anna" and, when a male vocalist missed a recording session, filled in on Turner's "Fool in Love" (Sue Records, 1960). The song was a hit and brought them from "race record" status to the Billboard rhythm and blues charts. Ike Turner redesigned the band and its live performances to feature Bullock, now named Tina Turner. The Ike and Tina Turner Revue, with heavy rhythm in music and dance routines, toured the country while a series of singles, such as "I Idolize You" and "Bold Soul Sister" for Sue and Blue Thumb, climbed the R&B charts.

The Ike and Tina Turner Revue achieved crossover success with the still-controversial single "River Deep, Mountain High." The pop song—by Ellie Greenwich, Jeff Barry and Phil Spector, as produced by Spector— was a number one hit in England and gained the Revue an engagement as the opening act for the Rolling Stones on their European and American tours. "River Deep, Mountain High," which *Rolling Stone* recently listed as number 30 in its top 100 singles of all time, was a flop in the United States, but the Rolling Stone tour brought the Turners to great prominence. At its peak in popularity, the Revue featured Ike Turner and the Kings of Rhythm in slicked-back hair, suits, and leather accessories while Tina Turner and her back-up singers, the Ikettes, wore microskirts, high boots, and wild wigs. *Rolling Stone* described it in 1984 as "everyone's favorite gutbucket soul revue."

The Revue defined itself in the song "Proud Mary," originally a pleasant paean to life on a riverboat recorded by Creedence Clearwater Revival. In her intro, Tina Turner warned that "We never do nothin' nice and easy . . . we're gonna do it nice and rough." In his "On-Stage" column in the *Village Voice* in 1971, critic John Lahr described her act as creating "the illusion of mythic gestures: Tina's presence is her power. . . . She knows she has energy and every performance is a

Born Anna Mae Bullock, November 26, 1939 (some sources say 1938, others say 1941) in Nutbush (some sources say Brownsville), Tenn.; father was a share-cropper; mother's name, Zellma; married Ike Turner (a musician), 1960 (some sources say 1956); divorced; children: one son by previous relationship; one son by Turner; two stepsons. *Religion:* Buddhist (since early 1980s).

Singer, 1956—. Performer with Ike Turner's Kings of Rhythm (name later changed to The Ike and Tina Turner Revue), 1956-76; solo performer, 1976—. Member of USA for Africa relief effort, 1985.

Awards: Winner of seven Grammy Awards, including 1971, (with Ike Turner) for best rhythm and blues vocal performance by a group, for "Proud Mary"; 1984, for record of the year and for best female pop vocal performance, for "What's Love Got to Do with It?," and for best female rock performance, for "Better Be Good To Me"; 1985, for best female rock performance, for "One of the Living"; 1986, for best female rock performance, for "Back Where You Started"; and 1988, for best female rock performance, for album *Tina Live in Europe.*

Addresses: *Manager*—Roger Davies, 3575 Cahuenga Ave. West, Los Angeles, CA 90068. *Agent*—Triad, 10100 Santa Monica Blvd., 16th Floor, Los Angeles, CA 90067.

performed in Europe and with the Rolling Stones' 1981 United States tour. Her single "Let's Stay Together" with members of the English synth-pop band Heaven 17, reached the top five in Great Britain and led Capitol Records to produce a new album.

In 1984 she was still appearing in small clubs and at McDonald's conventions when she returned to the top in England and the United States. Turner's comeback was assured with the overwhelming popularity of her album *Private Dancer* (1984), which went double platinum within the year. It spawned hit singles for the title song, "Let's Stay Together," "Better Be Good," and "What's Love Got to Do with It," which reached number one. In 1984 she won solo Grammys for best female pop vocal performance and for best female rock vocal performance, as well as taking record of the year honors.

Her vocal prowess was equalled by her performance power, which had even more impact on MTV and other cable music video shows as it had in live appearances. An HBO television special, also called "Private Dancer"

Tina Turner may be the only person on earth who does not like her distinct sound.

---

conquest which not only renews us but makes her stronger. . . . Whoever created her act knows how to make a myth and keep it gorgeously alive." The Revue's production values and insistent danceable beat brought the Turners to popularity in the United States, Europe, and Asia through their own tours, continuing Rolling Stones engagements, and the film "Gimme Shelter" which documented the groups' 1969 tour. "Proud Mary" was awarded the Grammy for best R&B vocal in 1971, and they released three major albums for United Artists—*Blues Roots* (1972), *Nutbush City Limits* (1973), and *The Gospel According to Ike and Tina* (1974).

Ike and Tina Turner's marriage and joint career broke up in 1976, and Tina Turner was forced to create a completely new act for herself. In her autobiography, she discussed the abuse that led to the split which occured during a national tour. She had released two solo albums, *Let Me Touch Your Mind* (1972) and *Tina Turns the Country On* (1974) before the final breakup and developed a single act. United Artists released an unsuccessful solo album, *Rough,* in 1978. Turner then

was aired in 1985. She performed in Azzedine Alaia dresses that were couture versions of her Ikette miniskirts. The Turner legs became as well known and admired as the Turner voice. Her next recordings, "Been There and Back" and *Break Every Rule,* added to her fame. Turner has also appeared in film roles that augment her stage personality, among them, the Acid Queen in the rock opera *Tommy* (1975) and Aunty Entity, the leader of a post-millenium civilization in "Mad Max Beyond Thunderdome" (1985).

Turner's popularity in Europe and the United States has, if anything, grown, thanks to the universality of video and recordings. *People* magazine described the frenzy of a Munich audience during the *Private Dancer* tour: "Under 30-foot high scarlet red letters that spelled her name, Tina Turner came galloping across the stage, white-hot, humming with energy, those incredible legs pumping, pumping, pumping. From that first moment, they belonged to her, 12,000 West Germans screaming with pure and mindless joy."

Turner has claimed that her 1987-1988 world tour will be her last, at least in the foreseeable future. She has discussed both a recording of ballads with *Interview*—"certain types of ballads . . . not real tearful, and not just with a piano, but with synthesizers and the electric sound"—and a return to "a raunchy rock album" with the *New York Times*. She plans to concentrate on filmmaking and stop live performance for the first time in more than thirty years.

Selected discography

Major single releases; with Ike Turner

"A Fool in Love," Sue, August, 1960.
"It's Gonna Work Out Fine," Sue, July, 1961.
"You Should'a Treated Me Right," Sue, June, 1962.
"River Deep, Mountain High," Philles, May, 1966.
"I've Been Loving You Too Long," Blue Thumb, April, 1969.
"The Hunter," Blue Thumb, July, 1969.
"Proud Mary," Liberty, 1971.

Major single releases; solo

"Let's Stay Together," Capitol, 1984.
"Private Dancer," Capitol, 1984.
"What's Love Got to Do with It?," Capitol, 1984.
"Better Be Good," Capitol, 1984.
"One of the Living," Capitol, 1985.

LPs; with Ike Turner; compilations

Get Back, Liberty, 1985.
Golden Empire, Striped Horse, 1986.
It's Gonna Work Out Fine, EMI America, reissued, 1986.
Workin' Together, EMI America, reissued, 1986.
The Ike and Tina Sessions, Kent, 1987.
The Best of Ike and Tina Turner, EMI America, 1987.

Cookin', JEM Classic Series.
The Dynamic Duo, Crown.
The Soul of Ike and Tina, Kent.

LPs; solo

Let Me Touch Your Mind, United Artist, 1972.
Tina Turns the Country On, United Artists, 1974.
Acid Queen, United Artists, 1975.
Love Explosion, United Artists, 1977.
Rough, United Artists, 1978.
Private Dancer, Capitol, 1984.
Break Every Rule, Capitol, 1986.
Tina Live In Europe, Capitol, 1988.

Sources

Books

Turner, Tina, and Kurt Loder, *I, Tina,* Morrow, 1985.

Periodicals

Ebony, November, 1986.
Interview, November, 1984.
New York Post, September 20, 1985; August 12, 1987.
New York Times, July 24, 1985; August 12, 1987.
People, July 15, 1985.
Rolling Stone, October 11, 1984; September 8, 1988.
Village Voice, April 8, 1971.

—Barbara Stratyner

Stevie Ray Vaughan

Guitarist

Stevie Ray Vaughan and Double Trouble's 1982 appearance at the Montreux Jazz Festival signalled the beginning of yet another blues revival and another guitar hero. Vaughan's mixture of Texas blues and Jimi Hendrix-inspired rock helped open the door for acts like the Fabulous Thunderbirds, Robert Cray, Los Lobos, and a host of other authentic roots bands.

Vaughan's earliest exposure to music came from his parents. While neither of them were musicians, they held many dance parties at their house in the Oak Cliff suburb of Dallas. At other times, members of Bob Wills's band (the Texas Playboys) would come over to play dominos and pick on their guitars, mixing popular hillbilly, swing, and country tunes of the day.

Following the lead of his older brother, Jimmie of The Fabulous Thunderbirds, Vaughan began playing the guitar in 1963, stealing practice time whenever his brother would set the instrument down. "Jimmy actually was one of the biggest influences on my playing," Vaughan told *Guitar Player*. "He really was the reason why I started to play, watching him and seeing what could be done." Both brothers dove into the blues head first, buying albums by B.B. King, Albert Collins, Buddy Guy, and all the masters, trying to absorb their feel and sound.

Starting his performing career in clubs at the age of fourteen, Vaughan played in a succession of bands, including Blackbird, the Shantones, the Epileptic Marshmallow, and Cracker Jack. He also played bass in Jimmie's band, Texas Storm, for a brief period. On New Year's Eve, 1972, one year before his high school graduation, he dropped out and moved to Austin, again following Jimmie who had been there since 1970. After forming the Nightcrawlers in 1973, Vaughan left for a rhythm and blues combo, the Cobras. "Actually, he was just too much of a guitar player for a band like that," former bandmate Denny Freeman offered in *Guitar Player*. "He'd do a solo and play all the guts out of a song."

The Cobras were offered a contract by Rounder records but, wary of being taken advantage of, never signed it. A year with them led Vaughan to the group Triple Threat in 1975, which consisted of five lead singers, including Lou Ann Barton. Three years later Vaughan and Barton left to start a new band, the original Double Trouble, named after the Otis Rush song.

Personnel changes saw Barton leave to start a solo career. Bassist Tommy Shannon had played with Vaughan previously in Blackbird and Cracker Jack, and more notably, with fellow Texan Johnny Winter's trio during the blues revival of the late 1960's. Along

For the Record. . .

Born c. 1956, in Dallas, Tex.; son of Jim (an asbestos worker) and Martha (Cook) Vaughan; divorced from wife, Lenny. *Education:* Left high school in 1972 to pursue a career in music.

Began playing guitar in 1963; began playing clubs in the Dallas, Tex., area at the age of fourteen; performed with a number of bands, including Blackbird, the Shantones, the Epileptic Marshmallow, Cracker Jack, and Texas Storm; moved to Austin, Tex., 1972, and performed with the Nightcrawlers, the Cobras, and Triple Threat; founder of Double Trouble, 1978; first recorded on David Bowie's album *Let's Dance,* 1983; signed by CBS and released first album, 1983; has toured extensively throughout the United States.

Awards: Named Blues Entertainer of the Year by W.C. Handy Blues Foundation, 1985; Grammy Award nomination, 1987, for *Live Alive!;* winner of numerous magazine readers poll awards.

Addresses: *Agent*—Classic Management, Inc., P.O. Drawer T, Manor, TX 78653.

with Chris "Whipper" Layton on drums, Stevie Ray Vaughan and Double Trouble began to astound audiences with their high-energy sound. "I'd call it rhythm and blues, but sometimes we get out there with it," Vaughan told Bruce Nixon. "A lot of people think of it as blues-rock, although I'd like to have it thought of as just music."

Whatever the label, around 1982 things started happening for the trio. Members of the Rolling Stones flew the band to New York to play a party at the Danceteria club. Next, record producer Jerry Wexler decided to pull some strings. While working on Lou Ann Barton's debut album, Wexler heard Vaughan performing in an Austin club and immediately got the band a spot at the 1982 Montreux Jazz Festival. They became the first band without a record ever to play there.

David Bowie heard the group's performance and asked Vaughan to play on his next album and the ensuing tour, with Double Trouble as the opening act. "From what I understand," Vaughan told *Guitar Player,* "Bowie was looking for somebody who played this style anyway, and I was the one he picked." The album, *Let's Dance,* was a major hit for Bowie. The six cuts that Vaughan played on showed a brand new audience the power of his Albert King-style licks. But in mid-May, just two days before the tour, Vaughan backed out.

Reasons for his departure vary, but according to Bowie in *Guitar World,* "Stevie didn't make it to the touring stage with us last tour because he had his own illustrious career to get on with, and he did very well, indeed."

Bowie and the Stones weren't the only artists to recognize Vaughan's talents. Jackson Browne jammed with him several times and offered Vaughan his own recording studio, Down Town, free of charge. The ensuing songs were purchased by none other than John Hammond (discoverer of Count Basie, Billie Holliday, Charlie Christian, Bob Dylan, Aretha Franklin, and Bruce Springsteen) who signed the group to CBS and became the executive producer of their first album. "I was so delighted by Stevie's sound," Hammond stated in *Guitar World.* "It's unlike anyone else's—and he's such a marvelous improviser, never repeating exactly the same thing twice. He's the kind of creative force one looks for but rarely finds."

The debut album, *Texas Flood,* was distributed by Epic in June of 1983. From the Chuck Berry-in-overdrive "Love Struck Baby" to the beautiful liquid tone of "Lenny", the album showed how different Vaughan's style was from his brother's, or for that matter, any other guitarist. As Dan Forte wrote, "He doesn't just play his guitar; he mauls it." With instrumentals that pinned listeners to the wall and enough unique licks to make even veteran bluesmen shake their heads, Vaughan was on a mission. The album won Best Guitar Album in the 1983 *Guitar Player* readers poll, and Vaughan was also voted Best New Talent and Electric Blues Guitarist (topping Eric Clapton and Johnny Winter).

Vaughan's 1984 follow-up, *Couldn't Stand the Weather,* laid to rest any flash-in-the-pan notions that may have been floating around. Jimmie was brought in on second guitar for the title cut, and there was even some jazzy sax on "Stang's Swang" (courtesy of Stan Harrison's tenor). But the real stopper was the unbelievable rendition of Hendrix's "Voodoo Chile (Slight Return)". For nearly fifteen years guitarists had been copying Jimi, but never before had anyone duplicated the sound of an entire song so expertly. Anyone who thought studio tricks were the secret needed only to see Vaughan live. Playing with the guitar behind his back, on the floor, or with hands *over* the fretboard, Vaughan tore into other Hendrix tunes with equal vengeance. Again he won the *Guitar Player* readers poll Guitar Albumn and Electric Blues categories.

In 1985 Vaughan had the opportunity to work with one of his idols and earliest influences, Lonnie Mack. The two had met years before when Vaughan was playing in a small club. Mack wanted to record Vaughn and have him play in his own band, but things didn't work out. As it was, Vaughan ended up producing and playing on

Mack's comeback effort, *Strike Like Lightning*. "They were his tunes and I just tried to help him by doing the best I could to do what he wanted to do with the record," Vaughan told *Guitar World*. "That's what I think producing is . . . just being there, and, with Lonnie, just reminding him of his influence on myself and other guitar players."

In addition to winning the *Guitar Player* readers poll Electric Blues category again, in 1985 Vaughan also became the first white artist to win the W.C. Handy Blues Foundation's Blues Entertainer of the Year award. Vaughan also released his third album, *Soul to Soul*. With the additon of Reese Wynans on keyboards as a permanent group member and Joe Sublett providing sax, the sound was fuller and more up-tempo. It contained the obligatory nods to Hendrix, "Come On" and an original wah-wah tour de force entitled "Say What!" But rather than just being vehicles for Vaughan's solos, the songs were now beginning to have more meaning, especially for Vaughan. He had been battling alcohol and cocaine for quite some time, trying to live

---

Vaughan was struggling to get a focus on his life without following [Jimi] Hendrix to his grave.

---

up to the superstar image. Vaughan was struggling to get a focus on his life without following Hendrix to the grave.

While touring to promote *Soul to Soul* and mixing tracks for an upcoming live album, Vaughan collapsed and fell off the stage in London. He had been stretching himself too thin and had to be checked into a clinic to seek help. In September of 1986 Vaughan entered the Marietta clinic under the supervision of Dr. Victor Bloom. Vaughan stayed there a month—with visits from Jackson Browne and Eric Clapton offering support—and then transferred to a treatment facility in Georgia.

His fourth album, *Live Alive!*, was released in 1986 and contained a remake of Stevie Wonder's "Superstition" which eventually became a video. Although a double album, critics like Gene Santoro complained: "It's not that the performances are uninspired, exactly; just that

they don't bring anything new to the material. And while the sound is ok, as often as not it's muddy an plagued by overloads." Regardless, *Live Alive!* received a Grammy nomination, and Stevie again won the *Guitar Player* readers poll for Electric Blues, beating Eric Clapton for the fourth year in a row (Jimmie Vaughan placed third).

Vaughan seemed to come to terms with his status and addictions and was back on the road playing with vigor and aggressiveness. "I can honestly say that I'm really glad to be alive today," Vaughan told Bill Bilkowski, "because left to my own devices . . . I would've slowly killed myself." In the future Vaughan plans to enter the studio with Jimmie to record an album.

Selected discography

With Double Trouble

Texas Flood, CBS, 1983.
Couldn't Stand the Weather, CBS, 1984.
Soul to Soul, CBS, 1985.
Live Alive!, CBS, 1986.

Other

Let's Dance (with David Bowie), EMI, 1983.
Soulful Dress (with Marcia Ball), Rounder, 1984.
Texas Twister (with Johnny Copeland), Rounder, 1984.
Blues Explosion (with others), Atlantic, 1984.
Strike Like Lightning (with Lonnie Mack), Alligator, 1985.
Heartbeat (with Don Johnson), Epic, 1986.
Twilight Time (with Bennie Wallace), Blue Note, 1986.
Back to the Beach (soundtrack), CBS, 1987.
Bull Durham (soundtrack), Capitol, 1988.
I'm in the Wrong Business (with A.C. Reed), Alligator, 1988.

Sources

Detroit Free Press, December 11, 1986.
down beat, May, 1987.
Guitar Player, August, 1983; September, 1983; January, 1984; October, 1984; January 1985; December, 1985; November, 1986; December, 1986.
Guitar World, September, 1983; May, 1984; May, 1985; November, 1985; April, 1987; July, 1987; September, 1988.

—Calen D. Stone

Herbert von Karajan

Conductor

Herbert von Karajan is hailed by many as the greatest living conductor of orchestral music. He is revered for eliciting overpowering beauty and precision from the Berlin Philharmonic, the orchestra with which he had been most closely associated from the mid-1950s until poor health forced his retirement in 1989. Many critics have noted his emphasis is on the sound of perfection—of note-perfect expressions of sheer, pure beauty. His conducting method is one of total authority and power. Many associates have noted his seemingly unequaled obsession with music, one that renders him a dynamic dictator when it comes to realizing his ambitions with orchestras. Gustav Kuhn, who studied conducting under von Karajan, told biographer Robert Vaughan that the vaunted maestro is "the greatest, the last great one, the last of the period that started with [Hans] von Beulow in 1850." Kuhn added: "He is the exception. No one can do it like he can. He is so egocentric, so clever; he uses all of his immense power to do the things he wants."

Von Karajan was born April 5, 1908, in Salzburg, Austria. He began studying piano in early childhood and first performed before the Salzburg public at age five. But teacher Bernhard Paumgartner found von Karajan too energetic and animated for the instrument and encouraged him to study conducting instead. In his mid-teens von Karajan saw the great maestro Arturo Toscanini and at that time vowed to conduct. But he also continued his piano studies, working under celebrated musician Josef Hofmann. Von Karajan later studied under another acclaimed artist, conductor Clemens Krauss, while attending Vienna's Academy for Music and the Performing Arts. Aside from his musical pursuits, von Karajan also studied philosophy at the University of Vienna.

In late 1928, von Karajan made his first conducting appearance by leading the student orchestra at the Academy. Soon afterwards, he arranged his own professional audition by hiring an orchestra. Attending that performance was the director of the Ulm Opera House, whose conductor, von Karajan had learned, was ill. In early 1929, von Karajan was hired as a late replacement conductor for a performance of Mozart's opera *The Marriage of Figaro*. Von Karajan then obtained the Ulm post and began developing the performances there. Aside from his strictly musical duties, he supervised technical aspects, such as lighting and staging as well. When the company was between seasons, von Karajan often returned to Salzburg to assist conductors such as Toscanini and composer Richard Strauss. Eventually, he led courses for other conductors at the Salzburg Festivals.

By the early 1930s, von Karajan's career was prospering, and he was enjoying increasing recognition as an

For the Record. . .

Born April 5, 1908, in Salzburg, Austria; son of Ernst (a surgeon) and Martha (Cosmac) von Karajan; married Elmy Holgerloef (a singer), 1938 (marriage ended, 1940); married Anita Guetermann, 1942 (divorced); married Eliette Mouret; children: Isabel, Arabel. *Education:* Attended Vienna Academy for Music and the Performing Arts and University of Vienna in the mid-1920s.

Ulm Opera House, Ulm, Germany, conductor, 1929-35; Aachen Opera House, Aachen, Germany, music director and conductor, 1935-c. 1942; Berlin State Opera, Berlin, Germany, music director and conductor, beginning 1938; Vienna Gesellschaft der Musikfreunde, artistic director for life; Philharmonic Orchestra, London, England, chief conductor, 1947-c. 1963; Salzburg Festival, Salzburg, Austria, adviser, 1946, member of board of directors, 1947, artistic director, 1956—; La Scala, Milan, Italy, music director and conductor, 1948-1955; Berlin Philharmonic, conductor, 1955-89; Vienna State Opera, artisitic director from 1956 until the 1960s. Conductor with various orchestras, worldwide, and at numerous festivals. Founder of Herbert von Karajan Research Institute at University of Salzburg, of Herbert von Karajan Foundation, and of film company Telemondial in Monaco.

Awards: Gold Medal from Royal Philharmonic Society.

Addresses: *Home*—Buchenhof, Austria; St. Moritz, Switzerland; and St. Tropez, France. *Office*—c/o Deutsche Grammophon, Polygram Classics, Inc., 810 Seventh Ave., New York, NY 10019.

impressive, multi-talented musician. The decade, however, was not entirely one that von Karajan recalls fondly. In 1935 he was named general music director of the Aachen Opera House. He has since claimed that for professional reasons he joined the Nazi Party at the time of the Aachen appointment. Nazi records, though, disclose that von Karajan had actually joined the party two years earlier, in 1933, within three months of Nazi leader Adolf Hitler's assumption of power in Germany. Von Karajan's actual association with the Nazis remains unclear, and many observers consider it likely that he made a professional, as opposed to a political, move to join the party.

The 1930s also marked the beginning of von Karajan's supposed feud with conductor Wilhelm Furtwangler, whose stature in Germany was such that he remained prominent despite his refusal to join the Nazi Party. As a result of his disdain for the Nazis, though, Furtwangler

left his position as director of the Berlin State Opera. By that time, von Karajan had already sparked great public interest in Berlin as a result of his stunning interpretation of Richard Wagner's opera *Tristan und Isolde*. When he returned there in 1938, he gained further enthusiasm with his rendition of Mozart's *The Magic Flute*. The acclaim, however, did not impress Furtwangler, who was apparently disgusted by von Karajan's seeming compliance with the Nazis. Furtwangler used his influence with Nazi culture minister Josef Goebbels to prevent von Karajan from conducting the Berlin Philharmonic.

Von Karajan nonetheless enjoyed great prominence in Berlin through his work with the Berlin State Opera, where he had replaced Furtwangler in 1938. But the acclaim and hectic pace were hardly conducive to von Karajan's art. "It was a dangerous time in my life," he later told biographer Vaughan. "Things were going so fast, I was having so much success that I was always apprehensive. Because wherever I went it was a sensation, people said it has never been like this. First, this put other conductors in opposition to me. Second, the expectations were at a level that one could not hope to fulfill. . . . And people began to say that I was a fast-burning candle, that I would soon burn out."

Von Karajan turned to yoga, and later to Zen, to stabilize himself. But his personal and professional activities, remained cause for anxiety. In 1942 von Karajan violated Nazi dictum by marrying a woman of Jewish ancestry. As a result he was dismissed from the party. He nonetheless continued to conduct in Berlin during World War II, constantly rescheduling concerts as bombings began to destroy the city. Von Karajan's activities during this period are obscured by his own privacy and lack of records. He apparently fled to Italy with his wife in 1944 and remained there until the war ended.

Following World War II, von Karajan underwent de-Nazification. For more than a year he was refused classification as a conductor by the Occupation government. In early 1946, however, he led the Vienna Philharmonic in concert. Record executive Walter Legge was awed by von Karajan's performance. In soprano Elisabeth Schwarzkopf's book *On and Off the Record*, Legge wrote: "I was absolutely astonished at what the fellow could do. The enourmous energy and vitality he had were hair-raising." Through Legge, von Karajan was able to record for a Viennese concert society, the Gessellscaft der Musikfreunde, of which he was eventually named artistic director for life. In 1947, von Karajan finally obtained de-Nazification status and resumed conducting in public, whereupon the Vienna Musikfreunde hired him for a series that evolved into an annual event.

The following year, he obtained an important post: music director and conductor at La Scala, the renouned opera house in Milan, Italy. At La Scala, where von Karajan remained until 1955, he enjoyed great success with such artists as soprano Maria Callas. He received further acclaim with his productions of Wagner's *Tristan un Isolde, Die Meistersinger von Nurmberg,* and the entire *Ring of the Nibulungen* cycle at Byreuth, West Germany, where festivals are devoted exclusively to Wagner's operas.

Von Karajan continued his return to prominence in the early 1950s through tours with the Philharmonic Orchestra and the Vienna Philharmonic. Perhaps the turning point in his career came in 1955 when Furtwangler died prior to a tour of America with his orchestra, the Berlin Philharmonic. Von Karajan agreed to tour with the orchestra on the condition that he be named conductor for life. Upon obtaining such an agreement, von Karajan led the Berlin Philharmonic on the tour, which proved enormously successful. The following year he was named artistic director of the Salzburg Festival, from

---

Herbert von Karajan is hailed by many as the greatest living conductor of orchestral music.

---

which Furtwangler had long succeeded in keeping him. Then he also became artistic director of the Vienna State Opera, where he had led a much praised production of Donizetti's *Lucia di Lammermoor* featuring Maria Callas.

By the end of the 1950s, von Karajan was known as much for his whirlwind schedule as for his musical prowess. And as if the pace of his concertizing were not exhaustive enough, he began recording extensively, producing highly prized interpretations of works by Beethoven, Tchaikovsky, Brahms, and Richard Strauss. Throughout the 1960s he continued to record constantly, repeating and even re-repeating portions of his burgeoning catalog. The records contributed greatly to his status as an unrivaled conductor—and to the Berlin Philharmonic's claim to the title of the world's greatest orchestra. Of course, von Karajan and the Philharmonic continued to triumph with their live performances. Par-

ticularly impressive were their four successive productions of Wagner's *Ring* cycle at the Salzburg Easter Festival, which von Karajan commenced in 1967.

In recent years, von Karajan sustained his reputation as one of the world's greatest—if not *the* greatest—of conductors. Artists such as soprano Leontyne Price and fellow conductor Seiji Ozawa are quick to offer their reverential praise, and many newcoming musicians cite him as a generous influence. Von Karajan recorded extensively—his canon now exceeds three hundred recordings, including five complete cycles of Beethoven's nine symphonies. In addition, he appeared on numerous radio and television broadcasts and was filmed many times. Among his many triumphs in the 1980s was a Salzburg Festival production of Mozart's *Don Giovanni* featuring soprano Kathleen Battle and baritone Samuel Ramey.

Health was the only obstacle to von Karajan's continued domination in classical music. He suffered a stroke in 1978 and was left partially paralyzed following emergency surgery in 1983. His health continued to worsen, and in April 1989 von Karajan announced his retirement from the Berlin Philharmonic after nearly 35 years as its conductor.

Selected discography

Johann Sebastian Bach, *Mass in B Minor,* Deutsche Grammophon.
Ludwig van Beethoven, *Nine Symphonies,* Deutsche Grammophon.
Hector Berlioz, *Symphonie fantastique,* Deutsche Grammophon.
Anton Bruckner, *Nine Symphonies,* Deutsche Grammophon.
Franz Joseph Haydn, *The Creation,* Deutsche Grammophon.
Gustav Mahler, *Symphony No. 5,* Deutsche Grammophon.
Felix Mendelssohn, *Five Symphonies,* Deutsche Grammophon.
Wolfgang Amadeus Mozart, *Requiem,* Deutsche Grammophon.
Giacomo Puccini, *Tosca,* Deutsche Grammophon.
Puccini, *Turandot,* Deutsche Grammophon.
Franz Schubert, *Symphony No. 8 ("Unfinished"),* Angel Records.
Robert Schumann, *Symphony No. 3 ("Rhenish"),* Deutsche Grammophon.
Jean Sibelius, *Symphony No. 2,* Angel Records.
Richard Strauss, *Der Rosenkavalier,* Angel Records.
Peter Ilyich Tchaikovsky, *Symphony No. 6 ("Pathetique"),* Angel Records.
Giuseppe Verdi, *Il trovatore,* Angel Records.
Richard Wagner, *Der Ring des Nibelungen* (contains *Das Rheingold, Die Walkure, Siegfried,* and *Goetterdammerung),* Deutsche Grammophon.

Sources

Books

Blyth, Alan, editor, *Opera on Record,* Hutchinson, 1979, Harper, 1982.

Schwarzkopf, Elisabeth, *On and Off the Record,* Scribner, 1982.

Vaughan, Roger, *Herbert von Karajan,* Norton, 1986.

Periodicals

Detroit Free Press, April 25, 1989.

High Fidelity, October, 1957; June, 1987; December, 1987; February, 1988; July, 1988.

Newsweek, October 25, 1982.

New York, July 18, 1988.

New York Times, April 29, 1988.

Stereo Review, March, 1987.

Tom Waits

Singer, songwriter, pianist

Saturday Review made this observation about Tom Waits: "No other musician creates a separate reality as engrossing, convincing, or terrifying as the one Tom Waits invents each time he makes a record. You don't just put on a Waits album. You think about it first. Then you pour yourself a drink." Tom Waits is well known for a lifestyle close to the fringes. He prefers to sleep in derelict hotels, eat in greasy spoons, drink in forgotten bars, and smoke Pall Malls. His songs are populated with the characters he meets in unsavory places.

Born in a taxicab in Pomona, Waits grew up in Southern California and then became the piano bar drifter whose life is so aptly characterized in his songs. He was "discovered" playing piano in a bar and released his first album, *Closing Time,* an acoustic set of blues and ballads, in 1977. He became well known for his gravely voice and jazz/blues-based songs with their sentimental, and starkly real, look at the other side of life. His albums held to this expected style, with an increasing use of backing instruments, until the release of the unusual *Swordfishtrombones* in 1983. *New Statesman* described the album as "junkyard orchestral deviation, . . . a series of fragments from a semi-legible journal in which Waits and his band play just about anything that comes to hand, as long as it makes noise."

In an interview in *Playboy* Waits commented on this move toward a less organized, more discordant sound: "I was cutting off a very small part of what I wanted to do. I wasn't getting down to things I was really hearing and experiencing. Music with a lot of strings gets like Perry Como after awhile. It's why I don't really work with the piano much anymore, like, anybody who plays the piano would thrill at seeing and hearing one thrown off a 12-story building, watching it hit the sidewalk and being there to hear that thump." *High Fidelity* looked at the album this way: "With *Swordfishtrombones* Waits turned minimalist in instrumental approach and surrealist in lyrical and general atmosphere, not so much eccentric as artistically ambitious. It was as if he imagined Kurt Weill and Captain Beefheart running into each other on an empty Hollywood sound stage while Coppola lurked in his computer programmed trailer ready to film the encounter in glorious living black and white and Waits himself transcribed the score."

The reference to filmmaker Francis Ford Coppola is apt. Waits began working with Coppola in 1982 when he wrote the soundtrack for "One from the Heart." The score was nominated for an Academy Award. Then he began his acting career, playing character roles in the Coppola films "Rumble Fish" (1983), "The Cotton Club" (1984), and "The Outsiders" (1987). He also played major roles in "Down by Law" (1986) and "Ironweed" (1987).

Waits met his wife, playwright Kathleen Brennan, in 1988. With her he cowrote the play "Frank's Wild Years," which was produced by Chicago's Steppenwolf Company in summer 1988. *Stereo Review* described the play: "*Frank's Wild Years* began as a song from *Swordfishtrombones* about a man who gets drunk one night and sets fire to his house with his wife and Chihuahua inside. 'Frank' then took on a life of his own in a musical play . . . about a down-and-out lounge singer who, sitting on a park bench in East St.Louis, is freezing to death and reliving his life in a semi-hallucinatory state. *Frank's Wild Years* [the album] includes many of the songs from the play, but it further develops the musical settings of Frank's reminiscences."

When asked by *Playboy* how his involvement with theater and film affected his music, Waits replied: "Just that I'm more comfortable stepping into characters in songs. On *Frank's Wild Years,* I did it in 'I'll Take New York' and 'Straight to the Top.' I've learned how to be different musical characters without feeling like I'm eclipsing myself. On the contrary, you discover a whole family living inside you." Waits saw the album *Frank's Wild Years* (1987) as the completion of a trilogy of albums, beginning with *Swordfishtrombones* (1983) and continued by *Rain Dogs* (1985). *Audio* had this observation about the album: "Now, Waits has ex-

plored the beaten-down, seedy, and desperate, but his subjects have never been quite this odd. His voice has always been scruffy, but here he contorts it into the most bizarre shapes it has ever assumed. *Frank's Wild Years* is disconcerting, challenging, even disturbing, as it dares you to explore dark places on its own terms."

Unlike most musicians who gravitate toward commercial compromises in their music, *Stereo Review* observed, Waits "abandoned what few commercial pretensions he had left and began to make music of ever-increasing eccentricity and conviction. No longer are his characters romanticized symbols of life on the edges. Now they are real." In the midst of this period when Waits was pushing the limits of his art, Electra released *Anthology,* an excellent retrospective of his best recordings from his years on the Electra/Asylum label.

In 1988 Waits returned to film, producing his major performance and story film "Big Time." Instead of a

> *Born in a taxicab in Pomona, Waits grew up in Southern California and then became the piano bar drifter whose life is so aptly characterized in his songs.*

character actor, in this film he is the star. Yet, he is still in character as a drifter who fantasizes about making the big time in music. He discussed the film with *Rolling Stone:* "What we tried to avoid is having a concert film that felt like a stuffed bird. I tried to film it like a Mexican cockfight instead of air-conditioned concert footage. Some of it felt like it was shot through a safari rifle. You forget about the cameras, which is what I was trying to do." *Rolling Stone* continued with this observation: "But in spite of media attention, Tom Waits has remained an outsider. It's exactly that lonesome-drifter persona that has always made his work so compelling. The seams were invisible between the desolate characters in his songs and the character standing onstage with a jazzman's goatee, a secondhand suit and a hobo's roar."

About his lack of drive for fame and awards, Waits told *Playboy:* I've gotten only one award in my life, from a place called Club Tenco in Italy. They gave me a guitar made out of tigereye. Club Tenco was created as an alternative to the big San Remo festival they have every year. It's to commemorate the death of a big singer who's name was Tenco and who shot himself in the heart because he'd lost at the San Remo Festival. For awhile it was popular in Italy for singers to shoot themselves in the heart. That's my award."

Writings

Co-author (with wife, Kathleen Brennan) of musical play "Frank's Wild Years," 1987.

Selected discography

On Elektra/Asylum, except as noted

Closing Time, 1973.
Looking for the Heart of Saturday Night, 1974.
Nighthawks at the Diner, 1975.
Small Change, 1976.
Foreign Affairs, 1977.
Blue Valentine, 1978.
Heart Attack and Vine, 1980.
Swordfishtrombones, Island, 1983.
Rain Dogs, Island, 1985.
Anthology, 1985.
Frank's Wild Years, Island, 1987.
Big Time, Island, 1988.

Sources

Audio, February, 1984; December, 1987.
down beat, March, 1986.
High Fidelity, December, 1985.
New Statesman, October, 1985.
People, October 21, 1985; September 28, 1987.
Playboy, March, 1988.
Rolling Stone, October, 1988.
Stereo Review, September, 1987.

—Tim LaBorie

Deniece Williams

Singer and songwriter

Singer-songwriter Deniece Williams emerged as an exciting new talent during the 1970s, captivating audiences with an engaging performing style and a stellar voice. Since that time, the vocalist has proven herself one of music's most popular entertainers, scoring hit singles, recording solo LPs, and even taking home a Grammy Award for her 1986 gospel album *So Glad I Know.* Indeed, with the ability to span four octaves, Williams, according to *US* reviewer Michael Musto, possesses "one of the most distinctive voices in pop—a high, vibrato-filled instrument capable of dazzling."

A native of Gary, Indiana, Deniece Williams, nicknamed Niecy, grew up as the eldest of four children born to working-class parents. Although the family didn't have much—Williams's mother was a nurse and her father served as part of the security team for a local business—they regularly attended the Church of God in Christ, where the youth got her musical start singing in the choir. She was also influenced by the impeccable articulation of singer Carmen McRae—later evident in her own precise enunciation—and at the age of seventeen the ambitious singer made her first single. The record only received air time in Gary, however, so the would-be vocalist decided to put her music career in abeyance and try nursing school.

Unsatisfied with that venture also, Williams eventually dropped out of school, married, and decided to start her family. But shortly thereafter one of her cousins, fortuitously employed by Stevie Wonder, scheduled Deniece for an audition with the musical great. He heard her, hired her to sing with his back-up group, Wonderlove, and the young singer finally found her professional career underway.

Williams spent the next several years touring with Stevie Wonder and refining her skills. She learned much from Wonder as well as from producer Maurice White, and by 1976 she was ready to launch her first solo album, *This Is Niecy.* Considered a stunning debut, the album provoked immediate acclaim and became a gold record in 1977. Williams followed it with a hit single in 1978, "Too Much, Too Little, Too Late," recorded with Johnny Mathis, and by 1983 she had secured a Grammy Award nomination for the rhythm and blues tune "It's Gonna Take a Miracle."

Since then, the vocalist has continued to outdo herself, consistently winning praise from the critics as well as attracting new fans. Writing for *Stereo Review,* Phyl Garland lauded her 1983 album *I'm So Proud* as both an artistic and a popular triumph, declaring the artist "the songbird of soul." According to Garland, Williams "has been able to attain popular success without compromising [because] she has forged a distinctive vocal

Full name, June Deniece Williams; born in 1951; grew up in Gary, Ind.; daughter of a security worker and a nurse; married first husband (divorced); married Christipher Joy (an actor and a minister), c. 1981 (marriage ended, 1982); married Brad Westering (a record producer and manager), c. 1986; children: (first marriage) Kenderick, Kevin; (third marriage) Forrest. *Education:* Attended Purdue University.

Singer and songwriter. Singer with Wonderlove, back-up group for Stevie Wonder, mid-1970s; has worked with many other artists, including back-up for Earth, Wind, and Fire, touring with Roberta Flack, and recording with Johnny Mathis, Thom Bell, and Elton John; solo recording artist, 1976—; founder of Christian Production Company, mid-1980s. Makes concert tours and occasional guest television appearances.

Awards: Grammy Award nomination from Academy of Recording Arts and Sciences, 1983, for "It's Gonna Take a Miracle"; Grammy Award for 1986 gospel album *So Glad I Know.*

Addresses: *Home*—Near Los Angeles, Calif.; *Office*—c/o Columbia Records, 51 W. 52nd St., New York NY 10019.

style that sizzles with brilliance." The album includes a duet with Mathis, "So Deep in Love," and also features several songs co-written by Williams. Among them are "Love, Peace and Unity" and "It's Okay," both considered strong contributions to the album.

Subsequent recordings have earned similar acclaim. Her 1986 *So Glad I Know,* the singer's first gospel album, finds Williams "in splendid voice, soaring heavenward with bird-like flutters, twists, and daring high notes," applauded a *Stereo Review* critic. *Stereo Review* also deemed her performance "heavenly," and the Academy of Recording Arts and Sciences concurred, honoring Williams with a Grammy Award for the album. One of the artist's most recent albums, *Water Under the Bridge,* returns to popular tunes. On this recording Williams has been praised for her still emo-

tional, but now mature and controlled approach to her material, with a *People* critic particularly commending "When Love Finds You" for its demonstration of the vocalist's "astonishing upper register."

Although a relative newcomer to contemporary music, Deniece Williams appears to have found an audience that only seems destined to grow. Gifted with a rich voice that admirers claim has a bird-like ability to dip and soar with ease, Williams combines emotion with technique to produce music of the highest integrity. Indeed, one critic has claimed that there is little music that is even worthy of the songstress's voice. But that shortcoming aside, fans should continue to be dazzled by a voice, described Garland, that pulls "high notes from the aural stratosphere with miraculous ease."

Selected discography

LPs

This Is Niecy, Columbia, 1976.
My Melody, Columbia, 1981.
Niecy, Columbia, 1982.
I'm So Proud, Columbia, 1983.
Let's Hear It for the Boy, Columbia, 1984.
So Glad I Know, Sparrow, 1986.
Water Under the Bridge, Columbia, 1987.
I Can't Wait, Columbia, 1988.

Also released numerous singles as well as several anthologies, including *Songbird,* 1977, and *When Love Comes Calling,* 1979.

Sources

Essence, May, 1985.
Jet, August 16, 1982; March 31, 1986; October 17, 1988.
People, June 18, 1984; June 29, 1987.
Rolling Stone, December 5, 1985.
Stereo Review, September, 1982; October, 1983; November, 1986; January, 1987.
US, June 22, 1982.

—Nancy H. Evans

Hank Williams, Jr.

Singer, songwriter, guitarist

Hank Williams, Jr. seems destined to achieve the unthinkable: a level of stardom and critical acclaim exceeding that of his famous father. Named Entertainer of the Year by both the Academy of Country Music and the Country Music Association for two consecutive years (1987 and 1988), the voluble Williams has finally come into his own as a performer and songwriter. *Philadelphia Inquirer* critic Ken Tucker contends that, given the weight of his father's legend in the music business, "it is remarkable that Hank Williams, Jr. even decided to become a country-music performer, let alone one who has run up a consistent string of hits in the last few years."

Tucker adds that the younger Williams has finally shaken "the lingering spirit of his father's style" and created "his own rough, raucous approach to country music." Williams has been singing professionally since he was eight, but only in the last decade has he forged a sound that can be called his own. That sound, "the purest example of the fusion between rock and country ever recorded," to quote *Esquire* contributor Michael Bane, has found a nationwide following of fans.

Randall Hank Williams, Jr. was born in Shreveport, Louisiana, in 1949. When he was only ten days old his father had a stunning six-encore debut at Nashville's Grand Ole Opry. Hank Williams, Sr. is still considered one of the most influential—and most loved—of country musicians, even though his days in the spotlight were few. Williams spent little time with Hank, Jr. as he toured the country and made records, and before the boy turned four, he was dead of an overdose of alcohol and drugs.

Death only increased Williams's fame, and Hank, Jr.'s mother, Audrey, decided that her son could capitalize on the legendary name he had inherited. At the age of eight Hank Williams, Jr. was put to work singing. Bane writes: "From the time he was old enough to hold a guitar, Hank Junior was The Living Proof, the reincarnation of the sainted Hank Williams, dead of pills and liquor. . . . He sang his daddy's songs, memorized his daddy's jokes, practiced his daddy's stage patter, and, ultimately seemed destined to repeat his daddy's nose dive."

Rick Marschall analyzes the pressures on Williams in *The Encyclopedia of Country and Western Music*. "To a creative artist," writes Marschall, "being accepted for wrong reasons is usually more frustrating than finding no acceptance at all. And such was the challenge to a very young Hank Jr. as he developed." Indeed, many of the songs Williams wrote in his twenties deal with his father either directly or indirectly. One of his first number one country hits, "Standing in the Shadows," describes his insecurity about his own accomplishments.

For the Record. . .

Full name, Randall Hank Williams, Jr.; born May 26, 1949, in Shreveport, La.; son of Hank, Sr. (a singer, songwriter, and musician) and Audrey Williams; married first wife (divorced); married Beck White (divorced); children: (first marriage) Shelton Hank; (second marriage) Hilary, Holly. *Education:* High school dropout.

Country singer, 1957—. Currently backed by The Bama Band. Sang soundtrack for motion picture based on his father's life, "Your Cheatin' Heart," 1964, and for motion picture based on his own autobiography, "Living Proof"; star of motion picture "A Time To Sing."

Awards: Holder of 15 gold and 3 platinum albums; Video of the Year Award from Country Music Association, 1986; Entertainer of the Year Award from Academy of Country Music, 1987 and 1988; Entertainer of the Year Award from Country Music Association, 1987 and 1988; Album of the Year Award, 1988, for *Born to Boogie.*

Addresses: *Office*—Hank Williams, Jr. Enterprises, P.O. Box 850, Highway 79, East Paris, TN 38242.

Another, "The Living Proof," asks rhetorically if the son will fall into all of his father's bad habits. For a time Williams seemed predisposed to do just that. He abused alcohol and pills, married and divorced twice, and even attempted suicide before he turned thirty. Finally, convinced that his audience "came to hear the reincarnation of Hank Williams, the one true son of the rural South," to quote Bane, Williams dropped out of the business temporarily, to concentrate on making himself unique.

According to Bane, in the early 1970s Williams threw himself into songwriting "with a vengeance, trying to piece his life together through the words of his songs. . . . The songs of Hank Junior became increasingly personal, honky-tonk vignettes frozen in amber." The music also picked up that fusion of rock and country that would become the earmark of the so-called "outlaw" or "urban cowboy" school. Williams was one of the first to experiment with that sound; his 1975 album *Hank Williams Junior and Friends* is considered a watershed recording in the "outlaw" style.

Bane notes that Williams wanted "no less than a reaffirmation of the old fusions—blues/country, R&B/country, rock/R&B, the kind of music that had powered southern honky-tonks since Day One." Ironically, just as *Hank Williams and Friends* was giving a needed

boost to his career, the young singer was nearly killed in an accident. He slipped while mountain climbing and fell nearly 500 feet, landing on a boulder. For more than a year he was incapacitated while surgeons reconstructed his face, which had been literally split in half. Then, with the accident behind him, a new Hank Williams, Jr. rose to the challenge of stardom.

From the late 1970s until the mid-1980s, Williams was known primarily for celebrating male rowdiness and nonstop rockabilly. Jack Hurst observes in the *Chicago Tribune* that Williams "used his loud guitar and versatile instrumental skills to become first a Stars and Bars-waving musical Dixie zealot. . . . This stance made him a god south of the Mason-Dixon line." Gradually, however, both Williams's personal lifestyle and his song lyrics began to reflect his maturity and a new-found awareness of political and social issues. "Instead of his former intense Dixie-ism," writes Hurst, "he expresses much more of a musical Americanism. Country music, he says, 'has to have' all sorts of sounds."

Bane elaborates: "With his own life filled with enough tragedy for a good dozen country tearjerkers, Hank

---

At the age of eight Hank Williams, Jr. was put to work singing.

Junior's viewpoint became wry and satiric rather than self-pitying. It was, in fact, the viewpoint of a survivor, the person left standing when all the shooting stopped." Nowhere is this sentiment more obvious than in Williams's number one hit "A Country Boy Can Survive," an earnest evocation of all the positive aspects of plain country life. Bane calls the song "the classic southern ethos—leave me alone or else—boiled down into three minutes or so, and it is a personal as well as a political statement. This particular country boy *has* survived."

Not only has Williams survived, he has flourished. In 1985 he hired a new manager, Merle Kilgore, who set about rehabilitating his rowdy, outlaw image and mending the bridges between Williams and the Nashville hierarchy. Properly humbled, and finally willing to participate politely in the Nashville scene, Williams has been embraced and has earned the industry's most prestigious awards. Williams told the *Chicago Tribune* that his new image is more than skin deep. "I may seem pretty square to some folks at this point in my life," he said, "but I get so sick of the damn drug thing, seeing it on the news and seeing it take a lot of great artists right to the bottom. I probably started feeling that way because of all my trips to the hospital, hearing doctors tell me to start being a tough s.o.b. and start taking care of myself. After you lose enough friends—and I've lost some, whether in car wrecks or drug overdoses or whatever—it just gets frightening.''

Williams has also become philosophical about the industry rejection he suffered until just recently. ''America loves an underdog,'' he told the *Chicago Tribune*. ''If I had gotten all the awards [before], I'd probably be like some of these other guys who today are selling insurance in Birmingham or something. And I don't want to do that.''

Writings

Living Proof (autobiography), Dell, 1983.

Selected discography

Hank Williams Jr. and Friends, Polydor, 1975; reissued, 1987.
Five-O, Warner Brothers, 1985.
Major Moves, Warner Brothers, 1985.
Greatest Hits Volume II, Warner Brothers, 1985.
The Early Years: 1976-1978, Warner Brothers, 1986.
Montana Cafe, Warner Brothers, 1986.
Blues My Name, Polydor, 1987.
Hank ''Live,'' Warner Brothers, 1987.

Born To Boogie, Warner Brothers, 1987.
Eleven Roses, Polydor, 1987.
Live at Cobo Hall, Polydor, 1987.
Luke the Drifter, Jr., Volume II, Polydor, 1987.
Standing in the Shadows, Polydor, 1988.
Wild Streak, Warner Brothers, 1988.

Also recorded *Pride's Not Hard To Swallow, The Last Love Song, After You, Family Tradition, 14 Greatest Hits, 40 Greatest Hits, Greatest Hits, Volume I, Habits Old and New, High Notes, Man of Steel, The New South, One Night Stands, The Pressure Is On, Rowdy, Strong Stuff, A Time to Sing,* and *Whiskey Bent & Hell Bound.*

Sources

Books

Marschall, Rick, *The Encyclopedia of Country and Western Music,* Exeter, 1985.
The Rolling Stone Encyclopedia of Rock 'n' Roll, Summit Books, 1983.

Periodicals

Chicago Tribune, October 18, 1987; October 2, 1988.
Esquire, March, 1982.
Philadelphia Inquirer, March 15, 1985.

—*Anne Janette Johnson*

Dwight Yoakam

Singer, songwriter

Country musician Dwight Yoakam has been dubbed the "honky-tonk savior" and the "Hank Williams of the 1980s" for his successful and almost singlehanded revival of traditional country forms. Yoakam, a native of rural Kentucky, makes "the sort of country music you might have thought wasn't made anymore—the Real Thing, complete with sweetly morose fiddles, howled vocals and songs about drowning romantic sorrows in the nearest distilled liquid," to quote *Philadelphia Inquirer* critic Ken Tucker.

Not only has Yoakam reaped praise from fans of "real" country, he has attracted a new generation of listeners, including punk rockers in America's biggest cities. "Yoakam sings country music the way a union organizer might seek to stir up the rank-and-file," wrote Tucker. "He extolls the virtues of country music with every twanging moan, with every sharp whine of the steel guitar that courses through his songs. 'Bill Monroe with drums,' is Yoakam's curt description of his music, and though not literally true . . . [his] implications are ringingly clear: This is a 29-year-old who aims to revitalize the verities."

Yoakam was born in Pikesville, Kentucky, the grandson of a coal miner. Although his parents moved to Ohio while he was still young, he retained a strong affection for his Appalachian roots, one which offers the primary fuel for his music. "Being born in Kentucky and having my mother's family there has left its imprint," he told the *Washington Post*. "I feel blessed by my exposure to that hillbilly culture. It's a vanishing part of America and I'll always be proud of it. I feel I have to acknowledge it because it's given me the subject matter and form for my music. I never could sing rock 'n' roll. I have a country voice." Yoakam also has a long abiding affinity for country performers such as Johnny Cash, Williams, and Buck Owens, whose music of the 1950s and 1960s had a strong regional appeal.

When he began making his own music, Yoakam drew without hesitation on the work of the predecessors he admired. Ironically, when he tried to sell his sound in Nashville in the late 1970s, he was told that he was "too country" and was turned away without a contract. Taking a clue from role models like Owens and Emmylou Harris, Yoakam journeyed to the West Coast and began a lengthy stint of club and bar performances. He worked in near anonymity—and near poverty—for more than eight years before finally landing a contract with Reprise, an eclectic subsidiary of Warner Bros.

The Nashville producers who rejected Yoakam initially must have found his success with a wide country *and* rock audience disconcerting. Equally embarrassing was the fact that Yoakam did not take great pains to hide his disdain for the type of country music that was

For the Record. . .

Born c. 1956, in Pikesville, Ky.; son of David and Ruth Yoakam. *Education:* Attended Ohio State University.

Country singer and songwriter, 1974—; unable to get a recording contract in Nashville, he moved to the West Coast during the late 1970s and performed in clubs and bars for eight years; began recording, 1986; has toured with backup band, The Babylonian Cowboys; has also made a number of appearances with singer-guitarist Buck Owens.

Awards: Gold Medal from New York Film Festival, and from American Music Awards, both 1987, both for video "Honky Tonk Man"; named best new male vocalist by American Academy of Country Music, 1987; two Grammy Award nominations, 1987.

Addresses: *Home*—Los Angeles, CA. *Office*—c/o Reprise Records, 3300 Warner Blvd., Burbank, CA 91505.

being promoted in the South. "There have been a few points in history when country music stopped being country music," Yoakam told the *Philadelphia Inquirer* in 1986. "It happened in the '60s, when you got a lot of Nashville producers putting violins onto country records to make them appeal to the pop-music audience. It happened a few years ago, when all you heard from the country-music industry was the necessity to 'crossover,' to make country records that could be played on pop radio stations. Country music then became this homogenized, all-things-to-all-people music, and it was terrible. It's the worst thing that can happen to a colloquial, ethnic, traditional art form, because it means that it loses its uniqueness."

Yoakam has striven to rebuild that traditional art form, finding it still valid and exciting. He told *Rolling Stone* that he is not surprised by the reaction his music gets from punk, New Wave, and rock fans. "At first glance it would appear to be a great irony," he said. "But not far below the surface, it starts to hit home that *this* is from whence [rock] music came. . . . Everybody knows rhythm and blues was the black predecessor to rock & roll, but from the white side of things, hillbilly music—when it came down into the cities—*was* rock & roll. It was the ostracized form of music that attracted kids. . . . These kids have picked up on that, which is why I owe them a debt for opening doors to me and the band. They're

part of the people who brought me to the dance. But all I have to do to satisfy that indebtedness is not bastardize my pure form of country music."

More recently Yoakam has become more diplomatic in his relations with Nashville, and the industry has responded in kind. Yoakam was named best new male vocalist by the Academy of Country Music in 1987, and although his duet with Buck Owens, "Streets of Bakersfield" was passed over for awards, it occasioned much positive critical comment. Yoakam is pleased to have helped revitalize Owens's career, which had fallen on hard times in the wake of a buffoon-like "Hee Haw" image. The two entertainers often travel and perform together, with Yoakam assuming the role of grateful apprentice. Tom Moon noted in the *Philadelphia Inquirer,* however, that Yoakam "is not an imitator. He's not Johnny Cash revisited. He's not reviving some lost art. Rather, he's reinventing the California honky-tonk sound, throwing together the elements of his background and re-combining them helter-skelter with an abandon usually exhibited by renegade avant-garde artists."

Whatever his methods, Yoakam is now finding the success he thought he might never achieve. According to Cameron Randle in *Rolling Stone,* Yoakam's "refusal to abandon traditional [country] forms is being vindicated." The critic concluded: "If Yoakam's early showing is any indication, his future might warrant equal optimism. On vinyl, as in concert, it is often difficult to tell which breaks more poignantly—his heart or his voice. . . . Yoakam may possess what it takes to become the Hank Williams of the Eighties."

Selected discography

Guitars, Cadillacs, Etc. Etc., Reprise, 1986.
Hillbilly Deluxe, Reprise, 1987.
Buenas Noches from a Lonely Room, Reprise, 1988.

Sources

Chicago Tribune, July 31, 1988; October 30, 1988.
Los Angeles Times, November 20, 1987; July 30, 1988.
People, August 4, 1986.
Philadelphia Inquirer, March 23, 1986; May 13, 1986; September 12, 1988; November 13, 1988.
Rolling Stone, May 22, 1986.
Washington Post, June 16, 1986.

—Anne Janette Johnson

Frank Zappa

Singer, songwriter, guitarist

"If you're not known as a popular musician, you don't exist," Frank Zappa told John Rockwell of the *New York Times*. "The audience that receives my music is a pop audience. If you don't appear as a pop musician, they don't even want to know what you're talking about. I've always assumed that anything I put on records would be bought by everybody in the world. I like my music, from the simplest to the weirdest. And I know that there are people out there who have the same idea of a good time as I have." In the 25 years since Frank Zappa first astonished an audience, he and his group have expanded the horizons of his personal fusion of electronic music.

Born in Baltimore in 1940, Zappa moved with his family to California where he first studied drums and guitar. He learned from the masters, as he told Rockwell: "Most musicians learn their trade by listening to records and imitating them. While we were first starting out, all we had was Chuck Berry." Zappa told *Guitar Player,* in an analytical profile of his own guitar style, that he had collected R&B records by guitar players "Gatemouth" Brown, "Guitar" Slim [Eddie Jones], Matt Murphy, and "Guitar" Watson. After an adolescent rock and roll group, he joined with Don Van Vliet, a.k.a. Captain Beefheart, in the early 1960s. Zappa switched to electric guitar at 21. His earliest pop song was "Memories of El Monte," with Ray Collins, which was recorded by the Penguins.

The first of the many variations of Zappa's band, the Mothers of Invention, began in 1964 as the Soul Giants. By 1966, when its first recording contract was negotiated, the group included Zappa, Collins, guitarist Elliot Ingber, keyboard player Ian Undrwood, bass guitarist Roy Estrada, and percussionists Billy Mindi and Jimmy Carl Black. Their first albums for Verve, *Freak Out!* (1966), *Absolutely Free* (1967), *We're Only in it for the Money* (1967), and *Cruisin' with Ruben and the Jets* (1968), were satirical, self-conscious records that used tape-montages and over-dubbings. *Lumpy Gravy* (1967) was Zappa's first to use a large orchestra.

It was the live performances that gave the Mothers of Invention their unique reputation and established Zappa as, in the words of *Rolling Stone,* incontestably the first of the pop freaks whose music had the impact to give his outrage real authority. "Rumours spread about incidents in the small theaters in which the Mothers of Invention played, but, as Zappa told David Rensin in *Circular* (a Warner Brothers press newsletter): "we played for whoever would come in and take part in what we were doing. We would involve the audience so that what we did was an extension of the personalities of the people in the group and in the audience instead of a locked-in spectacle type show. It was spontaneous, and our credo was that we weren't afraid to do anything as long as the audience was going to get off on it. I do weird things onstage, but nothing involving material discharges from the body or small animals subject to injuries. We've done some strange things, but we don't hurt people or animals, and it doesn't smell bad." His reminiscences were more specific in a 1968 interview in *Rolling Stone:* "We performed a couple of marriages on stage. We pulled people out of the audience and made them make speeches. One time we brought 30 people up on stage and some of them took out instruments and the rest of them sang 'Louie, Louie' as we left."

A contract with Warner Brothers gave Zappa his own label, DiscReet (originally called Bizarre and Straight), on which he also produced records by Captain Beefheart and the young Alice Cooper. His solo recordings—*Burnt Weeny Sandwich* and *Weasels Ripped My Flesh* (both 1970)—were instrumental with more jazz elements than in Mothers of Invention albums. The Mothers of Invention reformed in 1971 as an instrumental backup for Zappa's narratives—few if any of which could be played on the radio. His first hit single, "Don't Eat the Yellow Snow," from *Overnite Sensation* (1973), was probably aired only because its language was incomprehensible. Even the *New Grove Dictionary of*

American Music describes the Mothers of Invention's 1970's cannon as "scatological rock."

The jazz and rock fusion that Zappa had created depended on equal parts of surreal theatricality and expert instrumental playing. In the mid-1970's, critics complained that the Mothers of Invention were presenting just "a good if somewhat kinky rock-and-roll show," as Robert Palmer put it in the *New York Times*. A 1972 concert reviewed by Don Heckman in the *Times* garnered a more positive response: "Zappa gave [the audience] a mixed-bag of jazz-rock-classical music from a 20-musician ensemble." Heckman's list of musical genres evident in Zappa's concert ranged from Stravinsky, Shostakovitch, and Milhaud to rock rhythms, and it ended by labeling him "the Leonard Bernstein of rock." Chip Stern, writing in the *Village Voice* in 1984, created a similar list of influences: "The appeal for me . . . was Zappa's musical scope: anything from affectionate parodies of roots doo-wop to note, rhythm 'n' blues, Chicago-style lead guitar, modern jazz, psychedlia, electronics, opera and 20th cen-

---

"We've done some strange things, but we don't hurt people or small animals, and it doesn't smell bad."

---

tury classicism night turn up in his early albums—oftentimes simultaneously."

Zappa had legal problems with a succession of recording companies in the 1970's, ending up with a mail-order label, Barking Pumpkin, which is distributed by CBS. His novelty hit single, "Valley Girls," based on the slang of the teenagers in the San Fernando Valley, featured his daughter, Moon Unit. His eldest son, Dweezil, has also become a popular guitarist and rock singer. Zappa has also directed two films with his own scores—"200 Motels" (1971) and "Baby Snakes" (1980)—that have cult followings. He announced in 1988 that he would begin a series of video productions of "state of the art weirdness for the home market."

Electronic music is somewhat more acceptable in classical circles, and Zappa's instrumental works have been performed in concerts since 1981. He recognizes the influence of Edgar Varese on his works, as famed jazz critic Ralph Gleason noted in *BMI Many Worlds of Music,* prophecizing that "the more a serious music audience develops for Zappa's work, the sooner we will

---

have a concert in which he will expand his concepts of electronic music to include a diversification of sounds that should be astonishing." Zappa is also associated with Pierre Boulez' Ensemble InterContemporain, which commissioned his *The Perfect Stranger* in 1984. His music has also been championed by Kent Nagano's Berkeley Symphony, which performed his *Sinister Footwear* (1984), originally commissioned by the Oakland Ballet. Three works, including *The Perfect Stranger* are included on a album of electronic music in 1984— *Boulez Conducts Zappa* for Angel; the work has been revived by many ensembles, among them, the Juilliard Chamber Orchestra in 1988. Zappa ha experimented with the synclavier and has utilized its sampling ability in albums, such as his *Jazz from Hell* (Barking Pumpkin, 1988), producing sounds described in the *New York Times* as having an "almost fiendishly brittle, inhuman quality."

For a creative artist who has been described both as the "Leonard Bernstein of rock" in the *Village Voice* and as "the Orson Welles of rock" in the *New York Times*, Zappa has had a curious career. His music may become a staple in the classical repertory of the future or a document in the oddities of performance. He is, as he told the *Times*, a composer who deals with materials "that are not specifically musical."

Selected discography

Freak Out, Verve, 1966.
Absolutely Free, Verve, 1967.
We're Only in It for the Money, Verve, 1967.
Lumpy Gravy, Verve, 1967.
Cruisin' With Ruben and the Jets, Verve, 1967.
Mother Mania, Verve, 1969.
Uncle Meat, Bizarre, 1969.
Weasels Ripped My Flesh, Bizarre, 1970.
Chungas Revenge, Bizarre, 1970.
Hot Rats, Bizarre, 1970.
Burnt Weeny Sandwich, Bizarre, 1970.
Live at Fillmore East, Bizarre, 1971.

200 Motels, (film soundtrack), United Artists, 1971.
Just Another Band from LA, Bizarre, 1972.
The Grand Wazoo, Bizarre, 1972.
Waka Jawaka, Bizarre, 1972.
Overnight Sensation, DiscReet, 1974.
Apostrophe, DiscReet, 1974.
Roxy and Elsewhere, DiscReet, 1974.
One Size Fits All, DiscReet, 1974.
Rock Flashbacks, Verve, 1975.
Bongo Fury, DiscReet, 1975.
Zoot Allures, Warner Bros., 1976.
Mothers Day, Verve, 1977.
In New York, DiscReet, 1978.
Studio Tan, DiscReet, 1978.
Sheik Yerbouti, Zappa, 1979.
Sleep Dirt, DiscReet, 1979.
Orchestral Favourites, DiscReet, 1979.
Joe's Garage, Act 1, Zappa, 1980.
Joe's Garage, Acts 2 and 3, Zappa, 1980.
Zappa and the Mothers, Verve.
Tinseltown Rebellion, CBS, 1981.
You Are What You Is, CBS, 1981.
Shut Up 'n' Play Yer Guitar, CBS, 1981.
Ship Arriving Too Late, CBS, 1982.
Them or Us, EMI, 1984.
Boulez Plays Zappa, Angel, 1984.
Frank Zappa Meets the Mothers of Prevention, EMI, 1985.
Jazz from Hell, Barking Pumpkin, 1988.

Sources

BMI Many Worlds of Music, spring, 1969.
Circular, December 10, 1973.
Guitar Player, January, 1977.
New York Times, September 24, 1972; November 2, 1976; December 27, 1976; August 28, 1984; September 30, 1984; June 17, 1987; April 13, 1988.
Rolling Stone, July 20, 1968; July 4, 1974.
Village Voice, March 20, 1984.

—*Barbara Stratyner*

Subject Index

African
Ladysmith Black Mambazo
Sweet Honey in the Rock

Avant Garde
Anderson, Laurie
Glass, Philip
Monk, Meredith
Reed, Lou
Talking Heads
Zappa, Frank

Bandleaders
Eckstine, Billy
Santana, Carlos
Severinsen, Doc
Zappa, Frank

Banjo
Clark, Roy
Hartford, John

Bass
Fossen, Steve
   See Heart
Gentry, Teddy
   See Alabama
Hubbard, Preston
   See Fabulous Thunderbirds
Johnston, Bruce
   See Beach Boys
Jones, John Paul
   See Led Zeppelin
Sixx, Nikki
   See Mötley Crüe
Wilson, Brian
   See Beach Boys

Big Band/Swing
Eckstine, Billy
Fitzgerald, Ella
Severinsen, Doc
Sinatra, Frank

Bluegrass
Hartford, John
Monroe, Bill
O'Connor, Mark

Blues
Berry, Chuck
Charles, Ray
Clapton, Eric
Fabulous Thunderbirds
Hooker, John Lee
King, B.B.
Vaughan, Stevie Ray
Waits, Tom

Classical
Arrau, Claudio
Clayderman, Richard
Horowitz, Vladimir
Jarrett, Keith
von Karajan, Herbert

Composers
Bacharach, Burt
Davis, Miles
Glass, Philip

Hamlisch, Marvin
Jarrett, Keith
Jordan, Stanley
Kitaro
Mancini, Henry
Monk, Meredith

Conductors
Bacharach, Burt
Domingo, Placido
Jarrett, Keith
Mancini, Henry
von Karajan, Herbert

Country
Alabama
Berry, Chuck
Cash, Johnny
Charles, Ray
Clark, Roy
Denver, John
Gayle, Crystal
Hartford, John
Monroe, Bill
Nelson, Willie
O'Connor, Mark
Presley, Elvis
Rogers, Kenny
Williams, Hank Jr.
Yoakam, Dwight

Drums
Bonham, John
   See Led Zeppelin
Buck, Mike
   See Fabulous Thunderbirds
Christina, Fran
   See Fabulous Thunderbirds
Derosier, Michael
   See Heart
Frantz, Chris
   See Talking Heads
Herndon, Mark
   See Alabama
Lee, Tommy
   See Mötley Crüe
Lewis, Otis
   See Fabulous Thunderbirds
Wilson, Dennis
   See Beach Boys

Feminist Music
Near, Holly

Film Scores
Bacharach, Burt
Hamlisch, Marvin
Mancini, Henry
Waits, Tom

Flamenco
de Lucia, Paco

Folk
Baez, Joan
Denver, John
Hartford, John
Near, Holly
Redpath, Jean
Rogers, Kenny

Simon, Paul

Fusion
Davis, Miles
Jarreau, Al
O'Connor, Mark

Gospel
Charles, Ray
Cleveland, James
Cooke, Sam
Knight, Gladys
Little Richard
Presley, Elvis
Williams, Deniece

Guitar
Baez, Joan
Berry, Chuck
Byrne, David
   See Talking Heads
Cash, Johnny
Clapton, Eric
Clark, Roy
Cook, Jeff
   See Alabama
de Lucia, Paco
Denver, John
Diamond, Neil
Fisher, Roger
   See Heart
Hartford, John
Holly, Buddy
Hooker, John Lee
Jardine, Al
   See Beach Boys
Johnston, Bruce
   See Beach Boys
Jordan, Stanley
King, B.B.
Leese, Howard
   See Heart
Mars, Mick
   See Mötley Crüe
Nelson, Willie
O'Connor, Mark
Owen, Randy
   See Alabama
Page, Jimmy
   See Led Zeppelin
Presley, Elvis
Prince
Reed, Lou
Santana, Carlos
Simon, Paul
Townshend, Pete
Vaughan, Jimmie
   See Fabulous Thunderbirds
Vaughan, Stevie Ray
Williams, Hank Jr.
Wilson, Carl
   See Beach Boys
Wilson, Nancy
   See Heart
Zappa, Frank

Harmonica
Wilson, Kim
   See Fabulous Thunderbirds

Heavy Metal
Led Zeppelin
Mötley Crüe
Roth, David Lee

Jazz
Charles, Ray
Davis, Miles
Eckstine, Billy
Fitzgerald, Ella
Jarreau, Al
Jarrett, Keith
Jordan, Stanley
Mancini, Henry
Ross, Diana
Sanborn, David
Santana, Carlos
Severinsen, Doc
Waits, Tom

Keyboards, Electric
Charles, Ray
Cook, Jeff
See Alabama
Harrison, Jerry
See Talking Heads
Johnston, Bruce
See Beach Boys
Jones, John Paul
See Led Zeppelin
Kitaro
Wilson, Brian
See Beach Boys

Latin Music
Santana, Carlos

Mandolin
Hartford, John
Monroe, Bill

Minimalism
Glass, Philip

Musicals
Bacharach, Burt
Buckley, Betty
Hamlisch, Marvin

New Age
Kitaro

New Wave
Talking Heads

Opera
Cotrubas, Ileana
Domingo, Placido
Pavarotti, Luciano
von Karajan, Herbert

Performance Art
Anderson, Laurie

Piano
Arrau, Claudio
Bacharach, Burt
Charles, Ray
Clayderman, Richard
Cleveland, James
Glass, Philip
Hamlisch, Marvin
Horowitz, Vladimir
Jarrett, Keith
Little Richard
Waits, Tom

Pop
Bacharach, Burt

Beach Boys
Berry, Chuck
Bowie, David
Cash, Johnny
Charles, Ray
Cher
Clapton, Eric
Clark, Roy
Clayderman, Richard
Cole, Natalie
Cooke, Sam
Denver, John
Diamond, Neil
Ferry, Bryan
Fitzgerald, Ella
Gayle, Crystal
Gibson, Debbie
Hartford, John
Holly, Buddy
Jackson, Michael
Jarreau, Al
Knight, Gladys
Little Richard
Mancini, Henry
Martin, Dean
Nelson, Willie
Pavarotti, Luciano
Presley, Elvis
Prince
Robinson, Smokey
Rogers, Kenny
Ross, Diana
Roth, David Lee
Sanborn, David
Simon, Paul
Sinatra, Frank
Talking Heads
Townshend, Pete
Turner, Tina
Williams, Deniece

Producers
Prince
Wilson, Brian
See Beach Boys

Punk
Pop, Iggy
Reed, Lou
Smith, Patti

Record Company Executives
Near, Holly
Robinson, Smokey
Ross, Diana

Rhythm and Blues
Berry, Chuck
Charles, Ray
Cole, Natalie
Cooke, Sam
Fabulous Thunderbirds
Knight, Gladys
Prince
Robinson, Smokey
Turner, Tina
Vaughan, Stevie Ray
Williams, Deniece

Rock
Beach Boys
Berry, Chuck
Bowie, David
Cher
Clapton, Eric
Cooke, Sam
Ferry, Bryan
Holly, Buddy
Led Zeppelin

Little Richard
Mötley Crüe
Pop, Iggy
Presley, Elvis
Prince
Reed, Lou
Rogers, Kenny
Roth, David Lee
Simon, Paul
Smith, Patti
Townshend, Pete
Turner, Tina
Vaughan, Stevie Ray
Zappa, Frank

Rockabilly
Holly, Buddy
Presley, Elvis

Saxophone
Love, Mike
See Beach Boys
Sanborn, David

Songwriters
Bacharach, Burt
Baez, Joan
Berry, Chuck
Buckley, Betty
Cash, Johnny
Charles, Ray
Clapton, Eric
Cleveland, James
Cooke, Sam
Denver, John
Diamond, Neil
Ferry, Bryan
Gibson, Debbie
Hamlisch, Marvin
Hartford, John
Holly, Buddy
Jackson, Michael
Jarreau, Al
King, B.B.
Little Richard
Near, Holly
Nelson, Willie
Pop, Iggy
Presley, Elvis
Prince
Reed, Lou
Robinson, Smokey
Roth, David Lee
Simon, Paul
Smith, Patti
Townshend, Pete
Waits, Tom
Williams, Deniece
Williams, Hank Jr.
Wilson, Brian
See Beach Boys
Yoakam, Dwight
Zappa, Frank

Soul
Charles, Ray
Cooke, Sam
Knight, Gladys
Little Richard
Robinson, Smokey
Ross, Diana

Trumpet
Davis, Miles
Severinsen, Doc

Violin
Anderson, Laurie
Hartford, John
O'Connor, Mark

Musicians Index

Alabama
Anderson, Laurie
Arrau, Claudio
Bacharach, Burt
Baez, Joan
Barnwell, Ysaye Maria
　　See Sweet Honey in the Rock
Barton, Lou Ann
　　See Fabulous Thunderbirds
Beach Boys
Berry, Chuck
Bolade, Nitanju
　　See Sweet Honey in the Rock
Bonham, John
　　See Led Zeppelin
Bowie, David
Buck, Mike
　　See Fabulous Thunderbirds
Buckley, Betty
Byrne, David
　　See Talking Heads
Cash, Johnny
Charles, Ray
Cher
Christina, Fran
　　See Fabulous Thunderbirds
Clapton, Eric
Clark, Roy
Clayderman, Richard
Cleveland, James
Cole, Natalie
Cook, Jeff
　　See Alabama
Cooke, Sam
Cotrubas, Ileana
Davis, Miles
de Lucia, Paco
Denver, John
Derosier, Michael
　　See Heart
Diamond, Neil
Domingo, Placido
Eckstine, Billy
Fabulous Thunderbirds
Ferguson, Keith
　　See Fabulous Thunderbirds
Ferry, Bryan
Fisher, Roger
　　See Heart
Fitzgerald, Ella
Fossen, Steve
　　See Heart
Frantz, Chris
　　See Talking Heads
Gayle, Crystal
Gentry, Teddy
　　See Alabama
Gibson, Debbie
Glass, Philip
Hamlisch, Marvin
Harris, Evelyn
　　See Sweet Honey in the Rock
Harrison, Jerry
　　See Talking Heads

Hartford, John
Heart
Herndon, Mark
　　See Alabama
Holly, Buddy
Hooker, John Lee
Horowitz, Vladimir
Hubbard, Preston
　　See Fabulous Thunderbirds
Jackson, Michael
Jardine, Al
　　See Beach Boys
Jarreau, Al
Jarrett, Keith
Johnson, Shirley Childres
　　See Sweet Honey in the Rock
Johnston, Bruce
　　See Beach Boys
Jones, John Paul
　　See Led Zeppelin
Jordan, Stanley
Kahlil, Aisha
　　See Sweet Honey in the Rock
Karajan, Herbert von
　　See von Karajan, Herbert
King, B.B.
Kitaro
Knight, Gladys
Ladysmith Black Mambazo
Led Zeppelin
Lee, Tommy
　　See Mötley Crüe
Leese, Howard
　　See Heart
Lewis, Otis
　　See Fabulous Thunderbirds
Little Richard
Love, Mike
　　See Beach Boys
Lucia, Paco de
　　See de Lucia, Paco
Mancini, Henry
Mars, Mick
　　See Mötley Crüe
Martin, Dean
Mazibuko, Abednigo
　　See Ladysmith Black Mambazo
Mazibuko, Albert
　　See Ladysmith Black Mambazo
Mdletshe, Geophrey
　　See Ladysmith Black Mambazo
Methembu, Russel
　　See Ladysmith Black Mambazo
Monk, Meredith
Monroe, Bill
Mötley Crüe
Mwelase, Jabulane
　　See Ladysmith Black Mambazo
Near, Holly
Neil, Vince
　　See Mötley Crüe
Nelson, Willie
O'Connor, Mark

Owen, Randy
　　See Alabama
Page, Jimmy
　　See Led Zeppelin
Pavarotti, Luciano
Phungula, Inos
　　See Ladysmith Black Mambazo
Plant, Robert
　　See Led Zeppelin
Pop, Iggy
Presley, Elvis
Prince
Reagon, Bernice Johnson
　　See Sweet Honey in the Rock
Redpath, Jean
Reed, Lou
Robinson, Smokey
Rogers, Kenny
Ross, Diana
Roth, David Lee
Sanborn, David
Santana, Carlos
Severinsen, Doc
Shabalala, Ben
　　See Ladysmith Black Mambazo
Shabalala, Headman
　　See Ladysmith Black Mambazo
Shabalala, Jockey
　　See Ladysmith Black Mambazo
Shabalala, Joseph
　　See Ladysmith Black Mambazo
Simon, Paul
Sinatra, Frank
Sixx, Nikki
　　See Mötley Crüe
Smith, Patti
Sweet Honey in the Rock
Talking Heads
Townshend, Pete
Turner, Tina
Vaughan, Jimmie
　　See Fabulous Thunderbirds
Vaughan, Stevie Ray
von Karajan, Herbert
Waits, Tom
Weymouth, Tina
　　See Talking Heads
Williams, Deniece
Williams, Hank Jr.
Wilson, Anne
　　See Heart
Wilson, Brian
　　See Beach Boys
Wilson, Carl
　　See Beach Boys
Wilson, Dennis
　　See Beach Boys
Wilson, Kim
　　See Fabulous Thunderbirds
Wilson, Nancy
　　See Heart
Yoakam, Dwight
Zappa, Frank